Econometrics and
Quantitative Economics

Econometrics and Quantitative Economics

Edited by David F. Hendry
and Kenneth F. Wallis

BASIL BLACKWELL

First published 1984

Basil Blackwell Publisher Ltd
108 Cowley Road, Oxford OX4 1JF, UK

Basil Blackwell Inc.
432 Park Avenue South, Suite 1505,
New York, NY 10016, USA

British Library Cataloguing in Publication Data

Econometrics and quantitative economics.
1. Econometrics
I. Hendry, David F. II. Wallis, Kenneth F.
330'.0724 HB141
ISBN 0-631-13797-1

Library of Congress Cataloging in Publication Data

Econometrics and quantitative economics.
'Published works of J. D. Sargan': p. 315
Bibliography: p. 319
Includes index.
1. Econometrics – Addresses, essays, lectures.
2. Economics – Mathematical models – Addresses, essays, lectures. I. Hendry, David F. II. Wallis, Kenneth F.
HB139.E29 1984 330'.028 84-11085
ISBN 0-631-13797-1

Typeset by Unicus Graphics Ltd, Horsham
Printed in Great Britain by TJ Press Ltd, Padstow

for Denis Sargan

Contents

Contributors

MEGHNAD DESAI	Professor of Economics, London School of Economics
ANDREW C. HARVEY	Professor of Statistics, London School of Economics
DAVID F. HENDRY	Professor of Economics, Oxford University
GRAYHAM E. MIZON	Leverhulme Professor of Econometrics, Southampton University
STEPHEN J. NICKELL	Director, Institute of Economics and Statistics, Oxford University
ADRIAN R. PAGAN	Senior Fellow in Econometrics, Australian National University
JEAN-FRANÇOIS RICHARD	Professor of Econometrics, Université Catholique de Louvain
PRAVIN K. TRIVEDI	Reader in Economics, Australian National University
KENNETH F. WALLIS	Professor of Econometrics, University of Warwick

Preface

Contemporary discussion of economic problems at all levels is heavily influenced by the results of empirical econometric analysis. Yet econometrics textbooks seldom reflect the reality of empirical work. Textbooks often proceed as if the task of econometrics is limited to the statistical estimation of relationships given by economic theory. So they present a stylized account of the statistical theory that surrounds such estimation procedures, together with diagnostic tests for departures from the assumptions on which the statistical theory rests. Empirical researchers quickly recognize that such material provides only a partial account of the problems they encounter, and they have to develop rules of thumb to guide their search for a satisfactory description of the empirical phenomena under investigation. This book reflects the change of emphasis from estimation to modelling, and presents an account of recent work on empirical analysis in the face of specification uncertainty. Various facets of empirical modelling procedures that represent a constructive interplay of economics and statistics are explored by the nine authors, drawing on their research and teaching experience. The book is intended to be read by anyone engaged in or embarking on applied econometric research, working economist and graduate student alike. It is assumed that the reader has already been exposed to traditional econometric material of the kind referred to above.

The book is dedicated to Denis Sargan, with affection and respect, on the occasion of his sixtieth birthday. It also marks the twentieth anniversary of the publication of his Colston paper, reprinted herein with the kind permission of Butterworths and the Colston Research Society. That paper was an important contribution to the development of an empirical research strategy, involving the interaction of econometrics and quantitative economics and firmly based on the principles of statistical analysis, and it remains so today. It anticipated many subsequent developments in econometric modelling, yet has been surprisingly neglected, perhaps because the conference series in which it appeared is an unfamiliar outlet for econometric work. Nevertheless its general approach has strongly influenced the teaching and research in theoretical and applied econometrics of many who have followed, not least the present authors, all of whom have shared the privilege of having been, for shorter or longer periods, students and/or colleagues of Denis at the London School of Economics. The book was planned by Meghnad Desai, David Hendry and Kenneth Wallis, and royalties will be devoted to a fund to facilitate the travel of young econometricians to conferences and seminars at home and overseas, principally those organized by the Econometric Society, of which Denis was elected a Fellow in 1963, and which he served as President in 1980.

1

Editors' Introduction

1 Econometrics and Econometric Estimation

On the first appearance of the journal *Econometrica* in 1933, its editor, Ragnar Frisch, offered 'a word of explanation regarding the term econometrics' in the following way (Frisch, 1933, p. 2):

> ... there are several aspects of the quantitative approach to economics, and no single one of these aspects, taken by itself, should be confounded with econometrics. Thus, econometrics is by no means the same as economic statistics. Nor is it identical with what we call general economic theory, although a considerable portion of this theory has a definitely quantitative character. Nor should econometrics be taken as synonomous [*sic*] with the application of mathematics to economics. Experience has shown that each of these three view-points, that of statistics, economic theory, and mathematics, is a necessary, but not by itself a sufficient, condition for a real understanding of the quantitative relations in modern economic life. It is the *unification* of all three that is powerful. And it is this unification that constitutes econometrics.
>
> This unification is more necessary today than at any previous stage in economics. Statistical information is currently accumulating at an unprecedented rate. But no amount of statistical information, however complete and exact, can by itself explain economic phenomena. If we are not to get lost in the overwhelming, bewildering mass of statistical data that are now becoming available, we need the guidance and help of a powerful theoretical framework. Without this no significant interpretation and coordination of our observations will be possible.

> The theoretical structure that shall help us out in this situation must, however, be more precise, more realistic, and, in many respects, more complex, than any heretofore available. Theory, in formulating its abstract quantitative notions, must be inspired to a larger extent by the technique of observation. And fresh statistical and other factual studies must be the healthy element of disturbance that constantly threatens and disquiets the theorist and prevents him from coming to rest on some inherited, obsolete set of assumptions.
> This mutual penetration of quantitative economic theory and statistical observation is the essence of econometrics.

More than 50 years later, there is nothing in this explanation that would be seriously questioned. And statistical information is still accumulating at an unprecedented rate. But in much modern econometric writing it is hard to detect the essential fusion of the various strands sought by Frisch. Attention is frequently restricted to the formal procedures of statistical estimation and inference that have developed within econometrics, or to a style of reporting of empirical work that pays excessive respect to those formalities. Many textbooks have been written as if econometric estimation were the whole of econometrics.

Econometric estimation is often discussed in the following terms. A theoretical analysis, broadly based on economic principles, has produced a relationship between certain variables of interest; one or more are to be explained by others which are treated as given from outside the scope of the study. Data on these variables are collected and stored in the computer. A variety of assumptions about the nature of the data and the model are made, concerning the independence or otherwise of successive observations, the accuracy of the measurement process, the constancy of the posited relationship, the relevance of other interrelationships between these variables, and so on. Given sufficient assumptions and a specific objective, a method of estimating the numerical magnitudes of the unknown parameters can be derived from statistical theory and programmed on the computer. Finally the estimates are computed and compared in sign and size with the predictions of the original theory. If a good match is obtained, the exercise is deemed a success. In this approach the main role of econometric theory is to provide methods of estimation and inference which are applicable to the relationships of interest to economists, establish their properties and select those which function well in various specified circumstances.

That econometric practice sharply deviates from this model quickly becomes apparent. First, attempts to fit theory models to economic time series (the data form with which this book is principally concerned) tend to reveal a host of statistical problems. For example, successive errors are assumed to be independent, but the residuals appear to be highly autocorrelated; parameters anticipated to be positive are estimated as negative; the explanatory variables in the model seem to be more highly correlated among themselves than with the variables to be explained; and so on. In consequence, methods for diagnosing some of these problems and treating them if they are present have also been developed; perhaps the best-known examples are the Durbin–Watson test for first-order serial correlation and the Cochrane–Orcutt technique for treating it. By an appropriate selection of such methods, perhaps a good match of theory and data can be re-established, at least over the range of problems investigated. This process of revision raises new questions, some of which have begun to receive attention. Does the symptom have a unique cause, so that removing the symptom cures the disease? Does the order of treating problems matter? Does the validity or credibility of the final result depend on how many revision stages occur? What problems should be treated and which can be ignored? When should the process stop? And so on.

More generally, however, this continuing emphasis on statistical matters neglects other viewpoints emphasized by Frisch, and that this is only a part of an econometric research programme is widely recognized by empirical researchers. Economic theory is itself subject to a process of revision, as Frisch notes, and a judicious blend of economics, statistics and inspiration, if not serendipity, is required for a successful 'understanding of the quantitative relations in modern economic life'. In his explanation of econometrics Frisch does not use the word model, but the term econometric model is now commonly used to describe the mathematical representation of such quantitative relations. In seeking to discuss the essence of econometrics, as identified by Frisch, we are thus seeking to diminish the emphasis on estimation and to consider, more generally, modelling.

2 Econometric Modelling

Theories are designed to highlight the features of importance in an analysis, and are necessarily highly idealized abstractions. Often the variables of the theory are not directly observable, or even have no clear measurable counterparts. The data are usually the product of an administrative collection process with other objectives than producing material for later econometric study; moreover, they are generated passively, not experimentally, by a complicated dynamic system which is distinctly interdependent and subject to large interventions from various sources, not least domestic and foreign governments. The 'correct' formulation of the econometric model is not just highly uncertain, it may not even be a sensible concept.

In empirical econometrics, however, the emphasis is placed squarely on the operational – is the model adequate for the purposes to which it will be put? One does not ask an engineer if the 'correct' bridge was built, but rather if it will fulfil its functions satisfactorily; when the functions alter (carrying tanks rather than pedestrians) so will the adequacy. Next, there are many criteria influencing both the design and the evaluation of adequacy. Debates can concern the choice of design criteria, their relative weightings, their possible incompatibility, and the extent to which they are satisfied, but in econometrics, as in engineering, each stage is susceptible to analysis and evaluation. Further, treating symptoms rather than causes is generally disastrous; covering over cracks in bridges is not recommended! Finally, the checking of results (by numerical methods, including simulation) is a routine precursor to implementation: new methods and designs can be explored, but against a background of practical accumulated knowledge as to what has worked, and what 'laws' seem binding. Econometric modelling, like engineering, is a mixture of science, concerning what is established, and art, when the frontier is reached. In the remainder of this section we further elaborate its essential elements.

The potential uses of an econometric model are not often clearly stated, but generally include testing of some theoretical propositions, data summarization, forecasting and policy analysis. Where a specific purpose is singled out, a 'cheaper' product may be adequate (e.g. a simple time-series model, if forecasting in an unchanged environment is the objective). And given a specific purpose, a simple loss function can be defined (e.g. for forecasting, a minimum mean square error criterion is often deemed adequate). But in general, while multiple usage might be anticipated, it is not always possible to foresee the precise uses to which the model will be put. For example, parameter estimates from studies of production functions have later found their way into general equilibrium analyses of the effects of taxation policies, and various welfare calculations might rest on studies of consumer behaviour conducted with no advance knowledge of such an application. Given multiple usage of the econometric model, no specific loss function can be defined, and many design criteria are of potential relevance. We consider a minimal set of criteria of adequacy, although readers may agree that it is more extensive than that hitherto employed in much empirical research.

First, to consider criteria that assess adequacy directly, it is convenient to distinguish various kinds of information available:

(1) the observed data to be used in the exercise, comprising a sample of observations on a menu of variables. Within this, relative to a fixed point in time, we may further distinguish past, present and future observations;

(2) theoretical analysis of the economic behaviour being modelled, together with descriptions of the institutional setting, organizational features, and the impact of administrative and legislative arrangements;

(3) the measurement system, including changes in definition or method of collection, knowledge of identities, restrictions on the range of variables, and so forth;

(4) earlier empirical analyses, and the form and content of competing models.

Criteria appropriate to each subcategory of information have been developed along the following lines:

(a) to describe the relative past, the fit of the model should not deviate from the observed data systematically (absence of residual autocorrelation) or heterogeneously (absence of residual heteroscedasticity); models can be designed to satisfy these two criteria by appropriate specification of the lag structure and the functional form;

(b) to allow legitimate use of contemporaneous variables as explanatory factors requires that such variables be exogenous; sometimes this provides testable restrictions, although in other cases it is achieved by constructing the model in a specific way;

(c) adequately characterizing future data necessitates some form of time invariance, either of the 'fundamental parameters' or of the goodness-of-fit statistics; otherwise, predictive failure occurs (the eventual outcomes and the predictions are not deemed adequately close). Again, testable restrictions are generally implied.

(d) Certain aspects of theory consistency may be testable either directly (e.g. when the coefficients are significantly different from the values predicted by the theory) or indirectly (e.g. if the theory is imposed inappropriately on the data the resulting discrepancies in (a)–(c) may be investigated). Relevant economic theory may be of an equilibrium or comparative static kind, and so have relatively little to say about behaviour out of equilibrium or dynamic adjustment. Then the short-run and long-run implications of the model must be assessed separately.

(e) Measurement information often can be implemented directly (e.g. trading-day corrections) or imposed by design (e.g. logarithms ensure positive variables, identities enforce adding-up constraints) although conflicts with (a) might ensue (e.g. the residuals become heteroscedastic).

(f) Accounting for the results of rival models using one's own model is close to the requirement that the latter be a 'sufficient model' in the class; again this may be achievable by design on occasion, but yields testable implications otherwise.

Here, the concept of an adequate model is one which describes the historical data without producing a systematic misfit, has valid exogenous variables, fits equally well to the future, is consistent with the relevant theory and measurement system and accounts for (encompasses) alternative explanations of the same set of endogenous variables. These criteria of adequacy seem necessary but not sufficient; failure on any one criterion reveals a direction of inadequacy, whereas satisfying all the criteria does not guarantee that the model is adequate for some as yet unspecified purpose, nor that the next rival model will not reject the chosen specification. However, if the next model does encompass an existing adequate model and still satisfies (a)–(e), then it is both adequate and offers a 'better' explanation, that is, it accounts for more than the previously selected model. Consequently, progressive improvement of models becomes possible, each in turn providing a firmer basis from which others can be developed.

Auxiliary criteria are less easily categorized. Several that are commonly advocated are as follows; each is to be interpreted as applying when all other factors are equal:

(1) parsimony – it seems more useful to explain a lot by a little than vice versa;

(2) robustness – since we do not know in what aspects models are weakest and most susceptible to failure, they should be designed as far as possible to be protected against changes in features excluded from their formulations;
(3) orthogonal explanatory variables – large intercorrelations between explanatory variables mean that these are mainly acting as substitutes in accounting for the variability of the endogenous variables; this makes interpretations of parameters hazardous, as well as producing equations which show dramatic changes in parameter estimates for apparently small changes in data correlations (i.e. orthogonality is in part also one aspect of robustness);
(4) replication of results – methods which when applied by different investigators to a common framework yield the same or similar results are preferable to approaches in which a wide range of disparate outcomes could be achieved (encompassing helps circumvent some of the non-uniqueness problem).

A more systematic approach than the simple model discussed in section 1 seems feasible based on this analysis. Given the measurement system and the theoretical analysis, a general or maintained model is formulated. This should take account of existing empirical results (many of which might be nested special cases) and known salient data features (e.g. strong four-period lag reactions or rapid adjustment, etc.), and embed all the special cases which might be thought worthy of study. Should a still more general model transpire to be required in the end, one should at least be surprised and hence have learned important new information, albeit not what was initially sought. The general model is constrained in size by the number of available observations, and while collinearity may be a difficulty, a change in parameterization corresponding to a more nearly orthogonal set of variables might be sufficient at this stage. Estimation of the general model provides both the baseline goodness of fit and the unrestricted parameter estimates against which tests of restrictions can be conducted, so it acts as a set of sufficient statistics for the remaining analysis. Naturally, diagnostic tests of the general model remain worth while: its formulation could be inadequate and it is better to learn that at the outset than after substantial labour input, and so tests of (a)–(e) merit calculation at this stage.

Generally, the theory model will be a restricted special case of the maintained model and could be tested directly against the latter; alternatively, the maintained model could be sequentially simplified (each stage being an acceptable summarization of what is known) until a parsimonious and interpretable characterization results. Then this could be tested in turn for its ability to encompass rival models; in a least squares framework, a necessary condition is that an encompassing model must fit better than the alternatives.

This represents a directed model-building strategy that can claim some empirical success. Many issues remain to be investigated in order to clarify fully its properties, and a number of these are explored in the remaining chapters.

3 Overview

The chapters that follow reflect the general outline sketched above to emphasize the blend of economic theory, econometric analysis and data evidence in constructing useful quantitative economic models. Thus it is convenient to begin with a theory model, and in chapter 2 Stephen Nickell analyses the functioning of the labour market to offer a framework for models of wages and employment. He pays careful attention to the institutional setting of UK labour markets, which is common to many countries, and allows unions and collective bargaining to influence their functioning. He emphasizes the need to model wages and employment jointly, rather than focusing on the conventional linking of wages and prices. Of course, relevant theories are not strictly prior to data evidence, as noted by Frisch. Rather, theories are themselves part of an iterative strategy, formalizing and abstracting the salient features of existing evidence in a coherent framework, summarizing current understanding and seeking to predict or explain new phenomena, and this emerges clearly from Nickell's account. The result is directly relevant to applied work, as a basis for formulating a statistical model.

It is helpful to distinguish economic theory from statistical models, for a fully developed economic theory that would entail a complete statistical formulation is generally unattainable. Most economic theories leave unanswered a number of questions that arise in the transition to a statistical model. The relation between theory time and the data observation period, the mappings of the theory variables onto possible measured counterparts, aggregation over firms and households, and the arbitrary selection of functional forms all impinge on this transition. The net effect is that the econometric model is never more than an approximation to the way the variables under study are determined. Indeed, in purely statistical models variables that may not be stochastic are treated as stochastic, again as a convenient approximation. As noted above, the quality of some of these approximations can be assessed, and this is a theme to which later chapters return. But it is to a purely statistical model that we turn next.

In chapter 3 Andrew Harvey investigates the statistical formulation and analysis of models for characterizing time-series data. He presents an approach which seeks to unify a large class of potentially relevant models, based on the concept of the prediction error decomposition. First, the process generating the actual economic outcomes due to the behaviour of agents is formulated without confronting the issue of observability of the relevant variables. Then, the measurement system relating the observables to the state of the economy is defined, the whole being called a state-space representation. This two-stage formulation allows a close mapping of the theory model onto the state process and emphasizes the need to carefully formulate how the data are related to the latent variables of the state process (or theory). Using ideas based on the Kalman filter, Harvey is able to derive one-step-ahead prediction errors which fully incorporate all the existing information given a set of values for the parameters. Such errors allow the likelihood function to be obtained conveniently, and maximization of this yields all the statistics needed for estimation, inference and diagnostic checking.

The state-space formulation offers a convenient pedagogical device for understanding statistical models of time series. While it does not preclude the coefficients of the statistical model being dependent on a smaller subset of parameters of interest, certain classes of econometric model arise sufficiently often to merit specific analyses, which efficiently incorporate the restrictions on the coefficients. One of the most common models is that in which analysing the joint distribution of several variables is essential to sustain valid inference – i.e. simultaneous equations models of the kind arising in Nickell's chapter. This topic is considered by Jean-François Richard in chapter 4.

Again the emphasis is on a unifying and expository analysis, which considers both classical and Bayesian inference. There is broad common ground in these approaches to statistical inference, with the likelihood function being central to both, and Richard focuses on the similarities rather than the differences. Maximum likelihood and instrumental variables methods are analysed using the device of an estimator generating equation, which yields a large class of alternative estimators as different approximations to the score. The recent concepts of weak and strong exogeneity are explained and their respective roles in inference discussed, including testing for the validity of such assertions in practice. Richard illustrates all of these ideas in a model of money demand, and argues for the advantages of an instrumental variables approach to analysing submodels.

Both at the stage of formulating a general maintained model, and after developing a parsimonious representation, the issue of rigorously testing its adequacy must be confronted. As noted above, a model can first be diagnostically checked for a variety of departures from any set of formulation assumptions (criteria (a)–(e) for example). Secondly the model can be checked against other extant empirical models to see if it encompasses them and can become a summary representation of research to date (criterion (f)). These two aspects are treated in chapters 5 and 6 by Adrian Pagan and Grayham Mizon respectively.

First, Pagan presents a general analysis of a vast range of empirically important diagnostic tests, using the approach of augmenting regressions by adding suitably constructed variables. His framework provides easily implemented tests which use familiar tools and place minimal demands on computing resources for single structural equations. The basis of his theory is closely linked to that of the Lagrange multiplier principle, which has become the established technique for deriving diagnostic tests, and offers pedagogic advantages by highlighting the intuition behind the tests. Moreover, defects in *ad hoc* methods of obtaining test statistics are clearly revealed. Pagan considers a wide range of important tests corresponding to augmenting the mean and the variance of econometric equations, and his framework allows easy derivation of further tests as desired.

Accounting for the findings of other models can often be handled via variable addition (and Pagan briefly considers this case), but is sufficiently important to merit a separate treatment. The chapter on encompassing by Mizon develops the necessary concepts and tests, and relates encompassing tests to tests of non-nested hypotheses. Deeper insight into many familiar test statistics is obtained by re-interpreting and unifying these in an encompassing framework, in particular to see against which implicit rival models the tests are oriented. By appropriate development of encompassing tests, evaluation of rival views becomes possible, in terms of the extent to which each can or cannot account for the others' findings. A synthesis of the useful features of such models in the progressive research strategy noted above is possible, but even at a minimum it is important to understand the limitations of any claimed explanations of how economies function, and alternative models developed by those with different views seem well designed to highlight the potential weaknesses of one's own ideas.

Notwithstanding the rigour and generality of the initial economic theory and the care in formulating, estimating and testing the statistical model, it is almost inevitable that repeated estimation and iterative modelling will be needed in the process of developing useful data characterizations. In chapter 7, Pravin Trivedi analyses modelling strategies for time-series data when the prior information about the precise equation specification is uncertain. The main alternative approaches are discussed, including model revision based on testing, Bayesian methods (including 'rule of thumb' Bayesians), shrinkage techniques and the use of stochastic prior information. Intelligent model building undoubtedly reflects an informal Bayesian viewpoint, often with one's prior beliefs only being stimulated when unusual results are found. The presence of the multiplicity of criteria discussed above, the difficulty of handling high dimensional parameter spaces and our general inability to formalize a loss function or a complete prior distribution for any given problem all mitigate against simple formal modelling strategies. Trivedi explores the advantages and disadvantages of the alternatives, using the distributed lag model as the main vehicle, but noting that the issues are in no sense restricted to this case.

After these detailed theoretical analyses of the various aspects of modelling, in chapter 8 David Hendry presents an empirical modelling exercise, analysing the behaviour of house prices in the United Kingdom. Following an overview of the salient features of the data, static and dynamic theories of the main influences on house prices are discussed and a nonlinear price adjustment equation is posited to account for the extremely rapid price changes observed historically. A general model is formulated and tested, and a restricted version is developed using the various simplification criteria described in earlier chapters. This is estimated in three versions approximating the nonlinear price function and related to other existing models. As with most empirical studies, the results are a step towards an understanding of housing markets rather than a completed or definitive model, and the study also serves to illustrate the themes developed in other chapters.

Earlier chapters having reviewed many of the technical developments that followed Sargan's Colston paper, in chapter 9 Meghnad Desai reviews developments in the area in which it made an empirical contribution, namely the modelling of wages and prices. His account begins a little earlier with a paper written at LSE that has had a great impact on applied work, namely the original Phillips curve article. Desai first reappraises Phillips' theoretical framework and technical innovations, which have often been overlooked in the rush to replicate, enhance or deny the existence of the curve itself. Subsequent research, including Sargan's work, is then reviewed, and Desai finally evaluates attempts to build a more satisfactory subsystem, in the sense considered in earlier chapters.

Finally, Denis Sargan's Colston paper is reprinted (with the author's corrections). Some of the individual ideas it contains have been rediscovered since its publication and others have witnessed considerable technical developments. It was an important precursor in confronting the issues of modelling identified above and integrating economic theoretical insights into practical models. The operational aspect is firmly emphasized: if a new estimator is required, it is developed and its theoretical properties are evaluated; an appropriate algorithm is derived and its numerical performance assessed; associated test statistics are obtained and the whole is implemented in a computer program so that applications can proceed. The empirical implications accurately presaged later economic problems. It remains an outstanding example of the unification sought by Frisch, from which much can still be learned.

2

The Modelling of Wages and Employment

STEPHEN J. NICKELL

1 Introduction

The standard practice in the construction of economy-wide econometric models is to ignore the existence of markets. Nowhere is this made more clear than in the subsector of the model devoted to employment and wages. For example, in some of the key macroeconomic models of the British economy (those of the Treasury, the London Business School and the National Institute, among others), employment is a simple function of the level of activity and wages are determined by a string of variables which appear to have been selected more or less randomly and, as a consequence, differ markedly from one model to the next. For example the Treasury wage equation contains (lagged) wages, retail prices, producer prices, income taxes, employment taxes, output, unemployment, government employment, and company income at various lags up to and including 9 quarters. A recent London Business School wage equation, on the other hand, contains producer prices, import and export prices, output, the population of working age, employment, and the money stock. Finally a recent National Institute equation is somewhat more ascetic containing only (lagged) wages and earnings, retail prices, and income taxes. All three equations explain the rate of change of money wages.

The notion of a labour market obviously lies somewhere in the background in these models but it seems to have moved so far back that it has disappeared from view. The reasons for this are complex, indeed the topic is one which may well attract future historians of economic thought. However, two important and related factors immediately suggest themselves. These are the use of the income–expenditure framework as the basis of macro-econometric model building in its early years and the dominance of the Phillips curve in the modelling of wages. This curve started life in the seminal paper by Phillips (1958) as a historical correlation between a nominal variable, the rate of change in money wages, and a nonlinear function of a real variable, the unemployment rate. Given that both variables are outcomes of complex economic interactions and that one is nominal and the other is real, it is hardly surprising that the empirical Phillips curve has now disappeared from view with the consequences which we have already described. (The *theoretical* Phillips curve survives, however.)

Denis Sargan's Colston paper was one of the very first to try to make some theoretical sense of the Phillips correlation by pointing out that, at least in the long run, the Phillips curve must be about real and not nominal wages. This fundamental insight has, of course, been extended in a multitude of ways although not until the theoretical work of Friedman (1968), Phelps (1967, 1970), Mortensen (1970) and the empirical work of Lucas and Rapping (1969) was the *market* for labour returned to the centre of the stage. However, in spite of this latter paper, subsequent empirical work on wages has still been dominated by the Phillips curve paradigm with the labour *market* firmly in the background. By this I mean that wage equations are not typically treated in conjunction with their natural market partner, namely employment. Indeed, the usual partner of a wage equation is a price equation – thus we have the 'wage–price sector' where sector here refers to a part of a model rather than a sector of the economy.

So our purpose in this chapter is to drag the wage equation out of the 'wage–price sector' and put it back into the labour market where it belongs. Our intention is to set out a sequence of models which will provide some basis for the sensible discussion of employment and particularly wage equations. We begin by considering the standard market-clearing model with price-taking agents and this is followed by a discussion of models where the wage does not adjust in the short run to clear the market. We then introduce trade unions explicitly into the analysis looking at two models, the first where there is a union sector and a large, competitive market-clearing sector and the second where union collective agreements dominate wage determination throughout the economy. We conclude with some general remarks.

2 Demand and Supply in the Labour Market, and Market-Clearing Models

At the heart of any model of the labour market must be the labour demand and supply functions. Starting with the demand side we consider first a standard model of the demand for labour by a price-taking firm. At the expense of some slight additional complications we could equally well have considered an imperfectly competitive firm. The essence of the analysis would remain unaltered. Assuming that the capital stock is predetermined and that, apart from labour, there is one other variable factor of production which may be thought of as raw materials (plus energy), then the static demand for labour can be written in linear form as

$$n_t^d = \alpha_0 + \alpha_1 \frac{w_t}{p_{ft}} (1 + t_{1t}) + \alpha_2 \frac{p_{mt}}{p_{ft}} + \alpha_3 k_t;$$
$$\alpha_1 < 0, \alpha_2 < 0, \alpha_3 > 0 \quad (1)$$

where n_t^d is the demand for labour; w_t is the nominal wage; p_{ft} is the price of output; p_{mt} is the price of materials; t_{1t} is the tax rate on employment; and k_t is the capital stock. We treat this from now on as the *aggregate* demand for labour, where materials and energy are imported; the economy may, for example, be assumed to consist of a large number of identical firms.

A number of points are worth noting. First, lags will appear in this equation if, for example, there are costs associated with changing employment. Such costs will also imply that the demand for labour will depend on future expectations of the price variables (see Sargent 1978, for example). Since we do not wish to focus on this issue, we suppose that these have been substituted out. It is, however, worth remembering that as a consequence of this, a correctly specified 'reduced form' labour demand equation should contain all variables which are of value in forecasting prices. Second, we ignore the hours dimension of labour input; n, therefore, represents employment. Third, we can, of course, write down an alternative demand function which specifies employment conditional on output. Given our assumption that the firm is a price taker, current output is endogenous even at the firm level and for expositional purposes we therefore prefer to work with equation

(1). Thus we can read off the impact of wages on employment without having to specify a separate model to determine output. In the context of an economy-wide model this is not, of course, a problem and the output formulation may be preferred. Fourth, we are assuming that the firm is not 'output constrained'. If the firm is exogenously constrained in the amount of its product which can be sold, then output will be exogenous and must appear in the labour demand function. Equation (1) then becomes a 'notional' rather than an 'active' demand relation. Investigating this question involves modelling the market for output and since this takes us outside the topic of immediate concern we shall not pursue it further but simply stick with equation (1). Fifth, the price p_{ft} refers to gross output not value added. Were a value added price to be used then, at least under certain conditions, p_{mt} would not appear. We prefer the gross output formulation since p_{ft} then refers to prices of goods bought and sold in actual markets rather than to the price of some notional stuff (value added) which is bought and sold in some implicit market.

Turning now to the labour supply equation, we may simply write down the function which is consistent with intertemporal optimization on the part of individual agents (Lucas and Rapping (1969) give the two-period model and Sargent (1979, pp. 367–73) a general version). Thus we have

$$n_t^s = \beta_0 + \beta_1 \frac{w_t(1-t_{2t})}{p_{ct}} + \beta_2 W_t^n + \beta_3 r_t + \beta_4 z_t^s;$$

$$\beta_1 > 0,\ \beta_2 < 0,\ \beta_3 > 0 \quad (2)$$

where p_{ct} is the price of consumption goods; t_{2t} is the income tax rate; W_t^n is the 'normal' real wage; r_t is the real interest rate; and z_t^s is all exogenous factors influencing labour supply. These latter will include a measure of the 'at risk' population, the level of unemployment benefit, redundancy payments and the like, initial wealth and any other relevant labour supply variables. The normal real wage is simply a weighted sum of expected future real wages. So it is possible that fluctuations in the current real wage relative to this normal level could lead to a large labour supply response because of the intertemporal substitutability of leisure even if the long-run effect, $(\beta_1 + \beta_2)$, is small or negative. The positive real interest rate effect also arises from intertemporal substitution possibilities and is of considerable importance as we shall see. Finally, as with the demand model, we take (2) as the aggregate equation and lags may well arise either from costs of adjustment or habit persistence.

Suppose then that wages adjust to equilibrate the demand and supply of labour in every period. Then obviously, given the wage, employment will satisfy both equations (1) and (2). The equilibrium real wage in terms of producer prices, $(w_t/p_{ft})^*$, is then given by

$$\left(\frac{w_t}{p_{ft}}\right)^* = \left(\frac{\beta_1(1-t_{2t})}{(1+t_{3t})} - \alpha_1(1+t_{1t})\right)^{-1} \times \left((\alpha_0-\beta_0)+\alpha_2\frac{p_{mt}}{p_{ft}}+\alpha_3 k_t-\beta_0-\beta_2 W_t^n-\beta_3 r_t-\beta_4 z_t^s\right) \tag{3}$$

where we have assumed that the only wedge between producer prices and consumer prices is the tax rate on goods, t_{3t}. Thus

$$p_{ct} = p_{ft}(1+t_{3t}). \tag{4}$$

The following points are worth noting. First, the labour market determines *real* wages in terms of real variables some of which are not exogenous (e.g. p_{mt}/p_{ft}, r_t and possibly W_t^n which may be responsive to current real wages). Second, taxes of all kinds are very important. In particular it is worth noting that if we define the producers' real wage $W_t^f = w_t(1+t_{1t})/p_{ft}$ and the consumers' real wage $W_t^c = w_t(1-t_{2t})/p_{ct}$, then we have

$$W_t^c = \frac{(1-t_{2t})}{(1+t_{1t})(1+t_{3t})} W_t^f \simeq (1-T_t)\, W_t^f$$

where $T_t = t_{1t} + t_{2t} + t_{3t}$.

So the total tax 'wedge' is simply the sum of tax rates on employers, employees and goods as we might expect. Third, it appears at first sight that there is no room in this model for 'cyclical' fluctuations in employment where these are defined as fluctuations not arising from exogenous *labour* supply or *labour* demand shocks. It is, however, possible for aggregate demand shifts to influence employment essentially through the real interest rate term in labour supply. Thus a rise in government expenditure can, if it raises the real interest rate, both raise employment (and hence output) and lower the real wage. The role of the real interest rate is thus crucial in this kind of model.

However, nothing remotely resembling a Phillips-type relation will occur here in the sense that nominal shocks will not influence either real wages or employment unless one can make some argument concerning the normal real wage. (In order to allow nominal shocks to have an impact we require some informational deficiency: in the context of the labour market, Alogoskoufis (1982) provides a good example.) We shall, however, return to this issue later. Finally, it is worth noting that equation (3) provides the long-run solution for alternative disequilibrium models if they assume that wages adjust so as to attain the equilibrium real wage in the long run. The range of variables which should appear is extensive and if the real interest rate is substituted out, the set would become even more comprehensive. Most of the equations which purport to have this long-run property, in fact, omit a fair proportion of the relevant variables.

3 Disequilibrium Models

The adjective 'disequilibrium' in this context refers to the fact that the real wage does not satisfy equation (3). If this is the case we have a double problem. First, what then determines the real wage and, second, what determines employment, for if the real wage does not satisfy equation (3) then the demand and supply functions cannot be simultaneously satisfied. To solve the former problem involves constructing a theory of wage setting by the firm. One such theory is set out in Mortensen (1970) and is based on the so-called dynamic monopsony model. Here the firm adjusts its wage rate relative to external circumstances in order to regulate the flow of new workers. The Mortensen model also contains a theory of employment dynamics but the whole thing is a little difficult to operationalize. At this stage we simply bypass the question of a rigorous model of wage determination in a disequilibrium framework returning to it when we discuss the role of trade unions. It is clear, however, that there exists any number of *ad hoc* mechanisms through which the real wage might adjust towards $(w_t/p_{ft})^*$. One might consider an error correction mechanism of the form

$$\Delta\left(\frac{w_t}{p_{ft}}\right) = \delta_1 \Delta\left(\frac{w_t}{p_{ft}}\right)^* + \delta_2\left[\left(\frac{w_{t-1}}{p_{f,t-1}}\right)^* - \left(\frac{w_{t-1}}{p_{f,t-1}}\right)\right] \tag{5}$$

which reduces to simple partial adjustment if $\delta_1 = \delta_2$. Another way of writing this is to make use of equations (1), (2) and (3) to obtain (ignoring taxes)

$$\Delta\left(\frac{w_t}{p_{ft}}\right) = \frac{\delta_1}{(\beta_1-\alpha_1)(1-\delta_1)}\,\Delta(n_t{}^d - n_t{}^s) + \frac{\delta_2}{(\beta_1-\alpha_1)(1-\delta_1)}\,(n_{t-1}{}^d - n_{t-1}{}^s). \tag{6}$$

Again if we set $\delta_1 = \delta_2$ we have what is essentially a real wage Phillips curve, although the relationship between the excess demand for labour and the measured level of unemployment is somewhat tenuous, at least in the British context. For example, in Britain the unemployment rate at the very peak of the boom in 1973–4 would have been indicative of a disastrous slump 15 years before. Another interesting variant of equation (5), which is more conveniently considered if we assume a proportional or logarithmic adjustment process, is to suppose that we have periodic nominal wage contracts with the expected price used as the baseline. If we assume simple partial adjustment ($\delta_1 = \delta_2$) we obtain

$$\log\left(\frac{w_t}{p_t{}^e}\right) = \log\left(\frac{w_{t-1}}{p_{t-1}}\right) + \frac{\delta_1}{(\beta_1-\alpha_1)(1-\delta_1)}\,(n_t{}^d - n_t{}^s)$$

or

$$\Delta \log w_t = (\log p_t{}^e - \log p_{t-1}) + \frac{\delta_1}{(\beta_1-\alpha_1)(1-\delta_1)}\,(n_t{}^d - n_t{}^s) \tag{7}$$

which looks like an ‘expectations augmented’ Phillips curve.

Although these equations may be used as wage models in isolation, it is clear that given the number of possible variables which may enter the excess demand term, it is more efficient to consider them jointly with the employment equation. The specification of the employment equation may be done in a variety of ways. The simplest and least satisfactory is to assume that employment is always determined on the demand side. This is clearly at variance with the spirit of the model so we may consider the alternative where employment is set at min $(n_t{}^d, n_t{}^s)$. Thus employment is determined on the short side of the market. This model has been estimated by Rosen and Quandt (1978), for example, with some lack of success. On the basis of their estimates they conclude that the 1930s was a period of excess demand for labour and the 1960s mainly a period of excess supply, although more recent work (Romer, 1981) eliminates these unfortunate properties by changing the specification of the supply equation. One of the main objections to this approach is that there is not one large market for labour but many different submarkets some of which may be in excess demand while others are in excess supply. This suggests an extension which is hinted at in Muellbauer and Winter (1980) and which goes as follows. (This model is set out in Nickell (1980). Subsequently I discovered that it had also been written up in an unpublished manuscript by Kooiman and Kloek (1979), although they did not attach it to the wage equation.)

Suppose we have N separated labour markets with a uniform wage and demand and supply functions in the ith market given by

$$n_{it}{}^{d} = \tilde{X}_t\tilde{\alpha} + \tilde{u}_t + u_{it}; \qquad n_{it}{}^{s} = \tilde{Z}_t\tilde{\beta} + \tilde{v}_t + v_{it} \tag{8}$$

where $\tilde{u}_t$, $\tilde{v}_t$ are white-noise error terms, $\tilde{X}_t$, $\tilde{Z}_t$ are sets of variables including wages, and u_{it}, v_{it} are independently distributed across i. If we define U as the set of markets where firms are unconstrained (excess supply) and C as the set of markets where firms are constrained (excess demand), then we have

$$i \in U \text{ iff } v_{it} - u_{it} > \tilde{Y}_t\tilde{\gamma} + \tilde{\eta}_t; \qquad i \in C \text{ iff } v_{it} - u_{it} \leqslant \tilde{Y}_t\tilde{\gamma} + \tilde{\eta}_t$$

where

$$\tilde{Y}_t\tilde{\gamma} + \tilde{\eta}_t = \tilde{X}_t\tilde{\alpha} - \tilde{Z}_t\tilde{\beta} + \tilde{u}_t - \tilde{v}_t.$$

So, if λ_t is the proportion of labour markets in excess supply and N is 'large', we may write

$$\lambda_t = P(v_{it} - u_{it} > \tilde{Y}_t\tilde{\gamma} + \tilde{\eta}_t) = f_1(\tilde{Y}_t\tilde{\gamma} + \tilde{\eta}_t), \text{ say}$$

$$\sum_{i \in U} u_{it} = \lambda_t N \underset{i}{E}(u_{it} \mid v_{it} - u_{it} > \tilde{Y}_t\tilde{\gamma} + \tilde{\eta}_t) = \lambda_t N f_2(\tilde{Y}_t\tilde{\gamma} + \tilde{\eta}_t), \text{ say}$$

$$\sum_{i \in C} v_{it} = (1-\lambda_t)\, N \underset{i}{E}(v_{it} \mid v_{it} - u_{it} \leqslant \tilde{Y}_t\tilde{\gamma} + \tilde{\eta}_t)$$

$$= (1-\lambda_t)\, N f_3(\tilde{Y}_t\tilde{\gamma} + \tilde{\eta}_t), \text{ say.}$$

Note that $\Sigma_{i \in U} u_{it}$ is the sum of the market specific errors in the demand equation in those markets in excess supply. The conditional expectation f_2 is the average error in these markets which is likely to be negative because those markets which have negative demand errors are more likely to fall in the excess supply category.

An exactly similar argument applies with regard to the supply side errors in the excess demand markets.

Assuming that employment is determined on the 'short' side in each submarket we have aggregate employment, n, given by

$$\begin{aligned} n_t &= \sum_{i \in U} (\tilde{X}_t \tilde{\alpha} + \tilde{u}_t + u_{it}) + \sum_{i \in C} (\tilde{Z}_t \tilde{\beta} + \tilde{v}_t + v_{it}) \\ &= f_1 N(\tilde{X}_t \tilde{\alpha} + \tilde{u}_t) + \sum_{i \in U} u_{it} + (1 - f_1) N(\tilde{Z}_t \tilde{\beta} + \tilde{v}_t) + \sum_{i \in C} v_{it} \end{aligned}$$

or

$$n_t = f_1 N(\tilde{X}_t \tilde{\alpha} + \tilde{u}_t + f_2) + (1 - f_1) N(\tilde{Z}_t \tilde{\beta} + \tilde{v}_t + f_3). \tag{9}$$

Next we may generate aggregate equations by defining

$$N(\tilde{X}_t \tilde{\alpha} + \tilde{u}_t) = X_t \alpha + u_t, \qquad N(\tilde{Z}_t \tilde{\beta} + \tilde{v}_t) = Z_t \beta + v_t,$$
$$N(\tilde{Y}_t \tilde{\gamma} + \tilde{\eta}_t) = Y_t \gamma + \eta_t.$$

This adding-up procedure clearly involves either adjustment of the coefficient, if the variable is a (common) price, or adjusting the variable, if it is a quantity. Writing equation (9) out in full thus yields

$$\begin{aligned} n_t = f_1 \left(\frac{Y_t \gamma + \eta_t}{N} \right) (Y_t \gamma + \eta_t) + Z_t \beta + N f_1 \left(\frac{Y_t \gamma + \eta_t}{N} \right) f_2 \left(\frac{Y_t \gamma + \eta_t}{N} \right) \\ + N \left[1 - f_1 \left(\frac{Y_t \gamma + \eta_t}{N} \right) \right] f_3 \left(\frac{Y_t \gamma + \eta_t}{N} \right) + v_t. \end{aligned} \tag{10}$$

If we now suppose that v_{it}, u_{it} are bivariate normal with zero mean and parameters $(\sigma_1, \sigma_2, \rho)$, and define

$$\sigma_3 = N({\sigma_1}^2 + {\sigma_2}^2 - 2\sigma_1 \sigma_2 \rho)^{1/2}$$

then, by using standard results on conditional normal expectations (see Tallis, 1961), it may be shown that equation (10) reduces to

$$n_t = -\Phi \left(\frac{Y_t \gamma + \eta_t}{\sigma_3} \right) (Y_t \gamma + \eta_t) + X_t \alpha - \sigma_3 \phi \left(\frac{Y_t \gamma + \eta_t}{\sigma_3} \right) + u_t \tag{11}$$

where ϕ, Φ are the standard normal density and CDF respectively. Both σ_3 and $(Y_t \gamma + \eta_t)$ clearly play an important role in this equation which can be clarified if we rewrite equation (11) as

$$n_t = (X_t\alpha + u_t) - \left[\Phi\left(\frac{Y_t\gamma + \eta_t}{\sigma_3}\right)(Y_t\gamma + \eta_t) + \sigma_3\phi\left(\frac{Y_t\gamma + \eta_t}{\sigma_3}\right)\right]$$

$$= \text{aggregate demand for labour} - g(Y_t\gamma + \eta_t, \sigma_3)$$

where g is some non-negative function with the easily demonstrated properties that $g_1 > 0$, $g_2 > 0$. The variance of $(u_{it} - v_{it})$ is σ_3^2/N^2, and σ_3 thus indicates the variability of the extent of disequilibrium across markets, whereas $(Y_t\gamma + \eta_t)$ is a measure of the aggregate excess demand for labour. Thus for a given level of aggregate demand for labour, any increase either in the extent of aggregate excess demand or in the variability of excess demand across markets will lead to lower employment. These results are both in accord with intuition. Notice further that if both σ_3 and $(Y_t\gamma + \eta_t)$ are zero, g is zero and we have the equilibrium model. On the other hand if only σ_3 is zero, Φ takes on the value zero if $Y_t\gamma + \eta_t < 0$ and unity if $Y_t\gamma + \eta_t > 0$. Then equation (11) becomes

$$n_t = X_t\alpha + u_t \qquad \text{if } Y_t\gamma + \eta_t < 0 \text{ (aggregate excess supply)}$$

$$= Z_t\beta + v_t \qquad \text{if } Y_t\gamma + \eta_t > 0 \text{ (aggregate excess demand)}$$

and the model has the form $n_t = \min(n_t^d, n_t^s)$. Thus both the equilibrium model and the aggregate 'min condition' disequilibrium model are special cases of (11).

Estimating equation (11) alone is feasible, but identification is clearly weak, and using the wage equation as well will lead to enormous efficiency gains. Suppose we specify a wage equation with the partial adjustment form

$$\frac{w_t}{p_{ft}} = \delta_0 + \delta_1\left(\frac{w_t}{p_{ft}}\right)^* + (1-\delta_1)\left(\frac{w_{t-1}}{p_{f,t-1}}\right) + \sum_{i=2}\delta_i D_{it} \qquad (12)$$

where D_{it} are any other variables which are thought to maintain the real wage away from equilibrium (e.g. union effects).

Now if we ignore taxes for simplicity, we may write the demand and supply functions as

$$X_t\alpha + u_t = \alpha_1\left(\frac{w_t}{p_{ft}}\right) + X_t'\alpha' + u_t,$$

$$Z_t\beta + u_t = \beta_1\left(\frac{w_t}{p_{ft}}\right) + Z_t'\beta' + v_t \qquad (13)$$

simply separating out the wage terms. We have

$$\left(\frac{w_t}{p_{ft}}\right)^* = \frac{1}{\beta_1 - \alpha_1}\,(X_t{}'\alpha' - Z_t{}'\beta' + \eta_t) \tag{14}$$

or

$$\left(\frac{w_t}{p_{ft}}\right)^* = \frac{1}{\beta_1 - \alpha_1}\,(Y_t\gamma + \eta_t) + \frac{w_t}{p_{ft}}\,. \tag{15}$$

From equations (12) and (15) we can write

$$Y_t\gamma + \eta_t = \frac{\beta_1 - \alpha_1}{\delta_1}\left[\left(\frac{w_t}{p_{ft}} - \frac{w_{t-1}}{p_{f,t-1}}\right)(1-\delta_1) - \delta_0 - \sum_{i=2} \delta_i D_{it}\right]. \tag{16}$$

Substituting equations (14) and (16) into equations (12) and (11) respectively, we obtain the nonlinear two-equation model

$$n_t = -\Phi\left(\frac{A_t}{\sigma_3}\right) A_t + X_t\alpha - \sigma_3\phi\left(\frac{A_t}{\sigma_3}\right) + u_t \tag{17a}$$

$$\frac{w_t}{p_{ft}} = \delta_0 + \frac{\delta_1}{\beta_1 - \alpha_1}\,(X_t{}'\alpha' - Z_t{}'\beta') + (1-\delta_1)\left(\frac{w_{t-1}}{p_{f,t-1}}\right)$$

$$+ \sum_{i=2} \delta_i D_{it} + \frac{\delta_1}{\beta_1 - \alpha_1}\,\eta_t \tag{17b}$$

where

$$A_t = \frac{\beta_1 - \alpha_1}{\delta_1}\left[(1-\delta_1)\,\Delta\left(\frac{w_t}{p_{ft}}\right) - \delta_0 - \sum_{i=2} \delta_i D_{it}\right].$$

Thus not only does the wage equation enable us to obtain a far greater degree of identification, but it also allows us to eliminate the troublesome error, η_t, from the nonlinear sections of the employment function. So the model defined by equations (17a, b) seems fairly straightforward to estimate, and in joint work with Martyn Andrews we have already had some most encouraging preliminary results.

Finally the key lesson of this section is that if we are to estimate an *ad hoc* wage adjustment equation there are enormous gains in both clarity and efficiency to be had by considering the employment relation along with it.

4 A Market-Clearing Model with a Union Sector

In this section we consider a model where the union sector is not trivial but is not so large as to dominate completely the wage setting behaviour in the economy. The remaining sector is then assumed to be competitive and the wage in this sector adjusts to clear the market. This model is similar to that described in Minford (1983).

Our strategy here is to determine what adjustments have to be made to the demand and supply equations set out in section 2 if unions are considered explicitly. In particular we consider two key variables. The first is the proportion of (identical) firms which pay union rates, μ_t. This is the so-called coverage variable and must be sharply contrasted with the unionization rate which refers to the proportion of the workforce unionized. The latter variable is typically rather smaller than the former and serves as a useful measure of union power. As our second key variable, however, we shall use the mark-up of union over non-union wage rates. So if w_{ut} refers to the union wage rate paid in the covered sector and w_{nt} is the non-union wage rate, then the mark-up, m_t, is given by

$$w_{nt}(1+m_t) = w_{ut}. \tag{18}$$

We may also define the average wage rate, w_t, by

$$w_t = \mu_t w_{ut} + (1-\mu_t)\, w_{nt} \tag{19}$$

and then equations (18) and (19) imply

$$w_{nt} = \frac{w_t}{1+\mu_t m_t}, \qquad w_{ut} = \frac{w_t(1+m_t)}{(1+\mu_t m_t)}. \tag{20}$$

Equation (19) is not absolutely correct since the true average wage must be employment weighted and, since employment in the covered sector firms is lower than in the identical uncovered sector, the variable μ_t, which refers to the proportion of firms in the covered sector, is not the correct employment weight. It is, however, very close to it unless m_t is very large and so we ignore this problem. The best estimate of m_t for the British economy is around 8 per cent (see Stewart, 1983): this is the only estimate for Britain based on individual data.

Starting with the demand side we may write the demand for labour in firms in the two sectors as

$$\tilde{n}_{ut}{}^{d} = \tilde{\alpha}_0 + \tilde{\alpha}_1 \frac{w_{ut}}{p_t} + \tilde{\alpha}_2 \frac{p_{mt}}{p_t} + \tilde{\alpha}_3 k_t$$

$$\tilde{n}_{nt}{}^{d} = \tilde{\alpha}_0 + \tilde{\alpha}_1 \frac{w_{nt}}{p_t} + \tilde{\alpha}_2 \frac{p_{mt}}{p_t} + \tilde{\alpha}_3 k_t$$

where we have ignored taxes for simplicity of exposition. If there are N firms, with $\mu_t N$ in the covered sector, we may multiply the first equation by $\mu_t N$ and the second by $(1-\mu_t)N$ and add to obtain

$$n_t{}^{d} = N\tilde{\alpha}_0 + N\tilde{\alpha}_1 \left(\frac{\mu_t w_{ut} + (1-\mu_t)\, w_{nt}}{p_t}\right) + N\tilde{\alpha}_2 \frac{p_{mt}}{p_t} + N\tilde{\alpha}_3 k_t.$$

Setting $N\tilde{\alpha}_i = \alpha_i$, $i = 0, 1, 2, 3$, and using equation (19) we have:

$$n_t{}^{d} = \alpha_0 + \alpha_1 \frac{w_t}{p_t} + \alpha_2 \frac{p_{mt}}{p_t} + \alpha_3 k_t$$

which is the standard demand equation. Thus for linear models, the introduction of unions has no effect on the aggregate demand side. Of course in a log-linear model this would no longer be the case but even then the adjustments would be slight.

On the supply side, however, things are a little more complicated. Suppose we have an exogenous labour force L. Then the simplest assumption to make about the covered sector is to assume that individuals have an absolute preference for working in this sector as opposed to working in the uncovered sector or remaining unemployed. So whenever an individual who is either unemployed or working in the uncovered sector receives any job offer in the covered sector he or she immediately accepts it. Furthermore, we suppose that union wage bargaining essentially determines the mark-up. Which variables influence this mark-up we shall discuss later. As a consequence of these assumptions we may now limit our concern to the supply choices made by the $L - \mu_t N \tilde{n}_{ut}{}^{d}$ individuals who are not employed in the covered sector. The essential choice is either to remain unemployed or to work in the uncovered sector. Remaining unemployed may be desirable for a number of reasons. Apart from the obvious benefit argument, it may be the case that the probability of obtaining a covered-sector job is higher for the unemployed. This may be because they have greater access to information about jobs or because they can seize any opportunity immediately or because a job in the uncovered sector acts as a negative signal to employers. These are not very powerful arguments, however, and the first and third could easily go the other way.

Looking at the problem more formally we have the supply of labour to the non-covered sector, $n_{nt}{}^{s}$, given by

$$n_{nt}{}^{s} = (L - \mu_t N \tilde{n}_{ut}{}^{d}) f(.) \tag{21}$$

where f is the proportion of the available labour force willing to work. To determine the structure of f, consider first the position of an unemployed individual. Suppose the probability per period of his obtaining work in the covered sector is ϕ_u. Then if V_1 is his expected present value earnings, r is the discount rate and b the level of benefit, V_1 will satisfy

$$V_1 = \frac{b}{p} + \phi_u \frac{w_u}{rp} + (1-\phi_u) \frac{V_1}{1+r}$$

for the stationary, infinite horizon case. Thus V_1 satisfies

$$V_1 = \frac{1+r}{\phi_u + r}\left(\frac{b}{p} + \frac{\phi_u w_u}{rp}\right).$$

Similarly if V_2 is the expected present value for an employee in the non-covered sector and ϕ_e is his probability of obtaining a job at the union wage, we have

$$V_2 = \frac{1+r}{\phi_e + r}\left(\frac{w_n}{p} + \frac{\phi_e w_u}{rp}\right).$$

Then we may naturally assume that f is increasing in $(V_2 - V_1)$ which is given by

$$V_2 - V_1 = (1+r)\left[\frac{w_n}{p(\phi_e + r)} - \frac{b}{p(\phi_u + r)} + \frac{w_u}{rp}\left(\frac{\phi_e}{\phi_e + r} - \frac{\phi_u}{\phi_u + r}\right)\right].$$

So we may write f as the function

$$f = f\left(\frac{w_{nt}}{p_t}, \frac{b_t}{p_t}, \frac{w_{ut}}{p_t}\right) \tag{22}$$

with $f_1 > 0$, $f_2 < 0$, $f_3 \lesseqgtr 0$ as $\phi_u \gtreqless \phi_e$. Thus we have an aggregate supply function of the form

$$n_t{}^s = \mu_t N\tilde{n}_{ut}{}^d + (L - \mu_t N\tilde{n}_{ut}{}^d)\, f\left(\frac{w_{nt}}{p_t}, \frac{b_t}{p_t}, \frac{w_{ut}}{p_t}\right).$$

Our fundamental concern is the impact on aggregate supply of the parameters μ_t and m_t holding the average wage constant. These are given by

$$\frac{\partial n_t{}^s}{\partial \mu_t} = (1 - \overset{+}{f})\left(\frac{\overset{+}{n}_{ut}}{\mu_t} - \frac{\mu_t \alpha_1 w_t m_t (1+m_t)}{p_t (1+\mu_t m_t)^2}\right) - \frac{(L - \mu_t N\overset{+}{\tilde{n}}_{ut}{}^d)\, w_t m_t}{(1+\mu_t m_t)^2 p_t}\,[\overset{+}{f}_1 + f_3(1+m_t)].$$

This is likely to be positive unless f_1 is very large and/or f_3 is large and positive.

$$\frac{\partial n_t{}^s}{\partial m_t} = \frac{(1-f)\,\alpha_1 \mu_t w_t (1-\mu_t)}{(1+\mu_t m_t)^2 p_t} - \frac{(L - \mu_t N\overset{+}{\tilde{n}}_{ut}{}^d)\, w_t}{(1+\mu_t m_t)^2} \times [\overset{+}{f}_1 \mu_t + f_3(1-\mu_t)].$$

This is almost certain to be negative unless f_3 is extraordinarily perverse.

The consequence of this analysis is that, if we introduce a union sector into a market-clearing model, we may simply add a coverage measure and a mark-up measure into the aggregate supply equation. The latter variable is, however, unlikely to be readily available and therein lies a problem. The mark-up is clearly an endogenous variable. The relative wage in the union sector will emerge as the consequence of bargaining between firms and workers within this sector. The outcome of the bargain will depend, in general, upon all the factors affecting the demand for labour in this sector as well as the alternative opportunities available to workers in the competitive sector (see the next section for an explicit bargaining model). These outside opportunities are clearly influenced by the general employment situation in this sector which is, in its turn, affected by all the exogenous supply-side factors. The result is that the mark-up must be replaced by a function of all the exogenous variables directly relevant to the labour market as well as any direct exogenous measures of union power which are available. The resulting 'supply' function thus contains all exogenous labour market variables as well as direct measures of union power. This does not, of course, mean that it is unidentified since we still have exogenous variables available from the demand side of the goods market to serve as instruments. As we shall see, however, it does imply that this model is more or less indistinguishable from that discussed in the next section, where the economy is assumed to be completely unionized. (The model of Minford (1983) has a final form which is almost the same as that derived in the next section.)

5 A Model of a Unionized Economy

Our aim in this section is to consider a model suitable for an economy in which collective bargaining is the predominant mode of wage determination and where the uncovered sector is of negligible importance. It can be argued that the British economy has this form given that some 80 per cent of manual workers are covered by collective agreements and that wages councils and other regulatory bodies cover a considerable portion of the remainder. This leaves only tiny islands of competitive wage determination which are probably of little consequence.

In the light of this, we must specify precisely a bargaining model for the determination of wages. If we assume that the typical bargain occurs between each firm and its unionized employees we can write down the problem in stylized form as follows. Suppose the firm has a utility function over profit of the form $U(\pi(w, n))$ and the union has a utility function $u(w, n)$ where w is the real wage and n is employment. There are then three possible types of bargain we might consider. First, we might have the union setting the wage and the firm setting employment. Second, we might generalize this to the case where the firm and the union bargain about the wage and the firm sets employment. Third, we can have the case where the firm and the union bargain directly about both the wage and the level of employment. There has been extensive discussion in the literature on all of these possibilities, and some limited testing of the various alternatives: for theoretical discussions see McDonald and Solow (1981), Nickell (1982), Oswald and Ulph (1982), Grout (1983); for testing between alternatives see MaCurdy and Pencavel (1982) and Ashenfelter and Brown (1983).

Some of the key points are the following. The first model is the special case of the second in which the firm is powerless in a wage bargain. The third is the only one which will typically generate a Pareto efficient outcome. In the first two it is possible to rearrange employment and the wage in such a way as to make both parties better off. On the other hand, in the first two cases the firm is on its competitive demand for labour schedule at the given wage. In the third case, both the wage and the level of employment will emerge as direct functions of all the exogenous factors influencing the bargain. The strong empirically based argument against this type of bargain is that wages are typically set at relatively lengthy discrete intervals whereas employment is adjusted more or less continuously with no re-negotiation of the wage. It is almost inconceivable that the firm will engage in detailed bargaining over each adjustment, but will view the setting of employment as part of its 'right to manage'. This will, typically, only break down in the case where the outcome involves large-scale compulsory redundancies.

In the light of this, we consider only the second model here but the third may be developed very easily along the same lines. Since this second model has already been presented and estimated in Nickell and Andrews (1983), we concentrate only on the salient issues. Since the firm sets employment we suppose that, for any given wage outcome w, it chooses employment to solve $\max_n \pi(w, n)$, generating a known demand function $n^*(w)$. The wage bargain is assumed to be described by the solution to a Nash bargaining model. (McDonald and Solow (1981) discuss alternative bargaining models whose comparative static properties are generally rather similar to those of the Nash solution.) Thus w satisfies

$$\max_w \, [U(\pi(w, n^*(w))) - U(\bar{\pi})]^\beta [u(w, n^*(w)) - \bar{u}] \tag{23}$$

where $\bar{\pi}$, $\bar{u}$ are the levels of profit and union utility which may be obtained in the complete absence of any cooperation by the other side.

On the firm side we may write the real profit function as

$$\pi(w_t, n_t) = \max_{M_t} \frac{p_{ft}^{\,e}}{p_{ct}^{\,e}} \left(g(n_t, M_t, k_t) - \frac{p_{mt}}{p_{ft}^{\,e}} M_t \right) - \frac{w_t}{p_{ct}^{\,e}} (1 + t_{1t}) n_t \tag{24}$$

where g is the production function with n_t, k_t and materials/energy, M_t, as inputs. The fall-back profit, $\bar{\pi}$, we take as exogenous and the capital stock as predetermined. The superscript e refers to expectation over the coming period.

The union side is slightly more complex. We first assume that the union takes account of a fixed pool of workers of size l, which might be thought of simply as a parameter of the union's utility function reflecting, to some extent, the union's 'social responsibility'; it does not correspond to membership. For those staying with the firm, we specify utility as

$$v_t = v\left(\frac{w_t}{p_{ct}^e}(1-t_{2t}) - \bar{W}_t\right); \qquad v' > 0, v'' < 0. \tag{25}$$

$\bar{W}_t$ is a parameter of the utility function representing a baseline or 'subsistence' level of real wages. So utility is a function of real post-tax earnings relative to this baseline which we may expect to increase over time. This simply reflects the fact that an individual requires a higher real wage in 1980 than in 1960, for example, in order to have the same degree of well-being.

For those workers who do not gain employment within the firm during the next period, utility is specified as

$$\tilde{v}_t = \omega_t v\left(\frac{b_t^e}{p_{ct}^e} - \bar{W}_t\right) + (1-\omega_t)\, v\left(\frac{w_t^*}{p_{ct}^e}(1-t_{2t}) - \bar{W}_t\right). \tag{26}$$

ω_t is the proportion of the period spent unemployed receiving expected benefit b_t^e and $(1-\omega_t)$ is the proportion spent employed receiving an expected alternative wage w_t^*. We take union utility as the sum of all the utilities of the workers in the 'pool' and fall-back union utility $\bar{u}$ is that attained when all the workers have $\tilde{v}_t$. This gives

$$u(w, n) - \bar{u} = n_t v_t + (l - n_t)\,\tilde{v}_t - l\tilde{v}_t = n_t(v_t - \tilde{v}_t). \tag{27}$$

If we now substitute equations (27) and (24) into the Nash objective (23) we have a well-defined bargaining problem. The solution and comparative static results of a rather more general model are discussed in Nickell and Andrews (1983) so here we simply write down the log-linear approximation to the wage bargain generated:

$$\begin{aligned}\log(w_t/p_{ct}^e) = b_0 &+ b_1 \log(w_t^*/p_{ct}^e) + b_2 \log(b_t^e/p_{ct}^e)\\ &+ b_3\omega_t + b_4 \log \bar{W}_t + b_5 t_{1t} + b_6 t_{2t}\\ &+ b_7 \log(p_{ft}^e/p_{ct}^e) + b_8 \log \bar{\pi}_t\\ &+ b_9 \log k_t + b_{10} \log(p_{mt}/p_{ct}^e),\end{aligned} \tag{28}$$

where we expect $b_1 > 0$, $b_2 > 0$, $b_3 < 0$, $b_4 > 0$, $b_5 < 0$, $b_6 > 0$, $b_7 > 0$, $b_8 < 0$, $b_9 > 0$, $b_{10} < 0$.

The corresponding labour demand function has the standard form given by equation (1) although it is more convenient to approximate this in log-linear form.

The great advantage of equation (28) is that it provides some theoretical foundation on which to construct a 'disequilibrium' wage equation. In addition it provides a framework within which Phillips curve results can be interpreted. Several points are worth noting. First it is fundamentally a real wage model, indeed it could hardly be otherwise. Second it is a model which explains the *level* of real wages in period t although dynamics will enter naturally as we shall see. Third, it provides an explicit role for the unemployment rate through the term ω_t which is the length of time a worker can expect to remain unemployed if he is not given a job in the firm. Fourth, it provides a natural role for the level of benefits and taxes of all kinds. Fifth, we can expect all variables influencing the demand for labour to enter.

In order to transform equation (28) into an equation to be estimated we must specify all those regressors which do not directly correspond to observed variables. There are many possibilities but the following appear sensible. w_t^*/p_{ct}^e is the wage individuals can expect to obtain if they are thrown into the market. We might expect this to depend on the real wage in previous periods and, perhaps, on some general measure of the 'trend' level of labour productivity which we might specify by the capital stock normalized by the labour force to eliminate temporary cyclical fluctuations. Exactly the same argument can be applied to $\bar{W}_t$, the 'subsistence' real wage. Thus we might have

$$b_1 \log (w_t^*/p_{ct}^e) + b_4 \log \bar{W}_t = \gamma_0 + \sum_{j=1} \gamma_j \log \left(\frac{w_{t-j}}{p_{c,t-j}}\right) + \beta_1 \log (k_t/L_t). \qquad (29)$$

ω_t can be specified as a linear function of unemployment giving

$$\omega_t = \beta_0 + \beta_2 u_t, \ \beta_2 > 0 \qquad (30)$$

where u is the unemployment rate. The price ratio p_{ft}/p_{ct} is essentially equal to $1 - t_{3t}$, the tax rate on goods and we must normalize k_t if it is to refer to the aggregate capital stock. Again we use the labour force as a normalizing factor, some kind of normalization being essential if we take equation (28) to refer to the whole economy. Finally the level of fall-back profit $\bar{\pi}$ provides an avenue for union power variables since a more powerful union can clearly inflict greater damage to the firm if agreement is not reached. Thus we would specify

$$\log \bar{\pi}_t = \beta_0' + \beta_3 U_{pt}, \qquad \beta_3 < 0 \tag{31}$$

where U_{pt} is a measure of union power. The outcome of this discussion is that we may write equation (28) as

$$\begin{aligned}\log (w_t/p_{ct}^e) = \delta_0 + \delta_1 u_t + \delta_2 \log (b_t/p_{ct}) + \delta_3 t_{1t} + \delta_4 t_{2t} \\ + \delta_5 t_{3t} + \delta_6 U_{pt} + \delta_7 \log (k_t/L_t) \\ + \delta_8 \log (p_{mt}/p_{ft}) + \sum_{j=1} \gamma_j \log (w/p_c)_{t-j}.\end{aligned} \tag{32}$$

where we would expect $\delta_1 < 0$, $\delta_2 > 0$, $\delta_3 < 0$, $\delta_4 > 0$, $\delta_5 < 0$, $\delta_6 > 0$, $\delta_7 > 0$, $\delta_8 < 0$.

If we now combine equation (32) with a log-linear approximation to the labour demand of equation (1), we have a straightforward labour market model which, with minor adjustments, may be written as follows

$$\begin{aligned}\log n_t = \alpha_0 + \alpha_1 \log (w_t(1 + t_{1t})/p_{ft}) + \alpha_2 \log (p_{mt}/p_{ft}) \\ + \alpha_3 \log k_t,\end{aligned} \tag{33}$$

$$\begin{aligned}\log (w_t/p_{ct}) = \log (p_{ct}^e/p_{ct}) + \sum_{j=1} \gamma_j \log (w/p_c)_{t-j} + \delta_0 + \delta_1 u_t \\ + \delta_2 \log (b_t/p_{ct}) + \delta_3 t_{1t} + \delta_4 t_{2t} + \delta_5 t_{3t} + \delta_6 U_{pt} \\ + \delta_7 \log (k_t/L_t) + \delta_8 \log (p_{mt}/p_{ft})\end{aligned} \tag{34}$$

$$\log p_{ct} = \log p_{ft} + t_{3t}, \qquad u_t = (L_t - n_t)/L_t \simeq -\log (n_t/L_t).$$

Several points are worth noting about this model. First, it determines employment and the real wage conditional on the labour force, the capital stock, the real price of materials and energy plus a number of exogenous factors. Second, it has the great advantage of setting the wage equation in a theoretical context enabling us to interpret the role of unemployment, benefits, taxes and union power. These variables have often been added to Phillips curve models but in a relatively *ad hoc* fashion with, typically, only a random selection being included at any one time. Note that equation (34) can be made to look like a Phillips curve, if this is thought desirable, by writing

$$\Delta \log w_t = (\log p_{ct}{}^e - \log p_{ct}) + \Delta \log p_{ct} + (\gamma_1 - 1) \log (w/p_c)_{t-1} + \sum_{j=2} \gamma_j \log (w/p_c)_{t-j} + \ldots .$$

The real wage form of equation (32) is more closely related to the theory, but the alternative may have some advantages. Third, so long as $p_{ct}{}^e = p_{ct}$ in the long run, nominal variables have no long-run impact on employment or real wages. In this sense the model has a long-run neutrality property. The long-run (natural rate) level of employment can be deduced from this model in terms of tax rates, union power, benefits, the labour force, the capital/labour force ratio and the real price of materials. We would expect the last two variables to have a negligible long-run impact although 'income effects' on labour supply may prevent their being precisely zero. Furthermore we would expect long-run employment to be close to unit elastic with respect to the labour force.

Finally, it is of some interest to consider how aggregate shocks to the economy influence employment in this kind of model. Aggregate demand shocks which do not affect tax rates only influence employment through their impact on price forecasting errors $(\log p_{ct}{}^e - \log p_{ct})$. Thus an unexpected monetary/fiscal contraction will lead to prices rising by less than expected and hence to an increase in real wages and a fall in employment. Indeed the demand equation reveals that unless the shock influences taxes or the real price of materials, any impact on employment must come through the real wage. This is a property of any model which specifies a demand for labour function which is based on the profit maximizing behaviour of unconstrained price taking firms. Alternative formulations of labour demand will, of course, allow alternative channels for aggregate demand shocks. It is often asserted, for example, that firms are constrained in the goods market and this is taken as an excuse for including output in the demand equation. There are several objections to this procedure. First, it is difficult to disentangle the demand for labour from the production relation. Indeed the notoriously unstable employment–output relationships which are often presented as labour demand functions appear, in fact, to be more or less totally devoid of economic content. Their use simply serves to mask the important role of the labour *market* and the impact of wages on output is transferred elsewhere (to an export equation, for example). Second, there seems to be little reliable evidence which bears on the question of whether or not firms are constrained in the output market either some or all of the time. If this is thought to be an important issue then it must clearly be investigated in the appropriate fashion. Regressing employment on output is hardly the best place to start.

Another way of approaching the modelling of labour demand is to assume that firms are not price takers. This leads to the inclusion in the demand function of those exogenous factors which shift the firm's demand curve. This implies a labour demand function which directly incorporates aggregate demand shocks. Perhaps the most successful example of this approach is to be found in Sachs (1983) who finds significant effects of the (lagged) real money stock. Other attempts to proceed along these lines have been less successful (see Symons 1981, for example). Another promising alternative is suggested by the growing number of theoretical and empirical studies which investigate the constraints imposed on firms by banks and other corporate lenders (see Wadhwani (1984) for references and empirical investigation). These constraints are typically not neutral with regard to nominal changes and lead to a direct role for both nominal and real interest rates in determining the demand for labour. Suppose, for example, that borrowing limits for a firm are not indexed. Then a rise in inflation and rising nominal interest rates will raise the probability of bankruptcy and in order to reduce this probability, a plant is closed and employment is reduced. This direct role of interest rates in labour demand is thus another possible direct channel for monetary/fiscal policy in the labour market.

Thus the kind of model exemplified by equations (33) and (34) is capable of considerable extension without losing its fundamental characteristic, namely that it forms a simple coherent model of the labour market which serves to determine both real wages and employment. Such a model seems to me to be invaluable for understanding what is going on in the world and should not be lightly discarded.

6 Conclusion

To summarize, we have considered the ways in which wages and employment are determined in a variety of different models of the labour market. The important fact to bear in mind is that wage models are part of labour market models. If wages and employment are treated independently, information is lost and *ad hoc* specifications reign supreme. This is bad theory and bad practice and I hope this contribution goes some way towards eliminating it.

Acknowledgments

Many thanks are due to Meghnad Desai, David Grubb, Andrew Oswald and Pravin Trivedi for detailed comments on an earlier draft. Financial support was provided by the Economic and Social Research Council (in its earlier incarnation), the Department of Employment and the Esmee Fairbairn Trust, for which many thanks.

3

Dynamic Models, the Prediction Error Decomposition and State Space

ANDREW C. HARVEY

1 Introduction

This chapter is primarily concerned with the way in which the likelihood function for a model based on time-series observations can be constructed in terms of prediction errors. It is shown that this method of constructing a likelihood function is applicable to many models, including some which are nonlinear in a time-series sense. It is also shown how the state-space form of a model can be used as the basis for obtaining prediction errors in a wide range of cases. A number of specific topics will be touched on, including two of the areas in which Denis Sargan made important original contributions, namely continuous time models (Sargan, 1974) and missing observations in dynamic econometric models (Sargan and Drettakis, 1974).

1.1 The Prediction Error Decomposition

The classical theory of maximum likelihood estimation is based on a situation in which the T observations, $y_1, \ldots, y_T$, are independently and identically distributed. The joint density function $L(y; \psi)$ is therefore given by

$$L(y; \psi) = \prod_{t=1}^{T} p(y_t) \tag{1}$$

where $p(y_t)$ is the probability density function (pdf) of the tth observation and ψ is the $n \times 1$ vector of unknown parameters. Once the observations have been made, $L(y; \psi)$ is re-interpreted as a likelihood function and the maximum likelihood (ML) estimator of ψ is found by maximizing this function with respect to ψ.

The prime characteristic of a time-series model is that the observations are not independent. Hence equation (1) is not applicable. Instead the definition of a conditional probability density function is used to write

$$L(y;\psi)=\prod_{t=1}^{T} p(y_t|y_{t-1},\ldots) \tag{2}$$

where $p(y_t|y_{t-1},\ldots)$ denotes the pdf of y_t conditional on all the information up to and including time $t-1$.

Example 1 Consider the first-order autoregressive, AR(1), model

$$y_t=\phi y_{t-1}+\epsilon_t, \qquad t=1,\ldots,T \tag{3}$$

with $\epsilon_t \sim NID(0,\ \sigma^2)$. Conditional on y_{t-1}, y_t is normal with a mean of ϕy_{t-1} and a variance of σ^2. Hence

$$\log L(y)=-\frac{(T-1)}{2}\log 2\pi-\frac{(T-1)}{2}\log\sigma^2$$
$$-\frac{1}{2\sigma^2}\sum_{t=2}^{T}(y_t-\phi y_{t-1})^2+\log p(y_1) \tag{4}$$

where $p(y_1)$ is the unconditional pdf of y_1 since no observations are available at $t=0$. If $|\phi|<1$, then y_1 is normally distributed with a mean of zero and a variance of $\sigma^2/(1-\phi^2)$ and $\log p(y_1)$ can be written accordingly. As another possibility, y_1 can be assumed to be fixed, in which case $\log p(y_1)$ is simply dropped from equation (4).

When y_1 is fixed, maximizing the likelihood function is equivalent to minimizing the sum-of-squares function:

$$S(\phi)=\sum_{t=2}^{T}(y_t-\phi y_{t-1})^2=\sum_{t=2}^{T}\epsilon_t^2. \tag{5}$$

Note that when it appears in equation (5), ϵ_t is regarded as a function of ϕ.

If, conditional on the information at $t-1$, y_t has a finite mean and variance, its mean is the minimum mean square estimator (MMSE) of y_t at time $t-1$ (see Harvey, 1981, p. 13). The likelihood function can therefore be expressed in terms of the one-step-ahead prediction errors,

$$\nu_t=y_t-E(y_t|y_{t-1},\ldots), \qquad t=1,\ldots,T. \tag{6}$$

When $p(y_t | y_{t-1}, \ldots)$ is normal, the log-likelihood function is

$$\log L = -\frac{T}{2}\log 2\pi - \frac{T}{2}\sum_{t=1}^{T}\log f_t - \frac{1}{2}\sum_{t=1}^{T}\frac{\nu_t^2}{f_t} \tag{7}$$

where $f_t = \text{var}(y_t | y_{t-1}, \ldots)$. Since the optimal predictor of y_t is $E(y_t | y_{t-1}, \ldots)$, f_t is also the mean square error of this predictor.

In the AR(1) model, equation (3), the prediction error, ν_t, is the same as ϵ_t for $t = 2, \ldots, T$. In many models, however, there is not such a straightforward relationship between the prediction error and a disturbance term in the model.

Example 2 Suppose that an AR(2) process is observed with error, i.e.

$$y_t = y_t^{\dagger} + \epsilon_t \tag{8a}$$

where

$$y_t^{\dagger} = \phi_1 y_{t-1}^{\dagger} + \phi_2 y_{t-2}^{\dagger} + \eta_t \tag{8b}$$

and η_t and ϵ_t are independent white-noise disturbances. With

$$\phi(\text{L}) = 1 - \phi_1\text{L} - \phi_2\text{L}^2$$

where L is the lag operator, equation (8b) can be written as

$$\phi(\text{L})\, y_t^{\dagger} = \eta_t \tag{9}$$

and hence, substituting from equation (8a), we have

$$\phi(\text{L})\, y_t = \eta_t + \phi(\text{L})\, \epsilon_t. \tag{10}$$

The right-hand side of equation (10) is white noise, η_t, plus an MA(2) process and this is itself an MA(2) process. Thus equation (10) can be written

$$y_t = \phi_1 y_{t-1} + \phi_2 y_{t-2} + \xi_t + \theta_1 \xi_{t-1} + \theta_2 \xi_{t-2} \tag{11}$$

where ξ_t is a white-noise disturbance term. This is an ARMA(2, 2) process in which θ_1, θ_2 and $\text{var}(\xi_t)$ are functions of ϕ_1, ϕ_2, $\text{var}(\epsilon_t)$ and $\text{var}(\eta_t)$. It is sometimes referred to as the *canonical form* of equation (8) since it contains a single disturbance term, and by making suitable assumptions about the initial conditions this disturbance term can be identified with the one-step-ahead prediction error. (For example, if $\xi_1 = \xi_2 = 0$, then $\nu_t = \xi_t$ for $t = 3, \ldots, T$.) However, the disadvantage of obtaining the likelihood function from equation (11) is that this model is less parsimonious than equation (8) in that it contains five parameters rather than four. Furthermore, it is difficult to work in terms of the original parameters since θ_1, θ_2 and var(ξ_t) are complicated functions of them that cannot be written down in completely explicit form; see the discussions in Nerlove et al. (1979).

Example 3 Even if the model is in canonical form, the disturbance term can only be identified with the prediction error if suitable assumptions are made about starting values. In the MA(1) model

$$y_t = \epsilon_t + \theta\epsilon_{t-1}, \qquad t = 1, \ldots, T \tag{12}$$

with $\epsilon_t \sim NID(0, \sigma^2)$, the assumption that $\epsilon_0 = 0$ means that the residuals obtained from the recursion

$$\epsilon_t = y_t - \theta\epsilon_{t-1}, \qquad t = 1, \ldots, T, \tag{13}$$

are the same as the one-step-ahead prediction errors. However, this is not the case if $\epsilon_0 \sim N(0, \sigma^2)$. Here it can be shown that the prediction errors are given by the recursion

$$\nu_t = y_t - \theta\nu_{t-1}/f_{t-1} \tag{14}$$

where

$$f_t = 1 + \theta^{2t}/(1 + \theta^2 + \ldots + \theta^{2(t-1)}). \tag{15}$$

Using the ν_t from equation (14) in equation (7) gives what is usually referred to as the exact likelihood function.

Casting a model in state-space form enables prediction errors to be computed in many situations where their form is not obvious from inspection. Thus, it is straightforward to put equation (8) in state-space form and if this is done the likelihood function can be obtained directly in terms of the parameters of interest. In a similar way the MA(1) model (equation 12) can be expressed in state-space form. This leads to the prediction errors of equation (14) and therefore to the exact likelihood function.

1.2 *Missing Observations, Irregular Observations and Continuous Time*

The prediction error decomposition remains valid even if there are missing observations or the observations are irregularly spaced. Thus suppose that an observation is missing at time s, where

$1<s<T$. The likelihood function of $y=(y_1, \ldots, y_{s-1}, y_{s+1}, \ldots, y_T)'$ is

$$L(y) = \prod_{t \neq s} p(y_t | y_{t-1}, \ldots). \tag{16}$$

However, since y_s is missing, $p(y_{s+1}|y_s, \ldots)$ is replaced by $p(y_{s+1}|y_{s-1}, \ldots)$. The mean of this distribution is the optimal predictor two time periods ahead.

Example 4 In the case of an AR(1) model we have

$$y_{s+1} = \phi^2 y_{s-1} + \epsilon_{s+1} + \phi\epsilon_s. \tag{17}$$

Thus, conditional on the observations, the mean and variance at time $s+1$ are

$$E(y_{s+1}|y_{s-1}, \ldots) = \phi^2 y_{s-1},$$
$$\text{var}(y_{s+1}|y_{s-1}, \ldots) = E[(\epsilon_{s+1} + \phi\epsilon_s)^2] = \sigma^2(1+\phi^2).$$

In the above example, expressions for the prediction errors could be obtained directly by inspection. This is the exception rather than the rule. More complex patterns of missing observations and/or more complex models are best handled by putting the model in state-space form and applying the Kalman filter. Cases of temporal aggregation can also be handled by state-space methods.

Once models are set up in continuous time, the constraint that observations can only be made at equally spaced intervals is removed. Again, a state-space approach can be adopted; see section 4.

1.3 Linear and Nonlinear Models

Suppose that y_t denotes the stochastic part of a model, i.e. the part remaining after the systematic component, usually the mean, has been removed and/or a transformation, such as differencing, has been applied. A linear model has the characteristic that it can be written in the form

$$y_t = \sum_{j=0}^{\infty} \psi_j \zeta_{t-j} \tag{18}$$

where the ζ_t are independent random variables with zero mean and finite variance. If

$$\sum_{j=0}^{\infty} \psi_j^2 < \infty \tag{19}$$

the process is stationary; see, for example, Priestley (1980; 1981, pp. 141–3).

Example 5 If $|\phi| < 1$, the AR(1) process (equation 3) can be expressed in the form of equation (18) by writing

$$y_t = \sum_{j=0}^{\infty} \phi^j \epsilon_{t-j}. \tag{20}$$

One consequence of this is that if the ϵ_t are normally distributed, then the unconditional distribution of the y_t is also normal. By way of contrast the nonlinear model

$$y_t = \phi y_{t-1}^2 + \epsilon_t \tag{21}$$

cannot be written in the form of equation (18), and the assumption that $\epsilon_t \sim NID(0, \sigma^2)$ does not lead to the observations being normally distributed. However, the assumption that $\epsilon_t \sim NID(0, \sigma^2)$ is equivalent to the assumption that the conditional distribution of y_t, i.e. $p(y_t | y_{t-1}, \ldots)$, is $NID(0, \sigma^2)$. Thus if y_1 is fixed, the likelihood function of $y = (y_2, \ldots, y_T)'$ can still be written as a prediction error decomposition, i.e.

$$\log L(y) = -\frac{(T-1)}{2} \log 2\pi - \frac{(T-1)}{2} \log \sigma^2 - \frac{1}{2\sigma^2} \sum_{t=2}^{T} (y_t - \phi y_{t-1}^2)^2. \tag{22}$$

Maximizing this function is, of course, equivalent to minimizing the residual sum-of-squares function, $S(\phi) = \Sigma \epsilon_t^2$.

1.4 Non-Normality

Writing the joint density function of the observations in the form of equation (2) does not require that the conditional distributions of the observations be normal. However, if the disturbance terms in the model are not normal, it may be very difficult to determine the conditional distributions of the observations.

Example 6 For the model of equation (8), the disturbance term, ξ_t, in the canonical form (equation 11) is a linear combination of current and past ϵ and η. Unless both disturbance terms are assumed to be normal, it is difficult to derive the distribution of ξ_t and hence obtain the likelihood function in terms of the prediction error decomposition.

Example 7 In the AR(1) model with missing observations, it will be clear from equation (17) that non-normality of the disturbances leads to difficulties. As a general rule, non-normality can only be handled within a maximum likelihood framework if the model is in canonical form and suitable assumptions are made about the initial conditions. The second of these points is illustrated by an AR(1) model, in which the disturbances are independent with zero mean and constant variance, but are not normally distributed. Since the unconditional distribution of y_1 cannot, in general, be derived from such a specification, the usual course of action is to assume that y_1 is fixed.

Because a likelihood function is often difficult to construct when there are non-normal disturbances in the model, the assumption of normality is often adopted even when it is not taken seriously. Estimators obtained by maximizing the resulting 'likelihood' function are then referred to as Gaussian or quasi-maximum likelihood estimators.

1.5 The Prediction Error Decomposition and the Cholesky Decomposition

If the model is *linear* and if all the disturbances are normally distributed, then the full set of observations, y, has a multivariate normal distribution. If the mean vector and covariance matrix of y are denoted by μ and V respectively, this distribution can be written as

$$\log L(y) = -\tfrac{1}{2}T\log 2\pi - \tfrac{1}{2}\log|V| - \tfrac{1}{2}(y-\mu)'V^{-1}(y-\mu). \quad (23)$$

The Cholesky decomposition of V^{-1} consists of finding a $T\times T$ lower triangular matrix, H, with ones on the leading diagonal, such that $H'DH = V^{-1}$, where D is a $T\times T$ diagonal positive definite matrix. However, it can be shown that Hy is the vector of one-step-ahead prediction errors and that the tth diagonal element of D is f_t^{-1} for $t = 1, \ldots, T$. Thus substituting for V in equation (23) gives the prediction error decomposition form of the likelihood function in equation (7).

In many time-series models there is little point in working with equation (23) since by expressing the model in state-space form the likelihood function can be obtained very easily via the prediction error decomposition. However, a recognition of the link between state-space models and the Cholesky decomposition can sometimes lead to useful algorithms (see Wecker and Ansley, 1983).

2 State-Space Form

A state-space model for a single series of observations consists of a transition equation for the $m \times 1$ state vector, α_t, together with a measurement equation. The transition equation is of the form

$$\alpha_t = T_t \alpha_{t-1} + c_t + \eta_t, \qquad t = 1, \ldots, T \tag{24}$$

where T_t is an $m \times m$ transition matrix, c_t is an $m \times 1$ vector, and η_t is a vector of white-noise disturbances with zero mean and covariance matrix, Q_t. The measurement equation takes the form

$$y_t = z_t' \alpha_t + d_t + \epsilon_t, \qquad t = 1, \ldots, T \tag{25}$$

where z_t is an $m \times 1$ vector, d_t is a scalar and ϵ_t is a white-noise disturbance term with mean zero and variance h_t, which may be assumed to be distributed independently of η_t in all time periods, so that $E(\eta_t \epsilon_s) = 0$ for all t, s. In a linear state-space model, T_t, c_t, Q_t, Z_t, d_t and h_t are assumed to be fixed in repeated samples, i.e. they do not depend on any values of y_t $(t = 1, \ldots, T)$.

The Kalman filter consists of a set of recursive equations for updating estimates of the state vector as new observations become available. Given the mean and covariance matrix of the initial state vector α_0, the subsequent estimators of the α_t, computed by the Kalman filter, can be shown to be minimum mean square linear estimators (MMSLEs) or, if η_t and ϵ_t are assumed to be normal, minimum mean square estimators (MMSEs) (see, for example, Duncan and Horn, 1972; Anderson and Moore, 1979; Harvey, 1981). The relevance of the Kalman filter for maximum likelihood estimation is that it produces the one-step-ahead prediction errors, ν_t, together with their variances, f_t. Thus when the disturbances ϵ_t and η_t are normally distributed, the likelihood function can be constructed in the form of equation (7).

The way in which the Kalman filter is initialized depends on the structure of the model and on whether α_0 is assumed to be fixed or random. For example, if α_t is a stationary process, α_0 can be regarded as random, and a_0 and P_0 can be taken to be the mean and variance of the unconditional distribution of α_t. When this is not the case, other methods must be used for initializing the Kalman filter. For example, if α_0 is regarded as fixed, its elements can be treated as additional parameters to be estimated; see Rosenberg (1973) and the discussion in Harvey and Peters (1983).

Example 8 The MA(1) model (equation 12) can be put in state-space form by defining a 2×1 vector $\alpha_t = (y_t, \theta\epsilon_t)'$ which obeys the transition equation

$$\alpha_t = \begin{bmatrix} 0 & 1 \\ 0 & 0 \end{bmatrix} \alpha_{t-1} + \begin{bmatrix} 1 \\ \theta \end{bmatrix} \epsilon_t, \qquad t = 1, \ldots, T. \tag{26a}$$

The measurement equation is simply

$$y_t = (1 \quad 0)\, \alpha_t, \qquad t = 1, \ldots, T. \tag{26b}$$

Since the process is stationary, the starting values can be taken to be the unconditional mean and covariance, i.e. $a_0 = 0$ and

$$P_0 = \sigma^2 \begin{bmatrix} 1+\theta^2 & \theta \\ \theta & \theta^2 \end{bmatrix}. \tag{27}$$

The Kalman filter then gives the one-step-ahead prediction errors defined by equation (14).

Example 9 Putting model (8) in state-space form yields a transition equation

$$\alpha_t = \begin{bmatrix} \phi_1 & \phi_2 \\ 1 & 0 \end{bmatrix} \alpha_{t-1} + \eta_t, \qquad t = 1, \ldots, T \tag{28a}$$

where $\alpha_t = (y_t^{\dagger}, y_{t-1}^{\dagger})'$, and a measurement equation

$$y_t = (1 \quad 0)\, \alpha_t + \epsilon_t, \qquad t = 1, \ldots, T. \tag{28b}$$

Again an exact likelihood function can be computed by taking a_0 and P_0 to be the unconditional mean and variance of α_t.

Example 10 The following state-space model is important in univariate time-series forecasting since it provides a statistical rationale for projecting out a local linear trend:

$$y_t = \mu_t + \epsilon_t, \qquad t = 1, \ldots, T \tag{29a}$$

$$\begin{bmatrix} \mu_t \\ \beta_t \end{bmatrix} = \begin{bmatrix} 1 & 1 \\ 0 & 1 \end{bmatrix} \begin{bmatrix} \mu_{t-1} \\ \beta_{t-1} \end{bmatrix} + \begin{bmatrix} \eta_t \\ \zeta_t \end{bmatrix} \tag{29b}$$

where ϵ_t, η_t and ζ_t are independent white-noise disturbances; see Harvey (1981, 1983a) and Harrison (1967). The term μ_t can be regarded as the level of the process, and although y_t can also be expressed as an ARIMA(0, 2, 2) process the formulation in equation (29) is attractive in that it has a more direct interpretation. This point becomes even more apparent when seasonal and other effects are incorporated into the model; see Harvey and Todd (1983) and Harvey (1983a, b).

Because the state vector in equation (29b) is non-stationary, initialization of the Kalman filter must proceed in a different way from the previous two examples. Several possibilities are open. One is to regard α_0 as fixed and to estimate its elements along with the variances of the three disturbance terms; see Rosenberg (1973) or Wecker and Ansley (1983). A second is to regard y_1 and y_2 as fixed and to use these two observations to construct starting values a_2 and P_2 at time $t = 2$; see, for example, Harvey and Todd (1983). The second approach can be carried out indirectly by starting the Kalman filter at $t = 0$ with an arbitrary value for a_0 and a covariance matrix of the form $P_0 = \kappa I$, where κ is a large, but finite, number.

2.1 *Missing Observations*

The treatment of missing observations is straightforward for a model in state-space form. All that needs to be done is to bypass the updating equations in the Kalman filter. Equivalently, h_t, the variance of the measurement error in equation (25) can be set equal to a very large number. If estimates of the missing observations themselves are required, they can be obtained, once the parameters have been estimated, by using one of the smoothing algorithms associated with the state-space form; see Harvey and McKenzie (1984) and Harvey and Pierse (1984).

2.2 Nonlinear State Space Models

The state-space model, equations (24) and (25), can be extended by allowing T_t, c_t, Q_t, z_t, d_t and h_t to depend on observations up to and including time $t-1$. Although this results in the model being nonlinear, the Kalman filter can still be used to construct the likelihood function via the prediction error decomposition. This point is discussed further in section 3, where a number of applications are given.

More general nonlinearities arise when α_t is no longer a linear function of α_{t-1} in the transition equation and/or y_t is no longer a linear function of α_t in the measurement equation. Nonlinearities of this kind are much more difficult to handle since the Kalman filter can only be applied approximately by carrying out Taylor series expansions on the transition and measurement equations; see Anderson and Moore (1979, chapter 8). Similarly any likelihood function computed via the prediction error decomposition can only be approximate; see, for example, Harvey and Pierse (1984).

3 Nonlinear Models

This section examines a number of models, all of which are nonlinear in the sense that they do not satisfy equation (18). However, all of these models share the property that they allow a likelihood function to be constructed via the prediction error decomposition. Not all nonlinear models necessarily have this property.

3.1 Bilinear Models

Granger and Andersen (1978) describe the properties of a number of classes of nonlinear univariate time-series models. Some importance is attached to bilinear models, the simplest of which is

$$y_t = \phi y_{t-1} + \theta \epsilon_{t-1} + \beta \epsilon_{t-1} y_{t-1} + \epsilon_t, \qquad t = 1, \ldots, T. \qquad (30)$$

Given that the disturbances, ϵ_t, are independently distributed with a specified distribution, a joint density function can be written down subject to some assumptions about the initial conditions. The usual way of proceeding is to treat y_1 as fixed and suppose that $\epsilon_1 = 0$. The ϵ_t can then be obtained from the recursion

$$\epsilon_t = y_t - \phi y_{t-1} - \theta \epsilon_{t-1} - \beta \epsilon_{t-1} y_{t-1}, \qquad t = 2, \ldots, T. \qquad (31)$$

If $\epsilon_t \sim NID(0, \sigma^2)$, the ML estimates of ϕ, θ and β are obtained by minimizing the sum-of-squares function

$$S(\phi, \theta, \beta) = \sum_{t=2}^{T} \epsilon_t^2.$$

3.2 *ARCH Models*

The autoregressive conditional heteroscedastic (ARCH) model introduced by Engle (1982a) is a somewhat different kind of nonlinear time-series model in that the nonlinearity stems from the variance of the disturbance term. Suppose that y_t, $t = 1, \ldots, T$ are a sequence of independent random variables, such that conditional on the information available at time $t-1$, y_t is normally distributed with a mean of μ and a variance which depends on past observations, i.e. y_{t-1}, y_{t-2}, and so on. As a very simple example, we may have

$$\operatorname{var}(y_t | y_{t-1}, \ldots) = \alpha_0 + \alpha_1 y_{t-1}^2 \tag{32}$$

where α is an unknown parameter. The likelihood function for a model of this kind is

$$\log L = -\frac{T}{2}\log 2\pi - \frac{1}{2}\sum_{t=1}^{T} \log(\alpha_0 + \alpha_1 y_{t-1}^2) - \frac{1}{2}\sum_{t=1}^{T} \frac{(y_t - \mu)^2}{\alpha_0 + \alpha_1 y_{t-1}^2}. \tag{33}$$

More generally the mean of y_t may depend on a set of explanatory variables, x_t, as in a regression model, so that at time t, $\mu_t = g(x_t)$; this is, in fact, the case considered by Engle (1982a). The model could be further extended so that μ_t also depends on some function of the observations, i.e. the y_t, which are available at time $t-1$.

3.3 *Switching Regimes*

Suppose that at any given point in time, an observation is generated by any one of a number of models, say,

$$y_t = \phi^{(i)} y_{t-1} + \epsilon_t^{(i)}, \qquad i = 1, \ldots, N \tag{34}$$

where $\epsilon_t^{(i)} \sim NID(0, \sigma_i^2)$. Suppose also that the regime which is applicable depends in some way on the past observations. For example, if $N=2$, we might have $i=1$ if y_{t-1} is less than some 'threshold' value, y^*, and $i=2$ otherwise. Models of this kind have been used in the analysis of river flow data by Tong (1977) (see also Priestley, 1981, pp. 884–90; Tong and Lim, 1980). Similar ideas may also be applicable in econometrics, say in connection with markets in disequilibrium, possibly with the change in regime signalled by the value of the change Δy_{t-1}, rather than the level. However, provided the choice of regime depends only on past observations, the conditional form of the likelihood function remains valid.

3.4 *State-Space and Nonlinear Models*

The state-space model in equations (24) and (25) can be extended to allow z_t, d_t, h_t, T_t, c_t and Q_t to depend on any information which is available at time $t-1$. Thus, for example, we may write $c_t = c_t(y_{t-1}, \ldots)$ thereby denoting that c_t is some function of the past observations y_{t-1}, y_{t-2} and so on (see Anderson and Moore, 1979, pp. 43–4). In some cases this information may be expressed in terms of a_{t-1}, the estimate of the state vector at $t-1$.

Suppose that, conditional on the information available at time $t-1$, α_{t-1} is normally distributed with a mean of a_{t-1} and a variance of P_{t-1}. If the disturbances ϵ_t and η_t are also normally distributed, then the distribution of y_t conditional on y_{t-1} is also normal. This follows immediately by noting that

$$y_t - z_t' a_{t|t-1} = z_t' T_t(\alpha_{t-1} - a_{t-1}) - z_t' \eta_t + \epsilon_t. \tag{35}$$

Furthermore, the distribution of α_t conditional on the information at time t, i.e. the posterior distribution of α_t, is also normal. Thus the conditional distribution of α_{t+1} will also be normal and so on. This means that given an initial normal distribution for the state vector at time $t=0$, a likelihood function for the observations can be computed via the prediction error decomposition. A diffuse initial prior can be adopted as a limiting case.

Example 11 Consider a lagged dependent variable regression model with time-varying parameters, i.e.

$$y_t = \phi_t y_{t-1} + \beta_t x_t + \epsilon_t, \qquad \epsilon_t \sim NID(0, \sigma^2) \tag{36a}$$

$$\phi_t = \phi_{t-1} + \zeta_t, \qquad \zeta_t \sim NID(0, \sigma_\zeta^2) \tag{36b}$$

$$\beta_t = \beta_{t-1} + \eta_t, \qquad \eta_t \sim NID(0, \sigma_\eta^2) \tag{36c}$$

where x_t is a sequence of fixed and known variables. A model of this kind can be put in state-space form immediately, by defining $\alpha_t = (\phi_t \ \beta_t)'$ as the state vector and letting equations (36b, c) be the transition equations. The measurement equation is (36a) with $z_t' = (y_{t-1} \ x_t)$ (cf. Anderson and Moore, 1979, pp. 50–52). Although the model is a nonlinear one, estimation of σ^2, $\sigma_\eta{}^2$ and $\sigma_\xi{}^2$ can proceed via the prediction error decomposition exactly as in the fixed regressor case (cf. Harvey, 1981, section 7.3 or Garbade, 1977). The alternative approach of Cooley and Prescott (1976), which is based on generalized least squares, is no longer applicable. An application can be found in Sims (1982b).

Example 12 Allowing z_t, T_t, etc. to depend on past observations enables expectations of unobservables to be introduced into the model. As a simple example consider the model

$$y_t = \alpha_t + \epsilon_t, \qquad \epsilon_t \sim NID(0, \sigma^2) \tag{37a}$$

$$\alpha_t = \phi\alpha_{t-1} + \gamma \underset{t-1}{E}(\alpha_t) + \eta_t, \qquad \eta_t \sim NID(0, \sigma_\eta{}^2) \tag{37b}$$

where α_t is an unobservable variable, ϕ and γ are unknown parameters, and ϵ_t and η_t are independently distributed disturbance terms. The notation $E_{t-1}(.)$ indicates an expectation taken at time $t-1$, i.e. conditional on y_{t-1}, y_{t-2}, and so on. Such an expectation is rational since it is the conditional expectation implied by the model itself. Applying the conditional expectation operator to both sides of equation (37b) gives

$$\underset{t-1}{E}(\alpha_t) = \phi \underset{t-1}{E}(\alpha_{t-1}) + \gamma \underset{t-1}{E}(\alpha_t)$$

and on rearranging we have

$$\underset{t-1}{E}(\alpha_t) = a_{t|t-1} = \frac{\phi}{1-\gamma} a_{t-1}.$$

Thus equation (37b) gives

$$\alpha_t = \phi\alpha_{t-1} + \frac{\gamma\phi}{1-\gamma} a_{t-1} + \eta_t. \tag{38}$$

The likelihood function can be obtained from the prediction error decomposition. The conditions for identifiability are $\sigma^2 > 0$ and $\phi > 0$. If the first of these conditions does not hold, the model reduces to

$$y_t = [\phi/(1-\gamma)]y_{t-1} + \eta_t. \tag{39}$$

4 Models in Continuous Time

There is often a certain arbitrariness in specifying models in discrete time. This is illustrated by the fact that an AR(p) process for quarterly observations on a stock variable becomes an ARMA (p, $p-1$) process for annual observations (see Phillips, 1959; Brewer, 1973). A good deal of work has therefore been done on the formulation and estimation of continuous-time models in econometrics; see the papers in Bergstrom (1976). The aim of this section is to present some simple examples of continuous-time models in order to give the reader a flavour of the general approach.

4.1 Continuous Time Autoregressive Models

A continuous time white-noise process, $\zeta(t)$, with mean zero and variance σ^2 is defined in such a way that if

$$\zeta^*(r, s) = \int_r^s \zeta(t)\,\mathrm{d}t \tag{40}$$

then

$$E[\zeta^*(r, s)] = 0,$$
$$E[\zeta^*(t_1, t_2)\,\zeta^*(t_1, t_2)] = (t_2 - t_1)\,\sigma^2$$

and

$$E[\zeta^*(t_1, t_2)\,\zeta^*(t_3, t_4)] = 0 \qquad \text{for } t_1 < t_2 < t_3 < t_4;$$

see Priestley (1981, pp. 156–66) for a careful discussion of the concept. Using this definition a first-order continuous-time autoregressive process can be written as

$$(\mathrm{d}/\mathrm{d}t)\,y(t) = \rho y(t) + \zeta(t). \tag{41}$$

Solving this differential equation yields

$$y(t) = e^{\rho} y(t-1) + \int_0^1 e^{\rho(1-s)} \zeta(t-1+s)\,\mathrm{d}s. \tag{42}$$

If the observation at time t is y_t, then $y_t = y(t)$ and (41) can be written in discrete time as

$$y_t = \phi y_{t-1} + \zeta_t, \qquad t = 1, \ldots, T \tag{43}$$

where the parameter ϕ is given as

$$\phi = \exp(\rho) \tag{44}$$

and ζ_t is a white-noise process with mean zero and variance

$$\text{var}(\zeta_t) = \sigma^2(e^{2\rho} - 1)/2\rho. \tag{45}$$

The stationarity condition for the continuous-time model is $\rho < 0$, which corresponds to $\phi < 1$. Note that $\rho = -\infty$ corresponds to $\phi = 0$ so that negative values of ϕ are not permitted in equation (43).

The assumption of normality for $\zeta(t)$, and hence for ζ_t, leads directly to a likelihood function similar to equation (4). (The unconditional distribution of y_1 is normal with a mean of zero and a variance $\sigma^2/2\rho$.) The parameters in equation (43) can be estimated in the usual way and corresponding estimates of the continuous-time parameters, ρ and σ^2, can be obtained from equations (44) and (45).

Now suppose that the observations are spaced at irregular intervals. Let the τth observation be denoted by y_τ for $\tau = 1, \ldots, T$ and suppose that this observation is made at time t_τ. Let $t_\tau - t_{\tau-1} = \delta_\tau$. Then equation (42) becomes

$$y(t_\tau) = \exp(\rho\delta)\, y(t_{\tau-1}) + \int_0^\delta \exp[\rho(\delta - s)]\, \zeta(t_{\tau-1} + s)\, \mathrm{d}s \tag{46}$$

and so the discrete-time model is

$$y_\tau = \phi_\tau y_{\tau-1} + \zeta_\tau \qquad \tau = 1, \ldots, T \tag{47}$$

where the parameter ϕ_τ is given as

$$\phi_\tau = \exp(\rho\delta_\tau) \tag{48}$$

and the error variance is

$$\text{var}(\zeta_\tau) = \sigma_\tau^2 = \sigma^2(\phi_\tau^2 - 1)/2\rho\delta_\tau. \tag{49}$$

Thus the parameters ϕ_τ and σ_τ^2 in the discrete-time model are time varying, according to the time between observations δ_τ. However, the likelihood function can still be expressed in a similar form to equation (4) since the distribution of y_τ conditional on $y_{\tau-1}$, $y_{\tau-2}, \ldots$ is $N(\phi_\tau y_{\tau-1}, \sigma_\tau^2)$ for $\tau = 2, \ldots, T$.

The treatment of higher-order models is less straightforward. With equally-spaced observations, a continuous-time pth order process becomes an ARMA($p, p-1$) process in discrete time, but the $2p-1$ ARMA parameters are complicated functions of the p

continuous-time parameters; see Phadke and Wu (1974) for a discussion of the $p=2$ case, and Phillips (1959) for a derivation of the general result. The most satisfactory way of handling the problem is to put the model in state space form as in Jones (1981). This approach also allows a straightforward treatment of irregularly spaced observations and measurement errors.

Multivariate continuous-time models are discussed in Bergstrom (1976, 1983) and Harvey and Stock (1983).

4.2 Linear Trend Model

The continuous time analogue of the local linear trend model, equations (29a, b), consists of a level, $\mu(t)$, and a slope, $\beta(t)$, such that

$$(\mathrm{d}/\mathrm{d}t)\,\mu(t) = \beta(t) + \zeta_1(t) \tag{50a}$$

$$(\mathrm{d}/\mathrm{d}t)\,\beta(t) = \zeta_2(t) \tag{50b}$$

and the observations are given by

$$y_\tau = \mu(t_\tau) + \epsilon_\tau \qquad \tau = 1, \ldots, T. \tag{51}$$

The continuous-time white-noise disturbances, $\zeta_1(t)$ and $\zeta_2(t)$, are assumed to have variances $\sigma_1{}^2$ and $\sigma_2{}^2$ respectively, while the discrete-time white-noise disturbance, ϵ_τ, has variance σ^2. All three disturbances are taken to be independent of each other.

By defining $\alpha(t) = [\mu(t), \beta(t)]'$, the two equations (50a, b) can be written

$$(\mathrm{d}/\mathrm{d}t)\,[\alpha(t)] = A\alpha(t) + \zeta(t) \tag{52}$$

where $\zeta(t) = [\zeta_1(t), \zeta_2(t)]'$ and

$$A = \begin{bmatrix} 0 & 1 \\ 0 & 0 \end{bmatrix}. \tag{53}$$

The solution to equation (52) is

$$\alpha(t_\tau) = \exp(A\delta_\tau)\,\alpha(t_{\tau-1}) + \int_0^{\delta_\tau} \exp[A(\delta_\tau - s)]\,\zeta(t_{\tau-1}+s)\,\mathrm{d}s. \tag{54}$$

In view of the definition of a matrix exponential

$$e^A = I + A + \frac{1}{2!}A^2 + \frac{1}{3!}A^3 + \ldots \tag{55}$$

equation (54) becomes

$$\alpha_\tau = T_\tau \alpha_{\tau-1} + \zeta_\tau, \qquad \tau = 1, \ldots, T \tag{56}$$

where

$$T_\tau = \begin{bmatrix} 1 & \delta_\tau \\ 0 & 1 \end{bmatrix} \tag{57}$$

and

$$\operatorname{var}(\zeta_\tau) = \begin{bmatrix} \sigma_1^2 + \frac{1}{3}\delta_\tau^2\sigma_2^2 & \frac{1}{2}\delta_\tau\sigma_2^2 \\ \frac{1}{2}\delta_\tau\sigma_2^2 & \sigma_2^2 \end{bmatrix}. \tag{58}$$

Taken together with the measurement equation

$$y_\tau = (1 \quad 0)\,\alpha_\tau + \epsilon_\tau, \tag{59}$$

the transition equation (56) makes up the state-space model. The forecast function is a linear trend and hence the model is a continuous-time version of equations (29a, b).

An example of the use of the above model can be found in Jones (1984). In a slightly different context, Wecker and Ansley (1983) show that the same model can be used as the basis for fitting a spline function. Finally, Harvey (1983c) discusses extensions of this model to include seasonal and daily components.

5 Estimation and Testing

The prediction error decomposition can handle models where the structure changes from one observation to the next and the observations are irregularly spaced. The results presented below apply to the general form of the likelihood function given in equation (7), but the variables are subscripted τ, rather than t, to allow for irregular spacing, i.e.

$$\log L = -\frac{T}{2}\log 2\pi - \frac{1}{2}\sum_{\tau=1}^{T}\log f_\tau - \frac{1}{2}\sum_{\tau=1}^{T}\frac{v_\tau^2}{f_\tau} \tag{60}$$

5.1 Derivatives and the Information Matrix

When the likelihood function takes the form of equation (60) an explicit expression for the information matrix can be derived. This turns out to depend only on the *first* derivatives of f_τ and

ν_τ, and in many cases it is possible to evaluate these derivatives recursively without too much difficulty; see, for example, Pagan (1980) and Harvey and McKenzie (1984).

If ψ denotes the $n \times 1$ vector of parameters in the model, the score vector associated with (60) is, after some rearrangement,

$$\frac{\partial \log L}{\partial \psi} = -\frac{1}{2} \sum_{\tau=1}^{T} \frac{\partial f_\tau}{\partial \psi} \frac{1}{f_\tau} \left(1 - \frac{\nu_\tau^2}{f_\tau}\right) - \sum_{\tau=1}^{T} \frac{\partial \nu_\tau}{\partial \psi} \frac{\nu_\tau}{f_\tau} . \tag{61}$$

The information matrix is

$$-E\left[\frac{\partial^2 \log L}{\partial \psi\, \partial \psi'}\right] = \frac{1}{2} \sum_{\tau=1}^{T} \frac{1}{f_\tau^2} \frac{\partial f_\tau}{\partial \psi} \frac{\partial f_\tau}{\partial \psi'} + \sum_{\tau=1}^{T} \frac{1}{f_\tau} E\left[\frac{\partial \nu_\tau}{\partial \psi} \frac{\partial \nu_\tau}{\partial \psi'}\right] . \tag{62}$$

Dropping the expectation operator in the second term gives an expression which is asymptotically equivalent to equation (62) and which may, in some cases, be easier to evaluate.

In order to derive (62) it is easiest to write the likelihood function as

$$\log L = \sum_{\tau=1}^{T} l_\tau \tag{63}$$

where l_τ is the logarithm of $p(y_\tau | y_{\tau-1}, \ldots)$, and, to simplify the notation, to assume that there is only a single parameter ψ. First and second derivatives with respect to ψ can then be denoted by f', f'', and so on. Corresponding to equation (61) we have

$$l_\tau' = -\frac{1}{2} \frac{f_\tau'}{f_\tau} \left(1 - \frac{\nu_\tau^2}{f_\tau}\right) - \nu_\tau' \frac{\nu_\tau}{f_\tau} \tag{64}$$

and so the second derivative is

$$l_\tau'' = \frac{f_\tau'}{2f_\tau} \left(\frac{2f_\tau \nu_\tau \nu_\tau' - \nu_\tau^2 f_\tau'}{f_\tau^2}\right) - \frac{1}{2} \left(\frac{f_\tau f_\tau'' - (f_\tau')^2}{f_\tau^2}\right) \left(1 - \frac{\nu_\tau^2}{f_\tau}\right)$$
$$- \nu_\tau' \left(\frac{f_\tau \nu_\tau' - \nu_\tau f_\tau'}{f_\tau^2}\right) - \frac{\nu_\tau}{f_\tau} \nu_\tau'' . \tag{65}$$

The information matrix is, by definition,

$$-E\left[\frac{\partial^2 \log L}{\partial \psi^2}\right] = -E \sum_{\tau=1}^{T} l_\tau'' \tag{66}$$

but its evaluation in the present context is simplified considerably by noting that

$$E(l_\tau) = E\left[\underset{\tau-1}{E}(l_\tau)\right] \tag{67}$$

where $E_{\tau-1}$ denotes the expectation taken at $\tau-1$. Then consider a term such as $\nu_\tau \nu_\tau'$. Since

$$\nu_\tau = y_\tau - E(y_\tau | y_{\tau-1}, \ldots) = y_\tau - \underset{\tau-1}{E}(y_\tau) \tag{68}$$

it follows that $E_{\tau-1}(\nu_\tau') = \nu_\tau'$ and that $E_{\tau-1}(\nu_\tau'') = \nu_\tau''$. Furthermore, since $E_{\tau-1}(\nu_\tau) = 0$, any term of the form $\nu_\tau \nu_\tau'$ or $\nu_\tau \nu_\tau''$ disappears when the operator $E_{\tau-1}$ is applied. Bearing this in mind and recalling that $E_{\tau-1}(\nu_\tau^2/f_\tau) = 1$, expression (62) can be obtained almost immediately from equation (65).

5.2 *Large Sample Properties*

Given appropriate regularity conditions, the ML estimator of ψ is asymptotically normally distributed with a mean of ψ and a covariance matrix given by the inverse of the information matrix (equation 62). This result can be shown to hold by using Martingale theory; see Hall and Heyde (1980, chapter 6), Crowder (1976) and Pagan (1980). In fact it is not usually necessary to assume that the disturbances in the model are normally distributed in order to show that the estimator of ψ obtained by maximizing expression (60) is asymptotically normal with a mean of ψ and a covariance matrix equal to the inverse of $-E\{\partial^2 \log L/\partial\psi\, \partial\psi'\}$. This estimator is known as the quasi-ML or Gaussian estimator; see, for example, Bergstrom (1983). Note that the assumption of normality was not used in the derivation of the expression on the right-hand side of equation (62) and so this expression is valid for the Gaussian as well as the ML estimator.

Example 13 In the MA(1) model, equation (12), with $\epsilon_0 = 0$, $\nu_\tau = \epsilon_\tau$ and $f_\tau = \sigma^2$ as already noted. Since

$$\epsilon_\tau = y_\tau - \theta\epsilon_{\tau-1}, \qquad \tau = 1, \ldots, T$$

we have

$$\frac{\partial \nu_\tau}{\partial\theta} = \frac{\partial\epsilon_\tau}{\partial\theta} = -\epsilon_{\tau-1} - \frac{\theta\,\partial\epsilon_{\tau-1}}{\partial\theta} = -\sum_{j=0}^{\infty} (-\theta)^j \epsilon_{\tau-1-j}$$

and so

$$E\left[\frac{\partial \nu_\tau}{\partial \theta}\right]^2 = \sigma^2/(1-\theta^2).$$

Furthermore, $\partial \nu_\tau/\partial \sigma^2 = 0$, $\partial f_\tau/\partial \theta = 0$ and $\partial f_\tau/\partial \sigma^2 = 1$. Therefore

$$-E\left[\frac{\partial^2 \log L}{\partial \psi\, \partial \psi'}\right] = \begin{bmatrix} 0 & 0 \\ 0 & 1/2\sigma^4 \end{bmatrix} + \begin{bmatrix} 1/(1-\theta^2) & 0 \\ 0 & 0 \end{bmatrix}$$

and so

$$\text{asyvar}\,(\tilde{\theta}, \tilde{\sigma}^2) = \frac{1}{T}\begin{bmatrix} 1-\theta^2 & 0 \\ 0 & 2\sigma^4 \end{bmatrix}. \qquad (69)$$

5.3 *Test Statistics*

The Lagrange multiplier statistic is of the form

$$\text{LM} = \frac{\partial \log L}{\partial \psi'}\left[-E\,\frac{\partial^2 \log L}{\partial \psi\, \partial \psi'}\right]^{-1}\frac{\partial \log L}{\partial \psi} \qquad (70)$$

where the score vector and the information matrix are evaluated under a null hypothesis which places some restrictions on ψ. If there are m such restrictions, the LM statistic will be distributed as χ_m^2 under the null hypothesis.

Expressions (61) and (62) can be used directly in equation (70). Furthermore a test statistic which is asymptotically equivalent to LM can be computed by running a regression. In order to do this we define a dependent variable ν_j^*, $j = 1, \ldots, 2T$, such that

$$\nu_\tau^* = \frac{1}{\sqrt{2}}\{1-(\nu_\tau^2/f_\tau)\}, \qquad \tau = 1, \ldots, T \qquad (71a)$$

$$\nu_{T+\tau}^* = \nu_\tau/f_\tau^{1/2}, \qquad \tau = 1, \ldots, T. \qquad (71b)$$

Corresponding to this variable we have a regressor variable, z_j, $j = 1, \ldots, 2T$, such that

$$z_\tau = \frac{1}{\sqrt{2}}\,\frac{1}{f_\tau}\,\frac{\partial f_\tau}{\partial \psi} \qquad \tau = 1, \ldots, T \qquad (72a)$$

$$z_{T+\tau} = \frac{1}{f_\tau^{1/2}}\,\frac{\partial \nu_\tau}{\partial \psi} \qquad \tau = 1, \ldots, T. \qquad (72b)$$

The coefficient of multiple correlation in this regression is approximately (and in many cases, exactly) equal to the uncentred coefficient, i.e.

$$R^2 = \frac{(\Sigma \nu_j^* z_j)'(\Sigma z_j z_j')^{-1}(\Sigma \nu_j^* z_j)}{\Sigma \nu_j^{*2}} \tag{73}$$

with the summations running from $j = 1, \ldots, 2T$. The numerator of the right-hand side of equation (73) is the same as that in equation (70) evaluated using (61) and (62). Furthermore

$$\text{plim} \frac{\Sigma \nu_j^{*2}}{T} = \text{plim} \frac{1}{2T} \sum_{\tau=1}^{T} \{1-(\nu_\tau^2/f_\tau)\}^2 + \text{plim} \frac{1}{T} \sum_{\tau=1}^{T} \nu_\tau^2/f_\tau = 2,$$

since $\text{plim}\, \Sigma(\nu_\tau^4/Tf_\tau^2) = 3$ under the normality assumption, and so the statistic

$$\text{LM}^* = 2TR^2 \tag{74}$$

will have the same asymptotic distribution as (70).

If the assumption of normality of the disturbances is dropped, LM* will still be a valid test statistic under fairly general conditions; cf. Koenker (1981).

In many models the parameters in ψ can be separated into two sets, ψ_1 and ψ_2, such that $\partial \nu_\tau / \partial \psi_1 = 0$ and $\partial f_\tau / \partial \psi_2 = 0$ for all τ. The information matrix is then block diagonal. If the hypothesis to be tested involves only restrictions on ψ_1, the LM statistic is

$$\text{LM} = T.R^2 \tag{75}$$

where R^2 is the coefficient of multiple correlation obtained from regressing ν_τ^* on z_τ for $\tau = 1, \ldots, T$. If the null hypothesis involves only ψ_2, the test statistic is again of the form of equation (75) but based on a regression of $\nu_{T+\tau}^*$ on $z_{T+\tau}$ for $\tau = 1, \ldots, T$.

Example 14 In the MA(1) model, equation (12), with $\epsilon_0 = 0$, $\nu_\tau = \epsilon_\tau$ and $f_\tau = 1$ for all τ. Hence $\partial f_\tau / \partial \theta = 0$. Although a test of $H_0 : \theta = \theta_0$ based on equation (74) is valid, the more usual procedure is to regress ϵ_τ on $\partial \epsilon_\tau / \partial \theta$ for $\tau = 1, \ldots, T$ and to take the LM statistic as T times the R^2 from this regression; see, for example, Godfrey (1978d).

Example 15 The test of an ARCH specification for the variance of a disturbance term can be carried out by computing the TR^2 from a regression of (71a) on (72a). Thus in the model given by equation (32) the test statistic can be computed by regressing $1-\nu_\tau^2/\tilde{\alpha}_0$ on unity and y_{t-1}^2, where $\nu_\tau = y_\tau$ and $\tilde{\alpha}_0$ is given by

$$\tilde{\alpha}_0 = T^{-1} \sum_{\tau=1}^{T} y_\tau^2.$$

Alternatively, y_τ^2 can simply be regressed on $y_{\tau-1}^2$ and unity.

The test procedures for more conventional forms of heteroscedasticity are similar; see, for example, Breusch and Pagan (1979) or Harvey (1981a, pp. 170–1).

6 Conclusions and Extensions

The aim of this chapter has been to show how a wide variety of dynamic models, including nonlinear ones, can be handled via the prediction error decomposition. In many cases, the easiest way of computing the prediction errors is by means of the Kalman filter applied to the state-space form. The fact that the Kalman filter can be applied to nonlinear models opens up the possibility of handling several interesting econometric formulations, such as models involving rational expectations of unobservable components.

Although the results presented have been restricted to univariate models, multivariate models can be handled by similar techniques. The appropriate expressions for the first and second derivatives of the likelihood function can be found in Engle and Watson (1981).

Acknowledgments

I am grateful to David Hendry and Adrian Pagan for helpful comments on an earlier draft. Any errors, of course, remain my responsibility.

4

Classical and Bayesian Inference in Incomplete Simultaneous Equation Models

JEAN-FRANÇOIS RICHARD

1 Introduction

So-called 'incomplete' simultaneous equation models (SEM) are models in which the number of structural equations is less than the number of endogenous variables. This terminology is inherited from the usual, but statistically unsound, practice of randomizing deterministic models by adding disturbance terms to their equations. If instead the statistical assumptions are formulated directly in terms of the distribution of the endogenous variables, then the structural equations serve to characterize the linear manifold to which the (conditional) expectations of the endogenous variables belong, and there is no reason why their number should be equal to the number of endogenous variables. This is the approach followed e.g. in Florens et al. (1979), Richard (1980), Engle et al. (1983a) and Hendry and Richard (1983).

If the number of structural equations is less than the number of endogenous variables, then one is confronted with the presence of 'incidental' parameters. In the present chapter we only discuss the case in which these incidental parameters are themselves linear functions of a set of 'instrumental variables'. In the literature on SEM this assumption amounts to 'completing' the set of structural equations by 'unrestricted reduced form' equations. However, assuming from the beginning that the instrumental variables include all the 'predetermined' variables in the structural equations has important drawbacks:

(1) this assumption is typically incompatible with non-causality assumptions in the sense of Granger (1969) and strong exogeneity assumptions in the sense of Engle et al. (1983a)

whereby lagged values of some of the endogenous variables have to be excluded from the set of instrumental variables;

(2) incorporating all the predetermined variables in the list of instrumental variables may substantially increase the number of 'nuisance' parameters, which is generally undesirable given the small number of observations which are available in economics.

In this chapter, therefore, we allow for the exclusion of predetermined variables from the set of instrumental variables. We build upon earlier results derived in Florens et al. (1979) and Richard (1979) and also generalize results which are found in Lubrano et al. (1984) for single equation analysis. Special attention is paid to weak and strong exogeneity hypotheses in the sense of Engle et al. (1983a), for which a set of Instrumental Variables Likelihood Ratio (IVLR) statistics is proposed. Our analysis is naturally compatible with 'general to simple' modelling procedures and this is emphasized in the course of the discussion.

We proceed as follows: in section 2 we discuss the statistical model; in section 3 we derive the Estimator Generating Equations (EGE), in the terminology of Hendry (1976), for the Instrumental Variables Maximum Likelihood (IVML) estimators of the structural coefficients. IVLR test statistics are proposed for various hypotheses of interest within the context; in section 4 we apply Bayesian procedures, generalizing thereby so-called Bayesian limited information procedures; technical details are regrouped in an Appendix.

2 The Statistical Model

Let a time-sequential economic process be described by the following set of p 'structural' equations

$$B_\theta' y_t + \Gamma_\theta' x_t = e_t, \qquad e_t \sim IN(0, \Sigma), \qquad t = 1, \ldots, T \tag{1}$$

where: $y_t \in \mathbb{R}^n$ is a vector of endogenous variables; $x_t \in \mathbb{R}^m$ is a vector of variables describing the information set at time t and consisting of (weakly) exogenous variables, lagged values thereof and lagged values of y_t; Σ is a $p \times p$ unknown covariance matrix; B_θ and Γ_θ are $n \times p$ and $m \times p$ matrix functions of a vector of unknown parameters $\theta \in \Theta$, with rank $B_\theta = p \leqslant n$ almost surely in Θ.

When $p<n$ the system (1) is 'incomplete' in that it does not uniquely determine the conditional density of $y_t|x_t$. We, therefore, embed (1) within the linear Gaussian model:

$$y_t|x_t \sim IN(\eta_t, V), \qquad t=1,\dots,T \tag{2}$$

where η_t, the conditional expectation of $y_t|x_t$, belongs to the linear manifold defined by the identities

$$B_\theta{}'\eta_t + \Gamma_\theta{}'x_t = 0. \tag{3}$$

The formulation of equation (2) implies that the disturbances in (1) are sequentially independent, by properties of conditional expectations. We note that, as discussed in the literature on common factors (Sargan, 1964, 1980c; Hendry and Mizon, 1978) autoregressive error processes can usefully be re-interpreted in terms of restrictions on θ in equations (1) and (3). The problem of initial conditions will not be discussed here, see Richard (1979, section 2.2).

For $p<n$, the system of equation (3) allows infinitely many solutions. In order to characterize these solutions let S be an $n\times q$ selection matrix such that

$$Q_\theta = (B_\theta : S) \qquad (p+q=n) \tag{4}$$

is non-singular almost surely in Θ. The conditional expectation η_t may then be expressed as a linear function of x_t and $S'\eta_t$, a q-dimensional vector of 'incidental' parameters. The choice of S will be discussed below.

Florens et al. (1979) analyse the statistical properties of the above model, equations (2) and (3), and propose various solutions to deal with the incidental parameters $S'\eta_t$. Here we restrict our attention to the case where these parameters are themselves linear functions of a vector of 'instrumental variables', $z_t \in \mathbb{R}^k$:

$$S'\eta_t = P_2{}'z_t \tag{5}$$

where P_2 is a $k\times q$ unrestricted matrix of unknown coefficients (the reason for the subscript becomes obvious below). The unrestrictedness of P_2 is fundamental to our analysis and characterizes so-called 'limited information' and 'instrumental variables' methods. There is no loss of generality in assuming that z_t is a subvector of x_t since it is simply a matter of defining accordingly the restrictions in Γ_θ. Let therefore, x_t be partitioned as

$$x_t{}' = (z_t{}' : w_t{}') \tag{6}$$

where $w_t \in \mathbb{R}^l$ is a vector regrouping the $l = k - m$ variables in x_t which are excluded from the list of instruments. Γ_θ is partitioned conformably with x_t

$$\Gamma_\theta' = (C_\theta' : D_\theta') \tag{7}$$

where C_θ and D_θ are $k \times p$ and $l \times p$ matrix functions of θ.

Conventional simultaneous equation models (SEM) are characterized by the assumption that x_t and z_t coincide ($l = 0$). This assumption is computationally convenient. It is, however, often too restrictive, being incompatible with Granger non-causality and strong exogeneity assumptions (Engle et al., 1983a) whereby lagged values of some of the components of y_t are excluded from z_t even though they may be included in x_t. Also, as illustrated by the single equation application in Lubrano et al. (1984), incorporating all the variables in x_t in the set of instrumental variables may result in a lack of 'qualitative' identification at least with moderate sample sizes.

Collecting terms we can rewrite the model under consideration as

$$\begin{matrix} B_\theta' y_t + C_\theta' z_t + D_\theta' w_t = e_t \\ S' y_t - P_2' z_t = v_t \end{matrix}, \qquad \begin{pmatrix} e_t \\ v_t \end{pmatrix} \sim IN(0, \Phi) \tag{8}$$

with $\Phi = Q_\theta' V Q_\theta$. The analysis of this model is simplified by transforming e_t and v_t into independent random vectors. In much of the literature on 'exogeneity tests', starting with Wu (1973), this is (implicitly) achieved by including $S' y_t$ as additional explanatory variables in the structural equations. This amounts to factorizing the joint density of e_t and v_t into the product of the conditional density of $e_t | v_t$ and the marginal density of v_t. However, as we see below, the reverse factorization into the product of the marginal density of e_t and conditional density of $v_t | e_t$ proves analytically more convenient. Also we argue that the exogeneity tests which are based on the latter factorization probably have better finite sampling properties than those based on the former even though they are asymptotically equivalent. Let, therefore, Λ and Ω denote, respectively, the regression coefficients of v_t on e_t and the conditional covariance matrix of $v_t | e_t$:

$$E(v_t | e_t) = \Lambda' e_t, \qquad \operatorname{cov}(v_t | e_t) = \Omega. \tag{9}$$

Conditionally on θ, Φ and $(\Sigma, \Lambda, \Omega)$ are in one-to-one correspondence since, by properties of the multivariate normal density, we have the following identity

$$\Phi = \begin{pmatrix} \Sigma & \Sigma\Lambda \\ \Lambda'\Sigma & \Omega + \Lambda'\Sigma\Lambda \end{pmatrix}. \tag{10}$$

Also Φ is positive definite if and only if Σ and Ω are positive definite. Following the discussion in Engle et al. (1983a) components of $S'y_t$ are weakly exogenous for θ if the corresponding columns in $\Sigma\Lambda$ and, thereby, in Λ are zero.

The 'reduced form' of the model (equation 8) is given by

$$y_t = \Pi_\theta' x_t + e_t \qquad e_t \sim IN(0, V) \tag{11}$$

with

$$\Pi_\theta = -\begin{pmatrix} C_\theta & -P_2 \\ D_\theta & 0 \end{pmatrix} Q_\theta^{-1}. \tag{12}$$

It is assumed that θ is identified. A Likelihood Ratio (LR) test for overidentifying restrictions is proposed below.

It proves notationally convenient to rewrite the structural equation (1) in the following way:

$$A_\theta' \xi_t = e_t, \tag{13}$$

with $A_\theta' = (B_\theta' : \Gamma_\theta') = (B_\theta' : C_\theta' : D_\theta')$ and $\xi_t' = (y_t' : x_t') = (y_t' : z_t' : w_t')$. Note that, conditionally on θ, the model (8) takes the form of a restricted multivariate regression model, namely

$$\begin{aligned} A_\theta' \xi_t &= e_t \\ S' y_t &= P_2' z_t + v_t \end{aligned}, \qquad \begin{pmatrix} e_t \\ v_t \end{pmatrix} \sim IN(0, \Phi). \tag{14}$$

This analogy explains why, in order to keep notation as simple as possible, we first discuss inference within restricted multivariate regression models.

3 Sampling Theory

3.1 The Multivariate Regression Model

The unrestricted version of the model we now discuss is written as

$$y_t = \Pi' x_t + e_t, \qquad e_t \sim IN(0, \Phi), \qquad t = 1, \ldots, T. \tag{15}$$

Let Y and X represent the corresponding $T \times n$ and $T \times m$ matrices of observations. It is assumed that rank $X = m$, almost surely, and that $T \geqslant m + n$. The Maximum Likelihood (ML) estimators of Π and Φ are then given by

$$\hat{\Pi} = (X'X)^{-1}X'Y \qquad \hat{\Phi} = \frac{1}{T} Y'M_x Y \tag{16}$$

where $M_x = I_T - X(X'X)^{-1}X'$. We partition X and Π conformably with each other into

$$X = (Z:W) \qquad \Pi' = (P':R'). \tag{17}$$

The following formulae then prove useful in our analysis:

$$\hat{P} = (Z'M_w Z)^{-1}Z'M_w Y \tag{18}$$

$$\hat{R} = (W'W)^{-1}W'(Y - Z\hat{P}) \tag{19}$$

$$\hat{\Phi} = \frac{1}{T}(Y'M_w Y - \hat{P}'Z'M_w Z\hat{P}) \tag{20}$$

where $M_w = I_T - W(W'W)^{-1}W'$. These formulae are obtained by application of the formulae for the inverse of partitioned matrices.

Next partition y_t, x_t, Π and e_t conformably with each other into:

$$y_t = \begin{pmatrix} y_{1t} \\ y_{2t} \end{pmatrix} \quad x_t = \begin{pmatrix} z_t \\ w_t \end{pmatrix} \quad \Pi = \begin{pmatrix} P_1 & P_2 \\ R_1 & R_2 \end{pmatrix} = \begin{pmatrix} P \\ R \end{pmatrix} = (\Pi_1 : \Pi_2)$$

$$e_t = \begin{pmatrix} e_{1t} \\ e_{2t} \end{pmatrix} \tag{21}$$

where P_1, P_2, R_1 and R_2 are respectively $k \times p$, $k \times q$, $l \times p$ and $l \times q$ matrices ($k + l = m$ and $p + q = n$). The data matrices Y and X are partitioned conformably into $Y = (Y_1 : Y_2)$ and $X = (Z : W)$. We now analyse the restricted system ($P_1 = 0$)

$$\begin{aligned} y_{1t} &= R_1'w_t + e_{1t} \\ y_{2t} &= P_2'z_t + R_2'w_t + e_{2t}. \end{aligned} \tag{22}$$

Note that equations (22) generalize equation (14) by including w_t, with unrestricted coefficients, in the right-hand term. This generalization proves useful for discussing zero covariance restrictions and exogeneity assumptions.

Φ, the covariance matrix of e_t, is partitioned as in equation (10) conformably with y_t, so that $\operatorname{cov}(e_{1t}) = \Sigma$, $E(e_{2t} | e_{1t}) = \Lambda' e_{1t}$ and $\operatorname{cov}(e_{2t} | e_{1t}) = \Omega$. The (restricted) ML estimators of the parameters in equation (22) are denoted by the superscript $\tilde{}$. Their relationships with the unrestricted ML estimators $\hat{\Pi}' = (\hat{P}' : \hat{R}')$ and $\hat{\Phi}$, as given in equation (16), are described in the following theorem.

Theorem 1 The ML estimators of the parameters in equation (22) are given by

$$\tilde{P} = (0 : \hat{P}_2 - \hat{P}_1\hat{\Lambda}) = \hat{P} - \hat{P}_1(I_p : \Lambda) \tag{23}$$

$$\tilde{R} = \hat{R} - (W'W)^{-1}W'Z(\tilde{P} - \hat{P}) \tag{24}$$

$$\tilde{\Phi} = \hat{\Phi} + (1/T)\,(\tilde{P} - \hat{P})'Z'M_w Z(\tilde{P} - \hat{P}) \tag{25}$$

with $\hat{\Lambda} = \tilde{\Lambda} = (Y_1'M_x Y_1)^{-1}Y_1'M_x Y_2$. Also

$$|\tilde{\Phi}| = |\hat{\Phi}| \cdot (|\tilde{\Sigma}| \cdot |\hat{\Sigma}|^{-1}) \tag{26}$$

$$\tilde{\Phi}^{-1} = \hat{\Phi}^{-1} + \begin{pmatrix} \tilde{\Sigma}^{-1} - \hat{\Sigma}^{-1} & 0 \\ 0 & 0 \end{pmatrix} \tag{27}$$

with $\hat{\Sigma} = (1/T)\,Y_1'M_x Y_1$ and $\tilde{\Sigma} = (1/T)\,Y_1'M_w Y_1$. The Likelihood Ratio (LR) test statistic for the hypothesis $H_0 : P_1 = 0$ is given by

$$\phi = T(\log|\tilde{\Sigma}| - \log|\hat{\Sigma}|) \xrightarrow[H_0]{d} \chi^2(pk) \tag{28}$$

where d indicates convergence in distribution.

Proof The proof is relatively straightforward if, following equation (10), the joint density of y_t is factorized into the product of the marginal density of y_{1t} and the conditional density of $y_{2t}|y_{1t}$. The corresponding subsystems are given by:

$$y_{1t} = R_1'w_t + e_{1t} \qquad e_{1t} \sim IN(0, \Sigma) \tag{29a}$$

$$y_{2t} = \Lambda'y_{1t} + P_2'z_t + R_{2.1}'w_t + e_{2.1t} \qquad e_{2.1t} \sim IN(0, \Omega) \tag{29b}$$

with $R_{2.1} = R_2 - R_1\Lambda$ and $e_{2.1t} = e_{2t} - \Lambda'e_{1t}$. Note that (Φ, R) and $(\Sigma, \Lambda, \Omega, R_1, R_{2.1})$ are in one-to-one correspondence and are unrestricted except for the positivity of Φ, Σ and Ω. The subsystems (29a) and (29b) may, therefore, be analysed independently of each other. Note, furthermore, that the unrestricted system (15) may be factorized in a similar way except that (29a) then includes the additional factor $P_1'z_t$ and P_2 in (29b) is replaced by $P_{2.1} = P_2 - P_1\Lambda$. The proof takes full advantage of the similarities between the factorizations of the restricted and unrestricted models. The technical details are found in the appendix.

We consider next the covariance restrictions between y_{1t} and sub-vectors of y_{2t}. We, therefore, partition y_{2t} into $y_{at} \in \mathbb{R}^{q_a}$ and $y_{bt} \in \mathbb{R}^{q_b}$ with $q_a + q_b = q$. The matrices P_2, R_2, Λ, $R_{2.1}$ and Ω are partitioned conformably with y_{2t} into

$$P_2 = (P_a : P_b) \qquad R_2 = (R_a : R_b) \qquad \Lambda = (\Lambda_a : \Lambda_b)$$

$$R_{2.1} = (R_{a.1} : R_{b.1}) = (R_a - R_1\Lambda_a : R_b - R_1\Lambda_b) \tag{30}$$

$$\Omega = \begin{pmatrix} \Omega_{aa} & \Omega_{ab} \\ \Omega_{ba} & \Omega_{bb} \end{pmatrix}.$$

Let the superscript $^{-}$ denote the ML estimators of the parameters in equation (22) under the additional assumption that $\operatorname{cov}(y_{1t}, y_{at}') = \Sigma\Lambda_a = 0$, i.e. that $\Lambda_a = 0$.

Theorem 2 The ML estimators of the parameters in equation (22) under the assumption that $\Lambda_a = 0$ are given by

$$\bar{\Lambda} = (0 : \tilde{\Lambda}_b - \tilde{\Lambda}_a \tilde{\Delta}_{ab}) = \tilde{\Lambda} - \tilde{\Lambda}_a(I_{q_a} : \tilde{\Delta}_{ab}) \tag{31}$$

$$\bar{P} = (0 : \hat{P}_2 - \hat{P}_1\bar{\Lambda}) = \hat{P} - \hat{P}_1(I_p : \bar{\Lambda}) \tag{32}$$

$$\bar{R} = \tilde{R} - (W'W)^{-1}W'Z(\bar{P} - \tilde{P}) \tag{33}$$

$$\bar{\Sigma} = \tilde{\Sigma}, \quad \bar{\Omega} = \tilde{\Omega} + (1/T)(\bar{\Lambda} - \tilde{\Lambda})'Y_1'M_xY_1(\bar{\Lambda} - \tilde{\Lambda}) \tag{34}$$

with $\bar{\Delta}_{ab} = \tilde{\Delta}_{ab} = (Y_a'M_{\Xi_1}Y_a)^{-1}Y_a'M_{\Xi_1}Y_b$ and $\Xi_1 = (Y_1 : X)$. Also

$$|\bar{\Omega}| = |\tilde{\Omega}| \cdot (|\bar{\Omega}_{aa}| \cdot |\tilde{\Omega}_{aa}|^{-1}), \quad |\bar{\Phi}| = |\tilde{\Phi}| \cdot (|\bar{\Omega}_{aa}| \cdot |\tilde{\Omega}_{aa}|^{-1}) \tag{35}$$

$$\bar{\Omega}^{-1} = \tilde{\Omega}^{-1} + \begin{pmatrix} \bar{\Omega}_{aa}^{-1} - \tilde{\Omega}_{aa}^{-1} & 0 \\ 0 & 0 \end{pmatrix} \tag{36}$$

with $\tilde{\Omega}_{aa} = (1/T)\, Y_a'M_{\Xi_1}Y_a$ and $\bar{\Omega}_{aa} = (1/T)\, Y_a'M_x Y_A$. The LR test statistic for the hypothesis $H_0 : \Lambda_a = 0$ in equation (22) is given by

$$\phi_a = T(\log|\bar{\Omega}_{aa}| - \log|\tilde{\Omega}_{aa}|) \underset{H_0}{\xrightarrow{d}} \chi^2(q_a q_b). \tag{37}$$

Proof The proof is similar to that of theorem 1 except that the subsystem (29b) is also partitioned conformably with y_{2t} so that we have:

$$y_{1t} = R_1'w_t + e_{1t} \qquad e_{1t} \sim IN(0, \Sigma) \tag{38a}$$

$$y_{at} = P_a{}'z_t + R_{a.1}{}'w_t + e_{a.1t} \qquad e_{2.1t} = \begin{pmatrix} e_{a.1t} \\ e_{b.1t} \end{pmatrix} \sim IN(0, \Omega) \tag{38b}$$

$$y_{bt} = \Lambda_b{}'y_{1t} + P_b{}'z_t + R_{b.1}{}'w_t + e_{b.1t}\,. \tag{38c}$$

The assumption $\Lambda_a = 0$ does not affect the estimation of R_1 and Σ since e_{1t} and $e_{2.1t}$ are independent. We can, therefore, apply theorem 1 to the system (38b) and (38c) adapting the notation in consequence by comparison with equations (22). The results follow by appropriate regrouping. The technical details are found in the appendix.

3.2 *An IV Estimator Generating Equation*

Throughout this section the model (14) is taken as the maintained hypothesis. Conditionally on θ we can apply theorem 1. Since, however, (14) includes overidentifying restrictions, for which we derive test statistics in section 3.4, we use the superscript ˇ instead of ˆ to denote the IVML estimators of its parameters. The matrix of observations is denoted $\Xi = (Y : Z : W)$. Let

$$\check{P}_\theta = (\check{P}_{1\theta} : \check{P}_{2\theta}) = (Z'Z)^{-1}Z'(\Xi A_\theta : YS) \tag{39}$$

$$\check{\Pi}_\theta = -\begin{pmatrix} C_\theta & -\check{P}_{2\theta} \\ D_\theta & 0 \end{pmatrix} Q_\theta{}^{-1} \tag{40}$$

$$\check{\Phi}_\theta = \frac{1}{T}(\Xi A_\theta : YS)'M_z(\Xi A_\theta : YS) \tag{41}$$

$$\check{\Sigma}_\theta = \frac{1}{T}A_\theta{}'\Xi'M_z\Xi A_\theta \tag{42}$$

$$\check{\Lambda}_\theta = (A_\theta{}'\Xi'M_z\Xi A_\theta)^{-1}A_\theta{}'\Xi'M_zYS. \tag{43}$$

For notational convenience the fact that $M_z\Xi = (M_zY : 0 : M_zW)$ so that $\check{\Phi}_\theta$, $\check{\Sigma}_\theta$ and $\check{\Lambda}_\theta$ do not depend on C_θ is not made explicit. Let, furthermore,

$$\tilde{P}_\theta = \check{P}_\theta - \check{P}_{1\theta}(I_p : \check{\Lambda}_\theta) \tag{44}$$

$$\tilde{\Pi}_\theta = -\begin{pmatrix} C_\theta & -\tilde{P}_{2\theta} \\ D_\theta & 0 \end{pmatrix} Q_\theta{}^{-1} = \check{\Pi}_\theta - \begin{pmatrix} 0 & \check{P}_{1\theta}\check{\Lambda}_\theta \\ 0 & 0 \end{pmatrix} Q_\theta{}^{-1} \tag{45}$$

$$\tilde{\Phi} = \check{\Phi}_\theta + \frac{1}{T}(\tilde{P}_\theta - \check{P}_\theta)'Z'Z(\tilde{P}_\theta - \check{P}_\theta) \tag{46}$$

$$\tilde{\Lambda}_\theta = \check{\Lambda}_\theta \qquad \tilde{\Sigma}_\theta = \frac{1}{T} A_\theta{}' \Xi' \Xi A_\theta \tag{47}$$

$$\tilde{V}_\theta = Q_\theta{}'^{-1} \tilde{\Phi}_\theta Q_\theta{}^{-1}. \tag{48}$$

The concentrated log-likelihood function obtained by the application of theorem 1 to model (14) is given by

$$\tilde{L}(\theta;Y) = -\tfrac{1}{2} T \log |\tilde{V}_\theta|$$
$$= T \log \|Q_\theta\| - \tfrac{1}{2} T \log |\check{\Phi}_\theta| - \tfrac{1}{2} T \log |\tilde{\Sigma}_\theta| + \tfrac{1}{2} T \log |\check{\Sigma}_\theta|. \tag{49}$$

As shown in the next section, on system LIML estimators, formula (49) generalizes a variety of formulae which are available in the literature for special cases of the model (14). The IVML estimators $\tilde{\theta}$ of θ are those which maximize $\tilde{L}(\theta;Y)$ subject to the a priori restrictions on A_θ. Instead of proposing specific estimators we now generalize to the present formulation the notion of an Estimator Generating Equation (EGE) introduced by Hendry (1976) for 'complete' SEM and generalized by Hendry and Richard (1983) to 'incomplete' SEM (see also Lubrano, 1979). We only consider the case where A_θ is linear in θ so that $\partial A_\theta / \partial \theta_j = R_j$ $(j = 1, \ldots, J)$ is a matrix of known constants. $R_j{}'$ is partitioned conformably with $A_\theta{}' = (B_\theta{}' : \Gamma_\theta{}')$ into $R_j{}' = (R_{1j}{}' : R_{2j}{}')$. The score is

$$q'(\theta) = \frac{\partial \tilde{L}(\theta;Y)}{\partial \theta'} = (q_1{}'(\theta), \ldots, q_J{}'(\theta)). \tag{50}$$

The first-order condition $q(\theta) = 0$ for a maximum in (49) may be written as:

$$\operatorname{tr}[Q_\theta{}^{-1}(R_{1j} : 0)] - \operatorname{tr}[\check{\Phi}_\theta{}^{-1}(\Xi A_\theta : YS)' M_z (\Xi R_j : 0)]$$
$$- \operatorname{tr}(\tilde{\Sigma}_\theta{}^{-1} A_\theta{}' \Xi' \Xi R_j) + \operatorname{tr}(\check{\Sigma}_\theta{}^{-1} A_\theta{}' \Xi' M_z \Xi R_j) = 0$$
$$(j = 1, \ldots, J). \tag{51}$$

We can take advantage of the following identities:

$$\Xi R_j = Y R_{1j} + X R_{2j} = (Y - X\check{\Pi}_\theta) R_{1j} + X(\check{\Pi}_\theta : I_m) R_j \tag{52}$$

$$\operatorname{tr}[Q_\theta{}^{-1}(R_{1j} : 0)]$$
$$= \operatorname{tr}[\check{\Phi}_\theta{}^{-1} \check{\Phi}_\theta Q_\theta{}^{-1}(R_{1j} : 0)]$$
$$= \operatorname{tr}[\check{\Phi}_\theta{}^{-1}(\Xi A_\theta : YS)' M_z (\Xi A_\theta : YS - Z\check{P}_{2\theta}) Q_\theta{}^{-1}(R_{1j} : 0)]$$
$$= \operatorname{tr}\{\check{\Phi}_\theta{}^{-1}(\Xi A_\theta : YS)' M_z [(Y - X\check{\Pi}_\theta) R_{1j} : 0]\} \tag{53}$$

and reformulate equation (51) as

$$\operatorname{tr}\{\check{\Phi}_\theta{}^{-1}(\Xi A_\theta : YS)'M_z\,[X(\check{\Pi}_\theta : I_m)R_j : 0]\}$$
$$+\operatorname{tr}(\tilde{\Sigma}_\theta{}^{-1}A_\theta{}'\Xi'\Xi R_j - \check{\Sigma}_\theta{}^{-1}A_\theta{}'\Xi' M_z \Xi R_j) = 0 \qquad (j = 1, \ldots, J). \tag{54}$$

Equation (54) could be used, as it stands, for computation of the IVML $\tilde{\theta}$ of θ and, hence, of $\tilde{\Pi}$ and $\tilde{V}$ in formulae (45)–(48). However, an asymptotically equivalent, but simpler, form can be obtained by taking advantage of the following properties, derived from (14),

$$\operatorname*{plim}_{T\to\infty} \tilde{\Sigma}_{\tilde{\theta}} = \operatorname*{plim}_{T\to\infty} \check{\Sigma}_{\tilde{\theta}} = \Sigma \tag{55}$$

$$\operatorname*{plim}_{T\to\infty} [(Z'Z)^{-1}Z'\Xi] = \operatorname*{plim}_{T\to\infty} [G(\tilde{\Pi}_\theta : I_m)] \tag{56}$$

where $G = ((Z'Z)^{-1}Z'W : I_k)$ is a $k \times m$ matrix. Equation (44) is then reformulated as

$$\operatorname{tr}\{\check{\Phi}_\theta{}^{-1}(\Xi A_\theta : YS)'M_z[X(\check{\Pi}_\theta : I_m)\,R_j : 0]\}$$
$$+\operatorname{tr}[\tilde{\Sigma}_\theta{}^{-1}A_\theta{}'\Xi' ZG(\tilde{\Pi}_\theta : I_m)R_j] = 0 \qquad (j = 1, \ldots, J). \tag{57}$$

It is shown in the next section that if $k = 0$ (SEM), equation (57) reduces to equation (63) in Hendry and Richard (1983, section 4) whose discussion essentially covers the more general case under consideration. Therefore, a wide range of system IV estimators of θ can be generated as approximate solutions to the equations:

$$\operatorname{tr}[\Phi^{-1}(\Xi A_\theta : YS)'M_z(XFR_j : 0)] + \operatorname{tr}[\Sigma^{-1}A_\theta{}'\Xi' ZGFR_j] = 0$$
$$(j = 1, \ldots, J) \tag{58}$$

$$\Sigma = \frac{1}{T}A'\Xi'\Xi A \qquad F = (\Pi : I_m) \tag{59}$$

$$\Pi = \check{\Pi} - \begin{pmatrix} 0 & \check{P}_1\check{\Lambda} \\ 0 & 0 \end{pmatrix} Q^{-1} \tag{60}$$

$$\Phi = \check{\Phi} + \frac{1}{T}(P - \check{P})'Z'Z(P - \check{P}) \tag{61}$$

together with

$$\check{P} = (Z'Z)^{-1}Z'(\Xi A : YS) \qquad \check{\Pi} = -\begin{pmatrix} C & -\check{P}_2 \\ D & 0 \end{pmatrix} Q^{-1} \tag{62}$$

$$\check{\Phi} = \frac{1}{T}(\Xi A : YS)'M_z(\Xi A : YS)$$
$$\check{\Lambda} = (A'\Xi' M_z \Xi A)^{-1} A'\Xi' M_z YS. \tag{63}$$

Given Σ, Π and Φ equation (58) is linear in θ and so is easily solved. Moreover, given θ it is trivial to recompute Σ, Π and Φ by means of equations (59)–(63). Therefore, one can construe equation (58) as a method for generating IV estimators of θ, conditional on estimators of Σ, Π and Φ. Also

$$\operatorname*{plim}_{T\to\infty} \frac{1}{T}\bar{A}'\Xi' Z = 0 \tag{64}$$

$$\operatorname*{plim}_{T\to\infty} \frac{1}{T}(\Xi\bar{A} : YS)'M_z X = 0 \tag{65}$$

for all consistent estimators $\bar{A}$ of A. It follows that the asymptotic efficiency of an estimator of θ based on consistent estimators of Σ, Π and Φ is not affected by the efficiency of the latter. Consequently, a wide range of IV estimators of θ are obtained by varying the initial values selected for Σ, Π and Ω and the number of steps taken through the cycle (58)–(63), including not iterating at all. These IV estimators can be classified as follows:

(a) as efficient as $\tilde{\theta}$ if (Σ, Π, Φ) are estimated consistently;
(b) consistent for θ if a convergent estimator is used for (Σ, Π, Ω);
(c) asymptotically as efficient as can be obtained for a single equation of a system if $\Sigma = I_p$ and $V = I_n$ but Π is consistently estimated.

3.3 System LIML Estimators

The formulae in Richard (1979, section 3.1) and in Hendry and Richard (1983, section 4) apply to the case where $k = 0$ (conventional SEM). They can be derived from the more general formulae in section 3.2. Let

$$\hat{\Pi} = (Z'Z)^{-1}Z'Y, \qquad \hat{V} = \frac{1}{T}Y'M_zY, \tag{66}$$

We first have

$$\check{\Phi}_\theta = Q_\theta{}'\hat{V}Q_\theta \qquad \check{\Sigma}_\theta = B_\theta{}'\hat{V}B_\theta \qquad \check{\Lambda}_\theta = (B_\theta{}'\hat{V}B_\theta)^{-1}B_\theta{}'\hat{V}S \tag{67}$$
$$\check{P}_\theta = \hat{\Pi}Q_\theta + (C_\theta : 0) = (\hat{\Pi}B_\theta + C_\theta : \hat{\Pi}S) \tag{68}$$

$$\tilde{P}_{2\theta} = \hat{\Pi}S-(\hat{\Pi}B_\theta + C_\theta)\,(B_\theta'\hat{V}B_\theta)^{-1}B_\theta'\hat{V}S \tag{69}$$

whence, taking advantage of the identity

$$-C_\theta = \hat{\Pi}B_\theta - (\hat{\Pi}B_\theta + C_\theta)\,(B_\theta'\hat{V}B_\theta)^{-1}B_\theta'\hat{V}B_\theta, \tag{70}$$

we obtain successively

$$\tilde{\Pi}_\theta = \hat{\Pi}-(\hat{\Pi}B_\theta + C_\theta)\,(B_\theta'\hat{V}B_\theta)^{-1}B_\theta'\hat{V} \tag{71}$$

$$\tilde{P}_\theta = \hat{P}_\theta + (\tilde{\Pi}_\theta - \hat{\Pi})\,Q_\theta \tag{72}$$

$$\tilde{\Phi}_\theta = Q_\theta'\tilde{V}_\theta Q_\theta \tag{73}$$

$$\tilde{V}_\theta = \hat{V} + \frac{1}{T}(\tilde{\Pi}_\theta - \hat{\Pi})'Z'Z(\tilde{\Pi}_\theta - \hat{\Pi}). \tag{74}$$

Also $G = I_k$ and $M_zX = M_zZ = 0$ so that the concentrated log likelihood function (49) simplifies into

$$\begin{aligned}\tilde{L}(\theta;Y) &= -\tfrac{1}{2}T\log|\hat{V}| - \tfrac{1}{2}T\log|\tilde{\Sigma}_\theta| + \tfrac{1}{2}T\log|\check{\Sigma}_\theta| \\ &\propto \tfrac{1}{2}T\,(\log|B_\theta'Y'M_z YB_\theta| \\ &\quad -\log|(YB_\theta + ZC_\theta)'(YB_\theta + ZC_\theta)|).\end{aligned} \tag{75}$$

Formulae (75) generalize in an obvious way the well-known expression for the single equation LIML variance ratio. Also the first factor in the left-hand term of (54) drops out and the asymptotic first-order conditions for system LIML estimation are given by

$$\mathrm{tr}\,[\tilde{\Sigma}_\theta^{-1}A'\Xi'Z(\tilde{\Pi}_\theta : I_m)\,R_j] = 0, \qquad (j = 1, \ldots, J). \tag{76}$$

The corresponding EGE are

$$\mathrm{tr}\,(\Sigma^{-1}A'\Xi'ZFR_j) = 0 \qquad (j = 1, \ldots, J) \tag{77}$$

$$\Sigma = (1/T)\,(BY + CZ)'\,(BY + CZ) \qquad F = (\Pi : I_m) \tag{78}$$

$$\Pi = \hat{\Pi}-(\hat{\Pi}B + C)\,(B'\hat{V}B)^{-1}B'\hat{V} \tag{79}$$

$$V = \hat{V} + (1/T)\,(\Pi - \hat{\Pi})'Z'Z(\Pi - \hat{\Pi}). \tag{80}$$

We note that $\tilde{P}_\theta$, $\tilde{V}_\theta$, $\tilde{L}(\theta;Y)$ and the EGE no longer depend on the choice of the selection matrix S in (5), which is a well-known 'invariance' property within the context of LIML estimation. The same does not apply to the more general case where $k \neq 0$ since excluding explanatory variables from the instrumental variables equation (5) introduces an obvious asymmetry in the treatment of the endogenous variables. As discussed in Florens et al. (1979), there is much to say on conceptual grounds in favour of invariance with respect to the choice of S. In practice, however, sample sizes are limited and, as illustrated by the application in Lubrano et al. (1984), the dimensionality of P_2 has to be maintained within limits which are often incompatible with including all x variables in the instrumental variable equations (5). Also non-causality and strong exogeneity assumptions which are often of considerable interest to model builders are inherently asymmetric. A comparison between the EGE in sections 3.2 and 3.3 indicates that there are no major computational advantages in imposing $k = 0$. Whether this argument extends to the Bayesian approach is discussed in section 4.2 below.

3.4 Specification and Exogeneity IVLR Test Statistics

The model (14) incorporates overidentifying restrictions on the parameters of the structural equations (3) and zero restrictions on the parameters of the instrumental variable equations (5). Provided the sample size is large enough we may wish to test these restrictions. Starting from the unrestricted reduced form

$$y_t = \Pi' x_t + e_t \qquad e_t \sim IN(0, V) \tag{81}$$

the hypotheses of interest can be formulated as follows:

$$H_0^{(1)}: \Pi \in \mathscr{P}_1 = \{\Pi \mid \exists\, \theta \in \Theta,\ \Pi B_\theta + \Gamma_\theta = 0\} \tag{82}$$

$$H_0^{(2)}: \Pi \in \mathscr{P}_2 = \{\Pi \mid \exists\, P_2 \in \mathbb{R}^{kq},\ S'\Pi' = (P_2' : 0)\} \tag{83}$$

$$H_0^{(3)}: \Pi \in \mathscr{P}_3 = \mathscr{P}_1 \cap \mathscr{P}_2. \tag{84}$$

Let g denote the number of 'overidentifying restrictions' implicit in the definition of $\mathscr{P}_1$.

Under $H_0^{(1)}$, (81) may be reformulated as

$$\begin{aligned} A_\theta' \xi_t &= \epsilon_t \\ S' y_t &= P_2' z_t + R_2' w_t + v_t \end{aligned} \qquad \begin{pmatrix} \epsilon_t \\ v_t \end{pmatrix} \sim IN(0, \Phi) \tag{85}$$

where, as discussed in section 3.3, the choice of S does not affect the results since all the x are incorporated in the instrumental variable equations. Following formula (75), the LR test statistic for the hypothesis $H_0^{(1)}$ against (81) is given by

$$\phi_1 = T \min_\theta \left[\log |B_\theta' Y' M_x Y B_\theta| - \log |A_\theta' \Xi' \Xi A_\theta|\right] \xrightarrow[H_0^{(1)}]{d} \chi^2(g). \tag{86}$$

Under $H_0^{(2)}$, (81) may be reformulated as

$$\begin{aligned} B'y_t &= P_1'z_t + R_1'w_t + e_t \\ S'y_t &= P_2'z_t + v_t \end{aligned} \tag{87}$$

where B is an arbitrary selection matrix such that rank $(B : S) = n$. A straightforward application of formula (28) in theorem 1 yields the following expression for the corresponding LR test statistic against (81)

$$\phi_2 = T\,[\log|S'Y'M_zYS| - \log|S'Y'M_xYS|] \xrightarrow[H_0^{(2)}]{d} \chi^2(lq). \tag{88}$$

The LR test statistic for the joint hypothesis $H_0^{(3)}$ against (81) is derived from formula (49) and is given by

$$\phi_3 = T\,[\log|\check{\Phi}_{\tilde{\theta}}| - \log|\hat{\Phi}_{\tilde{\theta}}| + \log|\tilde{\Sigma}_{\tilde{\theta}}| - \log|\check{\Sigma}_{\tilde{\theta}}|] \xrightarrow[H_0^{(3)}]{d} \chi^2(lq+g)$$

where $\hat{\Phi}_\theta = Q_\theta'\hat{V}Q_\theta$ and $\tilde{\theta}$ denotes the IVML estimator of θ, i.e. precisely the value of θ which minimizes ϕ_3.

Taking now $H_0^{(3)}$ as the maintained hypothesis we may wish to test additional restrictions and, in particular, the weak and strong exogeneity of a subvector of $S'y_t$ for the structural coefficients θ. Let us, therefore, partition S as

$$S = (S_a : S_b) \tag{90}$$

where S_a and S_b are respectively $n \times q_a$ and $n \times q_b$ selection matrices $(q_a + q_b = q)$. Following theorem 4.3 in Engle et al. (1983a), the condition $\text{cov}(S_a'y_t,\ \epsilon_t') = 0$ is sufficient for the weak exogeneity of $S_a'y_t$ for θ. The concentrated likelihood function obtained by the application of theorem 2, conditionally on θ, to the model (14) under the assumption $\text{cov}(S_a'y_t, e_t') = 0$ is given by

$$\begin{aligned} \bar{L}(\theta; Y) = {} & T\log\|Q_\theta\| - \tfrac{1}{2}T\log|\tilde{\Phi}_\theta| - \tfrac{1}{2}T\log|\bar{\Omega}_{aa}| \\ & + \tfrac{1}{2}T\log|\tilde{\Omega}_{aa}{}^{\theta}| \end{aligned} \tag{91}$$

together with

$$\begin{aligned} |T\bar{\Omega}_{aa}| &= |S_a'Y'M_zYS_a| \\ |T\tilde{\Omega}_{aa}{}^{\theta}| &= |S_a'Y'M_{(\Xi A_\theta, Z)}YS_a| \\ &= |S_a'Y'M_zYS_a - S_a'Y'M_z\Xi A_\theta(A_\theta'\Xi'M_z\Xi A_\theta)^{-1} \\ &\quad \times A_\theta'\Xi'M_zYS_a| \end{aligned} \tag{92}$$

$$= |\check{\Sigma}_\theta|^{-1} |(\Xi A_\theta : YS_a)' M_z (\Xi A_\theta : YS_a)|$$
$$= |\check{\Sigma}_\theta|^{-1} |\check{\Phi}_{aa}{}^\theta| \tag{93}$$

or, equivalently, given (26),

$$\bar{L}(\theta;Y) = T \log \| Q_\theta \| - \tfrac{1}{2} T \log |\check{\Phi}_\theta| - \tfrac{1}{2} T \log |\tilde{\Sigma}_\theta|$$
$$+ \tfrac{1}{2} T \log |\check{\Phi}_{aa}{}^\theta| - \tfrac{1}{2} T \log |\bar{\Omega}_{aa}|. \tag{94}$$

We note that replacing $|\check{\Sigma}_\theta|$ in formula (49) by $|\check{\Phi}_{aa}{}^\theta|$ in formula (94) amounts to including YS_a in the list of exogenous variables, as one would expect heuristically. The EGE derived in section 3.2 can, therefore, easily be adapted for the computation of $\bar{\theta}$, the IVML of θ under the assumption that $S_a{}'y_t$ is weakly exogenous for θ. The LR test statistic for the weak exogeneity of $S_a{}'y_t$ against (14) is given by

$$\phi_4 = 2[\tilde{L}(\tilde{\theta};Y) - \bar{L}(\bar{\theta};Y)] \xrightarrow[\text{W.E.}]{d} \chi^2(pq_a). \tag{95}$$

The strong exogeneity of $S_a{}'y_t$ can be tested in a similar way simply by shifting variables from z_t into w_t. Doing this is conceptually simple but notationally tedious and so the strong exogeneity LR test statistic is not laid out in detail.

4 Bayesian Inference

As usual within the Bayesian framework, we have to find a compromise between the flexibility of the prior density and its numerical tractability. In the present treatment, we restrict the application of numerical methods to inference on θ, in line with our analysis in section 3. Our choice of (conditional) prior densities for the additional coefficients P_2 and Φ in (14) is, therefore, essentially restricted to so-called 'natural conjugate' prior densities, including limiting 'non-informative' versions thereof. Their inherent lack of flexibility represents the price to be paid in order to maintain analytical tractability within the limits which are characteristic of instrumental variables and limited information procedures. The approach described below unifies and extends earlier results in Richard (1973, 1979), Florens et al. (1979) and Drèze and Richard (1983). It generalizes the conventional Bayesian limited information analysis in three ways: (a) it applies to systems of structural equations ($1 \leqslant p < n$); (b) it covers the IV approach with $k \neq 0$; (c) it allows prior information on P_2 and Φ to be taken into account.

As in section 3 we first discuss the reduced form model (15) in order to separate the technical difficulties arising from the imposition of exclusion restrictions on the reduced form coefficients from those specific to the treatment of structural coefficients. This is the object of section 4.1. Although the technicalities of the Bayesian approach we develop below are similar in many ways to those of the classical approach in section 3.1, they are more demanding for readers unfamiliar with the Bayesian approach essentially because we manipulate density functions instead of point estimates. Section 4.1 has been written in a self-contained form hopefully accessible to readers who wish to follow the algebra of our analysis despite their lack of familiarity with the Bayesian approach. Readers who wish instead to get an overview of our Bayesian analysis of model (14) without entering its technicalities may skip section 4.1.

4.1 The Multivariate Regression Model

The likelihood function of the model (15) can be written as

$$L(\Pi, \Phi; Y) \propto |\Phi|^{-\frac{1}{2}T} \exp\left(-\tfrac{1}{2} \operatorname{tr} \Phi^{-1}[T\hat{\Phi} + (\Pi - \hat{\Pi})'N(\Pi - \hat{\Pi})]\right) \tag{96}$$

with $N = X'X$, $\hat{\Pi} = (X'X)^{-1}X'Y$ and $T\hat{\Phi} = Y'M_xY$. A minimal sufficient statistic is given by the moment matrix

$$\begin{pmatrix} X'X & X'Y \\ Y'X & Y'Y \end{pmatrix} = \begin{pmatrix} N & N\hat{\Pi} \\ \hat{\Pi}'N & T\hat{\Phi} + \hat{\Pi}'N\hat{\Pi} \end{pmatrix} \tag{97}$$

which, for $T \geqslant m + n$ and rank $X = m$, belongs almost surely to $\mathscr{C}_{m+n}$, the set of symmetric positive definite matrices of order $m + n$. Following the discussion in Raiffa and Schlaifer (1961) a 'natural conjugate' prior density for (Π, Ω) takes the functional form of the likelihood function associated with an 'hypothetical' independent sample, on which prior information is implicitly based, and may, therefore, be written as

$$D(\Pi, \Phi) \propto [|\Phi_0|^{\frac{1}{2}\nu_0}|N_0|^{\frac{1}{2}n}]|\Phi|^{-\frac{1}{2}(\nu_0+m+n+1)} \times \exp\left(-\tfrac{1}{2} \operatorname{tr} \Phi^{-1}[\Phi_0 + (\Pi - \Pi_0)'N_0(\Pi - \Pi_0)]\right) \tag{98}$$

with $N_0 \in \mathscr{C}_m$, $\Pi_0 \in \mathbb{R}^{mn}$, $\Phi_0 \in \mathscr{C}_n$ and $\nu_0 > n - 1$. The first two factors in the right-hand term of (98) are part of the integrating constant and are included for later reference. The joint density (98) factorizes into the product of a marginal inverted-Wishart density on Φ and a conditional matricvariate normal density on Π, given Φ:

$$D(\Phi) \propto |\Phi|^{\frac{1}{2}\nu_0}|\Phi|^{-\frac{1}{2}(\nu_0+n+1)} \exp(-\tfrac{1}{2}\operatorname{tr}\Phi^{-1}\Phi_0) \tag{99}$$

$$D(\Pi|\Phi) \propto |N_0|^{\frac{1}{2}n}|\Phi|^{-\frac{1}{2}m} \exp(-\tfrac{1}{2}\operatorname{tr}\Phi^{-1}(\Pi-\Pi_0)'N_0(\Pi-\Pi_0)). \tag{100}$$

In the rest of the chapter we use the notation $f_{IW}{}^{n}(\Phi|\Phi_0, \nu_0)$, $f_{MN}{}^{mn}(\Pi|\Pi_0, \Phi\otimes N_0{}^{-1})$ to represent the density functions in formulae (99) and (100). Properties of these density functions are discussed extensively in Drèze and Richard (1983, Appendix). For ease of reference, however, it proves convenient to discuss briefly the properties our analysis is based on, using the present notation. A matricvariate normal density on Π is in fact a normal density on $\operatorname{vec}\Pi$, the column expansion of Π, with a covariance matrix in the form of a Kronecker product. Let π_j denote the jth column of Π, so that $\operatorname{vec}\Pi = (\pi_1{}', \ldots, \pi_n{}')'$, and let ϕ^{ij} denote the (i, j)th element of Φ^{-1}. The quadratic form in formula (100) may then be rewritten as

$$\begin{aligned}\operatorname{tr}\Phi^{-1}(\Pi-\Pi_0)'N_0(\Pi-\Pi_0) &= \sum_{ij}\phi^{ij}(\pi_j-\pi_j{}^0)'N_0(\pi_i-\pi_i{}^0)\\ &= (\operatorname{vec}\Pi-\operatorname{vec}\Pi_0)'(\Phi^{-1}\otimes N_0)\\ &\quad\times(\operatorname{vec}\Pi-\operatorname{vec}\Pi_0).\end{aligned} \tag{101}$$

The expectation and covariance matrices of $\Pi|\Phi$ are, therefore, given by

$$E(\Pi|\Phi) = \Pi_0 \qquad \operatorname{cov}(\operatorname{vec}\Pi|\Phi) = \Phi^{-1}\otimes N_0. \tag{102}$$

All the properties of the multivariate normal distribution apply to the matricvariate normal distribution and those which preserve the Kronecker product form of the covariance matrix are of special interest to us. This is the case with the linear transformation

$$\Delta = A\Pi B \tag{103}$$

where A and B are arbitrary matrices of constants since, following e.g. Balestra (1975, p. 16),

$$\begin{aligned}\operatorname{vec}\Delta &= (I_r\otimes A)\operatorname{vec}(\Pi B) = (I_r\otimes A)(B'\otimes I_m)\operatorname{vec}\Pi\\ &= (B'\otimes A)\operatorname{vec}\Pi\end{aligned} \tag{104}$$

whence, in combination with (102),

$$E(\Delta|\Phi) = A\Pi_0 B \qquad \operatorname{cov}(\operatorname{vec}\Delta|\Phi) = B'\Phi^{-1}B \otimes AN_0^{-1}A'. \tag{105}$$

Useful choices of A and B are those which block-diagonalize N_0^{-1} and Φ. Let Π (and Π_0) be partitioned as in (21). Φ and N_0 are then partitioned conformably with Π as

$$\Phi = \begin{pmatrix} \Sigma & \Sigma\Lambda \\ \Lambda'\Sigma & \Omega + \Lambda'\Sigma\Lambda \end{pmatrix} \qquad \Phi^{-1} = \begin{pmatrix} \Sigma^{-1} + \Lambda\Omega^{-1}\Lambda' & -\Lambda\Omega^{-1} \\ -\Omega^{-1}\Lambda' & \Omega^{-1} \end{pmatrix} \tag{106}$$

$$\begin{aligned} N_0 &= \begin{pmatrix} E_0 + F_0'G_0F_0 & F_0'G_0 \\ G_0F_0 & G_0 \end{pmatrix} \\ N_0^{-1} &= \begin{pmatrix} E_0^{-1} & -E_0^{-1}F_0' \\ -F_0E_0^{-1} & G_0^{-1} + F_0E_0^{-1}F_0' \end{pmatrix}. \end{aligned} \tag{107}$$

If we take

$$A = \begin{pmatrix} I_k & 0 \\ F_0 & I_l \end{pmatrix} \quad \text{and} \quad B = I_n \tag{108}$$

then

$$\Delta = \begin{pmatrix} P \\ R + F_0P \end{pmatrix}, \qquad E(\Delta|\Phi) = \begin{pmatrix} P_0 \\ R_0 + F_0P_0 \end{pmatrix} \tag{109}$$

and

$$\operatorname{cov}(\operatorname{vec}\Delta|\Phi) = \Phi \otimes \begin{pmatrix} E_0^{-1} & 0 \\ 0 & G_0^{-1} \end{pmatrix} \tag{110}$$

whence

$$D(P|\Phi) = f_{MN}{}^{kn}(P|P_0, \Phi \otimes E_0^{-1}) \tag{111}$$

$$D(R|P, \Phi) = f_{MN}{}^{ln}(R|R_0 - F_0(P - P_0), \Phi \otimes G_0^{-1}). \tag{112}$$

If we take instead

$$A = I_n \quad \text{and} \quad B = \begin{pmatrix} I_p & -\Lambda \\ 0 & I_q \end{pmatrix}, \tag{113}$$

then

$$\Delta = (\Pi_1 : \Pi_2 - \Pi_1\Lambda), \qquad E(\Delta|\Phi) = (\Pi_1{}^0 : \Pi_2{}^0 - \Pi_1{}^0\Lambda) \tag{114}$$

and

$$\operatorname{cov}(\operatorname{vec}\Delta \mid \Phi) = \begin{pmatrix} \Sigma & 0 \\ 0 & \Omega \end{pmatrix} \otimes N_0^{-1} \tag{115}$$

whence

$$D(\Pi_1 \mid \Phi) = f_{MN}{}^{mp}(\Pi_1 \mid \Pi_1{}^0, \Sigma \otimes N_0^{-1}) \tag{116}$$

$$D(\Pi_2 \mid \Pi_1, \Phi) = f_{MN}{}^{mq}(\Pi_2 \mid \Pi_2{}^0 + (\Pi - \Pi_1{}^0)\,\Lambda, \Omega \otimes N_0^{-1}). \tag{117}$$

Those are the principles we rely upon in the analysis below. Also, as usual within the framework of normal distributions, our analysis can be conducted mostly in terms of first- and second-order moments. We use, in particular, the fact that a marginal covariance matrix equals the sum of the expectation of the conditional covariance matrix and the covariance matrix of the conditional expectations. For example, $\operatorname{cov}(\Pi_2 \mid \Phi)$ can be derived from (117) in the following way

$$\begin{aligned} \operatorname{cov}(\Pi_2 \mid \Phi) &= E[\operatorname{cov}(\Pi_2 \mid \Pi_1, \Phi)] + \operatorname{cov}[E(\operatorname{vec}\Pi_2 \mid \Pi_1, \Phi)] \\ &= \Omega \otimes N_0^{-1} + (\Lambda' \otimes I_m)(\Sigma \otimes N_0^{-1})(\Lambda \otimes I_m) \\ &= (\Omega + \Lambda'\Sigma\Lambda) \otimes N_0^{-1}. \end{aligned} \tag{118}$$

Not much need be said here about the properties of the inverted-Wishart distribution, which is a matrix generalization of the univarate inverted-gamma-2 distribution (Raiffa and Schlaifer, 1961). The property of interest to us lies in the transformation from Φ to $(\Sigma, \Lambda, \Omega)$ and is described in the course of lemma 3 below.

Multiplying together formulae (99) and (100) essentially amounts to replacing Φ_0 and ν_0 in (99) by $[\Phi_0 + (\Pi - \Pi_0)'N_0(\Pi - \Pi_0)]$ and $\nu_0 + m$. Integrating the resulting joint density $D(\Pi, \Phi)$ with respect to Φ yields, therefore, the marginal density $D(\Pi)$ in the form of the following 'matricvariate Student' density

$$D(\Pi) \propto |N_0|^{\frac{1}{2}n} |\Phi_0|^{\frac{1}{2}\nu_0} |\Phi_0 + (\Pi - \Pi_0)'N_0(\Pi - \Pi_0)|^{-\frac{1}{2}(\nu_0 + m)}. \tag{119}$$

The density (119) is denoted $f_{Mt}{}^{mn}(\Pi \mid \Pi_0, \Phi_0, N_0, \nu_0)$. Following (102) the first- and second-order moments of Π are given by

$$\begin{aligned} E(\Pi) &= \Pi_0 \\ \operatorname{cov}(\operatorname{vec}\Pi) &= E(\Phi) \otimes N_0^{-1} = \frac{1}{\nu_0 - n - 1}\,\Phi_0 \otimes N_0^{-1}. \end{aligned} \tag{120}$$

In accordance with the convolution rule for sufficient statistics which underlies the natural conjugate principle, the posterior density $D(\Pi, \Phi \mid Y)$ has the same functional form as the density (98). Its hyperparameters Π_*, Φ_* and N_* are defined by the identity

$$\begin{pmatrix} N_* & N_*\Pi_* \\ \Pi_*'N_* & \Phi_* + \Pi_*'N_*\Pi_* \end{pmatrix} = \begin{pmatrix} N_0 & N_0\Pi_0 \\ \Pi_0'N_0 & \Phi_0 + \Pi_0'N_0\Pi_0 \end{pmatrix} + \begin{pmatrix} X'X & X'Y \\ Y'X & Y'Y \end{pmatrix} \tag{121}$$

$$\nu_* = \nu_0 + T \tag{122}$$

whence, together with (97), we have

$$N_* = N_0 + X'X \qquad \Pi_* = N_*^{-1}(N_0\Pi_0 + N\hat{\Pi}) \tag{123}$$

$$\begin{aligned} \Phi_* &= \Phi_0 + \Pi_0'N_0\Pi_0 + Y'Y - \Pi_*'N_*\Pi_* \\ &= \Phi_0 + (Y - X\Pi_0)'(I_T - XN_*^{-1}X')(Y - X\Pi_0) \\ &= \Phi_0 + (Y - X\Pi_0)'(I_T + XN_0^{-1}X')^{-1}(Y - X\Pi_0). \end{aligned} \tag{124}$$

The 'marginal' likelihood function

$$L(Y) = \int L(\Pi, \Phi; Y)\, D(\Pi, \Phi)\, \mathrm{d}\Pi\, \mathrm{d}\Phi \tag{125}$$

is given by the ratio between the integrating constants of the prior and posterior densities of (Π, Φ):

$$\begin{aligned} L(Y) &\propto [|\Phi_0|^{\frac{1}{2}\nu_0}|N_0|^{\frac{1}{2}n}] \cdot [|\Phi_*|^{\frac{1}{2}\nu_*}|N_*|^{\frac{1}{2}n}]^{-1} \\ &\propto f_{Mt}^{Tn}(Y|X\Pi_0, \Phi_0, (I_T + XN_0^{-1}X')^{-1}, \nu_0). \end{aligned} \tag{126}$$

Under the assumption that the variables in x_t are *strongly* exogenous for Π and Φ, $L(Y)$ coincides, up to a multiplicative constant, with the *joint* predictive density $D(Y \mid X)$. Limiting 'non-informative' prior densities, whereby N_0 or Φ_0 are arbitrarily small compared with their sample counterparts, are commonly used. In the natural conjugate framework, however, it would be inherently unwise to combine an informative prior density on Π with a non-informative prior density on Φ, as discussed e.g. in Richard (1973, p. 181). The fact that, following (120), the prior covariance matrix of vec Π takes the form of a Kronecker product imposes severe constraints on the type of prior information for which the natural conjugate formulation is appropriate.

We partition y_t and Π conformably with each other into

$$y_t' = (y_{1t}' : y_{2t}') \qquad \Pi = (\Pi_1 : \Pi_2) \tag{127}$$

where Π_1 and Π_2 are respectively $m \times p$ and $m \times q$ matrices $(p + q = n)$. As in section 3, the joint density of $y_t | x_t$ is partitioned into the product of the densities of $y_{1t} | x_t$ and $y_{2t} | y_{1t}, x_t$. The corresponding systems of equations are given by

$$y_{1t} = \Pi_1' x_t + e_{1t} \qquad e_{1t} \sim IN(0, \Sigma) \tag{128a}$$

$$y_{2t} = \Lambda' y_{1t} + \Pi_{2.1}' x_t + e_{2.1t} \qquad e_{2.1t} \sim IN(0, \Omega) \tag{128b}$$

with $\Pi_{2.1} = \Pi_2 - \Pi_1 \Lambda$. The likelihood function (96) and the natural conjugate prior density (98) have similar functional form, by definition of the latter. It follows that the systems of equations (128a) and (128b) can be analysed independently of each other, as within the sampling theory framework. Lemma 3 collects together the results which are of interest to us. The matrices Φ and Φ_0 are partitioned as in (106) and Π_0 is partitioned conformably with Π, as in (127). Let also

$$\Pi_{2.1}^0 = \Pi_2^0 - \Pi_1^0 \Lambda_0. \tag{129}$$

Similar factorizations apply to Φ_*, Φ_*^{-1} and Π_*. In fact, since the prior and posterior densities have common analytical forms, the results which are reported below are formulated solely in terms of prior densities (except in case of ambiguities). Posterior densities are obtained simply by substituting posterior hyperparameters, subscripted with *, for prior hyperparameters, subscripted with 0 in the relevant expressions. The relationship between the two sets of hyperparameters is defined by the convolution rule (121) and factorizations such as (106) and (107) are applied in parallel to them.

Lemma 3 (a) The likelihood function of the model (15) can be rewritten as

$$L(\Pi_1, \Sigma, \Pi_{2.1}, \Lambda, \Omega; Y) = L_1(\Pi_1, \Sigma; Y) \cdot L_2(\Pi_{2.1}, \Lambda, \Omega; Y) \tag{130}$$

with

$$L_1(\Pi_1, \Sigma; Y) \propto |\Sigma|^{-\frac{1}{2}T} \exp(-\tfrac{1}{2} \operatorname{tr} \Sigma^{-1}(Y_1 - X\Pi_1)'(Y_1 - X\Pi_1)) \tag{131}$$

$$L_2(\Pi_{2.1}, \Lambda, \Omega; Y) \propto |\Omega|^{-\frac{1}{2}T} \exp(-\tfrac{1}{2} \operatorname{tr} \Omega^{-1}(Y_2 - Y_1\Lambda - X\Pi_{2.1})' \times (Y_2 - Y_1\Lambda - X\Pi_{2.1})). \tag{132}$$

(b) Under the prior density (98), (Π_1, Σ) and $(\Pi_{2.1}, \Lambda, \Omega)$ are a priori and a posteriori independent. Their joint prior density can be factorized into the product of the following densities

$$D(\Sigma) \propto f_{IW}{}^{p}(\Sigma|\Sigma_0, \nu_0 - q) \tag{133a}$$

$$D(\Pi_1|\Sigma) \propto f_{MN}{}^{mp}(\Pi_1|\Pi_1{}^0, \Sigma \otimes N_0{}^{-1}) \tag{133b}$$

$$D(\Omega) \propto f_{IW}{}^{q}(\Omega|\Omega_0, \nu_0) \tag{134a}$$

$$D(\Lambda|\Omega) \propto f_{MN}{}^{pq}(\Lambda|\Lambda_0, \Omega \otimes \Sigma_0{}^{-1}) \tag{134b}$$

$$D(\Pi_{2.1}|\Lambda, \Omega) \propto f_{MN}{}^{mq}(\Pi_{2.1}|\Pi_2{}^0 - \Pi_1{}^0\Lambda, \Omega \otimes N_0{}^{-1}). \tag{135}$$

(c) The posterior densities of $(\Sigma, \Pi_1, \Omega, \Lambda, \Pi_{2.1})$ have the same analytical form as the corresponding prior densities except that the subscript 0 is replaced by *.

(d) The 'marginal' likelihood functions $L_1(Y)$ and $L_2(Y)$ derived respectively from $L_1(\Pi_1, \Sigma; Y)$ and $L_2(\Pi_{2.1}, \Lambda, \Omega; Y)$ are given by

$$L_1(Y) \propto [|\Sigma_0|^{\frac{1}{2}(\nu_0 - q)}|N_0|^{\frac{1}{2}p}][|\Sigma_*|^{\frac{1}{2}(\nu_* - q)}|N_*|^{\frac{1}{2}p}]^{-1} \tag{136}$$

$$L_2(Y) \propto [|\Omega_0|^{\frac{1}{2}\nu_0}|\Sigma_0|^{\frac{1}{2}q}|N_0|^{\frac{1}{2}q}][|\Omega_*|^{\frac{1}{2}\nu_*}|\Sigma_*|^{\frac{1}{2}q}|N_*|^{\frac{1}{2}q}]^{-1}. \tag{137}$$

Proof These results can be found e.g. in Florens et al. (1979) or in Drèze and Richard (1983, Appendix). They follow from the principles discussed above in formulae (103)–(117). A short proof is given in the appendix for ease of reference.

The results in Lemma 3 call for the following comments which are essential to our analysis:

(a) The Bayesian results are fully coherent with the classical results derived in section 3 in the following sense: under a 'non-informative' prior density, whereby $\Phi_0 \cong 0$ and $N_0 \cong 0$, the posterior means of $(\Pi_1, \Sigma, \Pi_{2.1}, \Lambda, \Omega)$ coincide with the corresponding stepwise ML estimators. If indeed Φ_0 and N_0 are (relatively) negligible, then following (121)

$$N_* \cong X'X \qquad \Pi_* \cong \hat{\Pi} \qquad \Phi_* \cong T\hat{\Phi} \tag{138}$$

and, by application of the decomposition (106),

$$\Sigma_* \cong T\hat{\Sigma} \qquad \Lambda_* \cong \hat{\Lambda} \qquad \Omega_* \cong T\hat{\Omega}. \tag{139}$$

This analogy also applies to the other results which are derived below and usefully illuminates the close links between the sampling theory and the natural conjugate Bayesian frameworks, despite the apparent complexity of the Bayesian approach.

(b) The prior density $D(\Pi_{2.1}, \Lambda, \Omega)$ on the parameters of the *conditional* model (128b) is uniquely determined by the hyperparameters $(\Pi_1{}^0, \Pi_2{}^0, \Omega_0, \Lambda_0, \Sigma_0, N_0, \nu_0)$. These hyperparameters are in *one-to-one* correspondence with the hyperparameters $(\Pi_0, \Phi_0, N_0, \nu_0)$ which determine the prior density $D(\Pi, \Omega)$ on the parameters of the *joint* model (128). In other words a complete elicitation of the prior density $D(\Pi_{2.1}, \Lambda, \Omega)$ uniquely determines the joint prior density $D(\Pi, \Omega)$ and reciprocally. This property illustrates the lack of flexibility of the natural conjugate framework and, more fundamentally, reflects the fact that the moment matrix (97) is a sufficient statistic and contains, therefore, all the information originating from a (possibly hypothetical) sample. It contributes, however, a simplification of our analysis in the following sense. In order to gain flexibility we may consider replacing the prior density $D(\Pi_1, \Sigma)$, as given in (133), by an arbitrary prior density. Not only does this not affect our analysis of the conditional model (128b), in that the posterior density of $(\Pi_{2.1}, \Lambda, \Omega)$ is left unchanged but, furthermore, the corresponding prior or posterior hyperparameters are still related to each other by the convolution rule (121) and the factorization (106). This principle could lead to a recursive definition of a generalized natural conjugate prior density as proposed in Richard (1979, section 5). This is not our present object. The point is that, as soon as restrictions are imposed upon Π, as in theorem 1, the hyperparameters in the (conditional) posterior densities of (Π_1, Σ) and $(\Pi_{2.1}, \Lambda, \Omega)$ differ, even under the conditions of lemma 3. The object of lemma 4 below is, therefore, to generalize the above results in such a way that they can be applied to the analysis of the SEM (14), leading to a Bayesian analogue to theorem 1.

Lemma 4 Let the likelihood function of the model (15) be written as in (130). Let the joint prior density be the product of the prior density (134)–(135) with the following prior density on (Π_1, Σ):

$$D(\Sigma) = f_{IW}{}^p(\Sigma \mid \tilde{\Sigma}_0, \tilde{\nu}_0) \tag{140a}$$

$$D(\Pi \mid \Sigma) = f_{MN}{}^{mp}(\Pi \mid \tilde{\Pi}_1{}^0, \Sigma \otimes \tilde{N}_0{}^{-1}). \tag{140b}$$

Then

(a) the posterior density $D(\Pi_{2.1}, \Lambda, \Omega | Y)$ and the marginal likelihood function $L_2(Y)$ coincide with those which are obtained under the conditions of lemma 3;

(b) the posterior density $D(\Pi_1, \Sigma | Y)$ has the same analytical form as the prior density (140) with hyperparameters

$$\begin{pmatrix} \tilde{N}_* & \tilde{N}_*\tilde{\Pi}_1{}^* \\ \tilde{\Pi}_1{}^{*\prime}\tilde{N}_* & \tilde{\Sigma}_* + \tilde{\Pi}_1{}^{*\prime}\tilde{N}_*\tilde{\Pi}_1{}^* \end{pmatrix} = \begin{pmatrix} \tilde{N}_0 & \tilde{N}_0{}^0\tilde{\Pi}_1{}^0 \\ \tilde{\Pi}_1{}^{0\prime}\tilde{N}_0 & \tilde{\Sigma}_0 + \tilde{\Pi}_1{}^{0\prime}\tilde{N}_0\tilde{\Pi}_1{}^0 \end{pmatrix} + \begin{pmatrix} X'X & X'Y_1 \\ Y_1{}'X & Y_1{}'Y_1 \end{pmatrix}; \tag{141}$$

(c) the marginal likelihood function $\tilde{L}_1(Y)$ is given by

$$\tilde{L}_1(Y) \propto [|\tilde{\Sigma}_0|^{\frac{1}{2}\tilde{\nu}_0}|\tilde{N}_0|^{\frac{1}{2}p}] \cdot [|\tilde{\Sigma}_*|^{\frac{1}{2}\tilde{\nu}_*}|\tilde{N}_*|^{\frac{1}{2}p}]^{-1}; \tag{142}$$

(d) the prior expectations of (Π, Φ) and covariance matrix of $\operatorname{vec}\Pi$ are given by

$$E(\Pi) = \Pi_0 + (\tilde{\Pi}_1{}^0 - \Pi_1{}^0)(I_p : \Lambda_0) \tag{143}$$

$$\begin{aligned} \operatorname{cov}(\operatorname{vec}\Pi) = {} & \frac{1}{\nu_0 - q - 1}\begin{pmatrix} 0 & 0 \\ 0 & \Omega_0 \end{pmatrix} \\ & \otimes \left[N_0{}^{-1} + \frac{1}{\tilde{\nu}_0 - p - 1}\operatorname{tr}(\tilde{\Sigma}_0\Sigma_0{}^{-1})\tilde{N}_0{}^{-1}\right. \\ & \left. + (\tilde{\Pi}_1{}^0 - \Pi_1{}^0)\Sigma_0{}^{-1}(\tilde{\Pi}_1{}^0 - \Pi_1{}^0)'\right] \\ & + \frac{1}{\tilde{\nu}_0 - p - 1}\begin{pmatrix} \tilde{\Sigma}_0 & \tilde{\Sigma}_0\Lambda_0 \\ \Lambda_0{}'\tilde{\Sigma}_0 & \Lambda_0{}'\tilde{\Sigma}_0\Lambda_0 \end{pmatrix} \otimes \tilde{N}_0{}^{-1} \end{aligned} \tag{144}$$

$$\begin{aligned} E(\Pi) = {} & \frac{1}{\nu_0 - q - 1}\left[1 + \frac{1}{\tilde{\nu}_0 - p - 1}\operatorname{tr}(\tilde{\Sigma}_0\Sigma_0{}^{-1})\right]\begin{pmatrix} 0 & 0 \\ 0 & \Omega_0 \end{pmatrix} \\ & + \frac{1}{\tilde{\nu}_0 - p - 1}\begin{pmatrix} \tilde{\Sigma}_0 & \tilde{\Sigma}_0\Lambda_0 \\ \Lambda_0{}'\tilde{\Sigma}_0 & \Lambda_0{}'\tilde{\Sigma}_0\Lambda_0 \end{pmatrix}. \end{aligned} \tag{145}$$

The posterior moments have similar analytical forms except that subscripts 0 are replaced by *.

Proof (a) follows from the above discussion. (b) and (c) are obtained by the application of formulae (121) and (126) to the subsystem (128a). (d) is obtained by the application of the principles of analysis illustrated by formulae (103)–(118). The details are found in the appendix.

Under the conditions of lemma 3 ($\tilde{\Sigma}_0 = \Sigma_0, \tilde{N}_0 = N_0, \tilde{\Pi}_1{}^0 = \Pi_1{}^0, \tilde{\nu}_0 = \nu - q$) the expressions (143)–(145) for the moments of Π and Φ obviously simplify into the expressions in (120). Lemma 4 is central to our analysis in that it enables us to handle prior information which is specific to Π_1 such as the exact prior restriction $P_1 = 0$ in theorem 1. These restrictions can be handled in two formally different ways.

A first approach starts from an unconstrained prior density, as in lemma 3, on which the exact restriction $P_1 = 0$ is then imposed by conditionalization. Applying formulae (111) and (112) to the prior density $D(\Pi_1 | \Sigma)$, as given in (133b), we obtain

$$D(P_1 | \Sigma) = f_{MN}{}^{kp}(P_1 | P_1{}^0, \Sigma \otimes E_0{}^{-1}) \tag{146}$$

$$D(R_1 | P_1, \Sigma) = f_{MN}{}^{lp}(R_1 | R_1{}^0 - F_0(P_1 - P_1{}^0), \Sigma \otimes G_0{}^{-1}). \tag{147}$$

Multiplying $D(\Sigma)$ and $D(P_1 | \Sigma)$, as given respectively in formulae (140a) and (146), and regrouping the factors depending on Σ yields the following expression for $D(\Sigma | P_1)$:

$$D(\Sigma | P_1) = f_{IW}{}^p(\Sigma | \Sigma_0 + (P_1 - P_1{}^0)' E_0 (P_1 - P_1{}^0), \nu_0 + k - q). \tag{148}$$

Setting $P_1 = 0$ in (147) and (148) is then equivalent to choosing the hyperparameters in (140) in the following way

$$\tilde{\Sigma}_0 = \Sigma_0 + P_1{}^{0\prime} E_0 P_1{}^0 \qquad \tilde{\nu}_0 = \nu_0 + k - q \tag{149}$$

$$\tilde{\Pi}_1{}^0 = \begin{pmatrix} 0 \\ R_1{}^0 + F_0 P_1{}^0 \end{pmatrix} \qquad \tilde{N}_0{}^{-1} \cong \begin{pmatrix} 0 & 0 \\ 0 & G_0{}^{-1} \end{pmatrix}. \tag{150}$$

An alternative approach consists of setting $P_1 = 0$ in the subsystem (128a) and specifying a prior density on the remaining coefficients R_1 and Σ. This is *functionally* equivalent to assigning directly the hyperparameters in (140) in the following restricted form

$$\tilde{\Pi}_1{}^0 = \begin{pmatrix} 0 \\ \tilde{R}_1{}^0 \end{pmatrix} \qquad \tilde{N}_0{}^{-1} \cong \begin{pmatrix} 0 & 0 \\ 0 & G^{-1} \end{pmatrix}. \tag{151}$$

In all generality the second approach is preferable on conceptual grounds since it avoids the so-called 'conditionalization paradoxes' discussed e.g. in Kolmogorov (1956, p. 51). On the other hand the first approach allows for 'testing' first the prior restrictions $P_1 = 0$, e.g. by examining the unconstrained posterior density of P_1 derived under a tight prior density centred on $P_0^1 = 0$. In the present case, the two approaches are formally equivalent if $P_1^0 = 0$, $\tilde{R}_1^0 = R_1^0$, $\tilde{G}_0 = G_0$ and $\tilde{\nu}_0 = \nu_0 + k - q$. The second approach covers a wider class of prior densities at the cost of an elicitation procedure that might prove difficult to organize and could be based, for example, on the moments of Π and Φ, as given in formulae (143)–(145) in order to avoid reasoning in terms of such 'auxiliary' parameters as $\Pi_{2.1}$.

Strictly speaking the matrices $\tilde{N}_0^{-1}$ in formulae (150) and (151) are handled as limit cases of non-singular matrices with the effect that the sample information on P_1 is dominated by the prior information $P_1 = 0$. The convolution rule (141) is *de facto* replaced by

$$\begin{pmatrix} \tilde{G}_* & \tilde{G}_*\tilde{R}_1^* \\ \tilde{R}_1^{*\prime}\tilde{G}_* & \tilde{\Sigma}_* + \tilde{R}_1^{*\prime}\tilde{G}_*\tilde{R}_1^* \end{pmatrix} = \begin{pmatrix} \tilde{G}_0 & \tilde{G}_0\tilde{R}_1^0 \\ \tilde{R}_1^{0\prime}\tilde{G}_0 & \tilde{\Sigma}_0 + \tilde{R}_1^{0\prime}\tilde{G}_0\tilde{R}_1^0 \end{pmatrix} + \begin{pmatrix} W'W & W'Y_1 \\ Y_1'W & Y_1'Y_1 \end{pmatrix}. \tag{152}$$

Also the factors $|\tilde{N}_0|^{\frac{1}{2}p}$ and $|\tilde{N}_*|^{\frac{1}{2}p}$ which appear in the integrating constants of the prior and posterior densities of $\Pi_1|\Sigma$ and also in the marginal likelihood function $\tilde{L}_1(Y)$ are then replaced respectively by $|\tilde{G}_0|^{\frac{1}{2}p}$ and $|\tilde{G}_*|^{\frac{1}{2}p}$.

This concludes our rather lengthy discussion of the multivariate regression model with the advantage that, conditionally on θ, the Bayesian analysis of the SEM (14) is now straightforward.

4.2 *Incomplete SEM*

Conditionally on θ, the model (14) takes the form of a restricted multivariate regression model to which we can apply lemma 4. In fact the generality of lemma 4 enables us to analyse the model (14) at a level of flexibility whereby unrestricted columns in Γ_θ (constant terms, seasonal dummies, ...) would be incorporated in P_1 or R_1 (and dealt with analytically) and weak or strong exogeneity assumptions could be imposed, possibly after 'pretesting'. This level of generality can easily be exploited in the implementation of a computer program but complicates unnecessarily the argument at an expository level. We therefore limit ourselves to proposing a class of prior densities that are easily interpretable and yet can incorporate (stochastic) prior beliefs on the weak and strong exogeneity of components or subvectors of y_t.

It seems natural to formulate prior beliefs about variances and covariances in terms of V, the covariance matrix of $y_t|x_t$ in (2). Also assuming prior independence between V and θ obviously simplifies the elicitation of the prior density. Let us, therefore, consider prior densities of the form

$$D(V, P_2, \theta) = D(P_2| V, \theta) \cdot D(V) \cdot D(\theta) \tag{153}$$

where, in particular, $D(V)$ is an inverted-Wishart density

$$D(V) = f_{IW}{}^n(V | V_0, \nu_0) \quad \text{with} \quad E(V) = \frac{1}{\nu_0 - n - 1} V_0 \qquad (\nu_0 > n+1). \tag{154}$$

In order to embed the density (153) within the class of prior densities defined in lemma 4, we apply the transformation from V to $\Phi = Q_\theta' V Q_\theta$ and then to $(\Sigma, \Lambda, \Omega)$ as in (10), whereby

$$\Phi = \begin{pmatrix} B_\theta' V B_\theta & B_\theta' V S \\ S' V B_\theta & S' V S \end{pmatrix} = \begin{pmatrix} \Sigma & \Sigma\Lambda \\ \Lambda'\Sigma & \Omega + \Lambda'\Sigma\Lambda \end{pmatrix}. \tag{155}$$

Conditionally on θ, the transformation from V to Φ is linear and one-to-one so that

$$D(\Phi|\theta) = f_{IW}{}^n(\Phi | \Phi_0, \nu_0) \quad \text{with} \quad \Phi_0 = B_\theta' V_0 B_\theta. \tag{156}$$

It follows that, conditionally on θ, the prior density of $(\Sigma, \Lambda, \Omega)$ satisfies the assumptions of lemma 4 with the following choice of hyperparameters

$$\tilde{\Sigma}_0 = \Sigma_0 = B_\theta' V_0 B_\theta \qquad \tilde{\nu}_0 = \nu_0 - q \tag{157}$$

$$\Lambda_0 = \Sigma_0^{-1} B_\theta' V_0 S \qquad \Omega_0 = S' V_0 S - \Lambda_0' \Sigma_0 \Lambda_0. \tag{158}$$

Leaving $D(\Pi)$ unspecified for the moment, the specification of the joint prior density is completed by the assumption that

$$D(P_2 | \Lambda, \Omega, \Sigma, \theta) \equiv D(P_2 | \Lambda, \Omega, \theta)$$

in the form of the matricvariate normal density (135) with hyperparameters $P_1{}^0$ (typically set equal to zero), $P_2{}^0$ and N_0. (Since w_t is excluded from the right-hand side of (14), $\Pi = (\Pi_1 : \Pi_2)$ can be replaced by $P = (P_1 : P_2)$. Also P_2 need not be distinguished from $P_{2.1}$, *as long as* the restriction $P_1 = 0$ is maintained. The notation in section 4.2 onwards is adapted accordingly which avoids using the notation Π for a parameter which, in the notation of (14), no longer represents reduced form coefficients. We apologize to the reader for this source of confusion in our notation but, taking into account the limited supply of capital letters and our reluctance to use pairs of subscripts within partitioned matrices, we have not been able to think of a better notation.)

Note that, following the discussion at the end of section 4.1, we have imposed from the beginning the constraint $P_1 = 0$ and have specified a prior density solely for the remaining coefficients. Since, furthermore, we consider only the simplest case where w_t is excluded from the right-hand term of (14), $\tilde{P}_1{}^0$ $(=\tilde{\Pi}_1{}^0)$, $\tilde{N}_0{}^{-1}\tilde{P}_1{}^*$ $(=\tilde{\Pi}_1{}^*)$ and $\tilde{N}_*{}^{-1}$ are all set equal to zero in lemma 4. Also the determinants of $\tilde{N}_0$ and $\tilde{N}_*$ are deleted from the marginal likelihood function $\tilde{L}_1(Y)$, as given in (102), since they are implicitly arbitrarily large and equal.

The application of lemma 4, conditionally on θ, yields the following results:

(a) The conditional posterior densities of P_2, Λ, Ω and Σ, given θ, have the same analytical form as the corresponding prior densities. Their hyperparameters are given by

$$\nu_* = \nu_0 + T \qquad \tilde{\nu}_* = \nu_* - q \tag{159}$$

$$\tilde{\Sigma}_* = B_\theta{}' V_0 B_\theta + A_\theta{}' \Xi' \Xi A_\theta \tag{160}$$

$$N_* = N_0 + Z'Z \qquad P_* = N_*{}^{-1}[N_0 P_0 + Z'(\Xi A_\theta : YS)] \tag{161}$$

and taking advantage of the identity (124),

$$\Phi_* = \begin{pmatrix} \Sigma_* & \Sigma_* \Lambda_* \\ \Lambda_*{}' \Sigma_* & \Omega_* + \Lambda_*{}' \Sigma_* \Lambda_* \end{pmatrix} \tag{162}$$

$$= Q_\theta{}' V_0 Q_\theta + [(\Xi A_\theta : YS) - ZP_0]'(I_T - ZN_*{}^{-1}Z')$$
$$\times [(\Xi A_0 : YS) - ZP_0]. \tag{162}$$

(b) The posterior moments of P_2 and Φ are given by

$$E(\Pi_2 \mid Y, \theta) = P_2{}^* - P_1{}^* \Lambda_* \tag{163}$$

$$\operatorname{cov}(\operatorname{vec} \Pi_2 \mid Y, \theta) = \frac{1}{\nu_* - q - 1} \, \Omega_* \otimes [N_*{}^{-1} + P_1{}^* \Sigma_*{}^{-1} P_1{}^{*\prime}] \tag{164}$$

$$E(\Phi \mid Y, \theta) = \frac{1}{\nu_* - q - 1}\left(1 + \frac{1}{\tilde{\nu}_* - p - 1} \operatorname{tr}(\tilde{\Sigma}_* \Sigma_*{}^{-1})\right)\begin{pmatrix} 0 & 0 \\ 0 & \Omega_* \end{pmatrix}$$
$$+ \frac{1}{\tilde{\nu}_* - p - 1}\begin{pmatrix} \tilde{\Sigma}_* & \tilde{\Sigma}_* \Lambda_* \\ \Lambda_*{}' \tilde{\Sigma}_* & \Lambda_*{}' \tilde{\Sigma}_* \Lambda_* \end{pmatrix}. \tag{165}$$

(c) The posterior density of θ is given by

$$\begin{aligned} D(\theta \mid Y) &\propto D(\theta) \|Q_\theta\|^T \tilde{L}_1(Y)\, L_2(Y) \\ &\propto D(\theta) \|Q_\theta\|^T |\Phi_0|^{\frac{1}{2}\nu_0} |\tilde{\Sigma}_*|^{-\frac{1}{2}(\nu_*-q)} |\Omega_*|^{-\frac{1}{2}\nu_*} |\Sigma_*|^{-\frac{1}{2}q} \\ &\propto D(\theta) \|Q_\theta\|^{\nu_*} |\Phi_*|^{-\frac{1}{2}\nu_*} |\tilde{\Sigma}_*|^{-\frac{1}{2}(\nu_*-q)} |\Sigma_*|^{\frac{1}{2}(\nu_*-q)}. \end{aligned} \tag{166}$$

Comparing the concentrated likelihood function (49) and the posterior density (166) illustrates the close relationship between the classical and the natural conjugate Bayesian approaches and reveals how prior and sample information complement each other. Note also that the posterior density (166) is *marginalized* with respect to the 'nuisance' parameters in the q instrumental variable equations while the concentrated likelihood function (49) is *conditional* upon the ML estimators of those parameters. This difference in the treatment of nuisance parameters explains the correction for degrees of freedom in the exponents of $|\tilde{\Sigma}_*|$ and $|\Sigma_*|$ in the posterior density.

Φ_* depends in general on the choice of the selection matrix, in which case the posterior density (166) is not invariant with respect to the choice of S. As discussed already, this lack of invariance is inherent to the IV framework.

Invariance with respect to the choice of S is retrieved under a limited information framework ($k = 0$) in the following two cases.

(a) If we use a 'non-informative' prior density on P_2, i.e. if we set $N_0 = 0$, then formula (162) simplifies to

$$\Phi_* = Q_\theta' V_* Q_\theta \qquad V_* = V_0 + Y'M_z Y \tag{167}$$

and, since V_* does not depend on θ, the posterior density (166) takes the simpler form

$$D(\theta|Y) \propto D(\theta) \cdot [\,|\Sigma_*| \cdot |\tilde{\Sigma}_*|^{-1}]^{\frac{1}{2}(\nu_*-q)} \tag{168}$$

with

$$\begin{aligned} \Sigma_* &= B_\theta' V_* B_\theta \\ \tilde{\Sigma}_* &= B_\theta' V_0 B_\theta + (YB_\theta + ZC_\theta)'(YB_\theta + ZC_\theta). \end{aligned} \tag{169}$$

(b) If we use instead an 'informative' prior density on P_2 with hyperparameter $P_0 = \hat{\Pi}_0 Q_\theta + (C_\theta : 0)$, where $\hat{\Pi}_0$ is a matrix of constraints, then

$$(\Xi A_0 : YS) - ZP_0 = YQ_\theta + Z[(C_\theta : 0) - P_0] = (Y - Z\hat{\Pi}_0)\, Q_\theta \tag{170}$$

and Φ_* is rewritten as

$$\begin{aligned} \Phi_* &= Q_\theta' V_* Q_\theta \\ V_* &= V_0 + (Y - Z\hat{\Pi}_0)'(I_T - ZN_*^{-1}Z')(Y - Z\hat{\Pi}_0). \end{aligned} \tag{171}$$

The matrix $\hat{\Pi}_0$ plays the role of a prior expectation for the unconstrained reduced form (14), provided $k = 0$. Under (171), the posterior density of θ is also given by (168), together with (169) in which V_* is replaced by its expression in (171).

In all the cases under consideration, the analysis of the posterior density of θ and, therefore, the marginalization of the conditional moments of Π and Φ relies upon numerical procedures. This is no longer a binding constraint for models of 'moderate' size with no more than three or four structural equations but *as many* endogenous variables as required by the object of the analysis. Single equation IV Bayesian procedures are discussed in Lubrano et al. (1984). If $D(\theta)$ is multivariate Student, then $D(\theta|Y)$ belongs to a class of so-called 'poly-*t*' densities for which, as discussed in Richard and Tompa (1980), there exist efficient numerical methods of analysis. (These methods have been incorporated in a general 'Bayesian Regression Programme' (BRP) which is available from the author.) The analysis of models with more than one structural equation could be conducted by means of Monte Carlo numerical integration procedures which have been applied successfully to SEMs by Kloek and van Dijk (1978) and van Dijk and Kloek (1980). Their procedures would have to be adapted to the more general class of prior densities described in (166) but the principles of analysis would be unaffected. Following e.g. the suggestion by Morales (1971) one could compute the modal values and the corresponding Hessian matrix for the posterior density (166), by means of a generalization of the EGE described in section 3, and construct, from them, a normal approximation to the posterior density. This approximation could then be used as an 'importance function' from which random samples would be drawn for the estimations of the posterior moments of θ or functions thereof.

Finally there does not seem to be any more major computational arguments in favour of the SEM assumption ($k = 0$). For a single structural equation the assumption that $k = 0$ divides the cost of computation by a factor of 2 to 3 but, depending on the number of components in θ and on the accuracy requirement, an IV analysis takes only between 5 to 10 minutes on a minicomputer DG MV/8000, equipped with a floating-point accelerator. For larger models the Monte Carlo numerical integration procedures are unlikely to be very sensitive to the SEM assumption.

4.3 IV Bayes Factors

Bayes factors are the Bayesian analogue of LR test statistics and are defined within the following context. Let H_0 denote an hypothesis of interest and $H_1 = \Theta - H_0$ the alternative. Let the prior density be a 'mixed' prior density

$$D(\theta) = p_0 D(\theta \mid H_0) + p_1 D(\theta \mid H_1) \tag{172}$$

with $p_0 + p_1 = 1$, $D(\theta \mid H_0) = 0$ for $\theta \in H_1$, $D(\theta \mid H_1) = 0$ for $\theta \in H_0$ and

$$\int_{H_i} D(\theta \mid H_i) = 1 \qquad i = 0, 1. \tag{173}$$

The reason for using a mixed prior density lies in the fact that H_0 is typically of zero Lebesgue measure relative to Θ and would, therefore, be attached zero probability by continuous (prior and posterior) probability measures. Under (172) the posterior density $D(\theta \mid Y)$ is also a mixed density

$$D(\theta \mid Y) = p_0{}^* D(\theta \mid Y, H_0) + p_1{}^* D(\theta \mid Y, H_1) \tag{174}$$

with $p_0{}^* + p_1{}^* = 1$ and

$$\frac{p_0{}^*}{p_1{}^*} = \left[\frac{L_0(y)}{L_1(y)}\right] \frac{p_0}{p_1{}^0} \tag{175}$$

$$L_i(Y) = \int_{H_i} L(\theta ; Y)\, D(\theta \mid H_i)\, \mathrm{d}\theta \qquad i = 0, 1. \tag{176}$$

The ratio $L_0(Y)/L_1(Y)$ is the Bayes factor for H_0 against H_1 and serves to revise the prior odds for H_0. As discussed by Leamer (1978, chapter 4), careless use of 'non-informative' prior densities when H_0 is of zero Lebesgue measure relative to Θ yields 'nonsense' results. Bayes factors do not depend on the prior odds and may, therefore, be computed on their own for scientific reporting. In the absence of a decision context, one might, however, prefer to compare complete prior and posterior marginal densities for coefficients of interest under a continuous prior density, possibly centred on H_1. The application in Lubrano et al. (1984) follows this second approach and is evoked below in the context of exogeneity.

In section 3.4 we derived IVLR test statistics for a variety of hypotheses of interest. Conditionally on the structural coefficients, the numerators and denominators of the Bayes factors for these hypotheses are obtained by direct application of lemma 4, the generality of which is fully exploited at this stage of the analysis. Marginalizing these expressions, which are of the form of the posterior density (166), with respect to θ requires computing integrals which are precisely those whose numerical evaluation yields the integrating constants of the corresponding posterior densities, one for each competing hypothesis. This being said the derivation of the Bayes factors for each of the hypotheses in section 3.4 is straightforward but notationally demanding and need not be undertaken here.

4.4 Exogeneity

The prior density (153) can easily accommodate prior beliefs on the weak and strong exogeneity of components of $S'y_t$. In order to illustrate the argument, consider a situation where one wishes to construct a prior density such that $E(\Lambda) = 0$. Following formulae (134b) and (158), $E(\Lambda)$ is given by

$$E(\Lambda) = \int_{\Theta} E(\Lambda \mid \theta) D(\theta) \, \mathrm{d}\theta \tag{177}$$

with

$$E(\Lambda \mid \theta) = (B_\theta' V_0 B_\theta)^{-1} B_\theta' V_0 S. \tag{178}$$

Since $E(\Lambda)$ cannot be obtained analytically, one might have to try different combinations of V_0 and $D(\theta)$ and to evaluate numerically $E(\Lambda)$ at each step. Formula (178) suggests, however, that natural starting points for such a search are values of $M(B_\theta)$, the modal values of B_θ, and V_0 such that

$$M(B_\theta') \, V_0 S = 0. \tag{179}$$

For the single equation bivariate application in Lubrano et al. (1984) such starting values gave on every occasion marginal prior expectations of the scalar λ which were less than 0.01 in absolute values. No iterations were required. $E(\Lambda \mid Y)$ is evaluated by computing the posterior expectation of Λ_* as obtained from formula (162). The prior and posterior covariance matrix of vec Λ (and θ), as well as complete marginal densities for components of Λ are computed on similar principles.

If B_θ is a linear function of θ, then $E(\Lambda|\theta)$ and $E(\Lambda|Y, \theta)$ are *bounded* functions of θ and the integrability of the prior density $D(\theta)$ is sufficient for the existence of the prior and posterior (marginal) moments of Λ. This would *not* have been the case if, referring to our discussion of formulae (8) and (9), inference on the exogeneity of $S'y_t$ were based instead on the regression of e_t on v_t, say,

$$E(e_t|v_t) = \Delta' e_t. \tag{180}$$

Under the prior density (153), $E(\Delta|\theta)$ is given by

$$E(\Delta|\theta) = (S'V_0S)^{-1}S'V_0B_\theta. \tag{181}$$

Unless B_θ is bounded away from infinity, $E(\Delta|\theta)$ is an *unbounded* function of θ. Basing an exogeneity analysis on Δ instead of Λ requires, therefore, sharper *prior* information on θ (note that the factor which multiplies $D(\theta)$ in the expression (166) of the posterior density $D(\theta|Y)$ is typically homogeneous of degree zero in θ). This is, in our view, a major argument for preferring our approach to those which are (implicitly) based on the Δ-factorization. Given the close analogy between the classical and Bayesian IV procedures, we conjecture that $\tilde{\Lambda}$ has finite sample moments while $\tilde{\Delta}$ does not. Also the test statistics which are proposed in section 3.4 should have better finite sample properties than those which are typically found in the literature on exogeneity tests.

5 An Application

The procedures described in sections 3 and 4 are fully operational for single equation IV models and have been applied by Lubrano et al. (1984) to the analysis of an M3 demand for money equation in the UK. The institutional background led the authors to analyse separately the pre- and post-1971 period. For the purpose of illustration we report here the results of a typical run of computation for the period 1963(i)–1971(iii). The variables of interest are: M, the M3 personal sector monetary aggregate; Y, the real personal disposable income; P, the deflator of Y; R, the local authorities short-term interest rate; B, the level of reserves; and U, the unemployment rate. The data are seasonally unadjusted. Constant terms and seasonal dummies are not reported and are covered by the notation $\hat{C}_i$, $i = 1, \ldots, 4$. A 'progressive modelling' strategy based mostly on single equation specification searches resulted in the following IV estimation of a single (structural) equation bivariate model.

$$\begin{aligned}\Delta \log (M/P)_t = {} & \underset{(0.09)}{0.04}\, \Delta \log (M/P)_{t-1} - \underset{(0.13)}{0.49}\, \Delta \log P_t \\ & - \underset{(0.13)}{0.29}\, \Delta^2 \log P_{t-2} - \underset{(0.03)}{0.06} \log (M/PY)_{t-5} \\ & + \underset{(0.04)}{0.17}\, \Delta \log Y_t - \underset{(0.13)}{0.51}\, \Delta \log (1+R_t) \\ & - \underset{(0.09)}{0.25}\, \Delta^2 \log (1+R_{t-3}) \\ & - \underset{(0.06)}{0.13} \log (1+R_{t-5}) + \hat{C}_{i1} \end{aligned} \tag{182}$$

$$\begin{aligned}\Delta \log (1+R_t) = {} & -\underset{(0.08)}{0.25}\, \Delta \log (1+R_{t-2}) - \underset{(0.09)}{0.18}\, \Delta \log (1+R_{t-4}) \\ & + \underset{(0.10)}{0.26}\, \Delta^2 \log P_{t-2} - \underset{(0.00)}{0.02}\, \Delta^2 \log (1+U_t) \\ & - \underset{(0.01)}{0.03}\, \Delta^2 \log (1+U_{t-3}) - \underset{(0.00)}{0.01}\, \Delta_4 \log B_t \\ & - \underset{(0.01)}{0.01}\, \Delta^2 \log B_{t-1} + \underset{(0.08)}{0.03}\, \Delta \log M_{t-2} + \hat{C}_{i2} \end{aligned} \tag{183}$$

with $|\tilde{\Phi}| = 7.1 \times 10^{-10}$. The numbers in parentheses are asymptotic standard errors. The χ^2-test statistic for the weak exogeneity of the interest rate equals 3.5 against a 5 per cent critical value of 3.84. As indicated by equation (183) money does not Granger-cause the interest rate in any significant way.

The authors used a prior density on θ which is 'non-informative' except on b, the coefficient of the interest rate in (182). Different specifications were considered, including the relatively 'non-informative' Cauchy prior density

$$D(b) \propto [1.0 + 4.0(b+0.5)^2]^{-1} \tag{184}$$

for which $Pr(-1 \leqslant b \leqslant 0) = 0.5$, and the more informative Student prior density

$$D(b) \propto [1.0 + 0.75(b+0.5)^2]^{-11/2} \tag{185}$$

for which $Pr(-1 \leqslant b \leqslant 0) = 0.8$. Note that the Cauchy density (184) is integrable but that b has no finite prior (or posterior) moments of order $r \geqslant 1$. As discussed in section 4.4 this is precisely a situation for which the moments of Λ exist while those of Δ do not.

A first run of computation combines the prior density (184) with a non-informative prior density on (P_2, V) and serves to 'calibrate' sample information. The posterior moments of b do not exist. The posterior mean and standard deviation of λ are given by

$$E(\lambda \mid Y) = 0.37 \qquad \sigma(\lambda \mid Y) = 0.11. \tag{186}$$

Another run of computation combines the prior density (185) with an informative prior density on V which is constructed in the following way. The prior expectations of the diagonal elements of V are assigned on the basis of expected fits for the reduced form equations, respectively 80 per cent for $\Delta \log (M/P)_t$ and 60 per cent for $\Delta \log (1 + R_t)$. The prior belief that the interest rate is weakly exogenous serves to complete the elicitation of V_0 through equation (179) together with $M(b) = -0.5$. The degrees of freedom ν_0 associated with the prior density of V is set equal to 30 and is to be weighted against a sample size of 35 observations. The prior density on P_2 remains 'non-informative'. The posterior means and standard deviations of b and λ are then given by

$$E(b \mid Y) = -0.56 \qquad \sigma(b \mid Y) = 0.31 \tag{187}$$

$$E(\lambda \mid Y) = 0.27 \qquad \sigma(\lambda \mid Y) = 0.19. \tag{188}$$

These results together with others lead the authors to conclude that the acceptance of the weak exogeneity of the interest rate does not seem to require much prior information in favour of it. Also the IVML estimators in (182) and (183) do not differ in any significant way from the corresponding OLS estimators on which the specification search was concluded.

6 Conclusion

The IV approach described in the present chapter generalizes conventional single equation limited information procedures in three ways:

(a) It is applicable to systems of structural equations at a cost of computation which does not depend critically on the number of endogenous variables since nuisance parameters are dealt with analytically, preserving thereby the operational character of LI methods. (For a fixed number of structural equations, the total number of *structural* coefficients is not affected *per se* by the division into endogenous and exogenous variables. Note, however, that the coefficients in Γ_θ enter our formulae in a way which can be taken advantage of to reduce the cost of computation.)

(b) Predetermined variables can be excluded ($k \neq 0$) from the list of instrumental variables, e.g. in accordance with non-causality and strong exogeneity assumptions.

(c) Stochastic prior information on the coefficients of the IV equations can be accounted for, though in the relatively narrow framework of natural conjugate prior densities (noting, however, that the lack of flexibility of these densities originates from the specific structure of sample information itself).

The classical and Bayesian IV procedures bear close resemblance though the latter is computationally more demanding in so far as numerical integration is substituted for numerical optimization. The increase in the cost of computation represents the price to be paid for the incorporation of stochastic prior information and, more critically, for obtaining exact (versus asymptotic) results. Yet, given present computer technology, the Bayesian approach should be applicable to systems, with, say, no more than three structural equations.

The IV procedures have been shown to be quite flexible and can easily accommodate 'progressive modelling' strategies whereby overidentifying restrictions and the weak and strong exogeneity of subsets of the endogenous variables can be investigated. Except for minor technical details our analysis provides the results which are necessary for the development of general IV computer programs. In particular, the EGE equations derived in section 3.2 should enable one to adapt the choice of IV estimators to the circumstances. The formulae for the IVML estimators and the posterior densities of the reduced form coefficients are instrumental in our derivations, but can be used on their own for prediction (one-step ahead under weak exogeneity and several-steps ahead under strong exogeneity). In many ways, therefore, our paper provides technical complements to the methodological papers by Hendry and Richard (1982, 1983). Finally, applications such as the ones briefly discussed in section 5, illustrate the potentialities of the IV classical and Bayesian approaches.

Acknowledgments

This chapter collects and extends the results of research that was initiated in 1973. Over this period I have benefited from discussions with numerous friends and colleagues among whom L. Bauwens, J. Drèze, R. Engle, J. P. Florens, D. F. Hendry, M. Lubrano, G. Mizon, and M. Mouchart have co-authored with me several papers on which the present one heavily relies. The responsibility for errors and shortcomings remains entirely mine.

Appendix A Proof of Theorem 1

By application of formula (16) to the subsystems (29a) and of formulae (18)–(20) to its unrestricted counterpart we first have

$$\tilde{R}_1 = (W'W)^{-1}W'Y_1 \qquad \hat{R}_1 = \tilde{R}_1 - (W'W)^{-1}W'Z\hat{P}_1 \tag{A1}$$

$$\tilde{\Sigma} = \frac{1}{T}Y_1'M_wY_1 \qquad \hat{\Sigma} = \tilde{\Sigma} - \frac{1}{T}\hat{P}_1'Z'M_wZ\hat{P}_1. \tag{A2}$$

Similar procedures are applied to the subsystem (29b) and its unrestricted counterpart which differ only by the fact that P_2 is replaced by $P_{2.1}$ and we have

$$\tilde{P}_2 = \hat{P}_{2.1} = (Z'M_wZ)^{-1}Z'M_w(Y_2 - Y_1\hat{\Lambda}) = \hat{P}_2 - \hat{P}_1\hat{\Lambda} \tag{A3}$$

$$\tilde{\Lambda} = \hat{\Lambda} = (Y_1'M_xY_1)^{-1}Y_1'M_xY_2 \tag{A4}$$

$$\tilde{R}_{2.1} = \hat{R}_{2.1} = (W'W)^{-1}W'(Y_2 - Y_1\hat{\Lambda} - Z\hat{P}_{2.1}) \tag{A5}$$

$$\tilde{\Omega} = \hat{\Omega} = \frac{1}{T}(Y_2'M_xY_2 - \hat{\Lambda}'Y_1'M_xY_1\hat{\Lambda}). \tag{A6}$$

Combining formulae (A1) and (A5) yields successively

$$\tilde{R}_2 = \tilde{R}_{2.1} + \tilde{R}_1\tilde{\Lambda} = \hat{R}_{2.1} + [\hat{R}_1 + (W'W)^{-1}W'Z\hat{P}_1]\hat{\Lambda}$$
$$= \hat{R}_2 + (W'W)^{-1}W'Z\hat{P}_1\hat{\Lambda} \tag{A7}$$

$$\tilde{R} = \hat{R} + (W'W)^{-1}W'Z\hat{P}_1(I_p : \hat{\Lambda}) = \hat{R} - (W'W)^{-1}W'Z(\tilde{P} - \hat{P}). \tag{A8}$$

Combining formulae (A2), (A4) and A6) yields successively

$$\tilde{\Phi} = \begin{pmatrix} \tilde{\Sigma} & \tilde{\Sigma}\hat{\Lambda} \\ \hat{\Lambda}'\tilde{\Sigma} & \tilde{\Omega}+\hat{\Lambda}'\tilde{\Sigma}\hat{\Lambda} \end{pmatrix} = \hat{\Phi} + \frac{1}{T}\begin{pmatrix} I_p \\ \hat{\Lambda}' \end{pmatrix} \hat{P}_1{}'Z'M_w Z\hat{P}_1(I_p : \hat{\Lambda})$$

$$= \hat{\Phi} + \frac{1}{T}(\tilde{P}-\hat{P})'Z'M_w Z(\tilde{P}-\hat{P}) \qquad \text{(A9)}$$

and, finally

$$\tilde{\Phi}^{-1} = \begin{pmatrix} \tilde{\Sigma}^{-1}+\hat{\Lambda}\hat{\Omega}^{-1}\hat{\Lambda}' & -\hat{\Lambda}\hat{\Omega}^{-1} \\ -\hat{\Omega}^{-1}\hat{\Lambda}' & \hat{\Omega}^{-1} \end{pmatrix} = \hat{\Phi}^{-1} + \begin{pmatrix} \tilde{\Sigma}^{-1}-\hat{\Sigma}^{-1} & 0 \\ 0 & 0 \end{pmatrix} \qquad \text{(A10)}$$

$$|\tilde{\Phi}| = |\tilde{\Sigma}|\,|\hat{\Omega}| = |\tilde{\Sigma}|\,|\hat{\Phi}|\,|\hat{\Sigma}|^{-1}. \qquad \text{(A11)}$$

Appendix B Proof of Theorem 2

The results follow immediately from theorem 1 except for $\bar{P}$ and $\bar{R}$ for which we have, by application of formula (24)

$$\begin{pmatrix} \bar{P}_2 \\ \bar{R}_{2.1} \end{pmatrix} = \begin{pmatrix} \tilde{P}_2 \\ \tilde{R}_{2.1} \end{pmatrix} - (X'X)^{-1}X'Y_1(\bar{\Lambda}-\tilde{\Lambda})$$

$$= \begin{pmatrix} \tilde{P}_2 \\ \tilde{R}_{2.1} \end{pmatrix} - \begin{pmatrix} \hat{P}_1 \\ \hat{R}_1 \end{pmatrix} (\bar{\Lambda}-\tilde{\Lambda}). \qquad \text{(A12)}$$

Taking into account formula (23) and the fact that $\hat{\Lambda} = \tilde{\Lambda}$, we then have

$$\bar{P}_2 = \hat{P}_2 - \hat{P}_1\hat{\Lambda} - \hat{P}_1(\bar{\Lambda}-\tilde{\Lambda}) = \hat{P}_2 - \hat{P}_1\bar{\Lambda}. \qquad \text{(A13)}$$

Similarly, taking into account formulae (23), (24) and (A12) we have successively

$$\bar{R}_2 = \bar{R}_{2.1} + \bar{R}_1\bar{\Lambda} = \tilde{R}_{2.1} - \hat{R}_1(\bar{\Lambda}-\tilde{\Lambda}) + \tilde{R}_1[\tilde{\Lambda}+(\bar{\Lambda}-\tilde{\Lambda})]$$

$$= \tilde{R}_2 + (\tilde{R}_1 - \hat{R}_1)(\bar{\Lambda}-\tilde{\Lambda})$$

$$= \tilde{R}_2 + (W'W)^{-1}W'Z\hat{P}_1(\bar{\Lambda}-\tilde{\Lambda})$$

$$= \tilde{R}_2 - (W'W)^{-1}W'Z(\bar{P}_2-\tilde{P}_2) \qquad \text{(A14)}$$

from which (33) follows since $\bar{R}_1 - \tilde{R}_1 = \bar{P}_1 = \tilde{P}_1 = 0$. Note also that we can combine formulae (24) and (33) to obtain

$$\bar{R} = \hat{R} - (W'W)^{-1}W'Z(\bar{P}-\hat{P}). \qquad \text{(A15)}$$

Appendix C Proof of Lemma 3

Formulae (133b) and (135) coincide with formulae (116) and (117). Applying the transformation

$$A = I_T \quad \text{and} \quad B = \begin{pmatrix} I_p & -\Lambda \\ 0 & I_q \end{pmatrix} \tag{A16}$$

as in (113) to the matrix $(Y - X\Pi)$ yields

$$\begin{aligned} &\operatorname{tr}[\Phi^{-1}(Y-X\Pi)'(Y-X\Pi)] \\ &\qquad = \operatorname{tr}[\Sigma^{-1}(Y_1 - X\Pi_1)'(Y_1 - X\Pi_1)] \\ &\qquad\quad + \operatorname{tr}[\Omega^{-1}(Y_2 - Y_1\Lambda - X\Pi_{2.1})'(Y_2 - Y_1\Lambda - X\Pi_{2.1})] \end{aligned} \tag{A17}$$

from which (136) and (137) follow. The factorization of the inverted-Wishart density on Φ is obtained by applying formula (106) to Φ_0 and Φ^{-1} from which we obtain

$$\operatorname{tr}(\Phi^{-1}\Phi_0) = \operatorname{tr}(\Sigma^{-1}\Sigma_0) + \operatorname{tr}\{\Omega^{-1}[\Omega_0 + (\Lambda - \Lambda_0)'\Sigma_0(\Lambda - \Lambda_0)]\} \tag{A18}$$

and, since the Jacobian of the transformation from Φ to $(\Sigma, \Lambda, \Omega)$ is $|\Sigma|^q$, we also have

$$\begin{aligned} |\Phi|^{-\frac{1}{2}(\nu_0+m+n+1)}|\Sigma|^q &= |\Omega|^{-\frac{1}{2}(\nu_0+m+n+1)}|\Sigma|^{-\frac{1}{2}(\nu_0+m+p-q+1)} \\ &= [|\Omega|^{-\frac{1}{2}(\nu_0+q+1)}|\Omega|^{-\frac{1}{2}p}|\Omega|^{-\frac{1}{2}m}]. \\ &\quad \times [|\Sigma|^{-\frac{1}{2}(\nu_0-q+p+1)}|\Sigma|^{-\frac{1}{2}m}]. \end{aligned} \tag{A19}$$

Formulae (135a) and (136) follow from formulae (A17) and (A18).

Appendix D Proof of Lemma 4 (iv)

Taking advantage of the independence between (Π_1, Σ) and $(\Pi_{2.1}, \Lambda, \Omega)$ we first have

$$\begin{aligned} &E(\Pi_1) = \tilde{\Pi}^0 \qquad E(\Sigma) = \frac{1}{\tilde{\nu}_0 - p - 1}\tilde{\Sigma}_0 \\ &\operatorname{cov}(\operatorname{vec}\Pi_1) = E(\Sigma) \otimes \tilde{N}_0^{-1} \end{aligned} \tag{A20}$$

$$E(\Pi_2|\Pi_1, \Lambda, \Omega) = \Pi_2^0 + (\Pi_1 - \Pi_1^0)\Lambda$$
$$E(\Lambda|\Pi_1, \Omega) = \Lambda_0 \tag{A21}$$

$$\text{cov}(\text{vec}\,\Pi_2|\Pi_1, \Lambda, \Omega) = \Omega \otimes N_0^{-1}$$
$$\text{cov}(\text{vec}\,\Lambda|\Pi_1, \Omega) = \Omega \otimes \Sigma_0^{-1}. \tag{A22}$$

Let π_r' denote the rth row of Π_1 and $\tilde{n}_0^{rs}$ the (r, s)th element of $\tilde{N}_0^{-1}$. The following results are instrumental in the proof

$$\begin{aligned} &E[(\pi_s - \pi_s^0)' \Sigma_0^{-1}(\pi_r - \pi_r^0)] \\ &\quad = E\{\text{tr}[\Sigma_0^{-1}(\pi_r - \pi_r^0)(\pi_s - \pi_s^0)']\} \\ &\quad = \tilde{n}_0^{rs}\,\text{tr}[\Sigma_0^{-1}E(\Sigma)] + (\tilde{\pi}_s^0 - \pi_s^0)'\Sigma_0^{-1}(\tilde{\pi}_r^0 - \pi_r^0), \end{aligned} \tag{A23}$$

which implies

$$\begin{aligned} &E[(\Pi_1 - \Pi_1^0)\Sigma_0^{-1}(\Pi_1 - \Pi_1^0)'] \\ &\quad = \frac{1}{\tilde{\nu}_0 - p - 1}\,\text{tr}(\Sigma^{-1}\tilde{\Sigma}_0)\,\tilde{N}_0^{-1} + (\tilde{\Pi}_1^0 - \Pi_1^0)\Sigma_0^{-1}(\tilde{\Pi}_1^0 - \Pi_1^0)'. \end{aligned} \tag{A24}$$

Also

$$\begin{aligned} \text{cov}[\text{vec}(\Pi_1\Lambda_0)] &= (\Lambda_0' \otimes I_m)(E(\Sigma) \otimes \tilde{N}_0^{-1})(\Lambda_0 \otimes I_m) \\ &= \frac{1}{\tilde{\nu}_0 - p - 1}\Lambda_0'\tilde{\Sigma}_0\Lambda_0 \otimes \tilde{N}_0^{-1} \end{aligned} \tag{A25}$$

$$\text{cov}[\text{vec}(\Pi_1\Lambda_0), \text{vec}'\,\Pi_1] = \frac{1}{\tilde{\nu}_0 - p - 1}\Lambda_0'\tilde{\Sigma}_0 \otimes \tilde{N}_0^{-1}. \tag{A26}$$

The proof then follows by a recursive application of the marginalization principle underlying formula (118). We have successively

$$E(\Pi_2|\Pi_1, \Omega) = \Pi_2^0 + (\Pi_1 - \Pi_1^0)\Lambda_0 \tag{A27}$$

$$\begin{aligned} &\text{cov}(\text{vec}\,\Pi_2|\Pi_1, \Omega) \\ &\quad = \Omega \otimes N_0^{-1} + \text{cov}\{\text{vec}[(\Pi_1 - \Pi_1^0)\Lambda]|\Pi_1, \Omega\} \\ &\quad = \Omega \otimes N_0^{-1} + [I_q \otimes (\Pi_1 - \Pi_1^0)]\,\text{cov}(\text{vec}\,\Lambda|\Omega)[I_q \otimes (\Pi_1 - \Pi_1^0)'] \\ &\quad = \Omega \otimes [N_0^{-1} + (\Pi_1 - \Pi_1^0)\Sigma_0^{-1}(\Pi_1 - \Pi_1^0)'] \end{aligned} \tag{A28}$$

$$E(\Pi_2) = E(\Pi_2|\Omega) = \Pi_2^0 + (\tilde{\Pi}_1^0 - \Pi_1^0)\Lambda_0 \tag{A29}$$

$$\begin{aligned}
\operatorname{cov}(\operatorname{vec}\Pi_2\,|\,\Omega) &= \Omega\otimes\{N_0^{-1}+E[(\Pi_1-\Pi_1^0)\,\Sigma_0^{-1}(\Pi_1-\Pi_1^0)'\,|\,\Omega]\} \\
&\quad + \operatorname{cov}[\operatorname{vec}(\Pi_1\Lambda_0)\,|\,\Omega] \\
&= \Omega\otimes[N_0^{-1}+(\tilde{\Pi}_1^0-\Pi_1^0)\,\Sigma_0^{-1}(\tilde{\Pi}_1^0-\Pi_1^0)'] \\
&\quad + \frac{1}{\tilde{\nu}_0-p-1}\operatorname{tr}(\tilde{\Sigma}_0\Sigma_0^{-1})\,\tilde{N}_0^{-1} \\
&\quad + \frac{1}{\tilde{\nu}_0-p-1}\Lambda_0'\tilde{\Sigma}_0\Lambda_0\otimes\tilde{N}_0^{-1} \qquad \text{(A30)}
\end{aligned}$$

$$E(\Pi_1)=E(\Pi_1\,|\,\Omega)=\tilde{\Pi}_1^0=\Pi_1^0+(\tilde{\Pi}_1^0-\Pi_1^0) \qquad \text{(A31)}$$

$$\begin{aligned}
\operatorname{cov}(\operatorname{vec}\Pi_2,\operatorname{vec}'\Pi_1) &= E[\operatorname{cov}(\operatorname{vec}\Pi_2,\operatorname{vec}'\Pi_1\,|\,\Pi_1)] \\
&\quad + \operatorname{cov}[\operatorname{vec}(\Pi_1\Lambda_0),\operatorname{vec}'\Pi_1] \\
&= 0+\frac{1}{\tilde{\nu}_0-p-1}\Lambda_0'\tilde{\Sigma}_0\otimes\tilde{N}_0^{-1}. \qquad \text{(A32)}
\end{aligned}$$

Regrouping the results in formulae (A19) and (A28)–(A31) and taking expectations with respect to Ω yields formulae (143) and (144). Formula (145) is obtained by regrouping the following expressions

$$E(\Sigma)=\frac{1}{\tilde{\nu}_0-p-1}\tilde{\Sigma}_0 \qquad E(\Omega)=\frac{1}{\nu_0-q-1}\Omega_0 \qquad \text{(A33)}$$

and

$$E(\Sigma\Lambda\,|\,\Sigma)=\Sigma\Lambda_0 \qquad E(\Lambda'\Sigma\Lambda\,|\,\Sigma)=\Lambda_0'\Sigma\Lambda_0+\operatorname{tr}(\Sigma\Sigma_0^{-1}), \qquad \text{(A34)}$$

from which

$$\begin{aligned}
E(\Sigma\Lambda) &= \frac{1}{\tilde{\nu}_0-p-1}\tilde{\Sigma}_0\Lambda_0 \\
E(\Lambda'\Sigma\Lambda) &= \frac{1}{\tilde{\nu}_0-p-1}[\Lambda_0'\tilde{\Sigma}_0\Lambda_0+\operatorname{tr}(\tilde{\Sigma}_0\Sigma_0^{-1})].
\end{aligned} \qquad \text{(A35)}$$

5

Model Evaluation by Variable Addition

ADRIAN R. PAGAN

1 Introduction

Modelling was never meant to be easy. The 1970s taught many econometricians the worth of this aphorism but, strangely, there has grown up a conception that the principal lesson to be learned related to the utility of large-scale models. What should have come from this experience, however, was an appreciation of the weakness of the research strategy in evidence during the late sixties and early seventies. Four steps almost completely describe it: a model is postulated, data gathered, a regression run, some t-statistics or simulation performance provided and another 'empirical regularity' was forged. What was wrong with this approach? Depending upon the example there could be many specific factors, but three deficiencies are outstanding. First, it failed to be *critical*. Almost no attempt was made to discover weaknesses in the model selected, or at least to present them to an observer. Once a model agreeing with a priori conceptions of 'signs' and 'significance' was obtained, research terminated. Second, it failed to be *informative*. Few indices of model adequacy were given and very little discussion on the sensitivity of results was provided. Finally, in very few cases was an attempt made to *reconcile* the 'new' formulation with earlier research. In many instances, apart from obligatory references at the beginning of the article, a reader could well have gained the impression that there had been no previous research on the topic.

A good deal of attention has been paid by econometricians in the last 20 years to appropriate responses to these points. Indeed, as made explicit elsewhere in this volume, Sargan's Colston paper was a key element in stimulating much of this research. This chapter concentrates upon the second of the three needs identified above, the provision of indices of (in)adequacy for a given estimated model.

Two major approaches to the construction of such indices can be distinguished. In the first of these, measures are computed by the *addition* of selected variables to the model under scrutiny. Generally this strategy yields what have been termed 'diagnostic tests'. The second approach revolves around changes in the model induced by variable transformations. As these transformations are known, it is possible to describe their impact (in the population) exactly if the model under consideration is an adequate specification. A comparison of the predicted and actual *consequences* of these transformations then provides an estimate of how adequate the model is. Examples of test statistics generated by this latter approach would be the Berenblutt and Webb (1973) test for serial correlation, Farebrother's (1979) grouping test, King's (1982b) $S(\phi)$ tests for serial correlation and the differencing test of Plosser et al. (1982). Although we ignore this literature, it should not be inferred that variable addition is a superior strategy for the detection of inadequate models. Rather it reflects a decision to analyse what is relatively familiar rather than an area that has, to date, not received much exposure.

In the following section the basic framework is laid out. Decisions must be made concerning the characteristic of the model likely to be at variance with the evidence and the variables chosen to reveal that fact. A range of diagnostic tests emerges from this perspective, and are related to those currently proposed for the linear regression model. Section 3 follows the same pattern, but now for a structural equation. Finally, section 4 briefly examines some issues concerned with the combination of test statistics and small sample performance. Throughout, some statistical rigour has been sacrificed to exposition, and more formal proofs of many of the propositions can be found in Pagan and Hall (1983).

2 Model Evaluation by Variable Addition, Non-Structural Case

Under different guises, variable addition is the most common technique of model evaluation employed in econometrics. As will become apparent, the strategy of augmentation yields a diversity of measures of model performance for two reasons. Firstly, there are a number of *relationships* that might be augmented. Secondly, there are many *types of variables* that might be considered as candidates for 'completing' the relationship.

Turning first to the potential relations, an obvious way to characterize them is to focus upon the moments of the data explained by the model, i.e. one could describe inadequacies in a particular model by determining whether the assumptions made about the moments in the model are compatible with the behaviour of the sample moments. To make this more concrete, consider the ordinary regression model $y_t = x_t\beta + e_t$. In many instances the assumptions embodied in this model are that the mean conditional upon $\mathscr{F}_t = \{y_{t-j}\}_{j=1}^{\infty}, \{x_{t-j}\}_{j=0}^{\infty}$ is $E(y_t|\mathscr{F}_t) = x_t\beta$, the conditional variance $E[(y_t - E(y_t|\mathscr{F}_t))^2|\mathscr{F}_t]$ equals a constant σ^2 and the y_t are normal. Whether this model is adequate or not can then be re-phrased as whether the conditional mean is merely $x_t\beta$, whether the conditional variance is a constant σ^2 and whether higher-order conditional moments are connected to the lower-order ones in the postulated way. In what follows, model evaluation procedures are discussed by reference to the possibility of augmenting conditional moments. As only the first four moments have been considered as candidates for augmentation in the literature, the presentation that follows is truncated at that point as well. Within each category the range of variable types employed in the addition and their original purpose will be distinguished.

2.1 *Augmenting the Conditional Mean*

The regression equation discussed in the text above had conditional mean $E(y_t|\mathscr{F}_t) = x_t\beta$ which might be written in matrix form as

$$E(y|\mathscr{F}) = X\beta \tag{1}$$

where X is a $T \times K$ matrix of observations on x_t and β is a $K \times 1$ vector. If the model assumptions concerning the conditional mean are inadequate – *first-order* inadequacy borrowing Domowitz and White's (1982) term – it should be possible to augment (1) with a variable z_t, arranged in a $T \times K_1$ matrix Z. This creates a postulated alternative conditional mean

$$E(y|\mathscr{F}) = X\beta + Z\gamma \tag{2}$$

where $\mathscr{F}$ now contains $\{z_{t-j}\}_{j=0}^{\infty}$ as well. Expression (1) will then be incomplete if γ is non-zero, and some estimate of γ must therefore be obtained from the data in order to test this hypothesis. To do so, it will be assumed that the second-order conditional moment is constant at σ^2, setting aside until a later subsection what should be done if this presumption is unreasonable.

Imposing this last restriction yields

$$y = X\beta + Z\gamma + e \tag{3}$$

where $E(e|\mathscr{F}) = 0$, $E(ee'|\mathscr{F}) = \sigma^2 I$. From (3) it is immediately apparent that a test for the adequacy of the assumed conditional mean is available by regressing y against X and Z, followed by a decision based on the F-statistic that $\gamma = 0$. (Throughout we refer to t- and F- values, even though the regressors in X may contain lagged values of y and hence only asymptotic rather than small sample results are available. Section 4.2 of the paper looks at what has been discovered on small sample performance.)

An extension of this idea, looming large below, concerns an appropriate response if data on the suspected omitted variable Z are not available but data on a proxy $\tilde{Z}$ are. Manipulation of (3) produces the estimable form

$$y = X\beta + \tilde{Z}\gamma + e + (Z - \tilde{Z})\gamma = X\beta + \tilde{Z}\gamma + v. \tag{4}$$

Under the null hypothesis that $\gamma = 0$ nothing has changed; the error term remains e and a judgment on whether $\gamma = 0$ or not is available from the regression of y against X and $\tilde{Z}$. What then is the disadvantage of using $\tilde{Z}$ rather than Z? The answer lies in the fact that the *power* of the F-statistic for $\gamma = 0$ depends *inter alia*, upon the correlation of $\tilde{Z}$ and Z. When $\tilde{Z}$ is uncorrelated with Z poor power performance is likely, although, as section 4.2 details, power is determined by the nature of X as well. Cases where $\tilde{Z}$ are totally unrelated to Z are probably rare, and adding $\tilde{Z}$ to the model will yield *some* information concerning model adequacy. Obviously, constructing $\tilde{Z}$ in such a way that it is highly correlated with Z is very desirable.

In what follows tests are primarily differentiated through the nature of the Z or $\tilde{Z}$ adopted as added variables. There is a secondary consideration, though, in that there are a number of ways of formulating a test that $\gamma = 0$ in (3) and (4). Three options – A, B and C – will now be distinguished.

Option A: Fit (3) or (4) and test if $\gamma = 0$ using the F-statistic

Although Option A is relatively straightforward, it would be possible to provide variants of it, depending upon whether the test statistic used for determining if $\gamma = 0$ was the Wald, Lagrange Multiplier or Likelihood Ratio statistic; it is well known that only the first is the conventional F-statistic cited in Option A, but relations exist between the trio – see Breusch (1979) for an analysis. This further subtlety is ignored until section 3.1 in the interests of economy and the recognition that most invokers of Option A use the Wald or LM versions.

Option B arises by regressing y against X to get $\hat{\beta}$ and subtracting the predictions $X\hat{\beta}$ from both sides of (3) (or (4) if $\tilde{Z}$ replaced Z), making the new dependent variable the OLS residuals $\hat{u} = y - X\hat{\beta}$, i.e.

$$y - X\hat{\beta} = \hat{u} = X(\beta - \hat{\beta}) + Z\gamma + e. \tag{5}$$

Option B: Fit (5) and test if $\gamma = 0$ using the F-statistic

Since the transition from (3) to (5) only involves the subtraction of the same quantity from both sides, the estimators of γ and the associated F-statistics from (3) and (5) must be identical. Accordingly options A and B give identical answers to the query of whether $\gamma = 0$, but the distinction needs to be made because of the emphasis in many diagnostic tests upon the explanation of residuals.

The final formulation – option C – ignores $X(\beta - \hat{\beta})$ in (5), i.e. the equation estimated is

$$\hat{u} = Z\gamma + v^* \tag{6}$$

where $v^* = X(\beta - \hat{\beta}) + e$. What are the consequences of deleting X in the regression? From the definition of OLS applied to (6)

$$\gamma^* = (Z'Z)^{-1}Z'\hat{u} = \gamma + (Z'Z)^{-1}Z'X(\beta - \hat{\beta}) + (Z'Z)^{-1}Z'e. \tag{7}$$

Under the null hypothesis $\gamma = 0$, $\beta - \hat{\beta} = -(X'X)^{-1}X'e$, showing that the variance of the limiting distribution of $T^{1/2}(\gamma^* - \gamma)$ is

$$\operatorname*{plim}_{T \to \infty} \sigma^2 T(Z'Z)^{-1}Z'M_X Z(Z'Z)^{-1}$$

where $M_X = I - X(X'X)^{-1}X'$. Only if $Z'X = 0$ (or $T^{-1}Z'X \to 0$) does this variance become

$$\operatorname*{plim}_{T \to \infty} \sigma^2 T(Z'Z)^{-1},$$

revealing that a special computation of the variance of γ^* will normally be needed if valid inferences concerning γ are to be made. (This observation has wider relevance. Studies of causality in the Pierce and Haugh (1977) tradition suffer because of a failure to make the requisite adjustment. In their case $\hat{u}$ are the residuals from an ARMA model, Z are the lagged residuals from another ARMA representation of a second series and X, being functions of lags of the first variable, is almost never uncorrelated with Z.) These themes are collected now in the statement of Option C.

Option C: Fit (6) using $\sigma^2(Z'Z)^{-1}Z'M_XZ(Z'Z)^{-1}$ not $\sigma^2(Z'Z)^{-1}$ as the covariance matrix for γ^*, unless $T^{-1}Z'X \xrightarrow{p} 0$.

Having established the technology for determining if $\gamma = 0$, it is now necessary to consider the exact nature of Z (or $\tilde{Z}$). To do this requires a statement of the *types* of error that might be made in specifying the conditional mean. Six categories may be isolated: specification error, autocorrelation, functional form, comparisons with other models, model stability, and exogeneity.

By adopting the idea that variable addition is a powerful unifying principle for the detection of the inadequacies above, it is possible to reduce and relate most existing indices proposed to assess the validity of the conditional mean specification.

(a) *Specification error* Under this heading we are concerned with the idea of 'omitted variables', although there is no clear distinction between this type of problem and that discussed under functional form later. By far the most popular diagnostic test in this area has been the RESET test proposed by Ramsey (1969) and earlier in Anscombe (1961). It is constructed from an F-test that $\hat{y}^2, \hat{y}^3, \ldots, \hat{y}^L$ are insignificant in the regression of y against X and these variables, where $\hat{y}$ are the OLS predictions $X\hat{\beta}$. (Ramsey originally proposed a test that worked with BLUS rather than OLS residuals, but Ramsey and Schmidt (1976) subsequently showed that it was identical to the F-test from the stipulated regression.) In terms of (4) $\tilde{Z} = (\hat{y}^2, \ldots, \hat{y}^L)$ can be regarded as a proxy variable for the 'true' specification, and the utility of powers of $\hat{y}$ in the formulation of this diagnostic is largely dependent upon how closely it correlates with the omitted part of the conditional mean.

Various simulation studies of RESET are available (Ramsey and Gilbert, 1972; Thursby, 1979) with some suggestion that $L = 4$ is an optimal choice. There are at least two interesting applied studies. Loeb (1976) investigated investment equations, finding defects in a number of standard specifications. Ramsey and Alexander (1982) applied it to data from Blatt (1978). Blatt had generated data from a deterministic nonlinear model and had estimated it as if it were linear and stochastic. His contention was that, judged by traditional criteria, there was no evidence of a major specification error. Ramsey and Alexander found that RESET did indicate a serious failing in the assumed format and their conclusion is well worth repeating: '... obtaining a good fit, as measured by R^2 values, or significant t ratios with plausible signs is no way a guarantor of the use of appropriate statistical procedures, nor is it a guarantor of having reached even approximately reasonable inferences. Specification error tests, therefore, are an indispensible tool in our efforts to obtain useful inferences and to have some confidence in the robustness of our results over time.'

(b) *Autocorrelation* An alternative envisaged in this case might be that the errors of the maintained model, u_t, follow an autocorrelated process such as $u_t = \rho_j u_{t-j} + e_t$ or $u = u_{-j}\gamma + e$. Because the mean of y is conditional upon the past history of y and X, i.e. u_{-k}, the alternative conditional mean becomes

$$E(y\,|\,\mathscr{F}) = X\beta + u_{-j}\gamma = X\beta + Z\gamma. \tag{8}$$

Ideally evaluation would be accomplished by regressing y against X and $Z = u_{-j}$ as before. But u_{-j} is frequently an unobserved random variable, leading to its replacement by some proxy $\tilde{Z}$. One appealing candidate would be $\hat{u}_{-j} = y_{-j} - X_{-j}\hat{\beta}$ since, under the null hypothesis that $\gamma = 0$, $u_{-j} = e_{-j}$, and $\hat{e}_{-j}$ will be very highly correlated with e_{-j} in large samples. But other versions would be possible; a feature best appreciated by viewing $\hat{u}_{-j}$ as $\bar{A}\hat{u}$ where $\bar{A}$ is a matrix with unity in the jth diagonal below the main diagonal but zero elsewhere. With this orientation $\tilde{Z}$ can be taken as $A\hat{u}$, and a range of $\tilde{Z}$ generated by variations in the weighting matrix A. (There are some 'end effects' ignored in the following discussion. In practice all observations ($t = 1, \ldots, T$) would have been used to generate $\hat{\beta}$ and the fact that $\hat{u}_{-j}$ requires y_{-j} would mean that the new regression would be run over $j+1$ to T.)

Beginning with $j = 1$ and X exogenous, Option C might be invoked with $\tilde{Z} = \hat{u}_{-1}$ as regressor. Then $\gamma^* = (\hat{u}_{-1}'\hat{u}_{-1})^{-1}\hat{u}_{-1}'\hat{u} = \hat{\rho}_1$ estimates the first-order serial correlation coefficient between u_t and u_{t-1}. In these special circumstances $T^{-1}\tilde{Z}'X = T^{-1}\hat{u}_{-1}'X$ has probability limit zero, so that the covariance matrix of $\hat{\rho}_1$ may be taken as $\sigma^2(\tilde{Z}'\tilde{Z})^{-1} = \sigma^2(\hat{u}_{-1}'\hat{u}_{-1})^{-1} \simeq \sigma^2(T\sigma^2)^{-1} = T^{-1}$ under the hypothesis that $\gamma = 0$ (i.e. $u_t = e_t$). The t-test that $\gamma = 0$ from this regression is therefore just $\gamma^*(\sigma^2(\tilde{Z}'\tilde{Z})^{-1})^{-1/2} = T^{1/2}\hat{\rho}_1$, which is familiar as the diagnostic test for first-order serial correlation due to Bartlett (1946) and used extensively in Box and Jenkins (1976).

Instead of adopting $\hat{u}_{-1}$ as regressor, set $\tilde{Z} = (A_1 - 2I)\hat{u}$ where A_1 is the 'differencing matrix' in Durbin and Watson (1950). Both $\hat{u}_{-1}$ and $(A_1 - 2I)\hat{u}$ have the same correlation with u_{-1} in large samples and the $-2I$ correction term ensures that $T^{-1}\tilde{Z}'e^P \to 0$ and, hence, that γ^* is consistent. To relate this choice to an existing test we observe that $\gamma^* = (\tilde{Z}'\tilde{Z})^{-1}\tilde{Z}'\hat{u}$, and the t-test that $\gamma^* = 0$ could be equivalently viewed as a test that $\tilde{Z}'\hat{u} = 0$: the asymptotic covariance matrix of $\tilde{Z}'\hat{u}$ being $\sigma^2(\tilde{Z}'\tilde{Z})$ giving the χ^2-statistic $\sigma^{-2}\hat{u}'\tilde{Z}(\tilde{Z}'\tilde{Z})^{-1}\tilde{Z}'\hat{u}$. Inserting $\tilde{Z} = (A_1 - 2I)\hat{u}$ into $\tilde{Z}'\hat{u}$ leaves $\hat{u}'(A_1 - 2I)\hat{u}$ and $\tilde{Z}'\hat{u} = 0$ if $\hat{u}'A_1\hat{u} - 2\hat{u}'\hat{u} = 0$ or if $(\hat{u}'A_1\hat{u}/\hat{u}'\hat{u}) - 2 = 0$. But the ratio $(\hat{u}'A_1\hat{u})/(\hat{u}'\hat{u})$ is just the Durbin–Watson statistic, emphasizing its origins in variable addition. Of course the exact distribution of γ^* in small samples is unknown and many approximations have been derived for it in the literature; these endeavours are well set out in the comprehensive account provided by King (1983), where simulation studies of various diagnostic tests for autocorrelation are also reviewed.

Turning to the situation when X contains lagged values of y, Option B corresponds to the LM test for first-order serial correlation set out in Godfrey (1978b), Breusch (1978) and Durbin (1970) as his 'second method'. If Option C is used, the covariance matrix $\sigma^2(\tilde{Z}'\tilde{Z})^{-1}\tilde{Z}'M_x\tilde{Z}(\tilde{Z}'\tilde{Z})^{-1}$ is needed, as at least one of the elements in $\tilde{Z}'X$ is non-zero. Durbin (1970) worked with Option C with $T^{-1}\tilde{Z}'\tilde{Z}$ and $T^{-1}\tilde{Z}'X$ replaced by their probability limits in the covariance matrix expression and this constitutes his h-statistic (although the LM rather than the Wald test for $\gamma = 0$ in (6) is required).

Higher-order autocorrelation tests also involve the same three options that appear when $j = 1$. For example, when $j = 4$ Wallis (1972) and Vinod (1973) select Option C and $\tilde{Z} = (A_4 - 2I)\hat{u}$, with A_4 the 'fourth differencing matrix'; Godfrey (1978b) and Breusch (1978) have $\tilde{Z} = \hat{u}_{-4}$ with Option B. A complete treatment could therefore be presented for $j = 1, 2, 3, \ldots$ but only Vinod (1973) has explicitly done this, using Option C and $\tilde{Z} = (A_j - 2I)\hat{u}$ as the augmenting variable.

Autoregressive autocorrelation was of primary interest above, but this orientation is too narrow. At various times investigators might be interested in the moving average (MA) format

$u_t = e_t + \rho e_{t-j}$ or perhaps a nonlinear one such as $u_t = e_t + \rho e_{t-j} y_{t-j}$ (bilinear model) or $u_t = e_t + \rho e_{t-j}^2$ (nonlinear moving average). Little needs to be added to the discussion above. The conditional means under the alternative models would be

$$E(y_t | \mathscr{F}_t) = x_t \beta + \rho e_{t-j} \qquad \text{(MA)}$$
$$E(y_t | \mathscr{F}_t) = x_t \beta + \rho e_{t-j} y_{t-j} \quad \text{(bilinear)}$$

providing obvious proxies $\tilde{z}_t = \hat{u}_{t-j}$ and $\tilde{z}_t = \hat{u}_{t-j} y_{t-j}$ for the regressions associated with the three options. An item of some interest is that the proxy employed above to detect a jth order MA ($\hat{u}_{-j}$) is identical with that selected earlier to diagnose a jth order autoregression, giving the Durbin–Watson, h-statistics etc. a dual role – a result established in Breusch (1978) and Godfrey (1978b).

But is it sufficient to concentrate solely upon $j = 1$ – the most common choice – or $j = 4$? Many would argue that it might be impossible to characterize the autocorrelation well with a *single* parameter, and this has led to the proposal that a joint test for $\rho_1, \ldots, \rho_M$ being zero in the format $u_t = \rho_1 u_{t-1} + \ldots + \rho_M u_{t-M} + e_t$ be constructed. Application of Option A with augmenting variables $\hat{u}_{-1}, \ldots, \hat{u}_{-M}$ provides the LM-test for white noise across M-lags of the autocorrelation function established by Godfrey (1978b) or the portmanteau test given by Box and Pierce (1970).

Applications of the Durbin–Watson and h-statistic are myriad; those testing for fourth-order serial correlation are in smaller number but certainly available. Hendry (1983a) uses the LM test for white noise across $M = 6$ lags of the autocorrelation function in his study of consumption relations. A very much smaller range of studies is available once one departs from the linear process alternatives. Ashley and Granger (1979) found bilinear effects in the residuals of the St Louis model, Weiss (1983) has found similar evidence in models of a number of economic time series, and Pagan (1978) discovered a nonlinear effect in IBM stock price data.

(c) *Functional form* It is rare that the functional form is known in econometrics; linear or log-linear relations dominate, mainly because of their computational advantages but also because they sometimes have desirable attributes, e.g. imposition of non-negative restrictions upon variables. Suppose that the unknown functional form has the structure

$$y_t = g(x_t; \lambda, \delta) + e_t, \qquad (9)$$

specializing to a linear model when $\lambda = \lambda_0$. λ will be taken to be a scalar in the following exposition. A further restriction upon g is that it admits of a Taylor series expansion

$$y_t = x_t\beta + g_1(x_t;\lambda_0,\delta)\gamma + \sum_{k=2}^{\infty}(k!)^{-1}g_k(x_t;\lambda_0,\delta)(\lambda-\lambda_0)^k + e_t \tag{10}$$

where $g_j = \partial^j g/\partial\lambda^j$ and $\gamma = \lambda - \lambda_0$; $g(x_t;\lambda_0,\delta) = x_t\beta$ as the model is linear when $\lambda = \lambda_0$.

Under the null hypothesis of linearity ($\lambda = \lambda_0$) the error term in (10) is e_t and a test of the hypothesis that $\lambda = \lambda_0$ can be found by adding the variable $z_t = g_1(x_t;\lambda_0,\delta)$ to the conditional mean $x_t\beta$. To some extent the decision to include all higher-order derivatives than the first in the error is arbitrary; one could add the variables g_1 and g_2 for example, performing a joint test that their contribution is negligible. The argument for the division as in (10) is an asymptotic one: under the sequence of local alternatives $\lambda - \lambda_0 = T^{-1/2}\phi$, power is not increased by adding the higher-order derivatives. There may be some reason for their inclusion in small samples though.

Equations (9) and (10) highlight the fact that some family of functional forms needs to be specified as an alternative to enable the partial derivatives g_j to be obtained. Perhaps the most popular form has been the Box–Cox transformation $g(x_t;\lambda,\delta) = \lambda^{-1}(x_t{}^{\lambda} - 1)\delta$ as this incorporates both linear and log-linear formats. Andrews (1971) is an early reference exploiting the principle of variable addition in assessing functional form and Godfrey and Wickens (1981) followed up his work. This latter paper also examines the appropriate functional form for a consumption function.

Many other strategies for detecting functional form inadequacy may be interpreted in the above way, e.g. the regression of residuals against powers of x_t. An interesting application not in the Box–Cox framework is Kmenta (1967), in which a Cobb–Douglas production function specification is evaluated *vis-à-vis* the CES function by the addition of the variable $\log^2 k_t$, k_t being the capital–labour ratio.

(d) *Comparisons with other models* Sometimes the deficiency in a model might be expected to be more pervasive than the above classifications permit, i.e. it may be felt that a completely different conditional mean, $E(y\,|\,\mathscr{F}) = X_2\delta$, is really appropriate. Following the principle of augmentation, a proxy $\tilde{Z}$ for this alternative is needed. Various suggestions have been made. The classical F-test for model selection – discussed in Pesaran (1974) – sets $\tilde{Z} = X_2$. The J-test of Davidson and MacKinnon (1981) has $\tilde{Z} = X_2\hat{\delta}$ where $\hat{\delta} = (X_2'X_2)^{-1}X_2'y$, i.e. the proxy is the predictions from the alternative model. This latter procedure is asymptotically equivalent to Cox's (1961) test as interpreted for regression models by Pesaran (1974) and Pesaran and Deaton (1978).

Because an investigator is free to choose $\tilde{Z}$, it is sometimes possible to design it so as to simultaneously achieve high correlation with the alternative and yet exhibit some desirable small-sample property. Fisher and McAleer (1981) amend the J-test by taking $\tilde{Z}$ as the predictions from the regression of $X\hat{\beta}$ against X_2 rather than y against X_2; they refer to the resulting t-statistic for $\gamma = 0$ as the JA test. Asymptotically it has the same power as the J-test but in small samples it is exactly distributed as t. Whether this is an advantage or not is unclear. Godfrey and Pesaran (1983) consider adjustments that might be made to the J-test in small samples to obtain better performance, and this may be a better line of attack than adopting a particular $\tilde{Z}$ merely to ensure that an exact distribution is obtainable.

The additional variables for model comparisons are limited only by the imagination of an investigator in describing alternative conditional means for y. In many instances these arise naturally from the context. Harvey (1977) concentrates upon VES and CES production functions; McAleer et al. (1982) compare the relative performance of long- and short-run interest rates in money demand functions; Pesaran (1982) looks at whether a Keynesian or new classical model best describes the US economy (although note that Pesaran's results are probably biased in favour of the Keynesian model. He effectively augments Barro's (1977) equation with the predictions from a Keynesian model, finding that the t-statistic for the added variable is highly significant. As observed in Pagan (1984) the t-statistics from Barro-type models are overstated. No such effect occurs when the models are reversed). Sometimes deciding on a reasonable alternative conditional mean can be difficult and one solution would be to use the predictions from a time-series model for y_t. This proposal would formalize the notion that an adequate model should perform 'better' than a time series or 'naive' formulation.

(e) *Model stability* It is well established that a suspicion of coefficients exhibiting a break at a particular point in the sample may be checked by the addition of variables constructed as the product of an indicator variable with the regressor whose coefficient is believed to have changed. Most econometrics texts describe this approach, e.g. Stewart and Wallis (1981, p. 199).

The Chow test (1960) for model stability emerges as the special case where all coefficients of the regression are assumed to change.

A related development has been to infer model stability characteristics through predictive accuracy in a post-estimation sample of data. If the model is stable it is argued that the *one-step* prediction errors $\{\hat{y}_{T+j} - y_{T+j}\}_{j=1}{}^{q}$ should be insignificantly different from zero. Salkever (1976) formulates this connection as a possibility of variable addition; the variables $\tilde{Z}$ added to the model being indicator variables $d_{1,t}, \ldots, d_{q,t}$, where $d_{j,t}$ is zero except at $T+j$ when it is unity. Pagan and Nicholls (1984) generalize this notion to testing if the *multi-step* prediction errors were insignificantly different from zero by also adding constructed variables to the original model.

There have been a growing number of applications of the idea: Pagan and Volker (1981, p. 392) for a money demand function and Kirby (1981) for wage equations both explicitly adopt Salkever's method whilst the $z(k)$ variables in Davidson et al. (1978) provide an asymptotically equivalent test.

(f) *Exogeneity* The last assumption embodied in the classical linear model involves the exogeneity of X. At a very early stage in the growth of econometrics, studies were made of the consequences of replacing this supposition with one in which the equation was treated as part of a system. Thereupon X (or elements of it) could be regarded as variables determined elsewhere in the system.

Let W be a matrix of observations upon the predetermined variables of the system – sometimes called the instrumental variables. Conditioning performed in the definition of the moments of y is then naturally done in terms of W. Suppose that $E(X|W) = W\delta$ so that $E(y|W) = (W\delta)\beta$ and

$$y = (W\delta)\beta + e \tag{11}$$

where $E(e|W) = 0$ and $E(ee'|W) = \sigma^2 I$. Equation (11) describes the alternative model. It may be related to the maintained model by the addition and subtraction of $X\beta$:

$$y = X\beta + (W\delta - X)\beta + e = X\beta + Z\gamma + e, \tag{12}$$

which shows that a test for the exogeneity of X is available from the 'F-test' that $\gamma = 0$. When the maintained assumption of exogeneity for X is inadequate $\gamma = \beta \neq 0$.

In practice δ is unknown and $\hat{\delta} = (W'W)^{-1}W'X$ substitutes for it, making $\tilde{Z} = W\hat{\delta} - X$ the proxy for Z in the regression relation (12). If W represents all the predetermined variables of the system and $E(X \mid W)$ is linear, $X - W\hat{\delta}$ would be the reduced form residuals. However, most applications have recognized that W can never be known with complete certainty, leading to a further replacement of $W\hat{\delta} - X$ by $W_1\hat{\delta}_1 - X$ where W_1 is a subset of the total predetermined variables and $\hat{\delta}_1 = (W_1'W_1)^{-1}W_1'y$. Once again this last action does not affect the distribution under the null hypothesis, detracting only from power.

Hausman (1978) forms an exogeneity test from the regression of y against $\hat{X} = W\hat{\delta}$ and $X - \hat{X}$ rather than X and $X - \hat{X}$ as in (12). Nakamura and Nakamura (1981) demonstrate that the two approaches give identical answers. Durbin (1954) proposed a comparison of the OLS and instrumental variable estimates, and this has also been shown to be equivalent to the variable addition method in Hausman (1978); probably this last comparison represents, in an informal way, the most widespread method among applied researchers of gauging the adequacy of the exogeneity of X. There has been an increasing use of formal tests in recent years, however, e.g. Miller and Volker (1983) and Gregory and McAleer (1981), the first concerning the determination of female participation rates in Australia and the second money demand in Canada.

2.2 *Augmenting the Conditional Variance*

The second assumption underlying the standard regression model is that the conditional variance of the disturbances is a constant σ^2. Departures from this restriction can be usefully viewed as augmenting a constant conditional variance with some variables z_t, i.e. the alternative variance for the error u_t becomes

$$\sigma_t^2 = \sigma^2 + z_t\gamma. \tag{13}$$

Some test of whether $\gamma = 0$ or not is now desirable. To do that it is necessary to express (13) in terms of data. Suppose initially that the regression part $x_t\beta$ were zero making y_t and u_t identical. Equation (13) could then be re-written in the required format as

$$u_t^2 = \sigma^2 + z_t\gamma + u_t^2 - \sigma_t^2 = \sigma^2 + z_t\gamma + \bar{v}_t. \tag{14}$$

Under the null hypothesis that $\gamma = 0$, $E(\bar{v}_t) = 0$, $E(\bar{v}_t^2) = \mu_4 - \sigma^4$ where $\mu_4 = E(u_t^4 | \gamma = 0)$ and (14) is a regression equation with disturbances that are iid $(0, \mu_4 - \sigma^4)$. Accordingly, the F-statistic for $\gamma = 0$ from the regression of u_t^2 against unity and z_t would constitute a suitable test statistic.

Unfortunately, the likely presence of a non-zero mean for y_t makes it rare that $x_t\beta$ would be zero. With u_t^2 not directly observed, the regressand must be constructed from some estimate of it; in particular the OLS residuals $\hat{u}_t = y_t - x_t\hat{\beta}$ might be called upon to fit this role. With such a substitution the estimable analogue of (14) is

$$\hat{u}_t^2 = \sigma^2 + z_t\gamma + \bar{v}_t + \hat{u}_t^2 - u_t^2 = \sigma^2 + z_t\gamma + v_t. \tag{15}$$

Can the F-statistic of $\hat{\gamma}$ from the regression of $\hat{u}_t^2$ against unity and z_t be regarded as a proper test of γ being zero? For an affirmative answer it is necessary that $\hat{u}_t^2 - u_t^2$ contribute nothing to the asymptotic variance of $T^{\frac{1}{2}}(\hat{\gamma} - \gamma)$. When z_t and x_t are exogenous, Amemiya (1977) provides a formal proof; extensions to allow x_t and z_t to incorporate lagged values of y_t are dealt with in Nicholls and Quinn (1981) and the theorems there could be applied more generally.

Continuing with the same theme as in section 2.1, there is no certain knowledge of z_t, and a proxy $\tilde{z}_t$ will be used in lieu of it. Equation (15) then becomes

$$\hat{u}_t^2 = \sigma^2 + \tilde{z}_t\gamma + v_t + (z_t - \tilde{z}_t)\gamma \tag{16}$$

and a valid test for $\gamma = 0$ is available from the regression of $\hat{u}_t^2$ against unity and $\tilde{z}_t$. What differentiates tests for heteroscedasticity available in the literature therefore is the proxy variable $\tilde{z}_t$ chosen to augment the conditional second moment.

There are five major variations in the selection of $\tilde{z}_t$, each being constructed to diagnose a particular type of inadequacy in the variance assumption.

(a) σ_t^2 might equal σ_1^2 for $t = 1, \ldots, m$ and σ_2^2 for $m + 1, \ldots, T$, i.e. there is a single break at point m in the sample. $\tilde{z}_t$ for this situation is an indicator variable being unity for $t = 1, \ldots, m$ and zero for $t = m+1, \ldots, T$. Harrison and McCabe (1979) and Breusch and Pagan (1979, p. 1293) both make this proposal. In the latter reference the LM test statistic for heteroscedasticity is shown to be a scaling factor: the ratio $(\hat{u}'D\hat{u}/\hat{u}'\hat{u})$, where D is a diagonal matrix with only the first m elements being non-zero. Harrison and McCabe work with the ratio only. Pagan and Hall (1983) observe that this test statistic is asymptotically equivalent to the Goldfeld–Quandt test for heteroscedasticity. Where the break occurs at two points in the sample and the likelihood ratio rather than the Wald version of the test that $\gamma = 0$ in (16) is employed, BAMSET (Bartlett's M specification error test) discussed in Ramsey (1974, pp. 367–9) emerges.

(b) The RESET test in 2.1(a) treated z_t as powers of $E(y_t|\mathscr{F}_t)$. Analogues for the second moment could be $\sigma_t^2 = \sigma^2[E(y_t|\mathscr{F}_t)]^\gamma$ or $\sigma_t^2 = \sigma^2 + \gamma[E(y_t|\mathscr{F}_t)]^\delta$ (δ being a known scale factor). Because $E(y_t|\mathscr{F}_t)$ is unobserved it is replaced by $\hat{y}_t$. Taking the second form as example, $\hat{u}_t^2$ is regressed against unity and $\tilde{z}_t = \hat{y}_t^\delta$ to provide a test that $\gamma = 0$. Anscombe (1961) recommends this and Pagan et al. (1983) apply it in examining the level/variability debate over the effects of inflation (with $\delta = 1$).

(c) One scenario in which the conditional variance would not be a constant occurs when the coefficients of the regression are taken to be random, i.e. $\beta_t = \bar{\beta} + \eta_t$ where η_t is iid $(0, V)$ and independent of e_t. As $E(y_t|\mathscr{F}_t) = x_t\bar{\beta}$, the linear relation has the structure

$$y_t = x_t\bar{\beta} + x_t\eta_t + e_t = x_t\bar{\beta} + u_t \tag{17}$$

showing that the disturbances u_t are heteroscedastic with variance

$$\sigma_t^2 = \sigma^2 + x_t V x_t' = \sigma^2 + (x_t \oplus x_t) Q\gamma = \sigma^2 + z_t\gamma. \tag{18}$$

Here γ contains all the unknown elements in V, and Q is a known matrix such that $Q\gamma = \operatorname{vec} V$ (note that Q is not the identity matrix because of the symmetry of V). Regressing $\hat{u}_t^2$ against unity and z_t provides the test statistic for heteroscedasticity set out in White (1980) (note that the variance term corresponding to unity in V must be eliminated to avoid perfect collinearity with the regressor of unity attached to σ^2).

(d) Some researchers – for example Garbade (1977) – argue that coefficient variation in economic relationships will probably be much more systematic than that considered in (c). He concentrates instead upon an evolving form such as $\beta_t = \beta_{t-1} + \eta_t$. Taking β_t as a scalar the implied alternative model is

$$y_t = x_t\beta_0 + x_t \sum_{j=0}^{t-1} \eta_{t-j} + e_t = x_t\beta_0 + u_t \tag{19}$$

and

$$\sigma_t^2 = E(u_t^2) = \sigma^2 + t x_t^2 \sigma^2 \eta = \sigma^2 + z_t\gamma. \tag{20}$$

A test for this type of coefficient evolution is therefore available by considering whether the conditional variance may be augmented with the variable $z_t = tx_t^2$. Watson (1980) describes a similar test when $\beta_t - \bar{\beta} = \rho(\beta_{t-1} - \bar{\beta}) + \eta_t$ is the alternative evolutionary structure, while King (1982a) and Szroeter (1978) give diagnostic tests with $\tilde{z}_t = t$. (Since γ is a scalar the t-statistic for $\gamma = 0$ can be written as a multiple of $u'Bu/u'u$ where B is a diagonal matrix with $\tilde{z}_t - \bar{z}$ as diagonal elements.) A possible attitude toward the latter proposals could be that $\tilde{z}_t = t$ is being adopted as a proxy for $z_t = tx_t^2$.

(e) Engle (1982a) argues for the conditional variance to be related to the size of past errors, and he terms such formulations Autoregressive Conditional Heteroscedasticity (ARCH). A simple version could be

$$\sigma_t^2 = \sigma^2 + u_{t-1}^2\gamma = \sigma^2 + z_t\gamma \tag{21}$$

or, in terms of observed variables,

$$\hat{u}_t^2 = \sigma^2 + \hat{u}_{t-1}^2\gamma + v_t = \sigma^2 + \tilde{z}_t\gamma + v_t. \tag{22}$$

From (22) the regression of $\hat{u}_t^2$ against unity and $\hat{u}_{t-1}^2$ provides evidence on ARCH effects. For the special ARCH specification in (21), $\hat{\gamma}$ would be an estimate of the first-order serial correlation coefficient of the *squared* residuals, and that quantity is used by Granger and Andersen (1978) in attempting to detect bilinear models. This 'dual purpose' nature of the test once again illustrates the point that, although the variable added is frequently constructed to be powerful against a specific model deficiency, it can detect a much wider range of troubles. Clearly this is both a strength and weakness of the methodology.

Checks for constancy of the conditional variance are becoming more widespread. Engle (1982a) tests for an increase in the variance of US inflation whilst Gregory and McCurdy (1982) find evidence that the variance of disturbances entering an equation designed to enquire into the efficiency of the forward exchange market is not constant. Recently Engle et al. (1983b) draw attention to the relationship between risk premia and conditional variances; an increase in risk should cause a rise in the variance.

2.3 Augmenting Higher-Order Moments

In contrast to the activity surrounding the first two moments, there has been relatively little attention paid to the higher-order ones. To the best of my knowledge the only use of higher-order moments has been to assess the validity of any normality assumptions. Because of this emphasis, it has been the third and fourth moments that are the focus of attention.

Under normality the third moment of the disturbances e_t should be zero while the fourth moment will be three times the square of the second moment, i.e.

$$\mu_3 = 0 \tag{23}$$

$$\mu_4 - 3\sigma^4 = 0. \tag{24}$$

When disturbances are observable, equations (23) and (24) can be written as

$$u_t^3 = \gamma_3 + v_{3,t} \tag{25}$$

$$u_t^4 - 3\sigma^2 u_t^2 = \gamma_4 + v_{4,t} \tag{26}$$

where $v_{3,t} = u_t^3 - \mu_3$, $v_{4,t} = u_t^4 - \mu_4 - 3\sigma^2(u_t^2 - \sigma^2)$. γ_3 and γ_4 are both zero under the null hypothesis (23) and (24). Thus the question becomes whether it is possible to augment (25) and (26) with a constant term. Because the errors $v_{3,t}$ and $v_{4,t}$ have zero mean and constant variance, the OLS estimates $\hat{\gamma}_3$ and $\hat{\gamma}_4$ are the basis of appropriate test statistics.

A slightly different perpsective is available by basing tests not on $\hat{\gamma}_3$ and $\hat{\gamma}_4$ directly but rather on $\sqrt{\hat{b}_1} = \hat{\gamma}_3/\hat{\sigma}^3$ and $\hat{b}_2 = \hat{\gamma}_4/\hat{\sigma}_4$; these quantities being recognized as measures of skewness and kurtosis provided in many packages, e.g. SHAZAM. White and MacDonald (1980) give a comprehensive survey of the tests for normality based on $\sqrt{\hat{b}_1}$ and $\hat{b}_2$. Bowman and Shenton (1975) derive a joint test that $\sqrt{\hat{b}_1}$ and $\hat{b}_2$ are both zero – equivalent to a joint test that γ_3 and γ_4 are zero in the two equation system (25) and (26) – and Bera and Jarque (1981) demonstrate that the concomitant statistic coincides with the LM test for normality when the alternative distribution is a member of the Pearson family.

One qualification to these results needs to be recorded. When only residuals $\hat{u}$ rather than disturbances are available, the t-statistics for $\gamma_3 = 0$ and $\gamma_4 = 0$ computed from the regressions in (25) and (26) would be in error unless special adjustments are made to reflect the fact that $\hat{u}_t^3 - u_t^3$ contributes to the asymptotic distribution of $\hat{\gamma}_3$ and $\hat{\gamma}_4$. Thus, just as with Option C in section 2.1, it is not possible to obtain the correct test statistic from OLS output. The adjustments are simple, however, in that the true variances are just multiples of the estimated ones; the exact multiple can be found in Pagan and Hall (1983).

3 Augmenting Conditional Moments – the Structural Equation Case

3.1 Augmenting the Conditional Mean

When the equation is part of a simultaneous system the concept of a conditional mean needs more attention. As some of the elements in X are now endogenous there is little point in seeking to condition upon X itself. Instead, conditioning could be with respect to a set of variables W constituting the predetermined variables of the system. Defining the expectation of X, conditional upon W, as X^*, the equivalent of equation (1) for a structural equation $y = X\beta + e$ is

$$E(y \mid W) = X^*\beta. \tag{27}$$

(If any elements in X are predetermined they can be included in W. Hence it is not necessary to distinguish between the variables in X which are endogenous and those that are predetermined.)

In an identical fashion to section 2, the question of how adequate the conditional mean assumption is may be formulated as whether (27) is capable of being augmented with some extra variables. Defining $Z^* = E(Z \mid W)$ as these extra variables, the extended conditional mean is

$$E(y \mid W) = X^*\beta + Z^*\gamma \tag{28}$$

which can be rearranged as

$$y = X^*\beta + Z^*\gamma + y - E(y \mid W) \tag{29}$$

Converted to a relationship between observable variables

$$y = X\beta + Z\gamma + e + (Z^* - Z)\gamma \tag{30}$$

where $e = y - E(y \mid W) + (X^* - X)\beta$ has $E(e \mid W) = 0$, $E(ee' \mid W) = \sigma^2 I$ and we have the analogue of (3) for the structural equation case. When the null hypothesis that $\gamma = 0$ holds the error term in (30) is e, just as it was in (3).

Basic to the analysis of section 2.1 was a recognition that there were three options for the construction of a test statistic that $\gamma = 0$. These options recur here, but there is an extra complication in that both sets of regressors X and Z in (30) may be correlated with the error e. Accordingly all options must make allowance for this feature. In the statements of the three options to follow, $\tilde{Z}$ can be interchanged with Z, but for typographical reasons the distinction is not made explicitly. We ignore which of the LM, LR or Wald formulations might be used or what degrees of freedom adjustments might be made; Kiviet (1984) analyses these issues.

An instrumental variable estimator of $\delta' = (\beta'\gamma')$ with W (or a subset W_1) as instruments is consistent. Because of its generality the estimator adopted is Sargan's (1958) Generalized Instrumental Variable Estimator (GIVE), defined as $\tilde{\beta} = (\hat{X}'\hat{X})^{-1}\hat{X}'y$ where $\hat{X}$ are the predictions of X against W_1. Option A(S) for the structural equation case is

Option A(S): Apply GIVE to (30) with $W_1 \in W$ as instruments and test whether $\gamma = 0$ using the 'F-statistic' based on γ provided with GIVE programs.

Although Option A(S) is the simplest approach, in many instances test statistics presented have been based on the GIVE residuals $\tilde{u} = y - X\tilde{\beta}$, and this prompts an equivalent re-statement of it as Option B(S). To obtain $\tilde{u}$ as dependent variable, $X\tilde{\beta}$ is subtracted from both sides producing

$$\tilde{u} = y - X\tilde{\beta} = X(\beta - \tilde{\beta}) + Z\gamma + e + (Z^* - Z)\gamma. \tag{31}$$

Option B(S): Apply GIVE to (31) with $W_1 \in W$ as instruments and test whether $\gamma = 0$ using the 'F-statistic' based on γ provided with GIVE programs.

Sometimes the test statistic found in the literature comes from an analytic derivation of the 'F-statistic' of Option B(S). From Phillips and Wickens (1978) the covariance matrix of $T^{\frac{1}{2}}(\hat{\gamma} - \gamma)$ can be found by partitioned inversion to be

$$\operatorname*{plim}_{T \to \infty} T\sigma^2(\hat{Z}'\hat{Z} - \hat{Z}'\hat{X}(\hat{X}'\hat{X})^{-1}\hat{X}'\hat{Z})^{-1}$$

where $\hat{Z} = Z(W_1'W_1)^{-1}W_1'y$, giving the test statistic

$$[\hat{\gamma}'(\hat{Z}'\hat{Z} - \hat{Z}'\hat{X}(\hat{X}'\hat{X})^{-1}\hat{X}'\hat{Z})\,\hat{\gamma}/\sigma^2].$$

Some variation is induced by the existence of alternative estimators for σ^2. In Option B(S) σ^2 is estimated from the unrestricted model, whereas the analytic constructs generally estimate σ^2 from the residuals of the restricted model, i.e. $\tilde{u} = y - X\tilde{\beta}$. Both estimators are consistent under the null hypothesis, making the two statistics asymptotically equivalent.

In fact the estimate of the scaling factor represents the only difference between Options A(S) and B(S) as well. To see this observe that the regressions $(y; \hat{X}, \hat{Z})$ and $(\hat{u}; \hat{X}, \hat{Z})$ give identical estimates for γ where $\hat{u}$ are the residuals from the first regression and ';' separates regressand and regressors. But $(\hat{u}; \hat{X}, \hat{Z})$ and $(\tilde{u}; \hat{X}, \hat{Z})$ also give identical estimates as $\hat{X}'\hat{u} = \hat{X}'\tilde{u}$ and $\hat{Z}'\hat{u} = \hat{Z}'\tilde{u}$ because $\tilde{u} = y - X\tilde{\beta} = \hat{u} + (X - \hat{X})\tilde{\beta}$ and $\hat{X}'(X - \hat{X}) = \hat{Z}'(X - \hat{X}) = 0$ by construction. Consequently, as the cross-product matrix is the same in all regressions it is only the estimate of σ^2 that differentiates the test statistics.

Option C(S) follows as in section 2.1 by ignoring $X(\beta - \tilde{\beta})$ in (31). Provided Z consists of functions of predetermined variables alone, the least squares estimator $\gamma^* = (Z'Z)^{-1}Z'\tilde{u}$ is consistent – $T^{-1}Z'X(\beta - \tilde{\beta}) \xrightarrow{p} 0$ because $\tilde{\beta} \xrightarrow{p} \beta$ under the null hypothesis – but an adjustment to the covariance matrix of $T^{\frac{1}{2}}(\gamma^* - \gamma)$ is needed. Pagan and Hall (1983, equation (49)) show that $T^{\frac{1}{2}}(\gamma^* - \gamma)$ has limiting covariance matrix

$$\sigma^2 \operatorname*{plim}_{T \to \infty} T(Z'Z)^{-1}Z'\hat{M}_X\hat{M}_X{}'Z(Z'Z)^{-1}$$

where $\hat{M}_X = I - X(\hat{X}'\hat{X})^{-1}\hat{X}'$, allowing these elements to be collected in a statement of Option C(S).

Option C(S): Regress $\tilde{u}$ against Z to obtain $\gamma^* = (Z'Z)^{-1}Z'\tilde{u}$ and test if $\gamma = 0$ using γ^* with $\sigma^2(Z'Z)^{-1}Z'\hat{M}_X\hat{M}_X{}'Z(Z'Z)^{-1}$ as its covariance matrix.

Indices of inadequacy for the conditional mean specification when the equation of interest is part of a system are much fewer than in the ordinary regression case. For this reason the review below is brief, although it should be apparent that a wide range of tests might be constructed using the addition principle. Furthermore, as the motivation for alternate specifications is identical with that of section 2.1, it will not be repeated.

(a) *Specification error* An equivalent test to RESET could be generated in either of two ways. In the first, the predictions whose powers are to appear in $\tilde{Z}$ would be from the regression of y against W_1, i.e. the reduced form predictions for y if W_1 contained all predetermined variables. With the second, $X\tilde{\beta}$ forms the basis.

There seems no convincing reason why one should be chosen over the other, but option C(S) needs a GIVE rather than OLS estimate of γ in the second choice, as $\tilde{Z}$ is an endogenous variable.

(b) *Autocorrelation* A range of test statistics has been proposed for the detection of autocorrelation in the disturbances of a structural equation (or more precisely those of an equation which necessitates instrumental variable estimation). Much of the diversity can, however, be accounted for by differing choices of the three options described above.

In direct analogy with the single equation developments it would seem sensible to augment the maintained structural equation with lagged values of the GIVE residuals. Thereupon it is merely a matter of selecting one of the options A(S), B(S) or C(S) to compute the test statistic for the significance of this extra variable. Godfrey (1976) adopted Option B(S), i.e. he applied GIVE to an equation with $\tilde{u}$ as dependent variable and X and $\tilde{u}_{-1}$ as independent variables. Later, in Godfrey (1978a), he suggested Option C(S) – X is omitted from the second-stage relationship and an adjustment to the covariance matrix of γ^* is made instead. Finally, Breusch and Godfrey (1981) settle on Option A(S). Thus, what prima facie, are a variety of alternative test statistics are seen to be just different ways of assessing the importance of the same added variable.

One difficulty with Option C(S) is that the covariance adjustment is complex. It would be nice therefore if it could be waived. In the ordinary regression model the absence of lagged values of y among the regressors is a sufficient condition to allow the adjustment to be dispensed with. Of course it is scarcely surprising that this restriction also applies in the context of a structural equation, but it now needs to be strengthened. Formally, it is necessary that $T^{-1}Z'\hat{M}_X\hat{M}_X{}'Z - T^{-1}Z'Z \xrightarrow{p} 0$ which holds if $T^{-1}Z'X \xrightarrow{p} 0$. Because Z contains $\tilde{u}_{-1}$ this must generally mean there is no first-order serial correlation anywhere in the system, since the presence of any such autocorrelation will normally mean that the endogenous variables in X are correlated with $\tilde{u}_{-1}$. Hence, the covariance adjustment of Option C(S) may be viewed as making the test statistic robust to the presence of autocorrelation in equations of the system other than the one being examined.

(c) *Comparisons with other models* In section 2.1 (d) three variable addition tests were described to implement model comparisons – the F-test, the J-test and the JA-test. Analogues of each of these have been formulated when alternative structural equations are under consideration, with all proposals adopting Option A(S) as the preferred method of constructing test statistics.

Define the competing model as having conditional mean $E(y\,|\,W) = E(X_2\,|\,W)\,\delta$ rather than $E(y\,|\,W) = E(X_1\,|\,W)\,\beta$. Dastoor and McAleer (1983), in reviewing contributions to the area, argue the merits of augmenting the maintained structural equation with $Z = X_2$, this being the equivalent of the artificial nesting method. MacKinnon et al. (1983) add $X_2\bar{\delta}$ where $\bar{\delta}$ are the GIVE of δ obtained by estimating an equation with y as dependent and X_2 independent variables. This is the equivalent of the J-test. Godfrey (1983a) replaces this by $X_2\bar{\delta}^*$ where $\bar{\delta}^*$ is the GIVE of δ obtained by estimating an equation with $X_1\tilde{\beta}$ as dependent and X_2 independent variables. Such a test statistic would reduce to the JA test with a non-structural model.

(d) *Stability* In contrast to the extensive research on stability in regression models, there is a very limited amount for a structural equation. There would be little difficulty in repeating the analysis of section 2.1 (e) when the coefficients shifting are attached to predetermined variables; all this would require is the application of GIVE rather than OLS to the relationship augmented with the same variables as earlier. No satisfactory solutions exist, however, when it is the coefficients of endogenous variables which shift stochastically, although Pagan and Hall (1983) give some analysis of the issues involved in allowing coefficient variation in structural equations. Kiviet (1984) provides a test for structural change based on one-step-ahead prediction errors that is formulated as variable addition.

3.2 Augmenting Second and Higher-Order Moments

Augmenting the conditional variance. As with section 2.2 it is of interest to determine whether the restriction of the conditional variance to be a constant is appropriate. The alternative will be

$$E(e_t^2\,|\,W) = \sigma^2 + z_t\gamma. \tag{32}$$

In section 2.2 a regression was constructed in which the least squares residuals were related to unity and z_t, with the F-statistic for $\gamma = 0$ being used to assess departures from the maintained model. In line with that approach it seems reasonable to set up

(33) as the extension of (15) to the structural equation

$$\tilde{u}_t^2 = \sigma^2 + z_t\gamma + \tilde{u}_t^2 - u_t^2 + u_t^2 - \sigma_t^2. \tag{33}$$

For the ordinary regression case the term $\tilde{u}_t^2 - u_t^2$ contributes nothing to the asymptotic variance of $T^{\frac{1}{2}}(\hat{\gamma}-\gamma)$, but this is not necessarily the case when the equation is a structural one and $\tilde{u}_t$ are GIVE residuals. Kelejian (1982) shows that the t-statistic for $\hat{\gamma}$ from the regression of $\tilde{u}_t^2$ against unity and z_t is *only of the correct size if there is no heteroscedasticity anywhere in the simultaneous system.* Otherwise an adjustment similar to that encountered in the use of Option C(S) is needed. Pagan and Hall (1983) and White (1982b) describe this adjustment. Unfortunately, it cannot be implemented by the use of standard computer programs, although it is easy to program.

Augmenting higher-order conditional moments. There is a dearth of test statistics generated by augmenting conditional moments greater than the second. It is tempting to proceed as in section 2.3 and to test any normality assumptions about e_t. However, the use of GIVE residuals causes considerable complications in deriving the limiting distributions of $T^{\frac{1}{2}}\hat{\gamma}_3$ and $T^{\frac{1}{2}}\hat{\gamma}_4$. These are of a similar nature of those experienced when checking the constant variance assumption in section 3.2.1, but there is no longer any relatively simple adjustment to circumvent them. Under the strong assumption that y and any endogenous variables in X are jointly normal, Pagan and Hall (1983) observe that the conclusions in section 2.3 will hold, but that would seem a very strong assumption.

4 Joint Tests and Small-Sample Properties

4.1 Combining and Adjusting Test Statistics

Despite the implicit presumptions of the preceding analysis, departures from conditional mean assumptions rarely occur singly. For example, no really convincing argument is available to justify the restriction that the conditional variance is constant when assessing weaknesses in the conditional mean specification. This leads to a consideration of how the unidirectional tests distinguished earlier – to use Bera and Jarque's (1982) phrase – might be coordinated or modified to reflect the multidimensional departures possible from the standard regression assumptions. No detailed examination can be offered here, but the main themes will be presented.

A variety of solutions is available. One is to construct omnibus tests for all the specification errors deemed likely, e.g. a joint test for serial independence, heteroscedasticity, functional form and normality would be derived. Bera and Jarque (1982) explore this possibility. Cast in terms of variable addition it would involve the simultaneous estimation of equations (4), (16), (25) and (26) with the augmenting variables for each equation being selected to reflect the likely alternatives. Joint, rather than single, estimation of these equations then provides a complete resolution to the combinatorial issue.

Conceptually such a solution is satisfactory, but it ignores the fact that most computer packages only automatically compute unidirectional tests, and it would facilitate test construction if only such unidirectional information was needed. From the perspective of this chapter, the potential for simplification can be identified by isolating those situations when the coefficient estimators of the various γ are independent of one another. When there is independence, unidirectional tests provide all the requisite information. In particular, they may be added together to produce an omnibus test.

An example may clarify this contention. The error term in (4), under the null hypothesis of a correct mean specification, is e_t, while that in (16) is $e_t^2 - \sigma^2$ under the null hypothesis that the conditional variance is constant. With the extra restriction of normality for e_t, the errors in (4) and (16) will be uncorrelated since $E(e_t(e_t^2 - \sigma^2)) = E(e_t^3) = 0$. Following Zellner (1962), joint estimation of (4) and (16) reduces to single equation estimation. Thus a joint test of the adequacy of both conditional moments – with normality as part of the maintained hypothesis – is available by adding the individual tests. This additivity property has been extensively explored by Bera and Jarque (1982) and Pagan and Hall (1983).

Allocating the unidirectional tests to groups corresponding to the moment they are concerned with, it would be rare for intra-group tests to be additive (although tests for predictive failure and serial correlation represent intragroup tests that are additive). To see why, consider RESET and the Option A test for first-order serial correlation. Augmenting variables are $Z_1 = (\hat{y}^2, \ldots, y^L)$ and $Z_2 = \hat{u}_{-1}$ respectively, and the alternate relation is

$$y = X\beta + Z_1\gamma_1 + Z_2\gamma_2 + e. \tag{34}$$

Now for $\hat{\gamma}_1$ and $\hat{\gamma}_2$ to be independent it is necessary (assuming their asymptotic normality) that their covariance be zero, this in turn requiring Z_2 and Z_1 to be uncorrelated *and* either Z_2 uncorrelated with X or Z_1 uncorrelated with X. The last condition stems from the fact that the covariance between $\hat{\gamma}_1$ and $\hat{\gamma}_2$ is derived from the *inverse* of the matrix composed of *all* the cross products between X, Z_1 and Z_2. Satisfaction of these requirements must be rare; the presence of y_{t-1} in X for example makes RESET and the h-statistic correlated. Consequently the conclusion by Thursby (1981) that these tests seem independent is strongly dependent upon his Monte Carlo design, featuring regressors which are not lagged values of y. By contrast, inspection of equations (4), (16), (25) and (26) reveal that intergroup additivity is assured whenever the third moment of the errors is zero – perhaps not an unreasonable occurrence.

A number of doubts arise concerning the strategy outlined above. Of these, the most severe must be that there are too many possible univariate tests for them all to be combined together. Selection is necessary (perhaps even desirable) and with that act comes a certain arbitrariness in the procedure. To overcome the objection it may well be necessary to attempt to compensate the unidirectional tests for departures from the assumptions underlying their construction. Claims that test statistics such as RESET are robust to autocorrelation and heteroscedasticity (Thursby, 1979, 1982) are clearly incorrect. The OLS formula variance for γ is always estimated incorrectly in the presence of these defects and it forms the basis for tests such as RESET. Since the conditional mean test statistics are dependent only upon the assumption that the conditional variance be constant, these tests may be made robust by adjusting the F-statistic from the regression in (4) to account for heteroscedasticity of unknown form. Eicker (1967), Fuller (1975) and White (1980) all show how this may be done. Determining the limits to such action is still an open research area, but that constraints do exist can be ascertained by noting that tests for constancy of the variance require a specification of the conditional mean up to a white-noise term.

4.2 Small Sample Characteristics

Justification for the principle of variable addition primarily stems from asymptotic theory. There is some evidence, however, that this theory may be misleading as a guide to the magnitude of both

Type I and Type II errors, and this has led to various proposals aimed at improving such characteristics in small samples. A brief survey of some of that literature is now provided.

(a) *Type I error* The principal difficulty here is that the asymptotic prediction of $T^{\frac{1}{2}}(\hat{\gamma}-\gamma)$ being multivariate normal is likely to be incorrect in small samples. By analogy with ordinary regression theory, the distribution of the Wald statistic might be better approximated by formulating it as an F-statistic rather than treating it as a χ^2 variable. Both Harvey (1981) and Kiviet (1982) provide Monte Carlo evidence to support this viewpoint. A combination of the fact that degrees of freedom adjustments are almost certain to be required in small samples together with the ease of implementing the correction, almost certainly accounts for the widespread acceptance of this modification.

In standard regression theory the ability to construct a test statistic for $\gamma = 0$ that can be referred to the F-distribution originates in the assumption that X and $\tilde{Z}$ are composed of fixed numbers. Milliken and Graybill (1970) extend this result to allow $\tilde{Z}$ to be known functions of $X\hat{\beta}$. Because the RESET and JA tests discussed in section 2.1 have this property (assuming X_2 to be constants in the alternative model generating the JA-statistic), their exact small-sample distribution can be treated as F. But there will be few situations in which $\tilde{Z}$ possesses these properties. Nevertheless, the central idea of choosing the regressors to obtain a closer correspondence between nominal and actual sizes allows more possibility of extension. Godfrey and Pesaran (1983) follow this strategy in their work on the J-test. Because $\hat{\gamma}$ is biased in small samples with the $\tilde{Z}$ of the J-test, they re-formulate $\tilde{Z}$ so as to make it unbiased.

Although the bias corrections made by Godfrey and Pesaran achieve a considerable measure of success, the adjusted J-test still has a nominal size exceeding its actual size. As the test is based upon the Wald (W) statistic, it is natural to return to a remark of section 2.1 that a test for $\gamma = 0$ could be conducted as well with either the LM or LR variants. No consistent pattern of choice has emerged – although LR applications are very rare – but the existence of an inequality $\text{LM} \leqslant \text{LR} \leqslant \text{W}$ for regression models with linear restrictions (Berndt and Savin, 1977; Breusch, 1979) suggests that an appropriate response to overstatement of size by a W-test variant might be corrected by adopting the LM-test variant. Certainly this secondary issue in test construction by variable addition deserves greater attention than it has received. (Kiviet (1984) presents some Monte Carlo evidence that, when lagged dependent and jointly dependent variables are both present, the LM version seems preferable.)

All of the above approaches are aimed at modifying the regressors or statistics themselves so as to force a closer relation between the sampling distributions of test statistics for $\gamma = 0$ and standard ones such as F, χ^2, etc. But there do exist circumstances in which the exact Type I errors can be computed, albeit at some cost. More specifically, whenever the statistic can be written as the ratio of quadratic forms in normal variables, the exact distribution may be determined numerically by, say, Imhof's (1961) method. Durbin and Watson (1971) show that the Durbin–Watson statistic has the required structure while Breusch and Pagan (1979) note that some tests for heteroscedasticity based on variable addition also do.

Unfortunately, primary requirements for converting the test statistic to a ratio of quadratic forms in normal variables are that γ be a scalar and only the first and second moments are being augmented. Breusch and Pagan (1979, 1980) try to overcome this limitation by advancing a simulation technique for estimating Type I errors. The idea is very simple. Suppose that the variance of u_t in (14), under $H_0: \gamma = 0$ was known, and that u_t is assumed normal. Then u_t might be generated from a Gaussian number generator, $\hat{u}$ formed from $(I - X(X'X)^{-1}X')u$, and $\hat{u}_t^2$ regressed against unity and z_t to obtain $\hat{\gamma}$. Repeating this process many times, and counting the fraction of times the chosen test statistic for $\gamma = 0$ exceeded some value c, gives the Type I error for that critical value c. Moreover, it is not necessary to know σ^2; division of (15) by σ^2 re-parameterizes γ to $\gamma^* = \sigma^{-2}\gamma$, converts u_t to a standard normal deviate, but leaves the W, LM or LR test statistics for $\gamma^* = 0$ the same as for $\gamma = 0$. Breusch and Pagan (1979) compare the computational cost of this method with the Imhof solution, concluding that it is generally cheaper and just as accurate.

Finding Type I errors by computer simulation may be attractive as computer costs decline or if it proves hard to find simple modifications of test statistics that are capable of resolving nominal and actual size differentials. As the J-test of section 2.1 (d) appears to fall into this category, it is of interest that it too is invariant to the residual variance σ^2. To see this, observe that

$$\tilde{Z} = X_2(X_2'X_2)^{-1}X_2'y = X_2(X_2'X_2)^{-1}X_2'X\beta + X_2(X_2'X_2)^{-1}X_2'e$$

under the maintained model. Equivalently, the regression of y against $(X:\tilde{Z})$ could be thought of as a regression of y against $[X+X_2(X_2'X_2)^{-1}X_2'X\gamma:X_2(X_2'X_2)^{-1}X_2'e]$ which, when $\gamma=0$, is just that of y versus $[X:X_2(X_2'X_2)^{-1}X_2'e]$. Division of both sides of this regression by σ reveals that the regressor $X_2(X_2'X_2)^{-1}X_2'e$ can be constructed out of random numbers generated from a standard normal deviate. Hence, repeated application of Option B, in which $\hat{u}=y-X\hat{\beta}=(I-X(X'X)^{-1}X')\,e$ is regressed against X and $\tilde{Z}=(X_2'X_2)^{-1}X_2'e$, will enable the Type I error of the J-test to be determined exactly for given X and X_2.

A disadvantage of the simulation technique is its reliance on normality for e_t. Diaconis and Effron (1983) suggest a 'boot strap' method whereby $\hat{u}_t$ are treated as random numbers coming from an unspecified distribution. The idea appeals, although the error implicit in such an approximation is a function of sample size, and it may turn out to be more unacceptable than a normality assumption. In any case, none of the variations discussed can easily dispense with the requirement that X does not contain lagged values of y, and this may well represent the major challenge to be faced in the construction and use of tests based on variable addition.

(b) *Power* Almost all the test statistics generated by variable addition in this chapter can be shown to be asymptotically locally most powerful when Z is known. Intuitively such a conclusion must originate in the power properties of the F-test in the linear regression model, even though a direct extension of these to most variable addition tests is not possible. To discern why, consider testing the constancy of the second moment as in section 2.2. The regression relation based on equation (15) has, under the alternative hypothesis (and assuming normality), a variance of $2\sigma_t^4=2[\sigma^2+\gamma z_t]^2$. Only when the alternative is represented as a sequence of local alternatives $\gamma=T^{-\frac{1}{2}}\eta$ can this variance be treated as a constant, making the test only asymptotically locally most powerful.

A similar consideration emerges when Z is replaced by $\tilde{Z}$. From (4), $\hat{\gamma}=(\tilde{Z}'M_x\tilde{Z})^{-1}\tilde{Z}'M_xy$ and it is apparent that the limiting distribution of $T^{\frac{1}{2}}(\hat{\gamma}-\gamma)$ depends upon $T^{-\frac{1}{2}}\tilde{Z}'M_x(Z-\tilde{Z})\gamma$. Even if $\tilde{Z}$ and Z have the property that $T^{-1}\tilde{Z}'M_x\tilde{Z}-T^{-1}\tilde{Z}'M_xZ\xrightarrow{p}0$, i.e. the partial correlation between $\tilde{Z}$ and Z is unity in large samples, this term is not $0_p(1)$ unless $\gamma=T^{-\frac{1}{2}}\eta$. Statistics such as those for autocorrelation which use $\hat{u}_{-1}$ in place of u_{-1} therefore only possess an asymptotic power property. When Z is unknown, and a proxy $\tilde{Z}$ is employed which does not have a partial correlation of unity, there is a further loss of power. This loss may be measured by the difference in non-centrality parameters associated with the χ^2 statistics for testing $\gamma = 0$ when Z and $\tilde{Z}$ are used. Godfrey (1983b) gives this as

$$\sigma^2\eta'\{Z'M_x Z - Z'M_x\tilde{Z}(\tilde{Z}'M_x\tilde{Z})^{-1}\tilde{Z}'M_x Z\}\,\eta \geqslant 0,$$

highlighting the importance of Z, $\tilde{Z}$ and X in the determination of asymptotic power characteristics. One of the advantages of viewing diagnostic tests as variable addition is that a single formula can be exploited in making power comparisons of the efficacy of adding different variables for the detection of particular types of inadequacy.

Very little is known analytically concerning power performance in small samples, although there have been a large number of simulation studies. King (1983) surveys those on diagnostic tests for autocorrelation, Harvey and Phillips (1981) look at measures to detect heteroscedasticity in simultaneous equations, and so on. Perhaps the only established small-sample result is that due to King and Hillier (1980) who show that, when $\gamma \geqslant 0$ occurs in the alternative, the t-statistic that $\gamma = 0$ is locally most powerful invariant (provided $\tilde{Z} = Z$ of course).

5 Conclusion

Some years ago Denis Sargan made the following comment upon the nature of much applied work being done at that time: 'More generally, there are a range of tests for misspecification (including those for serial correlation) which are not very often used in applied work. Despite the problems associated with 'data mining' I consider that a suggested specification should be tested in all possible ways, and only those specifications which survive and correspond to a reasonable economic model should be used' (Sargan, 1975).

As many of the examples cited in this chapter attest, there is a substantial group in the profession now in agreement with this stance. But such a heightening of interest and experiment carries with it the danger of a confusion created by the existence and promulgation of a myriad of specification tests. Furthermore, it is not uncommon for researchers to emphasize what is unique or novel in their particular approach, and this can even lead to those whom it was designed to help despairing of assimilating such material. It would be tragic if it was the very proliferation and availability of methods which inhibited their widespread adoption.

The present chapter sought to rectify some of this imbalance. It concentrated upon the *common* characteristics of many tests for specification error. Such unity was achieved by exploiting the idea that existing diagnostic tests can be regarded as following simply from the addition of particular variables to a maintained relationship. Diversity in the measures was accounted for by the nature of the variable chosen for the addition, the relationship (moment) being augmented, the option chosen to estimate the expanded relation and the type of statistic constructed from these estimates. With this perspective, there should be little mystery attached to the origin of, and justification for, particular tests; an understanding of linear regression and instrumental variables would be a sufficient condition for researchers to appreciate and work with diagnostic tests in a wide variety of circumstances.

Specification errors were treated in this chapter as failures to specify correctly the conditional moments of the data. Thus, the presence of inadequacies such as autocorrelation, functional form and coefficient instability were interpreted as a divergence between the maintained and alternative first moments. Heteroscedasticity makes itself felt in the second moment, while distributional assumptions are frequently differentiated by higher-order moments. Section 2 of the chapter therefore classified diagnostic tests for the general linear regression model in this fashion, showing that the *principles* underlying the surveyed tests were extremely simple.

In section 3 the analysis was repeated, but this time allowing for the possibility that the equation under study was part of a system of simultaneous equations. These sections do little more than synthesize a wide range of existing work, and it was left to section 4 to take a brief look at a number of relatively new areas. Specifically, questions of independence and exact small-sample distributions were explored through the variable addition framework which is the unifying element of the chapter. More questions were posed than were answers provided, but it is to be hoped that an identification of the issues will stimulate further research on them.

It is worth ending by observing that the ideas presented herein are not restricted to regression models or structural equations. An example may clarify this contention. As Amemiya (1981) points out, models such as Logit or Probit have $E(y_t|x_t) = \Phi(x_t\beta)$ where Φ is the Logit or Probit function. Except for the complication that the conditional second moment is not constant in such models, the ideas in section 2.1 may be directly applied to assess whether this conditional mean is adequate or not. Of course the details will be different, but the guiding principles are the same. Such statistics are currently being developed, e.g. Jarque and Bera (1982) and Bera et al. (1982), from a likelihood viewpoint, but, as Chesher (1983) demonstrates, the notion of generalized residuals enables such tests to be re-interpreted in the framework of this chapter. Ultimately, it is to be hoped that a complete synthesis of diagnostic tests will be established; one that is both easy to communicate and upon which new developments can be made. The present chapter has been offered in that spirit.

6

The Encompassing Approach in Econometrics

GRAYHAM E. MIZON

> Empirical work that fails utterly to discriminate between competing explanations quickly degenerates into a sort of mindless instrumentalism, and it is not too much to say that the bulk of empirical work in modern economics is guilty on that score. Blaug (1980, p. 257)

1 Introduction

One of the most important activities in economics is the comparison of alternative theories and models. As in other disciplines, it is rare for there only to be one theory available to explain any particular phenomenon of interest. Coherence with the currently accepted general precepts of economic theory, and the requirement of logical consistency are obvious first yardsticks against which competing theories are measured. However, if a theory is to be useful and potentially durable, it must be empirically tested, and this is the role of econometrics. However, one of the important weaknesses characteristic of much empirical work published as part of the recent expansion of econometric activity has been a preoccupation with *confirming* theories (via 'correct' signs and magnitudes of estimated parameters, and high R^2 values) rather than *evaluating alternative* theories (using diagnostic test statistics to check for model inadequacies, and directly comparing alternative models). Thus Blaug (1980, p. 261) goes on to remark: 'In many areas of economics, different econometric studies reach conflicting conclusions and, given the available data, there are frequently no effective methods for deciding which conclusion is correct. In consequence, contradictory hypotheses continue to co-exist sometimes for decades or more.' Although this remark does not distinguish between comparison and selection, and it does not mention that the appropriate methods of comparison can be different when models are being used for different purposes, it does highlight the potential value of the encompassing principle, which is the main theme of this chapter.

The encompassing principle is concerned with the ability of a model to account for the behaviour of others, or less ambitiously, to explain the behaviour of relevant characteristics of other models. For example, consider one investigator who hypothesizes that the demand for money can be adequately explained as a function of real income, the price level, and the minimum lending rate, and a second investigator who believes that a model of the same form is appropriate except that the minimum lending rate is excluded, it being unimportant once the other two variables have been taken into account. It then follows that no matter what statistic the second investigator is interested in (e.g. an estimator of the income elasticity of money demand, or the one-period-ahead predictor of money demand) the first investigator using his model will be able to predict the behaviour (e.g. estimate the mean) of that statistic, and hence his model encompasses that of the second investigator. This follows automatically in this example, because the model of the second investigator is a special case of (or nested within) the first investigator's model. Trivial though this example (of one model encompassing another) is, it illustrates a property that the actual data generation process (DGP), whatever it may be, will always have. Hence one aspect of the encompassing principle is concerned with finding models that mimic this particular property of the DGP. However, a general model can always explain the behaviour of models that are restricted versions of it, and so a requirement that models encompass their rivals could lead to the adoption of the most general model feasible, given the data limitations. The principle of parsimony though militates against such action. Indeed a more interesting and valuable concept is that of a restricted model being able to perform as well as the model of which it is a special case, once account is taken of the difference in the degrees of freedom. If 'perform as well as' is interpreted in a hypothesis testing sense then this concept of encompassing leads directly to nested hypothesis testing. On the other hand if 'perform as well as' is interpreted in a model selection sense then the encompassing principle leads to selection criteria such as the *ad hoc* maximum $\bar{R}^2$ (Theil,

1961), minimum KLIC (Sawa, 1978) and minimum AIC (Akaike, 1973). Although the encompassing principle has been introduced and illustrated in the context of nested models many selection criteria, including those mentioned above, are intended to be applicable in comparing nested and non-nested models, and this is true of encompassing as well. In fact, it is one of the attractive features of the encompassing principle that it provides a simple framework for comparing nested and non-nested (or separate) models. Since general models always trivially encompass models which are restricted versions of them, and even when they are non-nested highly parameterized models are likely to encompass parsimoniously parameterized ones, attention will now be restricted to the parsimonious form of encompassing.

The comparison of models need not involve choosing a single preferred model: an important part of comparison is finding out what alternative models can (and cannot) do well, particularly in relation to the problem of interest. This was reflected above in the fact that the encompassing principle embraces both hypothesis testing and model selection, each having related, but distinct, roles in modelling. Hypothesis testing, whether part of specification searching (so that power against particular alternatives is important), or pure significance testing (e.g. tests of misspecification or diagnostic checks which do not have a single alternative in mind), is valuable in marshalling evidence for and against rival hypotheses. Model selection, on the other hand, uses evidence (such as that provided by hypothesis testing) to choose models which are preferred according to some criterion. Though hypothesis testing marshalls evidence and model selection uses evidence to take decisions, they are so closely related that the boundary between them is barely discernible at times, and this can lead to problems. For example, the fact that different models have very different policy implications can cause some economists to use model selection for 'practical purposes', when in fact the empirical evidence may not be sufficiently informative to allow clear discrimination between the models. In part, this misuse of model selection may arise because of the similarities of hypothesis testing and model selection being thought to be greater than they are as a result of the unfortunate terminology of significance testing – namely rejecting and accepting (strictly not rejecting) hypotheses (see Kendall and Stuart, 1967, p. 161).

In order to make the concept of model comparison operational it is necessary to choose a common distributional framework. This is discussed for different types of model, together with their relationship to the DGP, in section 2. Next, a basis of comparison must be chosen, which may be any statistic(s) of interest given the problem being analysed. For nested models, like the simple ones discussed above, obvious candidates are the log likelihood function, the score vector, and the parameter vector of the general model, the estimated value of each being compared under the restricted and the unrestricted hypotheses respectively. In fact, these choices lead to the three well-known asymptotically equivalent test statistics, likelihood ratio (LR), score or Lagrange multiplier (LM) and Wald (W), in this case. For example, consider the log likelihood function of the general model, denoted $L(\delta)$ when δ contains the parameters of that model. Hence, the statistic of interest from the general model is $L(\hat{\delta})$ when $\hat{\delta}$ is the maximum likelihood estimator of δ. Now if $\delta' = (\delta_1', \delta_2')$ and the restricted model corresponds to $\delta_2 = 0$, it follows that the restricted model will predict that $L(\hat{\delta})$ approaches $L(\delta^*)$ asymptotically, when $\delta^{*\prime} = (\delta_1', 0)$ which has $\tilde{\delta}' = (\tilde{\delta}_1, 0)$ as maximum likelihood estimator under the restricted hypothesis. Hence employing a basic idea from statistical inference (that of testing a theory by comparing the value of a statistic with an estimate of the theory's prediction of its value) the log likelihood ratio $L(\hat{\delta}) - L(\tilde{\delta})$ is obtained, and if its value is close to zero that is evidence in favour of the restricted model (though it does not confirm it), whereas poor agreement between $L(\hat{\delta})$ and $L(\tilde{\delta})$ is evidence against the restricted model. Since it is well known that $2[L(\hat{\delta}) - L(\tilde{\delta})]$ has a limiting $\chi^2(l_2)$ distribution on the restricted hypothesis, when l_2 is the dimension of δ_2, this immediately enables the restricted model to be compared with the general model using a significance test. For the other two 'obvious' statistics, the score vector $\partial L/\partial\delta$ and the parameter estimator $\hat{\delta}$, it is necessary to choose a metric in which to compare their values with the estimates of the restricted model's prediction of them. However, under suitable regularity conditions the differences (appropriately normed) have limiting normal distributions, so that quadratic forms having generalized inverses of the covariance matrices of these limiting distributions as metric, which have limiting χ^2 distributions, enable these statistics to be used in a significance test comparing the restricted with the unrestricted model. This approach is clearly similar to the use of χ^2 criteria for comparing models and generating estimators advocated by Berkson (1980). It is shown in section 3 that the Wald encompassing test statistic, developed along these lines, provides a unifying framework for a wide range of presently available test statistics, as well as being a generator of many more.

The use of the encompassing principle as part of a progressive modelling process is discussed in section 4. The encompassing approach does not require the existence of a stable and immutable DGP, nor is any model ever assumed to be the DGP. Rather a model, which has satisfied a wide range of model adequacy criteria as discussed elsewhere in this volume, is *temporarily* assumed to satisfy the axiom of correct specification (Leamer, 1978) in order that it can be used to make predictions about the behaviour of, and properties of statistics from, rival models. The accuracy of these predictions, which is an indication of the model's ability to encompass its rivals, is then a measure of that model's explanatory power as against that of competing models. The failure of one model to encompass another is instrumental in constructing 'better' models.

Before proceeding, we note an important topic that has been raised in the literature on sequential testing, and which is more widely relevant, namely the choice of an optimal significance level. That the unquestioning use of conventional (5 per cent or 1 per cent) significance levels may not be appropriate, became clear in pre-test estimation given its key role in the risk function (Toyoda and Wallace, 1976). Leamer (1978) draws attention to the limitations of the asymmetric treatment of the probabilities of Type I and Type II errors in classical hypothesis testing using conventional significance levels, namely that size is fixed at 0.05 or 0.01 whilst the power increases with sample size, and suggests that the chosen significance level should decrease with increases in the sample size. Noting that in econometrics all models are no more than approximations relative to the DGP, and that consistent tests are usually employed, it follows that such tests will tend to be conservative (i.e. reject the restricted model) for large enough sample size. Conversely, if a particular test statistic is known (perhaps from experience in its use or from Monte Carlo analysis) to have low power against important alternatives in finite samples, then it may be appropriate to increase the significance level in order to reduce the probability of Type II error; tests for unit roots (Sargan and Bhargava, 1983; Dickey and Fuller, 1981; Evans and Savin, 1981, 1984) appear to have low power against alternatives close to unity. Hence, in hypothesis testing generally and that discussed in this chapter care should be taken in the choice of significance levels, rather than adopting conventional levels unquestioningly.

2 Models and Model Comparison

The particular problem being analysed, the set of relevant competing theories and the measurement equations, provide a menu of variables for which observations are required. Let the full set of such variables be denoted by the vector w, a sample of n observations on them be denoted by $W_n^1 = (w_1, w_2, \ldots, w_n)$, and the process generating these variables be $D(W_n^1 | W_0, \Psi)$ where W_0 is the matrix of initial conditions and Ψ is a parameter vector. It is assumed that any marginalizations with respect to variables jointly determined with w, implicit in $D(W_n^1 | W_0, \Psi)$, are valid. Note that the DGP for W_n^1, namely $D(W_n^1 | W_0, \Psi)$, has all the empirical models associated with the competing economic theories as special cases, and so were it known it would provide a framework to interpret and determine the relationship between the competing empirical models. Although the DGP is not known, and given the limited sample evidence typically available is likely to remain unknown, the *concept* of a DGP remains useful since it provides a framework in which to interpret and compare alternative models. Moreover, the encompassing principle does not require the existence of a stable DGP with constant parameters, since all that it involves is the comparison of theory based predictions with observed values.

Alternative empirical models will rarely be concerned with all variables in w_t, and a typical empirical model M_α is characterized by: (a) a choice of jointly dependent variables y_t; (b) a choice of conditioning or exogenous variables z_t; and (c) a set of hypothesized density functions

$$f(y_t | z_t, Y_{t-1}, Z_{t-1}, \alpha), \qquad t = 1, \ldots, n$$

where α is a $k \times 1$ parameter vector, $Y_{t-1} = (Y_0, Y_{t-1}^1)$ and $Z_{t-1} = (Z_0, Z_{t-1}^1)$. Such an empirical model involves implicit marginalization with respect to those variables in w_t but not included in y_t and z_t, and requires z_t to be weakly exogenous – for further discussion of these points see Engle et al. (1983). In addition, models often incorporate conditional independence assumptions or hypotheses such as:

$$f(y_t | z_t, Y_{t-1}, Z_{t-1}, \alpha) = f(y_t | x_t, \alpha) \qquad t = 1, \ldots, n$$

when x_t includes all retained conditioning variables, i.e. conditionally on z_t, Y_{t-1} and Z_{t-1} the endogenous variables y_t are uncorrelated with those conditioning variables not included in x_t. These points, and the role of the general model (which is analogous to, though different from, the DGP), can be illustrated by the choice of regressors problem.

$$\begin{aligned} y &= X_1\beta + u_1 \qquad u_1 \sim N(0, \sigma^2 I_n) \\ y &= X_2\gamma + u_2 \qquad u_2 \sim N(0, \tau^2 I_n) \end{aligned} \tag{1}$$

when y is $n \times 1$, X_1 is $n \times k$, X_2 is $n \times l$ each of full column rank and (for simplicity only) having no variables in common. Clearly X_1 and X_2 are being treated as valid conditioning variables, but in which distributions? One possible interpretation of equation (1) is

$$\begin{aligned} y \mid X_1 &\sim N(X_1\beta, \sigma^2 I) \\ y \mid X_2 &\sim N(X_2\gamma, \tau^2 I) \end{aligned} \tag{2}$$

However, such an interpretation means that the two models involve different conditional distributions, and so the use of techniques which critically rely on competing hypotheses referring to a common distribution is precluded. Indeed, conventional hypothesis testing cannot be used to compare the models in (2), which is not surprising when it is realized that the first model has nothing to say about X_2. Furthermore, both models in (2) could be 'true' if y, X_1 and X_2 have a multivariate normal distribution. Comparing the error variance estimators $\hat{\sigma}^2$ and $\hat{\tau}^2$ might be useful in choosing between the models, but will *not* yield a significance test. A commonsense approach to discriminating between the models in (2) would test the least squares residuals for normality and heteroscedasticity, but this only provides an indirect test of one model against the other.

A more satisfactory interpretation of (1) is:

$$\begin{aligned} H_1 &: y \mid X_1, X_2 \sim N(X_1\beta, \sigma^2 I) \\ H_2 &: y \mid X_1, X_2 \sim N(X_2\gamma, \tau^2 I) \end{aligned} \tag{3}$$

so that the models represent conditional independence hypotheses on the distribution of y conditional on X_1 and X_2. Hence the two models in (3) involve testable hypotheses, and because they are both defined on a common distribution, hypothesis testing can be used to compare them. Though the distribution of y conditional on X_1 and X_2 provides a general framework in which the models of (3) can be compared, marginalization with respect to any other potentially relevant variables and the weak exogeneity of X_1 and

X_2 for the parameters of interest, need to be valid and should be tested where possible. The importance of considering the distribution of y conditional on X_1 and X_2 is further emphasized by noting that many of the diagnostic checks used in the process of model evaluation are concerned with properties (e.g. white-noise errors and mean innovation errors) that are defined with respect to an information set, and for the choice of regressors problem this set should include y, X_1 and X_2. However, it must be emphasized that whilst the distribution of y conditional on X_1 and X_2 (whatever form that distribution may take) provides the common distributional framework for comparing H_1 and H_2 in (3), the particular general model $y|X_1, X_2 \sim N(X_1\beta^* + X_2\gamma^*, \omega^2 I)$ need not be treated as a maintained model, in that even if H_1 and H_2 are found to be inadequate there is no necessity to take this general model as the 'preferred' model. Indeed, although the test for H_1 encompassing H_2 with respect to $\hat{\gamma} = (X_2'X_2)^{-1}X_2'y$ is later shown to take the same form as the conventional F-test of the hypothesis $\gamma^* = 0$ in the general model defined above, that particular general model has no essential role in the derivation of the encompassing test. The fact that the encompassing test and the conventional F-test take the same form in this case is of no importance, other than providing an alternative interpretation, and results from the special properties that normal linear models have.

The argument in favour of having a common distributional framework for model comparison applies to problems more general than the choice of regressors problem. Indeed, Mizon (1977a, b) and Hendry (1980) provide other examples, as well as emphasizing the role of the general model in a general-to-specific approach to specification searching. Note that the concepts of a common distributional framework and a general model are distinct. The specification of a common distributional framework does not give a particular form to the distribution, nor is it characterized by parameters. A general model on the other hand does involve the specification of a particular class of distributions and is characterized by parameters, some of which can act as indicators for the alternative models which are special cases of it – e.g. the elasticities of substitution in the two-level CES function of Sato (1967), or the weighting parameter of the Box and Cox (1964) transformation which embeds the linear and logarithmic forms in a single function. Furthermore, it is a common distributional framework that is essential for encompassing tests, not a general model. Although it is sometimes argued that general models lack a sensible economic interpretation, this is not an argument against having a coherent view of the distribution of the full set of variables being considered, rather it is an argument against concocting comprehensive models. General models are best obtained by specifying a particular form for the distribution of relevant variables, rather than being hybrid comprehensive models obtained via linear or exponential weighting of rival models (see Quandt, 1974; Pesaran, 1982). In addition, the fact that a general model may have few degrees of freedom and may overfit, is no argument against the interpretative and testing framework that the common distributional framework provides. It is rather an argument in favour of easily interpretable and data coherent simplifications of a general model, but it is knowledge of the common distributional framework that enables rival simplified models to be compared.

As a further illustration of the need for a clear specification of the distributions underlying rival models, consideration is now given to models with partially overlapping variables. Let y_t, z_t, $\{f(.)\}$, α, denote respectively the endogenous variables, the exogenous variables, the density functions, and the k parameters characterizing model M_α. The corresponding notation for a rival model M_δ is y^*, z^*, $\{g(.)\}$, δ when δ is $l \times 1$, it being noted that in practice there will usually be more than two competing models though most of the important issues can be dealt with using two models. For the purposes of this discussion it is assumed that it is desired to test whether M_α encompasses M_δ with respect to a statistic of interest under M_δ which therefore is a function of y_t^* and z_t^*. Firstly, note that if $y_t = y_t^*$, $f(.) = g(.)$ and $z_t^* \subset z_t$, with the additional conditioning variables z_t^{**} excluded from z_t^* because M_δ hypothesizes that y_t conditional on z_t is independent of z_t^{**} (as in the demand for money example discussed earlier), then M_δ is nested within M_α and so M_α automatically encompasses M_δ. However, if M_δ does not involve the conditional independence hypothesis, M_α and M_δ are not defined on a common distribution, and so they cannot be compared using significance tests without further information. In particular, it is necessary to know the joint distribution of y_t and z_t^{**} conditional on z_t^* so that z_t^{**} can be integrated out. That is, it is necessary to endogenize z_t^{**} and then marginalize with respect to z_t^{**}, in order to make M_α (strictly a modified M_α) and M_δ comparable. Secondly, if $y_t = y_t^*$, $f(.) = g(.)$, but z_t and z_t^* have no variables in common (e.g. the choice of regressors problem in (1)) then hypothesis testing cannot be used to compare M_α and M_δ unless each is a conditional independence hypothesis as in (3). In the conditional independence case the common distributional framework is the distribution of y_t conditional on z_t and z_t^*, which enables the comparison of M_α and M_δ using hypothesis tests. Note though that if M_α and M_δ are not conditional independence hypotheses then M_α and M_δ *per se* cannot be compared directly using hypothesis tests – they are non-comparable and in fact can be equally valid.

In the cases above it was assumed that M_α and M_δ were concerned with the same endogenous variables, i.e. $y_t = y_t^*$. If $y_t^* \subset y_t$ then no additional problems arise in considering tests for M_α encompassing M_δ, though clearly it will not be possible for M_δ to encompass M_α with respect to statistics involving endogenous variables not included in M_δ. Another possibility is that some of the endogenous variables in M_α are exogenous in M_δ and vice versa. Provided that the full set of variables in M_δ is a subset of those in M_α cases of this type cause no conceptual problems, since all statistics of interest under M_δ will be well-defined functions of variables whose status is unambiguous under M_α. However, the derivation of the distribution of the encompassing test statistics will not be able to rely on the conventional results about ML (maximum likelihood) and pseudo-ML estimators, since the sets of endogenous variables in M_α and M_δ differ. This means that each case will have to be dealt with separately rather than being able to use general results. An obvious alternative to this consists of 'reducing' each model to a common set of endogenous variables by conditioning in each model on all variables other than the common set of endogenous variables, and then applying the standard analysis to the submodels. This procedure offers the advantage that it requires no additional assumptions on M_α and M_δ, though the analysis is based on submodels not M_α and M_δ. With this limitation in mind, another alternative is to 'extend' M_α and M_δ to a common set of endogenous variables, though this might prove impractical when M_α and M_δ have been developed initially by independent modellers.

Turning now to cases in which $y_t \subset y_t^*$ and $z_t \subset z_t^*$ (when y_t^e and z_t^e denote the endogenous and exogenous variables excluded from M_α), obviously M_δ can be marginalized with respect to y_t^e so that the modified M_δ has the same endogenous variables as M_α. However, the variables in z_t^e cause more problems, since M_δ cannot be marginalized with respect to exogenous variables without 'endogenizing' them first. Modifications of M_δ of this type may be undesirable since they can give a misrepresentation of the gestalt of M_δ, especially if it was not developed by the modeller who wishes to compare M_α with it. The alternative, which is preferable generally is to extend M_α by making clear the position of z_t^e in it. A simple solution that can be considered is to incorporate z_t^e in the set of conditioning variables for M_α by means of a conditional independence hypothesis so that $f(y_t|z_t, \alpha) \equiv f(y_t|z_t, z_t^e, \alpha)$, $t = 1, \ldots, n$. If such a conditional independence hypothesis is inappropriate, then M_α has to be 'completed' by the specification of an additional distribution $f(z_t^e|z_t, y_t, \lambda^e)$, so that the status of z_t^e in M_α is made explicit. To the extent that this latter distribution was omitted from M_α initially because of uncertainty about its specification, the modeller may be uneasy with the outcome if the 'completed' M_α fails to encompass M_δ. To some extent this may be overcome by trying alternative specifications of $f(z_t^e|z_t, y_t, \lambda^e)$, though ultimately it has to be realized that the specification of such a distribution is necessary to 'complete' M_α, and it is only then that M_α and M_δ can be compared within a comprehensive framework – comparison otherwise must be within a framework of submodels.

The above examples have been concerned with finding a common distributional framework to enable M_α and M_δ to be compared when they differ in the set of variables they involve and possibly in their classification of them into endogenous and exogenous variables. It is also possible for rival models to specify different functional forms for the distributions $f(.)$ and $g(.)$, e.g. normal and log-normal densities. In some cases comparison of alternative distributions can be made on the basis of properties of the data, e.g. if the endogenous variable of interest can never be negative it makes less sense to consider it to be normally distributed (when the model can predict negative values) than it does to use a log-normal or similar distribution which is only defined for non-negative values. Similarly, if a variable is bounded between 0 and 1 a Logit or Probit model is likely to be more appropriate than a normal linear regression (Maddala, 1983). Hence the requirement that empirical models should yield predictions which satisfy with probability one the data constraints that characterize a variable can limit the range of admissible distributions $f(.)$ and $g(.)$. It has to be recognized though that it may be impossible to choose functions which satisfy all the data constraints relevant to a variable. One problem for which data constraints could provide sufficient evidence for a modeller to prefer one function rather than another is that of comparing a linear with a logarithmic model. This problem though has attracted a great deal of attention, and many test statistics have been proposed – see Evans and Deaton (1980), Godfrey and Wickens (1981), Poirier and Ruud (1979), among others. Since the endogenous variable in one model is the logarithm of the endogenous variable in the other, it is necessary to introduce the transformation Jacobian into one model in order to give them a common distributional framework. This is precisely what Sargan (1964) did in proposing a likelihood ratio criterion for discriminating between log and linear formulations. In general, if $y = h(y^*)$ then $f(y\,|\,z, \alpha)$ and $g(y^*\,|\,z^*, \delta)\,|\partial h/\partial y^*|$ provide the appropriate distributions (when account is taken of the differences between z and z^* as discussed above) for comparing M_α and M_δ in the framework of the distribution of y conditional on the variables in z and z^*.

Finally, note that in order to simplify notation, the possibility that M_α and M_δ contain lagged values of the endogenous and exogenous variables was not explicitly allowed for. Dynamic models are easily incorporated into the framework by augmenting the conditioning variables z_t and z_t^* by (Y_{t-1}, Z_{t-1}) and (Y_{t-1}^*, Z_{t-1}^*) respectively.

Once a common distributional framework has been chosen, and the rival models M_α and M_δ modified if necessary, it is possible to test the hypothesis that one model encompasses the other. In order to do this it is necessary to add to the common distributional framework a basis for comparison of the rival models. The framework for comparison consists of the common set of relevant variables, their classification into endogenous and exogenous or predetermined variables for each model, and maybe a transformation Jacobian. The basis of comparison is any statistic of interest in one model (say M_δ) which enables the possibility of another model (say M_a) encompassing M_δ to be assessed via its ability to explain the behaviour of this statistic. The implementation of this using Wald encompassing tests is discussed in the next section.

3 Encompassing Tests

Let $\tilde{b}$, an $r \times 1$ ($r \leqslant l$, when $l = \dim \delta$) vector, be a statistic relevant to the analysis of M_δ and hence a function of y^* and z^*, when z^* is now assumed to include exogenous and predetermined variables when appropriate. In view of the previous discussion of the need for a common distributional framework it is also assumed that, though the primary motive in selecting $\tilde{b}$ will be to choose a statistic of particular interest for the analysis of M_δ face-to-face with M_α, $\tilde{b}$ remains a well-defined function of variables whose status is unambiguous under M_α. As a consequence, it will be possible to consider $\tilde{b}$ which are functions of y and z as well as y^* and z^*, but it is essential that $\tilde{b}$ be a function of the latter variables if it is to be used as a basis of comparison of M_α and M_δ. Furthermore, let $b_\alpha = E_\alpha(\tilde{b})$ denote the expectation of b under M_α. If convenient E_α will be replaced by plim_α (i.e. plim under M_α) which in most cases will not affect the large-sample distributions of the statistics considered below. Note that b_α will be a function of α and the conditioning variables of M (suitably modified if necessary as discussed in section 2), and is therefore unknown since α is unknown. However, b_α can be estimated by replacing α by its maximum likelihood (or equivalent) estimator under M_α, namely $\hat{\alpha}$, to yield $b_{\hat{\alpha}} = E_\alpha(\tilde{b})_{\alpha=\hat{\alpha}}$. The ability of M_α to explain the behaviour of b can now be assessed by comparing $\tilde{b}$ with its prediction based on M_α, $b_{\hat{\alpha}}$. That is, comparison of the observed statistic $\tilde{b}$ with the estimate of its theoretical value under M_α, $b_{\hat{\alpha}}$, embodies the essence of the encompassing principle as applied to the comparison of M_α and M_δ with respect to $\tilde{b}$. However, since $\tilde{b}$ is a statistic of interest under M_δ (or at least characterizes a relevant aspect of the data employed in M_δ), it is appropriate to consider what in M_δ underlies $\tilde{b}$, i.e. evaluate $E_\delta(\tilde{b})$. Letting $b = E_\delta(\tilde{b})$ and $\phi = (b - b_\alpha)$ with $\hat{\phi} = (\tilde{b} - b_{\hat{\alpha}})$ leads to:

Definition 1 M_α encompasses M_δ with respect to $\tilde{b}$ iff $E_\alpha(\hat{\phi}) = 0$.

The obvious way to begin the derivation of a significance test of the encompassing hypothesis $E_\alpha(\hat{\phi}) = 0$, is to obtain the limiting distribution of $\sqrt{n}\hat{\phi} = \sqrt{n}(\tilde{b} - b_{\hat{\alpha}})$ under M_α. Before doing this for the general case consider the choice of regressors problem in (3). Taking the OLS estimator of γ in H_2 to be the basis for comparing H_1 and H_2 we have $\tilde{b} = \hat{\gamma} = (X_2'X_2)^{-1}X_2'y$. Hence

$$b_\alpha = E_1(\hat{\gamma}) = (X_2'X_2)^{-1}X_2'X_1\beta = \gamma_\alpha \text{ say,}$$

and

$$b_{\hat{\alpha}} = (X_2'X_2)^{-1}X_2'X_1(X_1'X_1)^{-1}X_1'y = \gamma_{\hat{\alpha}},$$

so that in this case $\hat{\phi} = (\tilde{b} - b_{\hat{\alpha}}) = (\hat{\gamma} - \gamma_{\hat{\alpha}}) = (X_2'X_2)^{-1}X_2'M_1y$ when $M_1 = I_n - X_1(X_1'X_1)^{-1}X_1'$. Note that γ_α is the pseudo-true value of $\hat{\gamma}$ (Sawa, 1978) which suggests that the existing results on the limiting distribution of pseudo-maximum likelihood estimators (Cox, 1961, 1962; Gourieroux et al., 1984; Huber, 1967; Kent, 1982; White, 1982a) might be helpful in obtaining the required test statistic. In fact, for this example these results are sufficient to obtain the limiting distribution under M_α of $\sqrt{n}(\hat{\gamma}-\gamma_\alpha)$, from which it is straightforward to derive those of $\sqrt{n}(\gamma_{\hat{\alpha}}-\gamma_\alpha)$ and $\sqrt{n}(\hat{\gamma}-\gamma_{\hat{\alpha}})$. Hence some of the existing results on pseudo-ML estimators, which prove helpful more generally than the choice of regressors problem, though they are not sufficient for all cases considered below, are now summarized and extended using our notation.

3.1 *Relevant Limiting Distributions*

Under the assumption that the process generating the full set of relevant variables W_n[1] is non-deterministic, covariance stationary and ergodic, with zero means and nonsingular contemporaneous covariance matrix, and under suitable regularity conditions (similar to those discussed by e.g. Huber (1967), Kent (1982) and White (1982a) for the iid case), the joint limiting distribution of the ML estimators $\hat{\alpha}$ and $\hat{\delta}$ on M_α is given by:

$$\begin{pmatrix}\sqrt{n}(\hat{\alpha}-\alpha)\\ \sqrt{n}(\hat{\delta}-\delta_\alpha)\end{pmatrix}\xrightarrow[M_\alpha]{d} N\left(\begin{pmatrix}0\\0\end{pmatrix},\begin{pmatrix}V(\hat{\alpha}) & C(\hat{\alpha},\hat{\delta})\\ C(\hat{\alpha},\hat{\delta})' & V_\alpha(\hat{\delta})\end{pmatrix}\right) \tag{4}$$

when $\hat{\alpha}$ and $\hat{\delta}$ are the ML estimators of α and δ under M_α and M_δ respectively, $L_f(\alpha)$ and $L_g(\delta)$ are the corresponding log-likelihood functions, $\delta_\alpha = E_\alpha(\hat{\delta})$, and when,

$$V(\hat{\alpha}) = \left(\lim_{n\to\infty} -\frac{1}{n}E\frac{\partial^2 L_f}{\partial\alpha\,\partial\alpha'}\right)^{-1}$$

$$C(\hat{\alpha},\hat{\delta}) = V(\hat{\alpha})\,D' \text{ with } D = \frac{\partial\delta_\alpha}{\partial\alpha'}$$

$$V_\alpha(\hat{\delta}) = H^{-1}JH^{-1} \text{ with } H = \left(\lim_{n\to\infty} -\frac{1}{n}E_\alpha\frac{\partial^2 L_g}{\partial\delta\,\partial\delta'}\right)_{\delta=\delta_\alpha} \tag{5}$$

and

$$J = \lim_{n\to\infty} E_\alpha\left(\frac{1}{n}\frac{\partial L_g}{\partial\delta}\frac{\partial L_g}{\partial\delta'}\right)_{\delta=\delta_\alpha}.$$

Mizon and Richard (1983) extend this result in a theorem which is re-stated here for convenience.

Theorem 1 Under the same conditions needed for the ML (or asymptotically equivalent) estimators $\hat{\alpha}$ and $\hat{\delta}$ to have the joint limiting distribution given in (4) and (5) on M_α, and provided that $\text{plim}_\alpha(\partial\delta_\alpha/\partial\alpha') = D$, an $l \times k$ matrix, and $\text{plim}_\alpha(\partial^2\delta_{\hat{\alpha}}/\partial\alpha\,\partial\alpha')$ are finite, the following results hold, where d indicates convergence in distribution:

(a) $\sqrt{n}(\delta_{\hat{\alpha}} - \delta_\alpha) \underset{M_\alpha}{\overset{d}{\longrightarrow}} N(0, V_\alpha(\delta_{\hat{\alpha}}))$ when $V_\alpha(\delta_{\hat{\alpha}}) = DV(\hat{\alpha})\,D'$

(*b*) $\sqrt{n}(\hat{\delta} - \delta_{\hat{\alpha}}) = \sqrt{n}\Delta \underset{M_\alpha}{\overset{d}{\longrightarrow}} N(0, V_\alpha(\hat{\Delta}))$

when $V_\alpha(\hat{\Delta}) = V_\alpha(\hat{\delta}) - V_\alpha(\delta_{\hat{\alpha}})$.

Returning to the choice of regressors problem, the distributional result (b) can now be used to obtain a test of H_1 encompassing H_2 with respect to $\hat{\gamma}$ (i.e. $H_1\mathscr{E}H_2(\hat{\gamma})$). Note that M_δ (i.e. H_2 in this case) has $\delta' = (\gamma', \tau^2)$ and so choosing $\hat{\gamma}$ as the statistic of interest means that the limiting distribution of $\sqrt{n}(\hat{\gamma} - \gamma_{\hat{\alpha}})$ under H_1 is required. This follows immediately from (b) as

$$\sqrt{n}(\hat{\gamma} - \gamma_{\hat{\alpha}}) = \sqrt{n}(X_2'X_2)^{-1}X_2'M_1 y \underset{H_1}{\overset{d}{\longrightarrow}} N(0, V_\alpha(\hat{\gamma} - \gamma_{\hat{\alpha}}))$$

when $M_1 = I - X_1(X_1'X_1)^{-1}X_1'$ and

$$\begin{aligned} V_\alpha(\hat{\gamma} - \gamma_{\hat{\alpha}}) &= V_\alpha(\hat{\gamma}) - V_\alpha(\gamma_{\hat{\alpha}}) \\ &= \text{plim}_\alpha\, n\sigma^2(X_2'X_2)^{-1}X_2'M_1X_2(X_2'X_2)^{-1} \end{aligned}$$

– see Mizon and Richard (1983, section 2.6). Hence

$$\begin{aligned} \eta_w(\hat{\gamma}) &= n(\hat{\gamma} - \gamma_{\hat{\alpha}})'\hat{V}_\alpha(\hat{\gamma} - \gamma_{\hat{\alpha}})^{-1}(\hat{\gamma} - \gamma_{\hat{\alpha}}) \\ &= y'M_1X_2(X_2'M_1X_2)^{-1}X_2'M_1 y/\hat{\sigma}^2 \underset{H_1}{\overset{d}{\longrightarrow}} \chi^2(l) \end{aligned}$$

provides a Wald encompassing test (WET) of $H_1\mathscr{E}H_3(\hat{\gamma})$. Furthermore, in this case a simple transformation of $\eta_w(\hat{\gamma})$ gives an encompassing test statistic which has an exact $F(l, n-l-k)$ distribution on H_1. The transformed test statistic is

$$\frac{(n-l-k)\,\sigma^2}{l(\hat{u}_1'M_{12}\hat{u}_1)}\,\eta_w(\hat{\gamma})$$

when

$$\hat{u}_2 = M_1 y,\ M_2 = I - X_2(X_2'X_2)^{-1}X_2',$$
$$M_{12} = I - X_{12}(X_{12}'X_{12})^{-1}X_{12}' \text{ and } X_{12} = M_2 X_1.$$

This transformed statistic is identical with the conventional F-statistic for testing the hypothesis $\gamma^* = 0$ in the model

$$H_3 : y \mid X_1, X_2 \sim N(X_1\beta^* + X_2\gamma^*, \omega^2 I),$$

even though H_3 played no role in obtaining the WET statistic. Indeed the only significance of this identity is that the F-statistic can be given an encompassing interpretation.

Alternatively, if the ML estimator of τ^2 under H_2, $\hat{\tau}^2$, was chosen as the basis for comparing H_1 and H_2 then (b) of Theorem 1 yields

$$\sqrt{n}(\hat{\tau}^2 - \tau_{\hat{\alpha}}^{\ 2}) = n^{-\frac{1}{2}}(n-l)\,((\hat{\tau}^2 - \hat{\sigma}^2) - \hat{\beta}'X_1'M_2X_1\hat{\beta}) \xrightarrow[H_1]{d} N(0, V_\alpha(\hat{\tau}^2 - \tau_{\hat{\alpha}}^{\ 2}))$$

when

$$n\hat{\tau}^2 = (n-l)\,\tilde{\tau}^2 = y'M_2 y,$$
$$n\tau_{\hat{\alpha}}^{\ 2} = (n-l)\,\sigma^2 + \hat{\beta}'X_1'M_2X_1\hat{\beta}, \qquad n\hat{\sigma}^2 = y'M_1 y,$$
$$\hat{\beta} = (X_1'X_1)^{-1}X_1'y,$$
$$\hat{V}_\alpha(\hat{\tau}^2 - \tau_{\hat{\alpha}}^{\ 2}) = \hat{V}_\alpha(\hat{\tau}^2) - \hat{V}_\alpha(\tau_{\hat{\alpha}}^{\ 2}) = 4\hat{\sigma}^2\hat{\beta}'X_1'M_2M_1M_2X_1\hat{\beta}/n.$$

Hence

$$\eta_w(\hat{\tau}^2) = n(\hat{\tau}^2 - \tau_{\hat{\alpha}}^{\ 2})^2/\hat{V}_\alpha(\hat{\tau}^2 - \tau_{\hat{\alpha}}^{\ 2})$$
$$= \frac{[(n-l)\,(\hat{\tau}^2 - \hat{\sigma}^2) - \hat{\beta}'X_1'M_2X_1\hat{\beta}]^2}{4\hat{\sigma}^2\hat{\beta}'X_1'M_2M_1M_2X_1\hat{\beta}} \xrightarrow[H_1]{d} \chi^2(1)$$

which is the WET for $H_1 \mathcal{E} H_2(\hat{\tau}^2)$. Mizon and Richard (1983) prove that this WET statistic is asymptotically equivalent to the Cox (1961) generalized likelihood ratio test, the Davidson and MacKinnon (1981) J-test, the Pesaran (1974) N^2-test, and the JA-test of Fisher and McAleer (1981), each of which is a $\chi^2(1)$ non-nested test for comparing H_1 and H_2 of (3).

Whilst H_3 has no role in the above analysis of the encompassing tests $\eta_w(\hat{\gamma})$ and $\eta_w(\hat{\tau}^2)$ – H_1 and H_2 are sufficient for that analysis – an obvious indirect way of comparing H_1 and H_2 is through H_3.

Since both H_1 and H_2 are special cases of H_3, H_3 automatically encompasses the other two models. In considering the more interesting concept of parsimonious encompassing though, it is possible to test for $H_1 \mathscr{E} H_3(\hat{\gamma}^*)$, $H_2 \mathscr{E} H_3(\hat{\beta}^*)$ and $H_1 \mathscr{E} H_3(\hat{\gamma})$, and for this, degrees of freedom adjustments might be expected to be relevant. Clearly if the asymptotic forms of the appropriate WET statistics are used, and only their asymptotic behaviour is being considered, degrees of freedom adjustments are unimportant. However, further analysis of the conventional F-statistic for H_1 being an acceptable simplification of H_3, which for all sample sizes is distributed as $F(l, n-l-k)$ on H_1, reveals the role of degrees of freedom adjustments. In particular, it is possible to show that the conventional F-test for $H_1 \mathscr{E} H_3(\hat{\gamma}^*)$ has the form $[(n-k)(\tilde{\sigma}^2 - \tilde{\omega}^2) + l\tilde{\omega}^2]/l\tilde{\omega}^2$ when $(n-k)\tilde{\sigma}^2 = y'M_1y$ and $(n-l-k)\tilde{\omega}^2 = y'M_*y$ with $M_* = I - X^*(X^{*\prime}X^*)^{-1}X^*$ and $X^{*\prime} = (X_1{}'X_2{}')$, so that $\tilde{\sigma}^2$ and $\tilde{\omega}^2$ are the degrees of freedom adjusted (unbiased) estimators of σ^2 and ω^2 under H_1 and H_3 respectively. Hence whenever $\tilde{\sigma}^2 < \tilde{\omega}^2$ (nb $y'M_1y \geqslant y'M_*y$) the conventional F-statistic will be less than unity and so the significance test will not reject $H_1 \mathscr{E} H_3(\hat{\gamma}^*)$. Similarly, $\tilde{\tau}^2 < \tilde{\omega}^2$ is a sufficient condition for the conventional F-test of $\beta^* = 0$ not to reject $H_2 \mathscr{E} H_3(\hat{\beta}^*)$. Thus degrees of freedom adjusted equation standard error dominance is in this case a sufficient condition for not rejecting model simplification. However, in the linear least squares framework degrees of freedom adjusted estimated residual variance dominance is not a sufficient condition in general for not rejecting encompassing. In fact, the transformed $\eta_w(\hat{\gamma})$ statistic can be written as

$$\frac{(n-k)(\tilde{\sigma}^2 - \tilde{\tau}^2) + l\tilde{\tau}^2 - k(\tilde{\tau}^2 - \bar{\tau}^2)}{l\bar{\tau}^2 + lk(\tilde{\tau}^2 - \bar{\tau}^2)/(n-l-k)}$$

when $k\bar{\tau}^2 = y'M_2X_{12}(X_{12}{}'X_{12})^{-1}X_{12}{}'M_2y$, from which it is clear $\tilde{\sigma}^2 < \tilde{\tau}^2$ is not a sufficient condition for the statistic to be less than unity. Note though that both $\tilde{\tau}^2$ and $\bar{\tau}^2$ are unbiased estimators of τ^2 under H_2, and they have equal expectations under H_1, so that if the transformed $\eta_w(\hat{\gamma})$ is less than unity, $\tilde{\sigma}^2 < \tilde{\tau}^2$ will be expected. It should be emphasized though, that in general it will be inappropriate to select models using a variance-dominance criterion (even if it is degrees of freedom adjusted), rather than adopting a strategy which seeks an encompassing model which will then usually have variance dominance as a property.

The above analysis of the choice of regressors problem illustrates the fact that many encompassing tests can be derived using the existing results for pseudo-ML estimators. There are though important cases for which this is not possible, e.g. Cox's generalized likelihood ratio test. Therefore, attention is now turned to cases in which $\tilde{b} = b(Y_n^1, \hat{\delta})$, which although more general than the cases considered earlier, will be able to make use of the known results for the pseudo-ML estimator $\hat{\delta}$. The following definitions are needed in order to state the required limiting distribution of $\sqrt{n}\hat{\phi}$ under M_α:

$$\bar{B}(\alpha, \delta) = \text{plim}_\alpha\, B(Y_n^1, \delta) \text{ when } B(Y_n^1, \delta) = \frac{\partial b(Y_n^1, \delta)}{\partial \delta'}$$

$$\phi^* = b(Y_n^1, \delta_\alpha) - b_\alpha - \Phi_\alpha(\hat{\alpha} - \alpha)$$

$$\Phi_\alpha = \lim_{n \to \infty} \frac{1}{n} E_\alpha\left(b(Y_n^1, \delta_\alpha) \cdot \frac{\partial L_f}{\partial \alpha'} \right).$$

Theorem 2 of Mizon and Richard (1983) is now re-stated:

Theorem 2 Assume that the r functions in $b(Y_n^1, \delta)$ are continuous and differentiable with respect to δ in the neighbourhood of $\delta = \delta_\alpha$ such that the $r \times l$ matrix $\bar{B}(\alpha, \delta_\alpha)$ is finite of rank r, and the $r \times l$ matrices $\text{plim}_\alpha (\partial B(Y_n^1, \delta)/\partial \delta_i)_{\delta^*}$ for $i = 1, 2, \ldots$ are finite when $\|\delta_\alpha - \delta^*\| < \epsilon$, $\epsilon > 0$. Then, under the conditions of Theorem 1

$$\sqrt{n}\hat{\phi} = \sqrt{n}\phi^* + \bar{B}(\alpha, \delta_\alpha)\sqrt{n}\hat{\Delta} + o_p(1)$$

and so if (a) $\sqrt{n}\phi^*$ is $o_p(1)$ then $\sqrt{n}\hat{\phi} = \bar{B}(\alpha, \delta_\alpha)\sqrt{n}\hat{\Delta} + o_p(1)$ so that

$$\sqrt{n}\hat{\phi} \xrightarrow[M_\alpha]{d} N(0, \bar{B}(\alpha, \delta_\alpha)\, V_\alpha(\hat{\Delta})\, \bar{B}(\alpha, \delta_\alpha)')$$

whereas if (b) $\sqrt{n}\phi^* \xrightarrow[M_\alpha]{d} N(0, V_\alpha(\phi^*))$ when $V_\alpha(\phi^*)$ is of rank r then

$$\sqrt{n}\hat{\phi} \xrightarrow[M_\alpha]{d} N(0, V_\alpha(\hat{\phi}))$$

with

$$V_\alpha(\hat{\phi}) = V_\alpha(\phi^*) + \bar{B}(\alpha, \delta_\alpha)\, V_\alpha(\hat{\Delta})\, \bar{B}(\alpha, \delta_\alpha)' + C_\alpha(\phi^*, \hat{\Delta})\, \bar{B}(\alpha, \delta_\alpha)' + \bar{B}(\alpha, \delta_\alpha)\, C_\alpha(\phi^*, \hat{\Delta})'$$

where $C_\alpha(\phi^*, \hat{\Delta})$ is the covariance between $\sqrt{n}\phi^*$ and $\sqrt{n}\hat{\Delta}$ in their joint limiting distribution under M_α.

Note that although $\tilde{b}$ was originally defined to be a statistic of interest in comparing M_α and M_δ and hence a function of y, z, y^* and z^*, since δ is the complete parameter vector of M_δ and $\hat{\delta}$ is a sufficient statistic for δ under M_δ, the dependence of $\tilde{b}$ on y^* and z^* can be captured through $\hat{\delta}$. This has the advantage of being able to make use of the known distribution of $\sqrt{n}(\hat{\delta}-\delta_\alpha)$ under M_α. Similarly, the dependence of $\tilde{b}$ on y and z could be captured through $\hat{\alpha}$, but since the behaviour of $\tilde{b}$ under M_α is being considered there would be no advantage in doing this. Furthermore, notice that the basis for comparing M_α and M_δ need not be confined to statistics $\tilde{b}$ which depend on y^*, and z^* via $\hat{\delta}$, when δ consists only of the parameters of M_δ as envisaged by the modeller who developed M_δ. This will be particularly important if M_δ does not yet satisfy all model evaluation criteria other than encompassing. For example, M_α might predict an autocorrelated error or parameter non-constancy in M_δ, and these should be tested for either directly within M_δ or by using the estimated serial correlation coefficient and the estimators of the augmented parameter set resulting from the hypothesized non-constancy of δ as the basis for an encompassing test. Therefore, the possibility that the parameter vector characterizing M_δ be augmented in the light of the predictions of M_α should be considered, and implicitly now δ is assumed to be so augmented. However, these considerations will only be relevant if each model is not tentatively acceptable (apart from encompassing), and so they increase the strength of the argument for adopting a comprehensive model evaluation strategy. Finally, note that to the extent that M_α predicts autocorrelated errors or parameter non-constancy in M_δ, M_δ is a special case of M_α, and so M_α ought to encompass M_δ automatically. In such situations the relevant and interesting question is whether M_δ encompasses M_α and not vice versa, and so δ need not be augmented. There will be cases though, in which for some features of the data M_α is a special case of M_δ, and yet for other features M_δ is a special case of M_α. Whilst this situation is likely to be common for models M_α and M_δ as originally specified by independent modellers, these difficulties can be resolved by modifying M_α and M_δ so that they can be compared in a common distributional framework as discussed in section 2.

3.2 Wald Encompassing Tests

In applying Theorem 2 to obtain Wald encompassing tests situations corresponding to (a) and those corresponding to (b) of the theorem need to be distinguished. Firstly, whenever $\sqrt{n}\phi^*$ is $o_p(1)$ the limiting distribution of $\sqrt{n}\hat{\phi}$ is derived straightforwardly from the distribution of the pseudo-ML estimator $\hat{\delta}$ as indicated in (a) of Theorem 2. This is in fact the case most commonly encountered, and some of the many examples of choices of $\tilde{b}$ for which $\sqrt{n}\phi^*$ is $o_p(1)$ are discussed below. The WET in this case takes the form

$$\eta_w(\tilde{b}) = n\hat{\phi}'[\bar{B}(\alpha, \delta_\alpha)\, V_\alpha(\hat{\Delta})\, \bar{B}(\alpha, \delta_\alpha)']^+\hat{\phi} \tag{6}$$

and

$$\eta_w(\tilde{b}) \xrightarrow[M_\alpha]{d} \chi^2(r^*),$$

r^* being the rank of $[\bar{B}(\alpha, \delta_\alpha)\, V_\alpha(\hat{\Delta})\, \bar{B}(\alpha, \delta_\alpha)']$ and '+' denotes a generalized inverse of this covariance matrix. Secondly, whenever $\sqrt{n}\phi^*$ is not $o_p(1)$ the limiting distribution of $\sqrt{n}\hat{\phi}$ is more difficult to derive. However, if $\sqrt{n}\phi^*$ has a limiting normal distribution on M_α (b) of Theorem 2 applies, and the WET statistic takes the form:

$$\eta_w(\tilde{b}) = n\hat{\phi}'V_\alpha(\hat{\phi})^+\hat{\phi} \tag{7}$$

with

$$\eta_w(\tilde{b}) \xrightarrow[M_\alpha]{d} \chi^2(r^{**})$$

when r^{**} is the rank of $V_\alpha(\hat{\phi})$. The limiting distribution on M_α of $\eta_w(\tilde{b})$ in (6) and (7) is unaffected if consistent estimators of $V_\alpha(\hat{\phi})$, $V_\alpha(\hat{\Delta})$ and $\bar{B}(\alpha, \delta_\alpha)$ are used, e.g. if α and δ_α are replaced by $\hat{\alpha}$ and $\delta_{\hat{\alpha}}$ respectively.

3.3 Relationship Between W, LR and LM Tests

The class of WET statistics defined by (6) and (7) generates a wide range of test statistics known in econometrics, and can be used as a generator of many more; as a result it unifies a vast and diverse literature on hypothesis testing. In addition, it yields some insights into the relationship between the Wald (W), likelihood ratio (LR) and score or Lagrange multiplier (LM) test statistics. For the usual situation in which $\sqrt{n}\phi^*$ is $o_p(1)$ the following score encompassing test (SET) statistic $\eta_s(\tilde{b})$ is asymptotically equivalent to $\eta_w(\tilde{b})$:

$$\eta_s(\tilde{b}) = q_{\hat{\alpha}}'H^{-1}\bar{B}(\alpha, \delta_\alpha)'[\bar{B}(\alpha, \delta_\alpha)\, V_\alpha(\hat{\Delta})\, \bar{B}(\alpha, \delta_\alpha)']^+\bar{B}(\alpha, \delta_\alpha)\, H^{-1}q_{\hat{\alpha}} \tag{8}$$

when

$$q = \frac{1}{\sqrt{n}} \frac{\partial L_g(\delta)}{\partial \delta}, q_{\hat{\alpha}} = \frac{1}{\sqrt{n}} \frac{\partial L_g(\delta_{\hat{\alpha}})}{\partial \delta}$$

and H is as defined in (5). The asymptotic equivalence between $\eta_w(\tilde{b})$ and $\eta_s(\tilde{b})$ is established by noting that

$$\frac{1}{\sqrt{n}} \frac{\partial L_g(\hat{\delta})}{\partial \delta} = 0 = \frac{1}{\sqrt{n}} \frac{\partial L_g(\delta_{\hat{\alpha}})}{\partial \delta} + \frac{1}{n} \frac{\partial^2 L_g(\delta_{\hat{\alpha}})}{\partial \delta \, \partial \delta'} \sqrt{n}\hat{\Delta} + o_p(1)$$

implies that $q_{\hat{\alpha}} = H\sqrt{n}\hat{\Delta} + o_p(1)$, and hence since $\sqrt{n}\hat{\phi} = \bar{B}(\alpha, \delta_\alpha) \times \sqrt{n}\hat{\Delta} + o_p(1)$ when $\sqrt{n}\phi^*$ is $o_p(1)$ by Theorem 2, it follows that $\sqrt{n}\hat{\phi} = \bar{B}(\alpha, \delta_\alpha) H^{-1} q_{\hat{\alpha}} + o_p(1)$. However, if $\sqrt{n}\phi^*$ is not asymptotically negligible $\eta_w(\tilde{b})$ and $\eta_s(\tilde{b})$ are not asymptotically equivalent, and $\eta_s(\tilde{b})$ will not in general have a limiting $\chi^2(r^*)$ distribution on M_α. Indeed, since $\sqrt{n}\hat{\phi} = \sqrt{n}\phi^* + \bar{B}(\alpha \cdot \delta_\alpha)\sqrt{n}\hat{\Delta} + o_p(1)$ in such cases a modified statistic which is asymptotically equivalent to $\eta_w(\tilde{b})$ in (6) is:

$$\eta_s(\tilde{b}) = (\bar{B}(\alpha, \delta_\alpha) H^{-1} q_{\hat{\alpha}} + \sqrt{n}\phi^*)' V_\alpha(\hat{\phi})^+ (\bar{B}(\alpha, \delta_\alpha) H^{-1} q_{\hat{\alpha}} + \sqrt{n}\phi^*).$$

It is inappropriate though to regard this as a score test given its form, especially since there are choices of $\tilde{b}$ for which $\bar{B}(\alpha, \delta_\alpha) = 0$. One such choice is $n\tilde{b} = [L_f(\hat{\alpha}) - L_g(\hat{\delta})] = \hat{L}_{fg}$ (say) which is the log-likelihood ratio. This choice of $\tilde{b}$ gives

$$\sqrt{n}\hat{\phi} = n^{-\frac{1}{2}}[L_{fg} - E_\alpha(L_{fg})_{\hat{\alpha}}] = \sqrt{n}T_\alpha \text{ (say)},$$

so that

$$\bar{B}(\alpha, \delta_\alpha) = \text{plim}_\alpha (-(1/n)\, \partial L_g(\delta_\alpha)/\partial \delta) = 0$$

and so $\sqrt{n}\hat{\phi} = \sqrt{n}\phi^* + o_p(1)$, yielding $\eta_w(\hat{L}_{fg}) = nT_\alpha{}^2/V_\alpha(\phi^*)$ which is precisely the generalized likelihood ratio test of Cox (1961) for separate hypotheses. $\eta_w(L_{fg})$, which is in effect the likelihood ratio encompassing test (LET), is such that

$$\eta_w(\hat{L}_{fg}) \underset{M_\alpha}{\overset{d}{\longrightarrow}} \chi^2(1)$$

irrespective of the dimensions of α and δ, as is well known for the Cox and other asymptotically equivalent non-nested test statistics, such as those of Pesaran (1974), Davidson and MacKinnon (1981) and Fisher and McAleer (1981). Hence for non-nested models the LET cannot be asymptotically equivalent to the WET and SET statistics in general. Furthermore, for non-nested hypotheses the usual form of the log-likelihood ratio test statistic, that is,

$-2[L_f(\hat{\alpha})-L_g(\hat{\delta})]$, does not have a limiting χ^2 distribution (Foutz and Srivastava, 1977; Kent, 1982). Note that the generalized likelihood ratio test is obtained by subtracting from it its mean under M_α, thus correctly centring it in order to have a limiting χ^2 distribution. Hence for non-nested models provided $\sqrt{n}\phi^*$ is $o_p(1)$ the WET and SET statistics are asymptotically equivalent, but in general the LET statistic will not be asymptotically equivalent to them. However, Trognon (1983) proposes pseudo-asymptotic W, LR and LM tests for the linear exponential family of distributions, which are asymptotically equivalent to each other, just as the usual W, LR and LM tests are for nested models.

3.4 *Example of a WET: An Information Criterion*

Another example of a WET statistic, which is closely related to that just considered with $n\tilde{b} = \hat{L}_{fg}$, is the information criterion discussed by Sawyer (1983). This information criterion is defined as $S_f(\hat{\alpha}) = n(\tilde{b}-b_{\hat{\alpha}})$ when $\tilde{b} = (1/n)\, E_\delta(\hat{L}_{fg})_{\delta=\hat{\delta}} = \hat{I}_{\hat{\delta}}(f\!:\!g)$ which is an estimator of $I_\delta(f\!:\!g) = (1/n)E_\delta(L_{fg})$ the Kullback–Leibler mean information criterion for discriminating between M_α and M_δ. Hence $nb_{\hat{\alpha}} = E_\alpha(E_\delta(\hat{L}_{fg})_{\delta=\hat{\delta}})_{\alpha=\hat{\alpha}}$ in this case, and

$$\sqrt{n}\hat{\phi} = \sqrt{n}(\tilde{b}-b_{\hat{\alpha}}) = n^{-\frac{1}{2}}S_f(\hat{\alpha}).$$

$S_f(\hat{\alpha})$ is expected to be zero under M_α and negative under M_δ, and so a ‘directional’ test is given by comparing

$$\frac{\sqrt{n}\hat{\phi}}{\sqrt{V_\alpha(\phi^*)}} = \frac{S_f(\hat{\alpha})}{\sqrt{nV_\alpha(\phi^*)}}$$

with a critical value from the standard normal distribution. Sawyer (1983) shows that

$$n^{-\frac{1}{2}}S_f(\hat{\alpha}) \xrightarrow[M_\alpha]{d} N(0,\, V_\alpha(\phi^*))$$

when $V_\alpha(\phi^*) = \Phi_\delta V_\alpha(\hat{\Delta})\,\Phi_\delta'$. ($\Phi_\delta$ is defined analogously to Φ_α.) This follows from Theorem 2 since $\sqrt{n}\phi^*$ and $\Phi_\delta\sqrt{n}\hat{\Delta}$ are asymptotically equivalent and $\bar{B}(\alpha, \delta_\alpha) = 0$ in this case. Though there is a close resemblance between the Cox and the Sawyer tests, in that they can both be obtained as encompassing tests with respect to $\tilde{b}$, with the choice of $\tilde{b}$ being $\hat{L}_{fg}/n$ and $E_\delta(\hat{L}_{fg})_{\delta=\hat{\delta}}/n$ respectively, they can behave quite differently. For example, for the choice of regressors problem of (3) it is well known (Pesaran, 1974) that the Cox test does not exist when X_1 and X_2 are orthogonal (i.e.

$X_1'X_2 = 0$), but Sawyer shows that the test based on $S_f(\hat{\alpha})$ does exist in this case and is equivalent to the F-test of $\gamma^* = 0$. However, this equivalence *only* holds when $X_1'X_2 = 0$, and so the Sawyer test is not in general equivalent to $\eta_w(\hat{\gamma}^*)$. The equivalence in the orthogonal case arises because δ_α and $\alpha_\delta = E_\delta(\hat{\alpha})$ are both zero, as is $b_{\hat{\alpha}}$ in each case, so that the F-test checks whether $\hat{\delta}$ is significantly different from zero and the information test equivalently checks whether $[L_f(0) - L_g(\hat{\delta})]$ is significantly different from zero.

3.5 *Example of a WET: Empirical MGF*

Epps et al. (1982) also propose a directional non-nested test analogous to the Sawyer test, which is also easily seen to be a special case of $\eta_w(\tilde{b})$ defined in (6). The statistic of interest to form the basis of the encompassing test in this case is

$$M(s) = \frac{1}{n} \sum_{t=1}^{n} \exp(sy_t)$$

which is the empirical moment generating function for y. In the notation of this paper $M(s) = \hat{\delta}$ so that $\delta_\alpha = \mu_\alpha(s, \alpha) = E_\alpha(e^{sy})$ the theoretical moment generating function under M_α. Hence $\sqrt{n}\hat{\phi} = \sqrt{n}(\hat{\delta} - \delta_{\hat{\alpha}})$ when $\delta_{\hat{\alpha}} = \mu_\alpha(s, \hat{\alpha})$ has a limiting normal distribution with zero mean and variance

$$V_\alpha(\hat{\Delta}) = V_\alpha(\hat{\delta}) - V_\alpha(\delta_{\hat{\alpha}}) = V_\alpha(M(s)) - DV_\alpha(\hat{\alpha})D'$$

under M_α when $D = \partial\mu_\alpha(s, \alpha)/\partial\alpha'$ (see Theorem 1). Therefore,

$$[\eta_w(M(s))]^{\frac{1}{2}} = n^{\frac{1}{2}}(M(s) - \mu_\alpha(s, \hat{\alpha}))/(V_\alpha(\hat{\Delta}))^{\frac{1}{2}}$$

is an asymptotically valid test of M_α for any s such that $0 < V_\alpha(\hat{\Delta}) < \infty$. So far M_δ has not been used, but Epps et al. (1982) suggest that s be chosen to maximize the power of the $[\eta_w(M(s))]^{\frac{1}{2}}$ test against the alternative M_δ. Their resulting test statistic is a one degree of freedom directional non-nested test for comparing M_α and M_δ, and as such is an alternative to the tests of Cox, Davidson and MacKinnon, and Sawyer. Epps et al. (1982) show that their test compares reasonably well with the Cox test in comparing the log-normal and exponential distributions, though both tests do not perform well in small samples.

In discussing WET and SET earlier it was noted that $\eta_w(\tilde{b})$ and $\eta_s(\tilde{b})$ are asymptotically equivalent whenever $\sqrt{n}\phi^*$ is $o_p(1)$. However, under this condition $\eta_s(\tilde{b})$ can be generated *exactly* as a WET of the form $\eta_w(\bar{B}(\hat{\alpha}, \delta_{\hat{\alpha}})H^{-1}q_{\hat{\alpha}})$. This is seen by comparing the forms of $\eta_w(\tilde{b})$ and $\eta_s(\tilde{b})$ in (6) and (8) respectively, noting $\sqrt{n}\hat{\phi}$ and $\bar{B}(\hat{\alpha}, \delta_{\hat{\alpha}})H^{-1}q_{\hat{\alpha}}$ are asymptotically equivalent under M_α, and so

$$\bar{B}(\hat{\alpha}, \delta_{\hat{\alpha}})H^{-1}q_{\hat{\alpha}} \underset{M_\alpha}{\overset{d}{\longrightarrow}} N(0, \bar{B}(\alpha, \delta_\alpha)\, V_\alpha(\hat{\Delta})\, \bar{B}(\alpha, \delta_\alpha)).$$

Hence for *generating* test statistics there is no real need for both the Wald and score principles: $\eta_w(\bar{B}(\hat{\alpha}, \delta_{\hat{\alpha}})H^{-1}q_{\hat{\alpha}})$ generates exactly $\eta_s(\tilde{b})$, where $\eta_s(\tilde{b})$ is only asymptotically equivalent to $\eta_w(\tilde{b})$, and there is no SET which will generate $\eta_w(\tilde{b})$ exactly. This does not deny the value of using the score principle to interpret tests, which can clearly be important – see Breusch and Pagan (1980). Ease of computation is a relevant consideration in comparing WET and SET statistics, and it has been suggested that the SET, because it does not require second derivatives of the log-likelihood function whereas the WET does, is easier to compute analytically and numerically. However, whilst it is true that if $\bar{B}(\alpha, \delta_\alpha)$ is nonsingular, in which case

$$\begin{aligned}\eta_s(\tilde{b}) &\equiv \eta_w(\bar{B}(\hat{\alpha}, \delta_{\hat{\alpha}})H^{-1}q_{\hat{\alpha}}) \equiv \eta_w(q_{\hat{\alpha}}) \\ &= q_{\hat{\alpha}}'(HV_\alpha(\hat{\Delta})H)^{+}q_{\hat{\alpha}} = \eta_s(\hat{\delta}),\end{aligned}$$

the SET statistic $\eta_s(\hat{\delta})$ need not involve H, since in the iid case with H nonsingular $(HV_\alpha(\hat{\Delta})H)$ and $(J-QV(\hat{\alpha})Q')$ are asymptotically equivalent when

$$Q = \lim_{n\to\infty} \frac{1}{n} E_\alpha\left(\frac{\partial L_g}{\partial \delta}\cdot\frac{\partial L_f}{\partial \alpha'}\right),$$

this is not true in general. In fact, whenever $\bar{B}(\alpha, \delta_\alpha)$ is non-square or singular, H will be required in calculating $\eta_s(\tilde{b})$.

3.6 Complete Parametric Encompassing (CPE)

The encompassing tests $\eta_w(q_{\hat{\alpha}}) \equiv \eta_s(\hat{\delta})$ (if $\sqrt{n}\phi^*$ is $o_p(1)$) and $\eta_w(\hat{\delta})$ which are asymptotically equivalent are 'good' statistics for testing $M_\alpha \mathcal{E} M_\delta(\hat{\delta})$, in that they have the correct asymptotic size when $\delta = \delta_\alpha$, and they are consistent for all fixed alternatives in which $\delta \neq \delta_\alpha$. In addition, since δ is the complete parameter vector for $g(y_t^* \mid z_t^*, \delta)$ of M_δ, and, as discussed in section 3, $g(.)$ and δ should be chosen to capture all aspects of the behaviour of $y_t^* \mid z_t^*$ (including features suggested as being relevant by M_α) of interest to the modeller responsible for M_δ, these tests are of particular interest. If M_α is able to account for the behaviour of $\hat{\delta}$ (the ML estimator of the complete parameter vector of M_δ) then $(\hat{\delta}-\delta_{\hat{\alpha}})$ will be close to zero, and this is strong evidence in favour of M_α as against M_δ. Furthermore, if $\delta = \delta_\alpha$ then $b(\delta) = b(\delta_\alpha)$ when $b(.)$ is continuous and not of higher dimension than δ. Hence, although $\hat{\delta} = \delta_{\hat{\alpha}}$, which means that $\tilde{b} = b(Y_n{}^1, \hat{\delta}) = b(Y_n{}^1, \delta_{\hat{\alpha}})$, does not necessarily imply that $\tilde{b} = b_{\hat{\alpha}}$, the hypothesis $\delta = \delta_\alpha$ is of considerable interest and is called complete parametric encompassing:

Definition 2 M_α has the property of complete parametric encompassing of M_δ iff $\delta = \delta_\alpha$.

Therefore, $\eta_w(\hat{\delta})$ and $\eta_s(\hat{\delta})$ are tests of complete parametric encompassing in comparing M_α with M_δ. It should be noted that there will be cases in which $(\hat{\delta}-\delta_{\hat{\alpha}})$ appropriately normed has a singular limiting distribution under M_α, and in such cases complete parametric encompassing remains as defined above, but is to be understood as being implemented via an encompassing test on a subvector of $(\hat{\delta}-\delta_{\hat{\alpha}})$ of the highest dimension having a non-singular distribution – or equivalently by the use of a generalized inverse.

Part of the value of tests for complete parametric encompassing is indicated by the following lemma which is proved in Mizon and Richard (1983):

Lemma A sufficient, but not necessary, condition for $M_\alpha \mathscr{E} M_\delta(\tilde{b})$ to $o_p(n^{-\frac{1}{2}})$ when $\bar{B}(\alpha, \delta_\alpha)$ is a finite $r \times l$ matrix of rank r and $(\hat{\delta}-\delta_\alpha)$ is $o_p(n^{-\frac{1}{2}})$, is that M_α provide a complete parametric encompassing of M_δ.

Hence, since δ is the complete vector of relevant parameters for the comparison of M_α and M_δ, all encompassing hypotheses $M_\alpha \mathscr{E} M_\delta(\tilde{b})$ will have $\tilde{b}$ which are functions of $\hat{\delta}$ (note the analogy with complete sufficient statistics). Therefore, complete parametric encompassing is a sufficient condition (to order $n^{-\frac{1}{2}}$) for all forms of encompassing $M_\alpha \mathscr{E} M_\delta(\tilde{b})$. However, this does not mean that if $\eta_w(\hat{\delta})$ does not reject $M_\alpha \mathscr{E} M_\delta(\hat{\delta})$ the statistics $\eta_w(\tilde{b})$, for any choice of $\tilde{b} = b(Y_n{}^1, \hat{\delta})$, will each fail to reject $M_\alpha \mathscr{E} M_\delta(\tilde{b})$, though most should. This simply reflects the fact that the induced acceptance region of a set of separate tests of the hypotheses which jointly form a particular composite hypothesis, does not in general coincide with the acceptance region of the direct test of the composite hypothesis, even when care is taken to ensure that the significance levels of the separate induced test and the direct test are similar, if not equal. Although a composite hypothesis can be factored into constituent hypotheses (e.g. $H_0^*: \beta_1 = \beta_2 = 0$ into $H_1^*: \beta_1 = 0$ and $H_2^*: \beta_2 = 0$) and separate induced tests applied to them, such a procedure is very rarely an optimal one. In fact, such optimality usually only applies in special situations, e.g. when the constituent hypotheses are naturally and uniquely ordered, as in the examples considered in Mizon (1977a). Indeed, the arguments in favour of a general-to-specific modelling strategy contained in Mizon (1977a, b) and Hendry (1980), are motivated by the desirability of having some test statistics which have power against a wide range of alternatives within the common distributional framework being used, rather than being arguments for the uncritical use of separate induced tests of a general model. In general, it seems sensible to apply a complete parametric encompassing test first, and then to exploit the potential for incomplete parametric encompassing tests ($\eta_w(\tilde{b})$ with $\tilde{b} \neq \hat{\delta}$), which might be tests of constituent hypotheses, to identify those aspects of M_δ that M_α cannot encompass.

(a) An application of CPE: choice of regressors. The choice of regressors problem of (3) provides an example to illustrate these points. The statistic for testing whether H_1 provides a complete parametric encompassing (CPE) of H_2 is $\eta_w(\hat{\gamma})$, or equivalently the modification of it discussed earlier which is identical with the conventional F-test of $\gamma^* = 0$ in H_3 and has an $F(l, n-l-k)$ distribution on H_1. This is established by Mizon and Richard (1983) who also show that the implicit null hypothesis of the F-test is $\gamma = \gamma_\alpha$, and that of the Cox test is $\gamma' X_2' X_2 \gamma = \gamma_\alpha' X_2' X_2 \gamma_\alpha$, so that the power properties of these tests for comparing H_1 and H_2 are very different. In fact, the Davidson and MacKinnon J-test, which is asymptotically equivalent to the Cox test, has $\gamma' X_2' X_2 (\gamma - \gamma_\alpha) = 0$ as its implicit null hypothesis, from which it is possible to see that the J-test will have power no greater than size for alternatives in which $\gamma \neq \gamma_\alpha$ but $\gamma' X_2' X_2 (\gamma - \gamma_\alpha) = 0$. The F-test though will have the correct size and have high power against all alternatives in which $\gamma \neq \gamma_\alpha$, as is to be expected of the CPE test for this problem. Also note that the F-test has high power for all linear combinations of its implicit null hypothesis $\gamma = \gamma_\alpha$ (or equivalently $\gamma^* = 0$) and so has power as a test of H_1 against alternatives involving X_1 and subsets of the X_2 variables. The J-test on the other hand has high power for one particular linear combination, for which it has higher power than the F-test. Hence in testing hypotheses it is important to choose test statistics which in addition to having the correct size on the null hypothesis have high power against the appropriate alternative. Simply to use a test statistic because it is provided by a computer package, or because it is easy to calculate, even though recent hardware and software developments mean that computation is usually not a serious constraint, is not good practice. The properties of alternative test statistics for the chosen null and alternative hypotheses should be compared before selecting a test statistic. The case for CPE tests is that they have high power against a wider range of alternatives than incomplete parametric encompassing tests. This is an argument in favour of the use of CPE tests as well as other tests because of their potential for detecting the presence of aspects of M_δ that M_α cannot encompass. It is not though an argument against the use of other incomplete encompassing tests, which if CPE is rejected may be capable of identifying the particular aspects of M_δ that M_α cannot account for.

(b) An application of CPE: COMFAC. Sargan (1964) proposed the testing of autoregressive error restrictions, as an important alternative to simply 'allowing for' serially correlated residuals by re-estimating the original model with the additional assumption that the errors are generated by an autoregressive process. Building on the work of Sargan (1964, 1980c), Hendry and Mizon (1978) consider testing the autoregressive error restrictions by testing for the presence of common factors (COMFAC) in the lag operator polynomials implicit in the unrestricted dynamic model. The CPE test in this case is equivalent to the COMFAC test, as can be seen by considering the following simple example.

$$M_\alpha:\ y_t = z_t{}'\beta + u_t$$

$$u_t = \rho u_{t-1} + \epsilon_t \qquad |\rho| < 1,\ \epsilon_t \sim NI(0, \sigma^2)$$

$$M_\delta:\ y_t = \lambda y_{t-1} + z_t{}'\gamma + z_{t-1}{}'\theta + v_t \qquad |\lambda| < 1,\ v_t \sim NI(0, \tau^2).$$

For this example $\alpha' = (\beta', \rho, \sigma^2)$ and $\delta' = (\lambda, \gamma', \theta', \tau^2)$ which are $(k+2)$ and $2(k+1)$ dimensional vectors respectively, when there are k regressors in z_t. Noting that M_α can be written alternatively but equivalently as:

$$M_\alpha:\ y_t = \rho y_{t-1} + z_t{}'\beta - z_{t-1}{}'\beta\rho + \epsilon_t$$

and comparing this form of M_α with M_δ it is easy to see that the k autoregressive restrictions are $\theta + \lambda\gamma = 0$. The common factor interpretation comes from noting that M_α and M_δ can be re-written using the lag operator L (i.e. $\mathrm{L}^p x_t = x_{t-p}$) as:

$$M_\alpha\colon\ (1-\rho\mathrm{L})\, y_t = (1-\rho\mathrm{L})\, \beta' z_t + \epsilon_t$$

$$M_\delta\colon\ (1-\lambda\mathrm{L})\, y_t = (\gamma + \theta\mathrm{L})' z_t + v_t$$

so that M_δ will have the same form as M_α if $(\gamma + \theta\mathrm{L}) = (1-\lambda\mathrm{L})\gamma$, i.e. the lag polynomials operating on y_t and z_t respectively have a common factor of $(1-\lambda\mathrm{L})$. OLS estimation of δ yields $\hat{\delta}$ which under M_α has $\delta_\alpha{}' = (\rho, \beta', -\rho\beta', \sigma^2)$ as its plim. Hence the CPE test is given by $\eta_w(\hat{\delta}) = n\hat{\Delta}' V_\alpha(\hat{\Delta})^+ \hat{\Delta}$ when $\hat{\Delta} = (\delta - \delta_{\hat{\alpha}})$, $\delta_{\hat{\alpha}}{}' = (\hat{\rho}, \hat{\beta}', -\hat{\rho}\hat{\beta}', \hat{\sigma}^2)$, $\hat{\alpha}' = (\hat{\beta}', \hat{\rho}, \hat{\sigma}^2)$ is the ML estimator (or asymptotic equivalent) of α, and $V_\alpha(\hat{\Delta}) = V_\alpha(\hat{\delta}) - V_\alpha(\delta_{\hat{\alpha}})$ which has rank k and so

$$\eta_w(\hat{\delta}) \xrightarrow[M_\alpha]{d} \chi^2(k).$$

In addition, note that $V_\alpha(\delta_{\hat{\alpha}}) = DV(\hat{\alpha})D'$ as usual, with

$$D = \begin{pmatrix} 0 & 1 & 0 \\ I_k & 0 & 0 \\ -\rho I_k & -\beta & 0 \\ 0 & 0 & 1 \end{pmatrix}$$

a $2(k+1) \times (k+2)$ matrix, and $V(\hat{\alpha})$ is the usual covariance matrix for autoregressive least squares (or the ML) estimator of α in M_α. Therefore, the CPE test is based on comparing $\hat{\Delta}$ with zero, i.e. whether

$$\begin{pmatrix} \hat{\lambda} & - & \hat{\rho} \\ \hat{\gamma} & - & \hat{\beta} \\ \hat{\theta} & + & \hat{\rho}\hat{\beta} \\ \hat{\tau}^2 & - & \hat{\sigma}^2 \end{pmatrix}$$

is significantly different from a zero vector. Since rank $V_\alpha(\hat{\Delta}) = k$ there are only k independent elements in $\hat{\Delta}$ under M_α, which is to be expected as $(\hat{\theta} + \hat{\lambda}\hat{\gamma})$ will be close to zero under M_α and $\mathrm{plim}_\alpha(\hat{\theta} + \hat{\lambda}\hat{\gamma}) = 0$. Hence the CPE test can be implemented either by $\eta_w(\hat{\theta})$ (which tests whether $(\hat{\theta} + \hat{\rho}\hat{\beta})$ is significantly different from zero), or by $\eta_w(\hat{\theta} + \hat{\lambda}\hat{\gamma})$ which is precisely the COMFAC test. That the latter two methods of implementing the CPE test are asymptotically equivalent should be no surprise, since $\eta_w(\hat{\theta}+\hat{\lambda}\hat{\gamma})$ is the Wald COMFAC test, whereas $\eta_w(\hat{\theta})$ is a likelihood ratio-type test based on the comparison of the restricted estimator $\hat{\rho}\hat{\beta}$ and the unrestricted estimator $\hat{\theta}$. It is also possible to derive the SET for CPE, which is $\eta_w(q_{\hat{\alpha}}) \equiv \eta_s(\hat{\delta})$, to express this in terms of elements of $\hat{\alpha}$, and to use the above results to show that it is asymptotically equivalent to $\eta_w(\hat{\theta}+\hat{\lambda}\hat{\gamma})$ and $\eta_w(\hat{\theta})$. In addition, since $-2(L_f(\hat{\alpha})-L_g(\hat{\delta})) = n \log(\hat{\sigma}^2/\hat{\tau}^2)$ in this case, and M_α is nested within M_δ, the likelihood ratio test of the autoregressive restrictions will be asymptotically equivalent to $\eta_w(\hat{\tau}^2)$ which is based on a comparison of $\hat{\tau}^2$ and $\hat{\sigma}^2$, i.e. on the final element of $\hat{\Delta}$. Unlike the case when M_α and M_δ are non-nested the likelihood ratio test and $\eta_w(\hat{\tau}^2)$ have limiting $\chi^2(k)$ distributions on M_α. Note that each of these tests is a WET, and they are easily interpreted, computed and compared in the encompassing framework. Furthermore, though there is an obvious similarity between the $\eta_w(\hat{\theta})$ test and a Hausman specification test (comparison of two alternative estimators), there are important differences between Hausman tests and WETs which mean that they are distinct and in particular have different interpretations, even though they can be based on a common statistic as in this case. These differences are discussed below.

If the hypothesis of CPE (i.e. $M_\alpha \mathscr{E} M_\delta(\hat{\delta})$), using any of the asymptotically equivalent tests mentioned above, is rejected then although $\theta+\lambda\gamma=0$ has been rejected it is not known whether $\lambda=0$ and/or $\gamma=0$ but $\theta \neq 0$, or alternatively that $\theta=0$ but $\lambda \neq 0$ and $\gamma \neq 0$, etc., which can be investigated using WET statistics for incomplete encompassing. Equally it is now possible to analyse tests of $H_0: \rho=0$ in this framework. Consider the model M_{α^*} when $\alpha^{*\prime} = (\beta', \sigma^2)$

$$M_{\alpha^*}: y_t = z_t'\beta + \epsilon_t \qquad \epsilon_t \sim NI(0, \sigma^2)$$

so that M_{α^*} can be thought of as $M_\alpha \cap H_0$. The WET statistic for CPE in this case is

$$\eta_w(\hat{\delta}) = n\hat{\Delta}^{*\prime} V_\alpha(\hat{\Delta}^*)^+ \hat{\Delta}^* \xrightarrow[M_{\alpha^*}]{d} \chi^2(k+1),$$

when

$$\hat{\Delta}^{*\prime} = (\hat{\delta}-\hat{\delta}_{\alpha^*})' = (\hat{\lambda}, (\hat{\gamma}-\tilde{\beta})', \hat{\theta}', (\hat{\tau}^2-\tilde{\sigma}^2))$$

since $\delta_{\alpha^*}{}' = (0, \beta, 0, \sigma^2)$, and when $\tilde{\beta}$ and $\tilde{\sigma}^2$ are the OLS estimators of β and σ^2 in M_{α^*}. Hence $\eta_w(\hat{\delta})$ in this case has the correct size and high power asymptotically for the joint hypothesis $\theta+\lambda\gamma=0$ and $\lambda=0$ against the alternative $\theta+\lambda\gamma\neq 0$ and $\lambda\neq 0$. This test can be implemented via $\eta_w(\tilde{b})$ choosing $\tilde{b}'$ to be either $(\hat{\lambda}, \hat{\gamma}')$, or $(\hat{\lambda}, \hat{\theta}')$, or $\hat{\tau}^2$. Furthermore, since under $M_{\alpha*}$, $C_{\alpha*}(\hat{\gamma}, \hat{\lambda})=0$ and $C_{\alpha*}(\hat{\theta}, \hat{\lambda})=0$ the WET statistic for CPE $\eta_w(\hat{\delta})$, no matter how it is implemented, factors into two asymptotically independent components, one having a limiting $\chi^2(k)$ distribution, and the other a limiting $\chi^2(1)$ distribution on $M_{\alpha*}$. This means that as far as the size of the test is concerned, the joint hypothesis $\theta+\lambda\gamma=0$ and $\lambda=0$ can be tested either directly using one of the test statistics which implement $\eta_w(\hat{\delta})$, or by a test of $\theta+\lambda\gamma=0$ and a separate test of $\lambda=0$. Moreover, since the joint hypothesis consists of two naturally ordered hypotheses (test first for a common factor and secondly test for the common factor having a zero root – see Mizon (1977a)) the separate induced procedure for testing the joint hypothesis will in this case have high asymptotic power as well.

(c) An application of CPE: Sargan misspecification test. The misspecification test statistic proposed by Sargan (1964) for checking the validity of instruments for the estimation of the parameters of a single equation from a simultaneous system, also has an immediate encompassing interpretation. In fact, it is the WET statistic for testing the hypothesis that the restricted (to take account of the overidentifying structural information) reduced form model encompasses the unrestricted reduced form model with respect to the unrestricted reduced form parameter estimates. Hence it is obtained as $\eta_w(\hat{\Pi}^v)$ when $\hat{\Pi}$ is the OLS (ML) estimator of the unrestricted reduced form coefficients, and 'v' denotes vectoring. The CPE test statistic is given by $\eta_w(\hat{\delta})$ when

$$\hat{\delta}=\begin{pmatrix}\hat{\Pi}^v\\ \hat{\Omega}^v\end{pmatrix}$$

with $\hat{\Omega}$ the MLE of the unrestricted reduced form error covariance matrix. However, $\eta_w(\hat{\delta})$ can be implemented via $\eta_w(\hat{\Pi}^v)$, and both have a limiting $\chi^2(N-m+1)$ distribution on the restricted hypothesis, when N is the number of instruments and m is the number of included endogenous and predetermined variables in the particular structural equation being considered. All other structural equations are treated as being just identified, so the only restrictions being taken into account are the overidentifying restrictions on the single structural equation.

(d) An application of CPE: simplification test. As a final example of the WET statistic for CPE, consider the choice of regressors problem and testing $H_1 \mathscr{E} H_3(\hat{\delta})$ when $\hat{\delta}' = (\hat{\beta}^{*\prime}, \hat{\gamma}^{*\prime}, \hat{\omega}^2)$ and

$$H_1: \ y \mid X_1, X_2 \sim N(X_1\beta, \sigma^2 I)$$

$$H_3: \ y \mid X_1, X_2 \sim N(X_1\beta^* + X_2\gamma^*, \omega^2 I).$$

Hence the hypothesis being tested is the parsimonious encompassing of H_3 by H_1, which is a test for a model simplification. $\eta_w(\hat{\delta})$ in this case has a limiting $\chi^2(l)$ distribution, and can be implemented via $\eta_w(\hat{\gamma}^*)$ or the conventional F-test for $\gamma^* = 0$ as discussed earlier. The reason for returning to this example here is to note the particular structure of the WET test, and to see its relationship to a Hausman test.

Note that:

$$\tilde{b} = \begin{pmatrix} \hat{\beta}^* \\ \hat{\gamma}^* \end{pmatrix} = \begin{pmatrix} \hat{\beta} + (X_1'X_1)^{-1}X_1'X_2\hat{\gamma}^* \\ (X_2'M_1X_2)^{-1}X_2'M_1y \end{pmatrix}$$

so that

$$b_\alpha = \begin{pmatrix} \beta \\ 0 \end{pmatrix} \quad \text{and} \quad \tilde{b} - b_{\hat{\alpha}} = \begin{pmatrix} (X_1'X_1)^{-1}X_1'X_2\hat{\gamma}^* \\ \hat{\gamma}^* \end{pmatrix}.$$

Hence $\sqrt{n}\hat{\phi} = \sqrt{n}(\tilde{b} - b_{\hat{\alpha}})$ in this case has a singular distribution on H_1, and

$$\eta_w(\tilde{b}) \underset{H_1}{\overset{d}{\longrightarrow}} \chi^2(l).$$

Therefore, if $k \geqslant l$ the CPE can be implemented by either $\eta_w(X_1'X_2\hat{\gamma}^*)$ which is a Hausman specification test, or by $\eta_w(\hat{\gamma}^*)$ which is proportional to the conventional F-test. However, in this case the two test statistics will be identical since the test based on the comparison of $\hat{\beta}^*$ and $\hat{\beta}$ is identical with that based on comparing $\hat{\gamma}^*$ with zero. On the other hand when $k < l$ the Hausman test

$$\eta_w(X_1'X_2\hat{\gamma}^*) \underset{H_1}{\overset{d}{\longrightarrow}} \chi^2(k)$$

whereas

$$\eta_w(\hat{\gamma}^*) \underset{H_1}{\overset{d}{\longrightarrow}} \chi^2(l)$$

and so they are not identical or even equivalent. Indeed, $\eta_w(X_1'X_2\hat{\gamma}^*)$ will have power no greater than size for fixed alternatives in which $X_1'X_2\gamma^* = 0$ but $\gamma^* \neq 0$ whereas $\eta_w(\hat{\gamma}^*)$ is consistent for all fixed alternatives in which $\gamma^* \neq 0$. This point was made by Holly (1982) in a more general context, and implies that the investigator must choose test statistics carefully in order to ensure that they have the correct size and high power for the null and alternative hypotheses of interest.

Finally, note that in general whenever $b = E_\delta(\tilde{b}) = 0$ implies that M_α and M_δ are identical, the WET statistic $\eta_w(\tilde{b})$ yields the nested test of $b = 0$. In the simplification example $b = \gamma^*$.

3.7 *Encompassing and Hausman Tests*

Especially, when $\tilde{b}$ is a parameter estimator, so that the WET statistic is based on comparing $\tilde{b}$ with the alternative estimator of that parameter under M_α, $b_{\hat{\alpha}}$, there appears to be a similarity between the encompassing and Hausman specification tests. However, they are not identical, and in fact have important differences. Firstly, the encompassing test uses $\tilde{b}$, a statistic of interest in M_δ, as the basis for comparison of M_α and M_δ, whilst the Hausman test uses $\hat{\alpha}$ (or a function of it) as the basis for comparison. Hence the roles of α and δ, as far as the basis for comparison is concerned, are reversed. Secondly, the Hausman test considers the possibility that, though α is the parameter of primary interest, M_α may be misspecified so that an estimator of α consistent under M_δ but inefficient under M_α may be a better estimator. This, however, requires α to be a meaningful parameter of M_δ. Hence if β in H_1 is the parameter of interest and misspecification in the direction of H_2 is being considered, it is required that β have meaning in H_2. If H_2 is regarded as a conditional independence hypothesis (i.e. $y \mid X_1,\ X_2 \sim N(X_2\gamma,\ \tau^2 I)$) then $\beta = 0$ in H_2 and so the Hausman test would be based on a comparison of $\hat{\beta}$ with zero, which is not an attractive way of comparing H_1 and H_2. Alternatively, if H_2 is interpreted as $y \mid X_2 \sim N(X_2\gamma, \tau^2 I)$ then β has no meaning in H_2 and a Hausman test is not available. The problem for which the Hausman test does have meaning in this context is that of checking for H_1 being misspecified in the direction of $H_3 : y \mid X_1, X_2 \sim N(X_1\beta^* + X_2\gamma^*,\ \omega^2 I)$. The Hausman test would then compare $\hat{\beta}$ and $\hat{\beta}^*$, and this yields an easily interpreted and sensible test for $H_1 \mathscr{E} H_3(\hat{\beta}^*)$ which has the correct size and high power for testing $X_1'X_2\gamma^* = 0$ against $X_1'X_2\gamma^* \neq 0$. Hence the Hausman test in this example is interpretable and can be generated as a WET statistic. However, because of the need for α to be a meaningful parameter in M_δ the Hausman test is only applicable when $M_\alpha \subset M_\delta$, i.e. for nested models. This particular point though means that the structure of the Hausman test makes explicit the need for a common distributional framework for comparing M_α and M_δ.

Moreover, note that the motivation provided for the Hausman test (Hausman, 1978), namely the desire to estimate α (or a function of it) consistently, taking into account the possible misspecification of M_α in the direction of M_δ, implies that the underlying problem is pre-test estimation rather than hypothesis testing. On the other hand the encompassing tests are very clearly hypothesis tests aimed at comparing M_α and M_δ, and are not concerned with estimation in itself. Finally, note that there is no necessity for $E_\delta(\tilde{b}) = b$ to have any meaning or be of particular interest in M_α. All that is required is that the common distributional framework enables $b_\alpha = E_\alpha(\tilde{b})$ (or $\text{plim}_\alpha(\tilde{b})$) to be evaluated. This contrasts with the need for α to be meaningful in M_δ for a Hausman test.

3.8 Specification Robust Tests

Kent (1982) and White (1982a) have shown how the results on pseudo-ML estimators can be used to obtain modified Wald and score test statistics for hypotheses of the form $H_0 : s(\delta) = 0$, when unrestricted and restricted ML estimators of δ under M_δ are used, even though it is possible that M_δ is misspecified. These tests can be cast in the encompassing framework by noting that account can be taken of the misspecification of M_δ by analysing the behaviour of the test statistics under M_α.

The basic idea is that since

$$\sqrt{n}(\hat{\delta} - \delta_\alpha) \xrightarrow[M_\alpha]{d} N(0, V_\alpha(\hat{\delta}))$$

and

$$\sqrt{n}\, s(\hat{\delta}) = \sqrt{n}\, s(\delta_\alpha) + S(\delta_\alpha)\sqrt{n}(\hat{\delta} - \delta_\alpha) + o_p(1)$$

it follows that on $M_\alpha \cap H_0$ *and* if CPE is assumed (i.e. $\delta = \delta_\alpha$)

$$\sqrt{n}\, s(\hat{\delta}) \xrightarrow[M_\alpha \cap H_0]{d} N(0, S(\delta_\alpha)\, V_\alpha(\hat{\delta})\, S(\delta_\alpha)')$$

and so

$$\eta_w{}^{\mathrm{CPE}}(s(\hat{\delta})) = ns(\hat{\delta})'[S(\hat{\delta})'V_\alpha(\hat{\delta})\,S(\hat{\delta})']^{-1}s(\hat{\delta}) \xrightarrow[M_\alpha \cap H_0]{d} \chi^2(r)$$

when $s(.)$ is $r\times 1$, $S(\delta) = \partial s(\delta)/\partial\delta'$ is $r \times l$ of rank r, and $\eta_w{}^{\mathrm{CPE}}(s(\hat{\delta}))$ is the WET statistic for $M_\alpha \mathscr{E} M_\delta(s(\hat{\delta}))$ when $\delta = \delta_\alpha$ is assumed. Note that $\eta_w{}^{\mathrm{CPE}}(s(\hat{\delta}))$ provides a test of $H_0 : s(\delta) = 0$ as a result of the unspecified M_α being assumed to provide a complete parametric encompassing of M_δ.

The corresponding score test is given by:

$$\eta_s{}^{\mathrm{CPE}}(s(\hat{\delta})) \equiv \eta_w{}^{\mathrm{CPE}}(S(\tilde{\delta})\,H^{-1}q_{\tilde{\delta}})$$

$$= q_{\tilde{\delta}}{}'H^{-1}S(\tilde{\delta})'[S(\tilde{\delta})\,V_\alpha(\tilde{\delta})\,S(\tilde{\delta})']^{-1}$$

$$\times\, S(\tilde{\delta})\,H^{-1}q_{\tilde{\delta}} \xrightarrow[M_\alpha \cap H_0]{d} \chi^2(r)$$

when $\tilde{\delta}$ is the restricted ML estimator of δ, and

$$q_{\tilde{\delta}} = \frac{n^{-\frac{1}{2}}\partial L_g(\tilde{\delta})}{\partial\delta}$$

Noting that $\eta_w{}^{\mathrm{CPE}}(s(\hat{\delta}))$ and $\eta_w{}^{\mathrm{CPE}}(S(\tilde{\delta})\,H^{-1}q_{\tilde{\delta}})$ are precisely the modified Wald and score test statistics respectively which were proposed by Kent (1982) and White (1982a), it is seen that these so called 'specification robust' test statistics can be interpreted and generated as WETs. Though CPE has to be assumed for $\eta_w(\tilde{b})$ to be able to generate these statistics, M_α is in fact assumed to be the unspecified and unknown DGP, and so it automatically encompasses M_δ. Given this, advantage is taken of the fact that $\hat{\delta}$ and $\tilde{\delta}$ are consistent estimators of δ_α, and of δ_α satisfying $s(\delta_\alpha) = 0$, respectively, to overcome the problem caused by M_α being unspecified and unknown (so that δ_α is also unknown), by replacing δ_α by $\hat{\delta}$ in $\eta_w{}^{\mathrm{CPE}}(s(\hat{\delta}))$ and by $\tilde{\delta}$ in $\eta_s{}^{\mathrm{CPE}}(s(\hat{\delta}))$ respectively.

4 Modelling and the Encompassing Principle

In a series of empirical studies, namely Davidson et al. (1978), Davidson and Hendry (1981) and Hendry (1980), the concept of encompassing has been used in an informal way. In particular, the authors of these papers have attempted to find models which were capable of accounting for the behaviour of all competing models, but without conducting any formal encompassing tests. The class of WET statistics proposed in Mizon and Richard (1983), and discussed in the previous section, provides the necessary testing framework for a formal use of the encompassing principle. Since the formal framework for developing, interpreting and using encompassing tests now exists it is relevant to discuss the role of such tests in modelling.

Noting that most economic variables are part of a complicated, interdependent, dynamic, stochastic, multidimensional and non-linear system, and the relative lack of information in the available data, it is unlikely that the DGP for the common set of data W_n^1 available to all investigators, will be discovered. Therefore, the aim in using econometric methods must be to find 'good' empirical models, that is models relevant to the problem being analysed which are statistically robust as well as being consistent with the appropriate economic theory. Hence comparison of alternative models will also be made according to their accuracy as representations of the chosen phenomena (which subsumes data admissibility and statistical checks of the model adequacy relative to the available data), their simplicity (the principle of parsimony), and their consistency with a theory model.

An essential characteristic of empirical modelling (and in fact the development of theory models) is that it is not a once-for-all event, but a process in which new information from theory and/or data leads to the modification of existing models. It seems reasonable to require, therefore, that this process be progressive rather than degenerate and use of the encompassing principle helps to ensure this.

For a given W_n^1 there will usually be a number of alternative models available as potentially adequate representations of the phenomena of interest. Furthermore, it is unlikely that any of these models will be the DGP for its variables. Hence it would be inappropriate to adopt a single selection criterion to choose one model from the small number of alternative models that is likely to be considered at any one time. Similarly it would be inappropriate to confine attention to the use of hypothesis tests which have been carefully selected to have high power against the alternatives representing the small number of models currently under consideration. For example, a test statistic designed to be powerful in testing M_α against a specific single alternative M_δ may have low power against other models involving the variables from W_n^1, even though some of these models may be preferable overall to M_α and M_δ. Hence it will generally be sensible to use test statistics which have power against models other than M_δ. *A fortiori* a complete parametric encompassing test (i.e. check whether $\hat{\delta} \simeq \delta_{\hat{\alpha}}$) would appear to be an essential first step in assessing the ability of M_α to encompass M_δ. However, should the hypothesis of complete parametric encompassing be rejected, analysis of more restricted forms of encompassing (i.e. with respect to $\tilde{b} \neq \hat{\delta}$) might be helpful in determining which features of M_δ cannot be encompassed by M_α.

There has been discussion in the literature on non-nested testing of the distinction between model selection and hypothesis testing, and it is a distinction worth emphasizing. Interpreting model selection as the use of a decision criterion to choose a model from a specified set, it is clear that the criterion will not consider models outside the specified set. Model selection, whether based on significance tests or not, has little role in the modelling strategy outlined above. Hence, for example, the use alone of one degree of freedom non-nested tests to *choose* between M_α and M_δ is inappropriate in the present framework, which, since neither M_α nor M_δ is likely to be the DGP, only uses hypothesis tests to *compare* the models rather than *choose* between them. In particular, if the hypothesis that M_α encompasses M_δ is rejected this does not necessarily lead to the acceptance of M_δ, nor to the rejection of M_α at that stage, though clearly it presents evidence against M_α. This applies particularly since, in a progressive modelling strategy, models are only rejected in favour of 'better' models, and the failure of M_α to encompass M_δ does not imply that M_δ is 'better'. This would be especially the case if M_δ were a 'nonsense' model. However, it should be emphasized that there is little point in using 'nonsense' models as alternatives in encompassing tests, since the failure of M_α to encompass the 'nonsense' model provides no evidence to enable a 'better' model to be constructed. Furthermore, models which M_α cannot encompass can always be found, if they are not required to be serious alternatives. The value of artificial nesting models is unclear for similar reasons.

Finally, it is the positive aspects of the encompassing principle, namely the fact that the failure of one model to encompass another is instrumental in constructing 'better' models, that makes it attractive for incorporation in a progressive modelling strategy. Furthermore, ability of M_α to encompass its rivals is very strong evidence in its favour.

5 Conclusion

This chapter has aimed to show that the simple and basic idea in statistics of evaluating a theory by comparing the value of an observed statistic with the theory's predicted value of it, can via the encompassing principle prove to be a very powerful tool in empirical modelling. The encompassing principle requires a model to be able to explain the characteristics of, or account for the behaviour of relevant statistics from, sensible rival models. In encompassing rival models a model is mimicking an important property of the DGP, which automatically encompasses all empirical models. Hence the encompassing principle should have a crucial role in modelling. Firstly, testing the ability of models to encompass rival models determines the relative strengths and weaknesses of alternative models. Such comparisons of models should be distinguished from the activity of selecting models, and they are feasible within the encompassing framework for nested and non-nested models since, as in all hypothesis testing, a common distributional basis is used for comparing the models. Secondly, models which cannot encompass serious alternatives are revealed to have important weaknesses, whereas finding that a model can encompass its rivals is powerful evidence in its favour, and ought at least to persuade other investigators that it should be taken seriously. Thirdly, the need to find a common distributional framework within which to compare models, means that the full underlying parameter vector (δ above) of a rival model is sufficiently general to enable the complete parametric encompassing test to have power against a wide range of relevant alternatives closely related to the two models under consideration.

The proposed class of Wald encompassing test statistics unifies a vast collection of test statistics in the literature on testing nested and non-nested hypotheses, and this facilitates the interpretation and comparison of alternative tests within a single framework. Complete parametric encompassing tests, especially when they factor into independent components, are particularly illuminating in this regard. Note that the existence of such a unifying framework is important, firstly because empirical models should be subjected to extensive and rigorous testing, and secondly, because it is inappropriate simply to use whatever test statistics happen to be provided by a computer program, or are fashionable, or are easy to calculate. The relative strengths and weaknesses of test statistics should also be analysed, and taken into account in selecting which of them to use.

Theorem 2 plays a crucial role in obtaining the required limiting distributions for the Wald encompassing tests. For example, the generalized likelihood ratio test (Cox, 1961), the information criterion test (Sawyer, 1983), the empirical moment generating function test (Epps et al., 1982), the COMFAC test (Sargan, 1964), and many other tests which have involved complicated derivations are obtained straightforwardly as WETs using Theorem 2. In addition, Theorem 2 enables the well-known results on pseudo-ML estimators to be used when possible, and also indicates when the limiting distribution of a statistic has to be derived by other means. This particular feature of Theorem 2 also enables it to cast light on the situations in which the Wald, likelihood ratio, and score (Lagrange multiplier) principles do and do not yield asymptotically equivalent test statistics. Furthermore, using the framework developed, it has been possible to identify the fundamental differences between Hausman specification tests and encompassing tests, and also the special nature of the specification robust tests. Finally, the equations defining the WET statistics in equations (6) and (7) together with Theorem 2 can be used as generators of test statistics for any models M_α and M_δ and any statistic $\tilde{b}$ which is to form the basis of comparison of M_α and M_δ.

Acknowledgments

I wish to thank the Statistics Department, Faculty of Economics, Australian National University for research support during a visit there when much of the material in section 3 was developed. The research support provided by a grant from the ESRC is also gratefully acknowledged. I am also grateful to David Hendry and Jean-François Richard for many helpful discussions. In this chapter I have drawn freely on the joint papers which the three possible pairings of Hendry, Mizon and Richard have produced, but retain sole responsibility for its deficiencies.

7

Uncertain Prior Information and Distributed Lag Analysis

PRAVIN K. TRIVEDI

1 Introduction

Distributed lags have a fundamental importance in applied macroeconometric work. Indeed Sims (1974) has stated that every model should be regarded as a distributed lag model until proven otherwise. Though the practical importance of distributed lags was recognized very early in econometrics, the emphasis of research has changed from time to time such that four reasonably distinct stages of development can be discerned.

The first stage began with Koyck (1954), following on the earlier work of Alt (1942) and in turn followed by Solow (1960), Almon (1965) and Jorgenson (1966), who were all very much concerned with increasingly general and flexible forms of distributed lags required to model dynamic responses based on quarterly time series. The second stage followed the first closely and focused predominantly on suitable techniques for estimating consistently single equation distributed lag models involving lagged dependent variables and serially correlated errors, many subsequent developments being anticipated by Sargan's Colston paper. The third stage was concerned with finding an economic theoretical basis for distributed lags and hence reducing arbitrariness in their specification. Nerlove (1972) argued forcefully in favour of (a research programme on) distributed lag models based firmly in dynamic optimization theory, in the hope that the resulting empirical specifications would be much less *ad hoc*, the restrictions on parameters much more tight and the relationship between underlying dynamic theory and the empirical models more transparent. He also sketched some of the steps that such a research programme would follow. The fourth and current stage of research on distributed lags is concerned with the difficult issue of selecting a subset of empirical specifications from numerous a priori probable and plausible specifications. It is a stage in which issues of model specification, estimation and selection are intimately linked, and so the problem becomes a microcosm of all applied econometric problems. In part this is due to the difficulty of achieving Nerlove's ambitious programme of linking dynamic optimization models and empirical research. There are severe limits to the extent to which prior theory can contribute to tight specification of distributed lags, and notwithstanding such theorizing much uncertainty remains about the character of most dynamic responses, which has profound implications for both specification and estimation of these models.

In this chapter I survey a variety of approaches to uncertainty surrounding the specification of distributed lags. The term distributed lags is used in a wide sense to encompass single equation structural dynamic models with lags on endogenous and/or exogenous variables and dynamic reduced and quasi-reduced forms, pure autoregressions and moving averages. The approaches considered have 'testimation' and Bayesianism at two ends of the spectrum. I use 'testimation' to describe a guided specification search strategy in which preliminary tests of significance are repeatedly and exhaustively used to arrive at a final specification which can be accepted as an adequate summary of the data. In the Bayesian approach certain aspects of uncertainty about distributed lags are encapsulated in a prior distribution; the posterior distribution of the parameters or moments of the posterior distribution are used to summarize the investigator's a posteriori opinions.

Between the two ends of the spectrum are several other approaches including (a) Bayesianism based on rules of thumb and priors of convenience, (b) vestigial Bayesianism based on minimal use of priors, (c) shrinkage estimation, and (d) estimation subject to stochastic constraints. Though each of these approaches has its own particular motivation, each is related to the others. The purpose of this chapter is to lay out the individual motivations and interrelationships and to comment on the strengths and weaknesses of each. A good deal of the discussion could relate to econometric modelling in general but it is both convenient and manageable to focus primarily on distributed lag models. The next section considers why our prior information about distributed lags is typically highly uncertain. The subsequent sections deal in turn with testimation, Bayesian analysis and several variants of the Bayesian approach.

2 Sources of Uncertainty in Specifying Distributed Lags

In empirical work finite and infinite lag parameterizations are equally common. In Almon's finite lag polynomial distributed lag (PDL) model the critical parameters are the length of lag and order of the polynomial, or the degree of smoothness; in the infinite lag rational distributed lag (RDL) model the order of the numerator and denominator polynomials in the rational lag function are the critical parameters. Fundamentally, uncertainty in distributed lag estimation concerns the dimensionality of the model. Intimately related to this are the following issues: Are there a priori reasons for preferring finite lag parameterization over the infinite one or vice versa? Is one of these a 'natural' specification? Are smooth lag distributions a priori more likely? Are fixed parameter lag distributions justifiable from an economic or statistical viewpoint? These and other related questions are not readily amenable to general answers. It is convenient, therefore, to discuss them by reference to some important ways in which distributed lags arise.

Costs of Adjustment

This is one of the major ways in which a genuinely dynamic element can be introduced into a model. The literature on investment contains some classic examples of which the following is an illustration. A present-value maximizing firm, which is a price taker in all markets, wants to determine a time path of investment to maximize

$$V = \int_0^\infty e^{-rt}[pF(K, L) - wL - qI - C(I)]\,dt, \tag{1}$$

subject to the production function and capital accumulation constraints

$$F(K, L) = Q \tag{2}$$

$$DK(t) = I(t) - \delta K(t) \tag{3}$$

respectively, where r denotes interest rate, p the price of output, w the wage rate, q the price of investment goods, K the capital input, L the labour input, I the rate of investment, $C(I)$ the cost of investment as a function of the rate of investment, Q the rate of output, D the differential operator d/dt and δ, $1>\delta>0$, the assumed constant rate of depreciation. The analytical problem of deriving the optimal investment rule in this problem is well known (Nickell, 1978) and a tractable solution is available only under rather special assumptions. For example, given constant returns to scale, constant expected future price vectors p and w and strictly convex adjustment costs such that $C'(I) > 0$, $\forall I > 0$ and $C''(I) > 0$, it can be shown that the capital stock adjusts according to a Koyck-type distributed lag model

$$\mathrm{D}K(t) = \delta[K^*(t) - K(t)] \tag{4}$$

where $K^*(t)$ is the desired capital stock.

In the more general and interesting case where there is uncertainty about all relevant future prices and where adjustment costs are not strictly convex, it is not known what characterization can be given to the optimal adjustment path. Whereas in broad qualitative terms uncertainty and convex adjustment costs lead to slow adjustment of actual to desired capital stock, the dynamic theory so far developed seems incapable of providing empirically useful restrictions on the adjustment path, even at the relatively well-defined level of the individual firm. It seems unlikely that this conclusion would be altered when less restrictive technological or expectational assumptions are employed.

When the assumption of convex adjustment costs is relaxed (see Nickell (1978) for a critique of that assumption) and an adjustment function with linear segments is admitted, which implies constant marginal cost of adjustment within specified ranges of investment, optimal investment behaviour is of the 'bang-bang' variety. That is, investment response is 'lumpy' and not distributed in time, so we get finite rather than infinite lags between stimulus and response. Of course, it is still possible to derive a distributed lag by aggregation over agents whose response lags differ in length, the longest lag being determined by the slowest agent. The point of this discussion, however, is that even in a microeconomic setting we have reasons for being somewhat uncertain about the nature of lagged response.

Unobserved Components and Signal Extraction

Lags in behaviour may arise from an economic agent responding to an unobserved component of a variable. For example, in the permanent income model the consumer adjusts his consumption to the unobserved value of permanent income. Since this is not directly observed the agent may be postulated to form an estimate of it by a process of signal extraction, see Nerlove (1967) and Nerlove et al. (1979). Signal extraction involves specification of a linear stochastic process generating the unobserved components of a time series and deducing the minimum mean square prediction error formula which will generate estimates of the unobserved component and then using this as a proxy for the unobserved component. Suppose, for example, that a de-trended, de-seasonalized time series on disposable income, denoted by y_t, has linear stochastic representation

$$y_t = \epsilon_t + \beta \sum_{i=1}^{\infty} \epsilon_{t-i} \tag{5}$$

$$0 \leqslant \beta \leqslant 1,\ E(\epsilon_t) = 0,\ E(\epsilon_t \epsilon_s) = \delta_{ts}\sigma^2,$$

then the minimum mean square error prediction of y_t, y_t^e, is given (Muth, 1960) by

$$y_t^e = \sum_{j=1}^{\infty} \beta(1-\beta)^{j-1} y_{t-j}. \tag{6}$$

Substituting this in a permanent income type relationship

$$c_t = \kappa y_t^e \tag{7}$$

yields the 'standard' consumption function:

$$c_t = \kappa\beta y_{t-1} + (1-\beta)\, c_{t-1}. \tag{8}$$

An observationally equivalent specification for income is

$$y_t = y_t^p + \eta_t; \quad E(\eta_t) = 0,\ E(\eta_t \eta_s) = \delta_{ts}\sigma_\eta^{\ 2} \tag{9}$$

$$y_t^p = y_{t-1}^p + \epsilon_t; \quad E(\epsilon_t) = 0,\ E(\epsilon_t \epsilon_s) = \delta_{ts}\sigma_\epsilon^{\ 2} \tag{10}$$

where the unobserved 'permanent' component of disposable (de-trended and de-seasonalized) income evolves according to a random walk. The minimum mean square prediction error formula is as above, with the parameter β given by

$$\beta = -\sigma_\epsilon^{\ 2}/2\sigma_\eta^{\ 2} + (\sigma_\epsilon/\sigma_\eta)\,(1 + \sigma_\epsilon^{\ 2}/4\sigma_\eta^{\ 2})^{\frac{1}{2}}. \tag{11}$$

There are a number of valuable insights that are obtained from the signal extraction approach. The first is that distributed lag weights reflect the properties of the stochastic process that generates the estimates of the unobserved component. The process may be such that the resulting lag structure can be smooth or jagged (Nerlove et al., 1979, p. 316); it all depends. Second, there should be no necessary presumption that the lag weights are constant. In the second of the two examples given above the lag weights depend upon $(\sigma_\eta/\sigma_\epsilon)$ (Okun's 'permanence presumption ratio') which in turn reflects the consumer's perception of the shocks to the permanent income arising from, *inter alia*, changes in taxes. If the consumer applies different signal extraction models to different income shocks (Dolde, 1975), no single signal extraction model will be adequate, and if the problem is truly serious the lag weights will be temporally unstable. Note that distributed lag weights arising from optimal signal extraction need not be positive, Nerlove et al. (1979) giving several examples. In summary, the signal extraction approach suggests that at the level of an individual agent distributed lags need not be time invariant or smooth or non-negative.

Production Lags

The existence of many firms which produce goods to specification, and in which the process of production extends over more than one data period, is a source of lags in many areas of econometric modelling. Examples are the lag between investment appropriations and investment expenditure, housing starts and completions, receipt of new orders and deliveries, prices of inputs and output, and many others. In many of these situations it is natural to consider a finite lag model as for example in the housing starts–completions case. A majority of the housing starts will end in completions within a finite time interval. Heterogeneity of the product itself (and possibly the method of recording data) would lead to the appearance of a finite distributed lag in the aggregate with the length of the lag determined by the longest construction period, as well as by the incentives operating on builders to speed up or slow down the construction process. At the level of an individual agent we can expect variable lags. At the aggregate level we can expect variable lags for the additional reason that population heterogeneity may vary over time. Once again therefore it is reasonable in absence of very detailed information to entertain only loose prior restrictions on distributed lags.

Habit Persistence and Behaviour Patterning

Distributed lags can arise from inertia, habit persistence and patterning of economic behaviour. In the context of consumption behaviour Deaton and Muellbauer (1980, p. 330) have observed: '... patterning of behaviour by households on other households takes time, particularly since there are recognition lags in perceiving what is the behaviour of the group with which the individual identifies. These lags in interactions result, when aggregated, in current purchase levels being dependent on past ones.' They give an example where a household has a demand function linear in income with the intercept depending upon the past consumption behaviour of all households. Linear aggregation over all households leads to an aggregate current demand as a function of current aggregate income and lagged aggregate demand.

Other examples of lags arising from patterning can be found in empirical studies on wage determination which deduce an aggregate wage equation from a model in which unions treat wages of other workers as reference wages (Trivedi and Rayner, 1978). Our interest in this approach to generating lags arises from the fact that it gives intuitive grounds for expecting smooth and (though not necessarily time invariant) infinite dimensional lag distributions more than just superficially akin to those which arise from tightly specified adjustment cost models with convex adjustment cost functions.

The preceding discussion has been concerned with economic theoretic issues which preclude a tight prior specification of distributed lags. We now turn to two statistical matters, viz. aggregation over time and aggregation over individuals, which are likely to cause misspecification even in the unlikely event that we begin with a tight prior theoretical specification. It can be shown that both these lead to inevitable misspecifications which increase one's uncertainty about the nature of the distributed lag response.

Temporal Aggregation

There are two convenient ways of handling this. In the first approach a stochastic dynamic, continuous time model is specified and a discrete time representation, suitable for measurement using either sampled and/or time-averaged data, is derived. This approach was used by Sargan (1974) and in several other papers listed in Bergstrom (1976). In the second approach one assumes that discrete data are available at some time interval which is longer than, and usually assumed to be a constant multiple of, the 'natural' interval. The data period may be a quarter whereas the decision period may be a month. Beginning then with a dynamic model specified in terms of the natural interval a model for the data interval is derived. Examples of this approach are Zellner and Montmarquette (1971), Brewer (1973) and Wei (1978) (see also Sims, 1971; Geweke, 1978). The resultant aggregated model will involve in general both temporal aggregation of flow variables such as sales or output per period, and systematic sampling of point variables such as prices, interest rates and stock levels. Irrespective of which of the two approaches is adopted certain common consequences follow from the process of aggregation. For convenience and concreteness let us suppose that the second approach has been followed and that we have aggregated an ARMAX (p, d, q) model to apply to a time interval 1, indexed by t, whereas the processes are observed at interval k, indexed by T, $T = tm$. That is, the original model is

$$\phi_p(\mathrm{L})(1-\mathrm{L})^d y_t = \xi_q(\mathrm{L})(1-\mathrm{L})^{d'} x_t + \mu_r(\mathrm{L})\epsilon_t \qquad (12)$$

where $\phi_p(\mathrm{L})$, $\xi_q(\mathrm{L})$ and $\mu_r(\mathrm{L})$ are polynomials of order p, q and r in the lag operator L, x_t is a stimulus variable assumed to be independent of ϵ_t, and d and d' are integers. A general method due to Wei (1978) can be used to express the ARMAX model in terms of the data interval T, which involves multiplying (12) through by a suitable polynomial function $P(\mathrm{L})$. If, however, the original model includes terms at lags $t \neq T$ then the aggregated model involves unobserved lagged terms in x at lags which are fractions of T, as well as aggregated values of x at lags T, say X_T. These unobserved terms may be absorbed into the error term of the equation and an efficient estimation procedure employed to estimate the model subsequently. Alternatively it may be possible to express the unobserved lagged values of x_t as a function of observed current lagged values of X_T and deduce the lag structure of the aggregate model. Some results obtained by Brewer (1973) and Weiss (1982) show that the lag structure on the X_T is in general quite complex being a function of $P(\mathrm{L})$, $\xi_q(\mathrm{L})$, m (usually unknown) and the parameters of the model generating the x_t. It is clear that we should have considerable uncertainty at the end of such an exercise as to what we might expect the distributed lag function to look like, the uncertainty being greater whenever our aggregation procedures are implicit rather than explicit. Rather than deduce the correct temporally aggregated model from an initial, assumed correct, specification, we may prefer that the uncertainty about the initial model, the relation between the true decision interval and the data interval and the process generating the x_t all be reflected simply in our willingness to entertain quite flexible and, on occasions, unexpected, lag distributions and autocorrelated error structures provided these are well supported by the sample information.

Aggregation over Agents

It is seldom that we see distributed lag analyses for microeconomic units; as a rule these models are used to analyse aggregate data. It has been suggested by a number of writers that observed lag distributions may reflect the distribution across a population of agents each of whom reacts to an economic stimulus with a fixed lag. For example the optimal response of an agent may be of the 'bang-bang' type, so that when an agent responds, which may be after a finite delay, he responds fully, but changes in economic incentives cause the delay time to vary. Then in interpreting estimated distributed lags one should be mindful not only of the 'typical' response of an agent but also of the statistical distribution of agents through the population. We now explore the implications of this intuitively appealing idea.

Let the discrete random variable z denote the number of periods ('dead time') that elapse between the occurrence of a stimulus and the response to that stimulus. $p(z=i\,|\,\phi)$ is the proportion of total response to the stimulus which occurs after i periods for an economic agent with parameter ϕ. $\{p(z\,|\,\phi),\ z=0, 1, 2, \ldots\}$ defines the entire lag weight sequence which we have assumed, rather restrictively given the results of the signal extraction theory, to be non-negative. Assume a population of heterogeneous economic agents, each one individually 'small' in the relevant sense, indexed by parameter ϕ. Take ϕ to be random, drawn from a *common* distribution dG with parameter ψ. The aggregate distributed lag response $\{p(z), z=0, 1, 2, \ldots\}$ is obtained by integrating out ϕ using the weighting density d$G(\psi)$ thus:

$$p(x) = \int_{R_\phi} p(x\,|\,\phi)\,\mathrm{d}G(\psi). \qquad (13)$$

Hence the resulting aggregate density will be characterized by the parameters of the weighting distribution. The idea can be generalized. Suppose that ϕ is drawn from not one but n distinct populations which occur in proportions $w_i, \ldots, w_n$, $\Sigma w_i = 1$. Let $F_i(\phi\,|\,\lambda_i)$ represent the ith distribution function. Then the finite mixture distribution

$$G(\phi) = \sum_{i=1}^{n} w_i F_i(\phi \mid \lambda_i) \tag{14}$$

can be used to generate the aggregate lag distribution. Assuming that a closed form expression for the latter exists, this distribution will be characterized by $\{(w_i, \lambda_i), i = 1, \ldots, n\}$. Many of the standard distributed lag models used in applied econometrics can be derived in this way. For example, the rational distributed lag model with non-negative weights can be generated by assuming that macroeconomic agents have Poisson lag distribution with mean lag λ and that the distribution of λ over the population can be represented by a finite mixture of gamma densities.

An implication of these aggregation considerations is that macro distributed lags need have no resemblance to their microeconomic counterparts. A well-specified dynamic optimizing model used to derive the latter is in itself insufficient to interpret distributed lags in macroeconometric work. Additionally information about the population diversity is required. In some situations only the information on the longest lag is required in order to specify the end-point of a finite lag distribution. In general, however, we can have only rather weak priors on both the length and shape of distributed lags. A second implication is that aggregation over agents is likely to produce a smooth distributed lag as has been noted informally by a number of writers. But can we be so certain when we aggregate temporally as well as over agents and when we take account of the stochastic characteristics of processes generating stimulus variables? The answer in general seems to be no, though an individual researcher with detailed information may be able to do better in specific situations. Smoothness of distributed lags is a commonly adopted assumption but it is an assumption of convenience.

My conclusion from this review is that there are very strong reasons for not imposing strong prior information in distributed lag analysis. The notion of a 'true' distributed lag is very tenuous. Whether one works with a finite or an infinite lag model, under a fixed or variable parameter assumption, in a continuous or discrete time format, with smooth or jagged lag distributions, it is doubtful whether one can claim to be doing any more than providing a rough-and-ready approximation to the way variables that we study are determined. Well specified microeconomic optimizing dynamic models are usually of limited use in the detailed determination of distributed lags. It seems inevitable and not at all unreasonable that practicing econometricians should resort to data-based priors.

Furthermore it is also desirable to employ fairly general (unrestrictive) stochastic specifications of the models to be estimated. Given initial uncertainty about precisely what to expect in terms of the serial correlation and heteroscedasticity, a sensible procedure is to use a computer program that provides a good set of diagnostics for evaluating the adequacy of the model in these respects, as discussed in chapter 5. If departures from serial independence and/or homoscedasticity are indicated, then, following a pre-test, corrective action will need to be taken. This may take the form of respecification of the model or application of a more suitable estimation technique. We now consider different approaches to estimation of distributed lags.

3 Testimation

What is Testimation?

The term testimation is intended to describe an empirical specification search involving a blend of estimation and significance tests. In the context of distributed lags it involves a purposive specification search in which one proceeds from the most general dynamic specification one is prepared to consider to the most restrictive, but still data coherent, each stage of the search being guided by (series of) significance tests applied at a conventional level. The implicit notion is that the most general data coherent dynamic specification at a conventional significance level is the 'correct' specification and that any alternative specification which either imposes restrictions inconsistent with the sample information, again at a conventional significance level, or which foregoes the opportunity to impose restrictions which would have been found to be data coherent, is to be avoided because in the first case they lead to statistical inconsistency and in the second to estimation inefficiency. Implicitly the approach attaches a penalty to a data incoherent restriction.

The approach is not atheoretic in the sense that its specifications lack a theoretical basis. Rather it is based on minimizing unnecessary assumptions and recognizing the limited applicability of dynamic theory in applied econometric work. Dynamic econometric modelling proceeds by a series of specification searches, whose main feature is that they are intended to be structured, not haphazard; furthermore one proceeds typically from a general to a special model (Mizon and Hendry, 1980; Hendry, 1983a).

Testimation does not espouse a parsimonious parameterization as an end since there is no necessary presumption that dynamic models ought to be simple. If the data support a simple model then it is adopted as 'tentatively adequate', but it will be abandoned when a larger and better data set enables one to reliably identify and estimate a more general model. The prior beliefs about the specification in the testimation approach are more akin to those based on the principle of scientific consistency and reliable differentiation recently advocated by Jones (1982), who defines a prior probability specification 'to be scientifically consistent with respect to a given set of data if it contains all parameters, hyperparameters, etc. which can be reliably differentiated by the data'. Jones defines a parameter to be reliably differentiated 'if it cannot be omitted without serious predictive distortion', but in the context of testimation the investigator's loss function is specified in terms of specification errors, not prediction errors. Avoidance of specification distortion, which in turn may induce distorted inferences, is paramount in the testimation approach. The choice of the significance level at which the tests are conducted must ultimately reflect the investigator's loss function. The use of a very low significance level naturally leads to a more parsimonious parameterization than if a high significance level is employed. This suggests that the significance level should be varied in accordance with the degree of prior beliefs in the validity of null hypotheses, a low value being chosen when the prior probability is low and a high value in the opposite case. But in many cases in distributed lag analysis it would seem hard even to do so and in any case may be contrary to the preferences of testimators.

We now turn to the application of the testimation approach.

PDL Models

In its simplest form the problem is to estimate the finite distributed lag model

$$y_t = \sum_{j=0}^{n} \omega_j x_{t-j} + u_t \qquad t = 1, \ldots, T \qquad (15)$$

where the coefficients ω_j are assumed to lie on the pth order polynomial

$$\omega_j = \alpha_0 + \alpha_1 j + \ldots + \alpha_p j^p, \qquad p \leqslant n \tag{16}$$

and u is the error term with properties $E(u_t) = 0$, $E(u_t u_s) = \delta_{ts}\sigma^2$. In matrix form the model is

$$y = X\omega + u \tag{17}$$

$$\omega = J\alpha \tag{18}$$

i.e.

$$y = XJ\alpha + u \tag{17a}$$

where X is a $T \times (n+1)$ matrix containing x_{t-j} as columns, $\omega' = [\omega_0, \ldots, \omega_n]$, $\alpha' = [\alpha_0, \ldots, \alpha_p]$ and J is an $(n+1) \times (p+1)$ Vandermonde matrix with $(i-1)^{j-1}$ in the ith row, jth column ($i = 1, \ldots, n+1$; $j = 1, \ldots, p+1$). The relations $\omega = J\alpha$ impose $(n-p)$ linear restrictions upon ω and this is the set formed by setting the $(p+1)$th differences of parameters to zero, i.e.

$$(1-\mathrm{L})^{p+1}\omega_j = \Delta^{p+1}\omega_j = 0, \qquad j = 0, 1, \ldots, n-p-1,$$

where L and Δ are respectively lag and difference operators. These linear restrictions may be written in the homogeneous form

$$R\omega = 0 \tag{19}$$

where R is an $(n-p) \times (n+1)$ matrix whose $(i, i+j)$th element is the coefficient of L^j in the expansion of $(1-\mathrm{L})^{p+1}$ ($i=1, \ldots, n-p$; $j = 0, \ldots, p+1$) with all remaining elements being zero (Shiller, 1973). If $p \geqslant 2$, the set of restrictions may be further enlarged by imposing one or both of the so-called 'end-point' restrictions $\omega_{-1} = \omega_{n+1} = 0$ which are designed to make the polynomial go smoothly through the end-points. The restricted least squares estimator is straightforwardly derived.

Since in general there is quite weak prior information, the testimation approach treats n, p and ω_j, $j = 0, \ldots, n$ as unknown parameters. There are a number of possible approaches of which the following seem particularly worth mentioning:

(a) Choose the 'best' p by some criterion conditional on a given n. See Godfrey and Poskitt (1975), Trivedi and Pagan (1979), Amemiya and Morimune (1974).

(b) Initially impose no restrictions, i.e. set $n=p$. Choose the best n by some criterion and then choose the best p, $p<n$ for a given n. For example, see Pagano and Hartley (1981), who do not, however, employ the optimal Anderson procedure of testing against the immediately preceding model, but test each hypothesis against the original maintained hypothesis (Terasvirta, 1982).

(c) For given ranges of integers of n and p estimate all possible models and choose the best (n, p) according to some criterion. For example, see Terasvirta and Mellin (1983).

(d) Iteratively select n and p. For example, see Sargan (1980a).

The key issue is clearly the choice of the criterion and the properties of the procedure adopted in applying the criterion, the key distinction being between sequential and non-sequential procedures. Given the relative simplicity of (a) we discuss it first.

Suppose n is fixed and it is desired to choose a value of p conditionally. Then, beginning with the maintained hypothesis $H_0: p=p^*$, the alternative hypotheses $H_j: p=p^*-j$, $j=1, \ldots, n-p^*+1$, constitute a uniquely ordered and nested sequence of linear hypotheses each of which can be tested using the F-criterion $Q_j=[(n-p^*-j)s^2]^{-1}\hat{\omega}R'[R(X'X)^{-1}R]^{-1}R\hat{\omega}$ where s^2 is the OLS estimate of residual variance. Under H_0,

$$p=p^*-j,\ Q_j \sim F_{n-j,\,T-n-1}.$$

Beginning with the largest p^* that the investigator is prepared to admit, the F-test is applied sequentially until the first significant test is made at which point the procedure terminates. If there are, say, S steps in the sequence and the significance level at step i is γ_i then the significance level of the test of H_0 against H_S is

$$1-\prod_{i=1}^{S}(1-\gamma_i)$$

so that the choice of a constant conventional five per cent significance level may lead to a quite high significance level for the procedure as a whole if a large number of tests are made. Consequently, even in this otherwise straightforward nested case, one has to balance the probability of ending up with too high a value of p^* by choosing γ_i 'too large' against the probability of failing to learn that a high value of p^* is required by choosing γ_i 'too small'. Clearly the choice of the significance level is critical and we need to know what the optimal choice should be. It seems difficult to answer this without a decision theoretic criterion.

In the more realistic case where both n and p have to be determined, the choice is slightly more complicated because (say) increasing n with p constant leads to non-nested hypotheses. Given p and considering two successive values n and $n+1$ from (16), it is clear that in the second case not only do we have an additional restriction but that the restrictions themselves are different. This is especially clear if the polynomial restrictions are written in the form $(1-L)^S \omega_0 = 0$, $S = p+1, \ldots, n$ (Sargan, 1980), which has the advantage that when we increase p we are merely removing one constraint. If we increase (decrease) n and p simultaneously, we add (remove) one constraint but we also remove (add) one. Hence the constraint set is non-nested. One may therefore choose between the two specifications using one of the many available tests of non-nested models or, alternatively, following Sargan (1980a) reformulate the problem in terms of computationally more convenient nested hypotheses as follows. Maintaining the restrictions at (19) introduces unconstrainedly an additional lagged variable x_{t-n-1} and using a t-test (a) test if $\omega_{n+1} = 0$, and (b) test whether ω_{n+1} is on the p-degree polynomial. If we obtain insignificant t-test for both (a) and (b) but the probability of (b) is higher than (a), we may impose the end-point constraint $\omega_{n+1} = 0$. If the t-test is significant in both cases we should consider abandoning the maintained model in favour of a more general model possibly by increasing the degree p. However, in this last case because of our uncertainty about the maximum lag the matter does not end there and we may at that stage wish to consider yet larger maximum lags, say $n+2$. What is the appropriate strategy: To maintain existing polynomial restrictions, introduce additional lags unconstrainedly and test whether the additional lagged variables should be retained or to begin again by increasing the degree p and testing whether $(n+2)$ lag should be introduced? The t-test on the marginal (last) lag obviously does not provide an answer to this question and, moreover, if the second strategy involving trying different constraint sets is adopted we end up not only with having to do more computation but with the difficult problem of deciding on the appropriate significance level to use in any one of a sequence of t(or F)-tests.

In summary, testimation resolves the problem of simultaneous choice of lag length and polynomial order in the PDL model satisfactorily when the hypotheses have a unique nested form or alternatively when we have some reason to limit the maximum lag length to a small number of values, say two or three. In that case significance testing helps in quickly ruling out data incoherent alternatives. But where a large number of combinations (n, p) must be considered, computational and power considerations make testimation less appealing. Now it is not unusual in applied work to find examples where one has to fix the polynomial and lag lengths simultaneously on two or three explanatory variables. This poses substantial difficulties because there is no complete unique nested ordering of the hypotheses. Even the number of non-nested models to be compared can become large with the attendant problems of the choice of optimal significance level in the tests. It seems attractive at this stage to resort to one of the many model selection criteria (Judge et al., 1980, chapter 11) in preference to hypothesis testing. However, a number of these criteria are explicitly or implicitly decision theoretic (Schwarz, 1978). In so far as a particular criterion favours say a parsimoniously parameterized model, or that based on predictive mean square error, any exponent of testimation who claims not to espouse such a loss function ought not to use it.

Rational Distributed Lags

A simple example of the RDL, also sometimes called the ARMAX model, with a single forcing variable x_t and white-noise error ϵ_t, is

$$y_t - \mu_1 y_{t-1} - \ldots - \mu_{p_1} y_{t-p_1} = \omega_0 x_t + \omega_1 x_{t-1} + \ldots + \omega_{p_2} x_{t-p_2} + (\epsilon_t + \rho_1 \epsilon_{t-1} + \ldots + \rho_{p_3} \epsilon_{t-p_3}) \quad (20)$$

or

$$\mu(\mathrm{L})\, y_t = \omega(\mathrm{L})\, x_t + \rho(\mathrm{L})\, \epsilon_t \quad (21)$$

where $\mu(\mathrm{L})$, $\omega(\mathrm{L})$ and $\rho(\mathrm{L})$ are polynomials of degree p_1, p_2 and p_3 respectively. The problem is to identify and estimate $\mu(\mathrm{L})$, $\omega(\mathrm{L})$ and $\rho(\mathrm{L})$ given that p_1, p_2 and p_3 are unknown.

The testimation approach to this problem is set out clearly in Mizon and Hendry (1980) who take Sargan's Colston paper as their antecedent. The stochastic term is autoregressive not moving average. We now sketch the testimation approach they propose and indicate some of its difficulties.

Suppose we choose initially p_1 and p_2 sufficiently large that $\rho(L)$ can be set to unity. Then the maintained model can be compactly written as

$$\theta(L)'z_t = \epsilon_t \tag{22}$$

where $\theta(L)' = [\mu(L) : \omega(L)]$, $z_t' = [y_t : x_t]$. In the first stage one tries to determine whether, beginning with the largest values of p_1 and p_2 one considers a priori, the model can be specialized to a lower-order data coherent dynamic model with polynomials $\mu^*(L)$ and $\omega^*(L)$, respectively of degree p_1^* and p_2^*, $p_1^* \leqslant p_1$, $p_2^* \leqslant p_2$. Assuming that this difficult task has been accomplished we write the result in the obvious notation

$$\theta^*(L)'z_t = v_t \tag{23}$$

Next we see whether this representation can be further specialized to a simpler data coherent model in which the system dynamics and error dynamics can be separated. If $\theta^*(L)'$ contains a common factor polynomial $\rho(L)$, a polynomial of degree a_1 such that $\theta^*(L) = \rho(L)\cdot\alpha(L)'$ then the dynamic model can be written in the form

$$\alpha(L)'z_t = u_t \tag{24a}$$

$$\rho(L)\, u_t = \epsilon_t \tag{24b}$$

where (24a) corresponds to the system dynamics in which presumably the typical applied econometrician is interested and (24b) corresponds to error dynamics which inconveniently, but not unexpectedly, arise in dynamic models (Sargan, 1980c, p. 879). Here we have assumed an autoregressive error process as an approximation to a more general mixed autoregressive moving average process. A simple and well-known example of this two-step procedure is the following.

Let $p_1 = p_2 = 2$ whence the starting point is the model

$$y_t - \theta_1 y_{t-1} - \theta_2 y_{t-2} - \theta_3 z_t - \theta_4 z_{t-1} - \theta_5 z_{t-2} = \epsilon_t;$$

suppose that the restriction $\theta_2 = \theta_5 = 0$ is found to be data consistent at a conventional level of significance whence we deduce that the appropriate unrestricted model is

$$E(y_t \mid y_{t-1}) = \theta_1^* y_{t-1} - \theta_2^* z_t - \theta_3^* z_{t-1}.$$

Next we test to see whether the model can be further specialized thus: $\theta_1^* = \rho$, $\theta_2^* = \omega_0$ and $\theta_3^* = -\rho\omega_0$. If so then the common factor restriction is accepted and the model reduces to the static model $y_t = \omega_0 x_t + u_t$ with autoregressive error $u_t = \rho u_{t-1} + \epsilon_t$. Finally one can test whether the extracted common factor has a zero root. If the common factor restriction is rejected, then we accept the model at that stage as an adequate dynamic representation of the way y_t is generated.

If the restriction $\theta_2 = \theta_5 = 0$ is not accepted, the procedure is to determine whether the model

$$y_t - \theta_1 y_{t-1} - \theta_2 y_{t-2} - \theta_3 z_t - \theta_4 z_{t-1} - \theta_5 z_{t-2} = \epsilon_t$$

can be specialized to one of the following: (a) model with first-order systematic dynamics and first-order error dynamics (b) model with zero-order systematic dynamics and second-order error dynamics. That is, in general, the problem is one of testing a sequence of hypotheses of the form:

$$\rho_r(\mathrm{L})\,\alpha_{m-r}(\mathrm{L}) = \theta_m(\mathrm{L}) \qquad \text{for } r = 0, 1, 2, \ldots, \min(p_1, p_2).$$

An alternative testimation strategy is to omit the first step in the above procedure. Sequential tests are first applied for reducing the length of lags on all variables until the (Wald) test criterion exceeds the critical value at a pre-chosen significance level and then to use the common factor approach to determine and extract the common factors. Even if two investigators begin with the same unrestricted model and each uses one of these two procedures and the same test criterion, say the Wald criterion, and a common significance level at each stage in the procedure, it is not clear that they would end up with the same dynamic model at the end especially if the initial unrestricted model is high dimensional and does not permit a unique ordering of the sequential tests. A convenient computational feature of the testimation procedures as outlined is that within each procedure hypotheses can be tested sequentially, given the unique ordering. Provided that testing is carried out at a carefully chosen significance level it is possible to ensure the conventional 5 per cent or 10 per cent significance level for the procedures as a whole (although many tests are asymptotic and the nominal significance level may not provide an adequate guide to the correct size of the test in finite samples). However, note that when four or five sequential tests are involved and a constant significance level of 5 per cent is used at each stage the overall significance level will be in the order of 25 per cent, so that it would be advisable to use low significance level, say 1 per cent or 0.5 per cent throughout the procedure. This issue is discussed well by Mizon and Hendry (1980).

There are several difficulties with the testimation procedure. The first concerns the choice of the test procedure itself. If the maximum lag length and/or the common factor restrictions were to be tested via the likelihood ratio procedure, considerable computation would be involved as various restricted and unrestricted models would have to be estimated. The alternative Wald test based on the unrestricted estimates alone seems attractive particularly if the Sargan–Sylwestrowicz (1976) algorithm can be exploited, but otherwise this too is computationally difficult (Mizon and Hendry, 1980, p 25). The really troublesome issue is, however, that the outlined testimation approach deals solely with the problem of the order of dynamics and the number of common factors. When we admit uncertainty about variables in the model, alternative measures of a given set of included variables, the possibility of temporal variation in the parameters and alternative functional forms, it becomes difficult to uniquely order the hypotheses corresponding to a sequence of increasingly restricted models. Depending upon how the hypotheses are ordered different investigators might arrive at different final models. It might then be argued that the choice between non-nested hypotheses be made on the basis of tests of the kind discussed in Mizon and Richard (1983) but since typically to fix several distributed lags, a large number of tests must be made and testing takes place simultaneously at several margins, it would seem difficult to choose the significance level of each test or to determine the power for the *procedure as a whole*. At the final stage the problem is not simply that of comparing two non-nested models but several, each of which may have been arrived at after considerable pre-testing involving repeated application of significance tests in a situation where we have inadequate guidance about what the appropriate significance level should be. In short we are not in the situation in which the Neyman–Pearson hypothesis testing approach leads to optimal decisions.

One attraction of testimation lies in its flexibility, especially in dealing with nuisance parameters, and in its avoidance of strong, possibly arbitrary, prior information which could be in conflict with sample information. Given uncertain prior information testimation incorporates it in a sensible and non-dogmatic fashion. In certain situations, but by no means all, it leads to a structured contracting interpretive search which provides an informative summary of the sample likelihood and is not subject to the full force of Leamer's (1983) strictures of whimsy and subjectiveness in reporting. The weakness of testimation involving a large number of significance tests at essentially arbitrary significance levels is apparent in the context of model selection from a large set of possibly non-nested, competing models.

4 Bayesian Approaches

Preliminaries

Since in the Bayesian framework one treats both the observations and the parameters as random, it seems a natural framework for handling uncertain prior information. Given a vector-valued random variable y and parameter vector θ, the joint pdf $p(y, \theta)$ can be factorized as $p(y\,|\,\theta) \propto p(\theta\,|\,y)\,p(y)$ whence we obtain the well-known Bayes Theorem, $p(\theta\,|\,y) \propto p(\theta)\,p(y\,|\,\theta)$ where $p(\theta\,|\,y)$, the posterior pdf, is proportional to the product of the prior pdf $p(\theta)$ and the sample likelihood function $p(y\,|\,\theta)$. If a suitable prior density $p(\theta)$ can be formulated to reflect the investigator's uncertainty about θ prior to analysing the sample at hand, and if this is combined with sample information in accordance with Bayes' Theorem, the posterior density will reflect how the prior information is modified by the sample information. In many situations the econometrician will want point estimates of θ, $\hat{\theta}$, and also the posterior distribution $p(\theta\,|\,y)$. In the Bayesian approach the optimal point estimator, $\hat{\theta}_{\mathrm{B}}$, is derived as a solution to the minimization problem (see Zellner, 1983)

$$\min_{\hat{\theta}} EL(\theta, \hat{\theta}) = \min_{\hat{\theta}} \int L(\theta, \hat{\theta})\,p(\theta\,|\,y)\,\mathrm{d}\theta \tag{25}$$

where $L(\theta, \hat{\theta})$ denotes the investigator's loss function with θ random and $\hat{\theta}$ non-random and $EL(\theta, \hat{\theta})$ is the expected posterior loss obtained by weighting the losses with posterior probabilities. The optimal Bayes point estimate therefore depends on the investigator's loss function and the prior pdf. For example, it is well known that if the loss function is quadratic, i.e.,

$$L(\theta, \hat{\theta}) = (\theta - \hat{\theta})'W'W(\theta - \hat{\theta})$$

where $W'W$ is a symmetric positive definite matrix, the optimal Bayes esimator is the posterior mean.

Properties of Bayes estimators have been discussed elsewhere, see Zellner (1983). An important property that needs to be mentioned is that of *admissibility*. Under fairly general conditions, usually but not necessarily including a proper prior distribution, the Bayes estimator is admissible, i.e. for a given loss function its risk is no higher than that of any non-Bayes estimator. Conversely every admissible estimator is a Bayes estimator under some prior distribution. Though this makes Bayes estimators generally attractive the problem of specifying the loss function and the prior distribution is difficult. According to the usual arguments the choice of the loss function ought to depend upon the use to which the estimators are to be put, e.g. prediction. However, quite often no particular use of econometric estimates is intended and estimation is simply a part of an evaluation of the data coherency of some particular theory. The implicit loss function in this case is one which assigns a penalty to imposition of a restriction if, at a conventional significance level, that restriction is data incoherent. The more usual quadratic loss function can be justified as a local approximation to any arbitrary loss function and is in any case more appropriate if the goal of estimation is prediction. But to those, like some exponents of testimation, who see no intrinsic merit in a quadratic loss function optimality relative to it has no specific attraction. However, in view of the discussion of section 2 it appears that distributed lag estimation almost always involves a more or less poor approximation and the notion of a correct specification seems tenuous. Therefore, the adoption of a quadratic loss function is defensible. In any case, the quadratic loss function has been widely used both in the Bayesian and in the empirical Bayesian literature.

Prior Distributions

The choice of a suitable prior distribution poses even more difficulties than the loss function since one simultaneously seeks flexible, non-arbitrary, informative and uncontaminated (by sample evidence) priors that lead to tractable posteriors on a possibly high-dimensional parameter space. The difficulty is accurately encapsulated by Leamer (1972, p. 1064) who, in his Bayesian analysis of a distributed lag model of US imports, notes that 'the logic of the Bayesian case requires the prior to reflect reasonably well the state of knowledge prior to data analysis' but notes later that he 'has, of course, read several studies of import demand which employ the same data set ... but he has attempted to purge that information from his mind in order to construct a prior which is unpolluted by "sneak peeks" at the sample evidence'. We now turn to issues of non-arbitrariness and tractability of priors beginning with the PDL model (15).

Given n the model (15) is in the standard regression format and Bayesian analysis of the regression model (Zellner, 1971, chapters 3–4), can be exploited. A variety of non-informative ('diffuse' or 'vague') and informative priors on ω and σ^2 are available. Beginning with the situation where there is little a priori information and following Jeffreys' invariance principle, and assuming the sample likelihood to be multivariate normal so that

$$p(\omega, \sigma) = p_1(\omega) p_2(\sigma) \propto 1/\sigma, \qquad (26)$$

the marginal posterior distribution is well known to be the multivariate Student-t form

$$p(\omega, \sigma) = p_1(\omega)\, p_2(\sigma) \propto \{(T-n-1)s^2 + (\omega-\hat{\omega})'X'X(\omega-\hat{\omega})\}^{-T/2} \qquad (27)$$

where $\hat{\omega} = (X'X)^{-1}X'y$ and $s^2 = (y-X\hat{\omega})'(y-X\hat{\omega})/(T-n-1)$.

In this case the main advantage of a Bayesian analysis is that it allows one to do interesting things to the joint likelihood such as marginalizing it. Usually, however, one desires a marginal posterior density of each component of ω and this will typically involve computationally expensive and inconvenient high-dimensional numerical integration, though the recent advances in integration by Monte Carlo methods (Kloek and van Dijk, 1978), would reduce the force of this argument. Even if this could be achieved it is very doubtful if the end product of such an exercise would be very useful for the usual reasons of multicollinearity between columns of X. The assumption of a vague prior in the context of a high-dimensional distributed lag model is simply inadequate, and we turn to informative priors.

Informative Priors

Several insightful analyses of finite distributed lags, conditional on n, have been carried out, under standard assumptions $\tilde{\omega} \sim N(\omega, H^{-1})$ where $H = \sigma^2(X'X)^{-1}$ and the conjugate normal prior distribution on ω is $\omega \mid y, \sigma^2, n \sim N(\omega^*, H^{*-1})$ where ω^* is the prior location vector and H^{*-1} is the prior covariance matrix. Examples of studies which use normal–gamma prior theory are Leamer (1972), Shiller (1973), Zellner and Williams (1973). For expositional reasons only the analysis below is carried out conditionally on σ^2. The following lemma is also useful:

$$(\omega-\omega^*)'A(\omega-\omega^*) + (\omega-\hat{\omega})'B(\omega-\hat{\omega}) = (\omega-\omega^{**})'(A+B)(\omega-\omega^{**}) + (\omega^*-\omega^{**})'AB(\omega^*-\omega^{**}),$$

where A and B are square symmetric matrices and

$$\omega^{**} = (A+B)^{-1}(A\omega^* + B\hat{\omega}).$$

It is then straightforward to show that the posterior distribution of ω is $\omega \mid y, \sigma^2 \sim N(\omega^{**}, H^{**\,-1})$, with location vector

$$\omega^{**} = (H+H^*)^{-1}(H\hat{\omega} + H^*\omega^*), \tag{28}$$

posterior precision $H^{**} = (H+H^*)$, so ω^{**} is a matrix-weighted average (MWA) of the sample mean $\hat{\omega}$ and the prior mean ω^{**}. If H and H^* are given up to a scale factor, then the MWA ω^{**} forms a one-dimensional curve in R^{n+1} between $\hat{\omega}$ and ω^*. Leamer (1978) has called this curve the 'information contract curve' and has given it a geometrical interpretation, viz. the locus of tangencies between the family of ellipsoids around the location $\hat{\omega}$, $(\omega^{**} - \hat{\omega})'H(\omega^{**} - \hat{\omega}) = c_1$ and $(\omega^{**} - \omega^*)'H^*(\omega^{**} - \omega^*) = c_2$, where c_1 and c_2 are given constants. This geometrical interpretation highlights that the Bayesian posterior mean is obtained by pooling prior and sample means with prior and sample precision matrices being used as weights. Tight and weak prior information implies that we are in the neighbourhood of ω^* and $\hat{\omega}$ respectively. See figure 3.1 in Leamer (1978).

Leamer's application of a normal–gamma prior to an import demand function with four lags on each of the two variables, income and relative prices, also involves a relaxation of the assumption that σ^2 is given. Specifically he assumes an inverted gamma prior for σ^2, independent of the means, but this elaboration while clearly important in practice need not detain us here. The important point is that even if σ^2 were treated as given, the prior mean and variance parameters, ω^* and H^*, have to be specified and this raises the questions: Where is such information to come from? How can it be entered flexibly into the analysis? Leamer (1972) provides an example where a prior is constructed for ten lag coefficients in the US import demand equation involving two variables, income and relative prices. He considers a variety of priors involving decaying as well as humped distributed lags and constructs the prior variance matrix H^* by an appealing principle of proportionality. Furthermore he carries out a sensitivity analysis to show the impact of prior assumptions on posterior distributions. Finally, whereas the unrestricted least squares estimates in his example are quite imprecise, the posterior mean estimates are shown to be meaningful and acceptable. However, some, such as Hendry and Richard (1982), who regard serial correlation in residuals as implying invalid conditioning, possibly arising from the choice of a wrong class of models (numerator distributed lags), may complain that his model choice is too restrictive and that the fitted models do not adequately describe the data.

Leamer's empirical example notwithstanding, the construction of a prior density in a high-dimensional space is difficult. Even in his fully-reasoned article, there is an implicit presumption that the lag weight sequence is unimodal and the weights in any one sequence are all of the same sign; but aggregation and seasonality will in many cases lead to bimodality in the weighting pattern. Moreover, rational expectations arguments will in many cases lead to a mixture of positive and negative weights. Furthermore construction of a prior variance matrix, an already complex task in Leamer's own example, becomes even more complex if we admit greater uncertainty about the elements in the location vector. Indeed there do not appear to be many examples besides Leamer's in which a prior has been carefully constructed for a high-dimensional model. Leamer admits in a more recent contribution (Leamer, 1983, p. 37), 'I am *quite* uncomfortable using a prior distribution, mostly I suspect because hardly anyone uses them.' Furthermore it is also conceded that the construction of a prior covariance matrix involves many arbitrary decisions whose individual impact on the posterior distribution cannot be assessed. There is the additional issue of convenience and flexibility with respect to priors. An investigator who is simultaneously uncertain about the length of the lag and the shape of the lag distribution would want to separate the two issues, which in practice means that his analysis must be conditional on prechosen lag length. Presumably he should carry out a sensitivity analysis under alternative prior distributions and alternative lag lengths and choose from this possibly large set of models. On the other hand, the Bayesian investigator who uses a posterior odds ratio to select between a pair of models will need to specify a priori probabilities attached to different models. The present author has not seen any applied work in which probabilities attached to different models were anything other than equal, which may be convenient but hardly compelling. Finally there is the important point that conjugate priors cannot highlight data incoherency satisfactorily. This is because (Leamer, 1978, pp. 78–9) in the context of the normal regression model the posterior distribution associated with a conjugate prior on ω is unimodal and the mode is located at

ω^{**}. In this procedure there is no distinction between sample and prior information because a conjugate prior is equivalent to a previous sample of the same process. Exponents of testimation as well as others who prefer to obtain a precise idea of the degree of data consistency of a prior distribution will rightly regard this as a drawback. A conflict between prior information and sample information ought to be reflected in a multimodal posterior density and this requires us to move away from the convenient conjugate priors to, for example, an alternative such as Dickey's (1975) Student-t prior which leads in general to a multimodal poly-t posterior density. The task of computing high-dimensional poly-t marginal posterior densities at present is not trivial (Dreze, 1977).

It follows from above that without further modification the Bayesian approach based on conjugate normal priors may not be sufficiently flexible, non-arbitrary or computationally convenient. We therefore turn our attention to variants of the Bayesian approach which attempt to overcome some of these difficulties.

Vestigial Bayesianism

This is a term which I use to describe a methodology for reporting regression results that has been advocated by Leamer (see especially Leamer and Leonard (1983)). It is called vestigial Bayesianism because it eschews the usual Bayesian decision-theoretic framework for point estimation and instead concentrates on a certain subset of location estimates obtained using conjugate normal theory. It is essentially a method of conducting a sensitivity analysis designed to throw light on the following question: Given the normal regression model $y \mid \omega, \sigma^2 \sim N(X\omega, \sigma^2 I_T)$ and the prior distribution $\omega \mid \omega^*, H^{*-1} \sim N(\omega^*, H^{*-1})$, how does the posterior mean ω^{**} defined by equation (28) vary as we change the prior location vector ω^* and the precision matrix H^*? More narrowly, in the above context, what are the extreme values of the posterior mean generated for a fixed σ^2 and an arbitrary H^*? Leamer and Chamberlain have shown (Leamer, 1978, chapter 5.8) that the posterior mean ω^{**} is constrained to lie in the feasible ellipsoid

$$(\omega^{**}-(\hat{\omega}+\omega^*)/2)'H(\omega^{**}-(\hat{\omega}+\omega^*)/2) \leqslant (\hat{\omega}-\omega^*)'H(\hat{\omega}-\omega^*)/4 \qquad (29)$$

which has the midpoint $(\hat{\omega}+\omega^*)/2$. Note that unlike the posterior mean the feasible ellipsoid depends neither on σ^2 nor on

H^*. Thus the difficult problem of having to specify H^* that faces the Bayesian investigator can be circumvented by the vestigial Bayesian who is prepared to specify ω^* but not H^* and to settle for less than the marginal posterior distribution of ω, specifically the extreme bounds of ω^{**}. This procedure, known as extreme bounds analysis (EBA), is intended to provide information on the sensitivity of the posterior mean to continuous variation in the prior location vector ω^*. Any constraints whose impact an investigator wishes to study can be analysed by an appropriate choice of ω^*. This is clearly the nub of the matter. In the testimation approach the investigator makes discrete choices on exclusion or inclusion and is not interested in all possible combinations of including and excluding variables but rather makes a judgment on the direction of search guided by pre-tests. EBA is intended to supplant this judgmental approach. There are not many applications available yet but Leamer and Leonard (1983) have provided one. In contrast with EBA the utility of information contract curve analysis, especially in the case where a Shiller-type prior is used is quite immediate. I take up this issue below.

The Hyperparameter Approach

A very useful way to broaden the set of prior distributions and to avoid some of the difficulties of having to specify in detail the prior means and variances is to use multistage or hierarchical priors. An illustrative example is provided by our PDL model. Suppose we write this as follows:

$$\begin{aligned} y \mid \omega, \sigma^2 &\sim N(X\omega, \sigma^2 I_T) \\ \omega \mid \alpha, J, H^* &\sim N(J\alpha, H^{*-1}) \end{aligned} \tag{30}$$

where the second statement represents a first-stage informative prior, and we adopt a vague second-stage prior on α (on hierarchical priors, see Lindley and Smith, 1972). The main difference between this specification and the Almon specification is that the polynomial restrictions are not treated as exact but uncertain. Parameters in the higher-stage prior such as α are referred to as hyperparameters. Non-Bayesians can interpret the first-stage prior as a stochastic representation of polynomial restrictions. The second-stage vague prior on α then is a non-dogmatic representation of our limited knowledge. By adopting it the investigator is admitting that the first-stage prior is chosen for convenience and that there is some uncertainty about the prior parameters themselves. It can be shown that the posterior distribution of ω has mean given by

$$\omega^{**} = (H + H^{*})^{-1}(H\hat{\omega} + H^{*}J\hat{\alpha}) \tag{31}$$

where all symbols have been defined except $\hat{\alpha} = (J'X'XJ)^{-1}(J'X'y)$, the least squares estimates of the polynomial coefficients. In words, the posterior mean in this case is a MWA of the unrestricted least squares vector $\hat{\omega}$ and the (Almon) restricted least squares estimator $J\hat{\alpha}$. Thus in this hierarchical approach we avoid having to specify the prior distribution and exploit Almon-type restrictions in a flexible fashion, which should appeal to the Bayesian and non-Bayesian alike since no one can seriously believe in the polynomial restrictions except as convenient fiction. The fact that the posterior mean is a MWA of sample estimates ensures that the prior is data-based and potentially data-coherent. Further, it can be shown that if a first-stage normal–gamma conjugate prior on ω and $1/\sigma^2$, and a vague second-stage prior on the hyperparameters are combined to derive a joint prior on all parameters, and if the hyperparameters are integrated out of the expression, the resulting density is of the Student-*t* type and hence when combined with normal likelihood leads to a posterior marginal poly-*t* density (Drèze, 1977, pp. 343–4). The posterior density will in general be multimodal and can potentially reveal a conflict between prior and sample information. This feature of the Bayesian analysis reflected in hierarchical priors should appeal to non-Bayesians. Note, however, that to discover the conflict one should examine the marginal posterior density fully and not simply focus on the posterior mean or modal values. This involves a numerical integration, the difficulties associated with which have already been mentioned.

If the hierarchical prior set-up is accepted the question of the number of stages in the hierarchy arises. This choice itself involves considerations of the investigator's loss function. When is it not worth while for the investigator to enter further hyper-hyper-parameters in his model? Jones (1982) has suggested that the criterion of reliable differentiation (see p. 184 above) be used as a stopping rule. Additional parameters are to be introduced if they lead to substantially different predictions. He calls the method of conducting such a comparison 'generalized hypothesis testing'. The Bayesian, like the frequentist, therefore, faces the problem of having to specify what constitutes a substantial difference. On the other hand it may be argued that this implicitly refers to a decision. Some, like Leamer, may prefer to have a general 'over-parameterized' model for inference and simplify it later when a decision is made. Analysis of hyperparameter models due to De Groot and Goel (1981) indicates that when trying to learn from data about hyperparameters at each level of prior distribution, for a wide class of information measures, the information decreases as one moves to higher levels of hyperparameters. Both considerations therefore suggest that for the Bayesian as well there is a need for the prior probability specification to depend upon the data. The Bayesian concerned with flexibility and non-arbitrariness of his priors will end up data snooping. This feature may at first appear distasteful to orthodox Bayesians but it does bring the Bayesian approach more in line with testimation. An important difference is the greater computational complexity of the hyperparameter approach (especially if the marginal posterior densities are to be reported).

5 Rule-of-thumb Bayesianism

We use this term following Shiller's (1973) discussion of rules of thumb. Rule-of-thumb Bayesians (RTBs) are motivated by considerations of convenience, flexibility and robustness. They are prepared to use data-based priors and hence come up with estimators which can be readily interpreted in a hierarchical (hyperparameter) framework. Shiller has, for example, suggested a Bayesian formulation of the PDL model in which the lag weights lie almost but not exactly on a chosen degree of polynomial. In fact his suggestion is exactly equivalent to (30) though his parameterization of the polynomial restrictions is different. However, writing $y|X,\ \omega,\ \sigma^2 \sim N(X\omega,\ \sigma^2 I_T)$, $R\omega|\sigma_\omega{}^2 \sim N(0,\ \sigma_\omega{}^2 I_{n-q})$ the posterior distribution is easily shown to be normal with mean

$$\omega^{**} = [X'X + \sigma^2/\sigma_\omega{}^2(R'R)]^{-1}(X'X\hat{\omega}) \qquad (32)$$

which is exactly equivalent to (31). In practice one relaxes the assumption that σ^2, $\sigma_\omega{}^2$ are known. Orthodox and rule-of-thumb Bayesians differ in the way they approach this issue. The former will include a prior distribution on σ^{-2}, say a gamma, obtain a joint posterior density for ω and σ^2 and derive the marginal posterior distribution of ω by integrating out σ^2. The RTBs will typically not take this route but treat the posterior mean and variance formulae derived by assuming known σ^2, $\sigma_\omega{}^2$ as approximately valid after some sensible estimates for them have been inserted in the formulae. The argument can be formally justified along the lines of Zellner (1971) who analyses the normal approximation to a Student-t posterior density. Essentially in this spirit Shiller proposes to replace σ^2/σ_ω^2 in the expression (32) by $s^2/\hat{\sigma}_\omega^2$ where s^2 is the sample residual variance estimate from the unrestricted least squares estimate of the distributed lag model and $\hat{\sigma}_\omega^2$ is an estimate of the variance of the qth differences of ω and hence is not independent of the units of measurement. Shiller refers to his estimator of σ_ω^2 explicitly as a rule of thumb and demonstrates by a numerical example the insensitivity of estimates to the choice of σ_ω^2. Akaike (1983) improves on it by providing a maximum likelihood type estimator for estimating σ^2/σ_ω^2. In fact when one has gone this far it is hard to see the difference between the Bayesian and likelihood approaches.

Recently Litterman (1980) has considered the estimation of a vector autoregression (VAR) model in the same spirit as Shiller. As is well known the problem of high dimensionality in a VAR model is generally quite severe, especially when the investigator explicitly acknowledges uncertainty about the lag structure and is not prepared a priori to rule out a high-order autoregression. To tackle the degrees of freedom problem, however, he must introduce some simplifying assumptions and try some method of reducing the dimensionality. In a Bayesian spirit Litterman imposes the prior that 'a reasonable approximation of the behaviour of an economic variable is a random walk around an unknown deterministic component. All equations in the system are given the same form of prior distribution . . . . The parameters are all assumed to have means of zero except the coefficient on the first lag of the dependent variable which is given a coefficient of one'. That is, for the ith equation the prior distribution is centred around the specification

$$Y_{i,t} = Y_{i,t-1} + d_{i,t} + \epsilon_{i,t}$$

where d represents the deterministic component.

Other details of Litterman's prior will not be given here; Sims (1982a) has a valuable discussion. Observe, however, that he uses an approximation to the posterior mean as his point estimator, in much the same way as Shiller, for generating forecasts and he shows that these are not very sensitive to the choice of certain parameters in his prior. The Litterman prior is a rule of thumb, justifiable from the viewpoint of flexibility and robustness. Given the forecasting focus of his paper the concentration on the (approximate) posterior mean with an implicit quadratic loss function also seems appropriate.

The RTBs are not vulnerable to the criticism that distorted inferences may result from their priors. Subject to the choice of maximum dimension they also have a more appealing attitude to inclusion and exclusion of lags compared with testimators. However, in practice the choice of maximum dimension and avoidance of a poor class of models (e.g. number of variables in a VAR or the maximum lag) is extremely important if distortions are to be avoided so that even the RTBs should not avoid experimenting with different models in the same way as testimators. They are probably more likely to embrace explicitly a decision-theoretic criterion for model choice at the final stage.

6 Shrinkage Estimation

Why Shrink?

Shrinkage estimation of distributed lags has been often considered (Spencer, 1976; Maddala, 1977; Lee, 1979; Trivedi, 1978). Shrinkage also involves imposition of constraints in an attempt to reduce the dimensionality of the model. Shrinkage can be uniform or non-uniform, continuous or discontinuous. Exclusion of variables from the model after a pre-test is an example of non-uniform discontinuous shrinkage since some coefficients judged to be negligible are completely excluded from the model. Bayesian estimation with informative priors is an example of continuous shrinkage estimation since, in general, unrestricted estimates are moved in the direction of the prior location vector. In general all Bayesian estimators with informative priors are shrinkage estimators. Leading examples of shrinkage estimators are the James–Stein (1961) estimator and the ridge regression estimators both of which involve continuous shrinkage, in the latter case usually towards zero.

There are several variants of the James–Stein estimator (Judge and Bock, 1978, pp. 229–57) of which two are particularly worth mentioning here. They are

$$\omega_{\mathrm{JS1}} = (1-\tilde{\alpha}(1-R^2)/R^2)\,\hat{\omega} \qquad (33)$$

$$\omega_{\mathrm{JS2}} = (1-\tilde{\alpha}(F)/(1+F))\,(\hat{\omega}-\omega_A) + \omega_A \qquad (34)$$

where R^2 is the coefficient of multiple correlation in the unrestricted OLS estimation of (15), F is the usual F-statistic associated with the test of the linear hypothesis $H_0: R\omega = 0$, ω_A is the Almon estimator of ω, $\tilde{\alpha}$ is a suitably chosen constant and $\tilde{\alpha}(F)$ is a function of F. The factor which multiplies $\hat{\omega}$ in (33) and $(\hat{\omega} - \omega_A)$ in (34) is the shrinkage factor. The shrinkage factor is stochastic and in (34) it depends upon, *inter alia*, the chosen significance level. It has to be chosen in such a way that it leads to an estimator which is superior to $\hat{\omega}$ in terms of the loss function $(\omega - \tilde{\omega})'X'X(\omega - \tilde{\omega})$. In (33) the shrinkage is towards the origin, in (34) towards ω_A. In the first case ω_{JS1} can be regarded as a stochastically weighted average of $\hat{\omega}$ and the zero vector, in the second of $\hat{\omega}$ and ω_A. The existence of a suitable $\tilde{\alpha}$ is not guaranteed but rather depends upon certain features of the matrix $(X'X)$. The extent to which the shrinkage estimator improves upon $\hat{\omega}$ or ω_A depends upon $\tilde{\alpha}$ and the significance level of the pre-test.

The simple ridge regression estimator, ω_R, has the form

$$\begin{aligned} \omega_R &= (X'X + k^* I_{n+1})^{-1} X'y \qquad k > 0 \\ &= (I_{n+1} + k^*(X'X)^{-1})^{-1}\, \hat{\omega} \equiv V(k^*)\, \hat{\omega} \end{aligned} \tag{35}$$

where the term inside the parentheses is the shrinkage factor. It is easily seen that as $k^* \to \infty$, $\omega_R \to 0$ and as $k^* \to 0$, $\omega_R \to \hat{\omega}$. For any $k^* > 0$ shrinkage is towards the origin. If k^* is non-stochastic the properties of ω_R are very easy to work out. In practice k^* is stochastic which makes it difficult to obtain exact standard errors of ω_R. Conditional on k^*, $\mathrm{var}(\omega_R) = \sigma^2 V(K^*)(X'X)^{-1}V(K^*)$. Most shrinkage estimators can be derived as approximations to Bayes posterior means with respect to some informative prior. Viewing them in this manner has the obvious advantage that it makes clear the nature of the prior assumptions employed. For example consider the MWA in (28).

(a) Set $\omega^* = 0$, $H^* = \sigma_\omega^{-2} I_{n+1}$ which yields

$$\omega^{**} = ((X'X) + \sigma^2/\sigma_\omega^2 I_{n+1})^{-1} X'y;$$

this is the so-called *ridge regression* estimator. In this case the shrinkage is towards the origin. As $\sigma^2/\sigma_\omega^2 \to \infty$, $\omega^{**} \to 0$.

(b) Set $\omega^* = 0$, $H^* = \mathrm{diag}(\sigma_{\omega_i}^{-2})$, $i = 1, \ldots, n+1$; which yields

$$\omega^{**} = (X'X + H^*)^{-1}(X'y);$$

this is the *generalized ridge regression* estimator. In this case the shrinkage is also towards the origin but different elements of $\hat{\omega}$ get pulled towards the origin at different rates.

(c) Set $\omega^* = 0$, $H^* = \sigma_\omega^{-2}(X'X)$ which yields

$$\omega^{**} = (1+\sigma^2/\sigma_\omega^2)^{-1}\hat{\omega}$$

which shrinks all components $\hat{\omega}$ towards the origin at a uniform rate; substituting an estimator for σ^2/σ_ω^2 leads to a variant of the James–Stein estimator (see also Zellner (1980)).

(d) Set $\hat{\omega} = J\alpha$ as in (31), $H^* = \sigma_\omega^{-2}(X'X)$; this yields

$$\omega^{**} = \phi\hat{\omega} + (1-\phi)\,\omega^*$$

where $\phi = \sigma^2/(\sigma^2 + \sigma_\omega^2)$ which also is a variant of the James–Stein estimator.

Historically, however, shrinkage estimators have been motivated differently. Shrinkage along the ridge regression lines has been justified by emphasizing that ridge regression 'combats multicollinearity' and leads to an estimator with a smaller squared length (Hoerl and Kennard, 1970) and along the James–Stein lines by arguing that the maximum likelihood estimator is in general not admissible relative to quadratic loss. The multicollinearity argument amounts to saying that its existence leads to uncertainty about the parameters which can only be reduced by introducing prior information and ridge regression incorporates such prior information. If ω^{**} is computed for different value of the ratio σ^2/σ_ω^2 we obtain what is known as the *ridge trace*, or in Leamer's terminology the *information contract curve*. Choice of a particular point on this curve amounts to incorporation of a particular ratio of σ^2/σ_ω^2. If this choice is data-based then the approach is not strictly Bayesian. Rule-of-thumb Bayesians (RTBs) choose σ^2/σ_ω^2 in such a way that a good approximation to the posterior mean ω^{**} is obtained without the need to compute the marginal posterior density and the estimates are robust to that choice. Substitution of an estimate of σ^2/σ_ω^2 is equivalent to an approximation of the posterior density which is of normal–Student-t type (Zellner, 1971, chapter 4, Appendix B) by the leading normal term. The resulting point estimator is not a Bayes rule and cannot be admissible but it may have good properties if σ^2/σ_ω^2 is well chosen (Vinod, 1978). Exponents of shrinkage estimation attempt to choose a value of σ^2/σ_ω^2 so as to approximate minimum expected quadratic loss estimator. But the posterior mean has the minimum expected quadratic loss relative to the prior. It follows therefore that 'shrinkers' and RTBs are after the same thing, though they often appear to set about the task differently. The literature on ridge regression contains extensive discussion of how to choose the ridge parameter (Vinod and Ullah, 1981, chapters 7 and 8). Most of these adopt a quadratic loss function.

In Zellner and Vandaele (1975) Stein-like estimators are motivated from minimum MSE considerations. Let v_0 and v_1 be scalars and $\tilde{\omega} = v_0 l + v_1 \hat{\omega}$ be an estimator for ω, for alternative choices of v_0 and v_1 where l is a unit vector. We seek values of v_0 and v_1 such that the risk associated with $\tilde{\omega}$ is no greater than that associated with $\hat{\omega}$, i.e.

$$\begin{aligned} R(\omega, \tilde{\omega}) &\equiv E(\omega-\tilde{\omega})'Q(\omega-\tilde{\omega}) \\ &\leqslant E(\omega-\hat{\omega})'Q(\omega-\hat{\omega}) \equiv R(\omega, \hat{\omega}). \end{aligned} \tag{36}$$

Substituting for $\tilde{\omega}$ and differentiating with respect to v_0 and v_1 we can determine the optimal values of v_0 and v_1, say v_0^* and v_1^*. Of course the optimal values will be functions of unknown parameters ω and σ^2 and hence $\tilde{\omega}$ is not operational. If these optimal values are substituted into $\tilde{\omega}$ we obtain an expression for $\tilde{\omega}$ of the form

$$\tilde{\omega} = \bar{\omega} l + \left[1 - \frac{R(\omega, \hat{\omega})}{R(\omega, \hat{\omega}) + (\hat{\omega}-\bar{\omega}l)'Q(\hat{\omega}-\bar{\omega}l)}\right](\hat{\omega}-\bar{\omega}l) \tag{37}$$

where $\bar{\omega} = l'Q\omega/l'Ql$, a weighted average of elements of ω (Zellner and Vandaele, 1975, p. 610). A 'sensible' procedure would be to substitute estimates of ω and σ^2, but if this is done then the inequality at (36) need not be satisfied, i.e. the operational version of minimum MSE estimator is not itself minimum MSE and may in fact be inferior to $\hat{\omega}$. If, however, the scalars v_0 and v_1 have been estimated 'well' then the operational version of $\tilde{\omega}$ will dominate the estimator $\hat{\omega}$ relative to a simple quadratic loss function in some region of the parameter space. The task of selecting estimators of v_0 and v_1 which perform generally satisfactorily (i.e. at all points in the parameter space of interest) seems quite difficult. Most of the guidance comes from sampling experiments which indicate the possibility of improving on the OLS estimator within points in the parameter space and for certain data matrices.

Critique of Shrinkage

There are a number of difficulties with the adoption of shrinkage methods in distributed lag estimation. The first and fundamental difficulty concerns the choice of the necessary prior and loss function. But the quadratic loss function does not have intrinsic or universal appeal except on utilitarian grounds. As regards the prior, certain types of priors common in the shrinkage literature do not have a strong appeal in the context of distributed lag estimation. The simple ridge method for example seems reasonable when one is modelling a single long-tailed lag distribution but not when modelling several short ones. The variant of James–Stein estimator which leads to uniform shrinkage seems rather contrary to the usual practice of not tinkering with well-determined coefficients but shrinking poorly determined ones. In other words, the implicit prior in this case does not seem sufficiently flexible.

A second difficulty arises from the fact that a great deal of the shrinkage literature is concerned with estimation of a given specification. This is equivalent to having a procedure to apply at the final stage of a sequential search. But what about the sequential search itself? Should shrinkage not be considered at each stage in that search? Sometimes, as in Judge and Bock (1978), shrinkage along the James–Stein lines is advocated as an alternative to pretesting on the grounds that the pre-test estimator is inadmissible relative to quadratic loss. But I have already suggested in section 3 that the reasons for pre-testing are probably inconsistent with a quadratic loss function anyway. There is in any case the problem of choosing the parameters $\tilde{\alpha}$ and $\tilde{a}(F)$ in (33) and (34). Furthermore, in the context of distributed lag models at any rate, one of the necessary conditions for the existence of a James–Stein estimator which dominates the OLS estimator is unlikely to be satisfied in practice (Trivedi, 1978) and even if it is the reduction in loss may not be that great. We note that most of the shrinkage literature, because it refers to the normal regression model, has an applicability only to the finite distributed lag model. When dealing with models with lagged dependent variables, we would not in general wish to impose the priors implicit in simple ridge regression. Much of the theory and properties of the shrinkage estimators have only been developed for the standard regression model so we have an insufficient basis for extending them to the important class of rational distributed lags. Finally we note that where the shrinkage factor is stochastic, exact standard errors of the estimates are hard to obtain; as a result point estimation rather than hypothesis testing is emphasized in applications of shrinkage methods.

7 Stochastic Constraint Formulation

Some Examples

The stochastic constraint approach has been developed largely in the context of the finite PDL model and is largely motivated by the desire to free the constraints implicit in the Almon PDL formulation. An example due to Ullah and Raj (1979) helps to make the discussion concrete. Ullah and Raj specify the following variant of the PDL model

$$y_t = \sum_{i=0}^{n} \omega_{it} x_{t-i} + u_t \qquad t = 1, \ldots, T \tag{38}$$

$$\omega_{it} = \bar{\omega}_i + \epsilon_{it} \tag{39}$$

$$\bar{\omega}_i = \alpha_0 + \alpha_1 i + \ldots + \alpha_q i^q + \eta_i \qquad i = 0, \ldots, n \tag{40}$$

where ϵ_{it} and η_i are independent random zero mean, homoscedastic disturbances with variances σ_ϵ^2 and σ_η^2 respectively. This specification says that the distributed lag weights vary randomly over time around a mean level $\bar{\omega}_i$; $\bar{\omega}_i$ $(i = 0, \ldots, n)$ deviate randomly from a polynomial of order q. If the ϵ_{it} are assumed constant, the model specializes to the Shiller formulation and if ϵ_{it} and η_i are both constant we get the Almon formulation. Since we have already seen that the Shiller formulation can be interpreted in the Lindley–Smith hierarchical prior format it follows that the Ullah–Raj formulation is in one respect also more general than the Lindley–Smith formulation. By substituting (39) and (40) into (38) and writing the result in matrix notation introduced earlier we obtain

$$y = XJ\alpha + w \tag{41}$$

where the elements of w,

$$w_t = u_t + \sum_{i=0}^{n} (x_{t-i}\epsilon_{it} + x_{t-i}\eta_i),$$

are heteroscedastic and $E(ww') = \Omega$ is a diagonal matrix. From the viewpoint of estimation therefore the main impact of the Ullah–Raj generalization is to introduce heteroscedastic error terms, albeit in their specification this can be handled relatively easily by a GLS type procedure. The Ullah–Raj assumption of serial independence of ϵ and η seems quite restrictive. In practice $\{x_t\}$ is likely to be a strongly serially correlated process, hence we might expect ω to be serially correlated and heteroscedastic. Estimation of such models is discussed by Cragg (1982) and Nicholls and Quinn (1982).

The hierarchical prior model itself allows a random coefficient interpretation. For example we can write the two-stage hierarchical model as follows. Let

$$y = X\omega + u, \qquad u \sim N(0, \sigma_u^2 I_T) \tag{42}$$

$$\omega = J\alpha + \epsilon, \qquad \epsilon \sim N(0, \sigma_\epsilon^2 I_{n+1}) \tag{43}$$

$$\alpha = \bar{\alpha} + \eta, \qquad \eta \sim N(0, \sigma_\eta^2 I_{q+1}) \tag{44}$$

where ω is a random drawing from a normal distribution with mean $J\alpha$ (J given) variance σ_ϵ^2 and α itself is a random drawing from another normal distribution with mean $\bar{\alpha}$ and variance σ_η^2. This type of specification has been exploited to deal with seasonal patterns in distributed lags in Trivedi and Lee (1981). But it does not of course introduce into the picture temporal observed or unobserved variation in ω as in the Ullah–Raj formulation.

The stochastic constraint formulation can be used to provide an alternative derivation of a Shiller-type estimator. Terasvirta (1980) writes the polynomial constraints (40) more generally in the form

$$r = R\omega + \psi, \; E\psi = 0, \; E(\psi\psi') = \sigma_\psi^2 I, \; E(u'\psi) = 0 \tag{45}$$

In this set-up R, whose elements are known coefficients of the differencing polynomial, is interpreted as a set of fictitious observations, and r is observed zero. Combining (45) and (38) in a single model and deriving the least squares estimator for ω we have

$$\omega_m(k) = (X'X + \sigma_u^2/\sigma_\psi^2 R'R)^{-1}(X'y + (\sigma_u^2/\sigma_\psi^2)\, X'r) \tag{46}$$

which is the so-called Theil–Goldberger mixed estimator and which reduces to Shiller's estimator if $r \equiv 0$ which implies $\sigma_\psi^2 = 0$. This derivation, which motivates the problem from a non-Bayesian viewpoint, is not insightful. An alternative way of making the polynomial restrictions stochastic (mentioned by Terasvirta (1980)) assumes that the coefficients ω lie on or within an ellipsoidal cylinder so that they satisfy the inequality restrictions

$$\|R\omega\| \leqslant c^2. \tag{47}$$

Minimizing $(y-X\omega)'(y-X\omega)$ subject to (47) then yields a Shiller-type estimator $(X'X+kR'R)^{-1}X'y$ where k is the Lagrange multiplier associated with the constraint (47) and is inversely related to c. When (47) takes the form $\|\omega\| \leqslant c^2$, which confines elements of ω to lie on or within a hypersphere of radius k, we obtain the simple ridge estimator. Clearly the smaller is c the tighter is the constraint.

Estimators derived from stochastic constraint formulations are close to Bayesian posterior means under an appropriate prior. For those with a philosophical preference for the sampling theory framework it provides an alternative route to empirical Bayes or RTB estimators. However, in some situations they also permit a further broadening of prior assumptions. As yet the stochastic constraint formulation has not been applied to the rational distributed lag model. It is easy to verify by reference to the Koyck model that random parameter variation in the coefficient of the lagged dependent variable will introduce complex nonlinearities, in the handling of which we have as yet little practice experience. (For some discussion of tests for detecting this kind of variation see chapter 5.)

8 Conclusion

This chapter is not concerned with the technicalities of econometric estimation but rather with the general principles on which different approaches to distributed lag analysis are based. In a typical distributed lag model we face a problem of parametric estimation in a high-dimensional parameter space with multicollinear data. If reasonably precise information about individual parameters is to be obtained, it is essential to introduce some prior information first. However, the considerations outlined in section 2 suggest that we do so in a flexible and robust fashion. I have attempted to show how different approaches cope with this difficult task and to indicate the weaknesses and strengths of each approach. There appears to be considerable mystery and even prejudice surrounding a number of these approaches, e.g. the shrinkage approach, despite the fact that the widely practised method of pre-testing involves precisely that. On the other hand there is a widespread suspicion of testimation as a methodology based on dubious principles. Hopefully I have shown that each of these approaches has its own motivation and should be evaluated in terms of the investigator's loss function, the acceptability of the implicit or explicit characterization of prior information and the completeness of the data summary provided by it, rather than in terms of widely used but essentially arbitrary criteria.

Acknowledgment

I am indebted to A. C. Harvey, D. F. Hendry, E. E. Leamer, B. M. S. Lee, C. A. Sims, T. Terasvirta and A. Ullah for comments and suggestions which have led to improvements. I alone remain responsible for the contents.

8

Econometric Modelling of House Prices in the United Kingdom

DAVID F. HENDRY

1 Introduction

The prices at which housing transactions take place have major impacts on the wealth holdings of individuals, the composition of their portfolios and the interpersonal distribution of wealth, as well as on the costs of obtaining any given flow of housing services, and on the level of activity in the new-construction sector (thus influencing several major industries which supply construction materials). It is an unsurprising consequence that house prices should have assumed political importance after a decade which witnessed massive fluctuations in both the nominal and the real prices of houses. These arguments alone suffice to justify a study of the 'average' behaviour over time of house prices in the UK.

To an econometrician, however, there are also intrinsic interests in modelling this variable. The volatility of UK house prices makes their study a challenging one for econometric methods – can we only model simple phenomena whose systematic determinants are relatively obvious, or are dynamic modelling methods sufficiently powerful to allow 'good' explanations of rapidly changing variables? If so, can house price changes be predicted *ex ante* sufficiently accurately to sustain profitable 'speculation'? Will the market functioning alter in the light of such information to arbitrage away any excess profit? And so on. All the usual pitfalls of econometric modelling also await the unwary: issues of measurement, specification, efficient inference, etc. The whole offers a most interesting prospect.

A natural starting point is to see what phenomena have occurred and what merits explanation, albeit that this presupposes both implicit measurement systems and embryonic theories. However, a time series ostensibly measuring the prices at which second-hand houses are transacted (via mortgage advances from Building Societies) is recorded in various issues of *Housing and Construction Statistics* and *BSA Bulletins*, and the quarterly observations for 1959(i)–1982(ii) are shown in figure 8.1 where 1959(iv) = 20, 1964(iv) = 40 etc. While we later question the accuracy of this series, it is an adequate index of housing prices for illustrating the salient data features (see *Economic Trends*, October 1982) and is denoted Ph, with $ph = \log Ph$.

Clearly, nominal house prices have risen dramatically in the last quarter century, by over *twelvefold* all told. However, the dominant trend in figure 8.1 makes it difficult to see short-period variation so the quarter-to-quarter proportional changes are shown in figure 8.2. This series is an erratic one, but is generally positive (the concomitant of the previously noted trend) and exhibits apparent 'cyclical' behaviour. Such a phenomenon is more easily seen in the plot of annual price changes (*i*th quarter of one year to the *i*th quarter of the succeeding year), again using the symmetrical proportional change advantages of the log transforma-

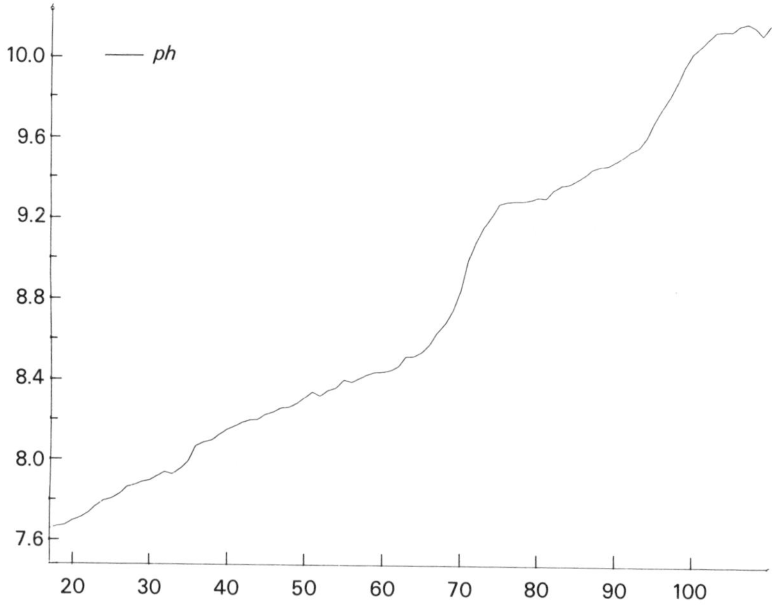

Figure 8.1 Second-hand house prices, based on *Housing and Construction Statistics* and *BSA Bulletin*, quarterly from 1959(i) to 1982(ii), log scale.

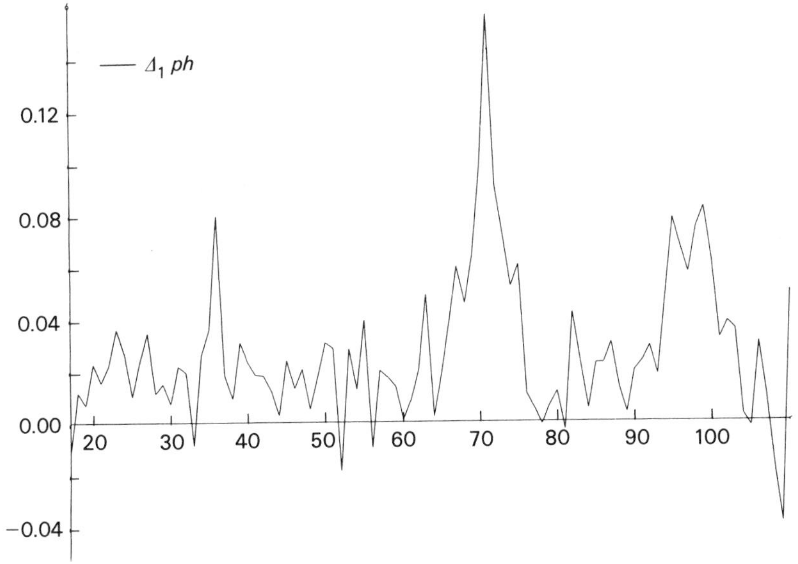

Figure 8.2 Proportional changes in second-hand house prices on a quarter-to-quarter basis.

tion. By way of comparison, annual changes in the retail price index also are plotted in figure 8.3. Several more data phenomena are suggested: the rate of change of house prices is much more volatile than that of the RPI, and the two series are remarkably asynchronous, seemingly showing house price changes both leading general inflation by several years, and on average exceeding the rate of increase of the RPI. Thus, real house prices (i.e. house prices measured in constant purchasing power terms) must have risen and figure 8.4 confirms such an inference: real house prices have increased by over 50 per cent during the sample period. However, in contrast to figure 8.1, the general trend is not at all monotonic – large falls in real house prices have occurred (up to 40 per cent over the four-year period 1973–7).

Since house purchases are frequently the largest financial transactions in which most individuals will participate during their lives, the prices of owner-occupied houses must be related to the incomes of their owners (note that our house-price data relate only to owner-occupiers' purchases). Thus, the next data description we consider is the ratio of house prices to incomes. At the

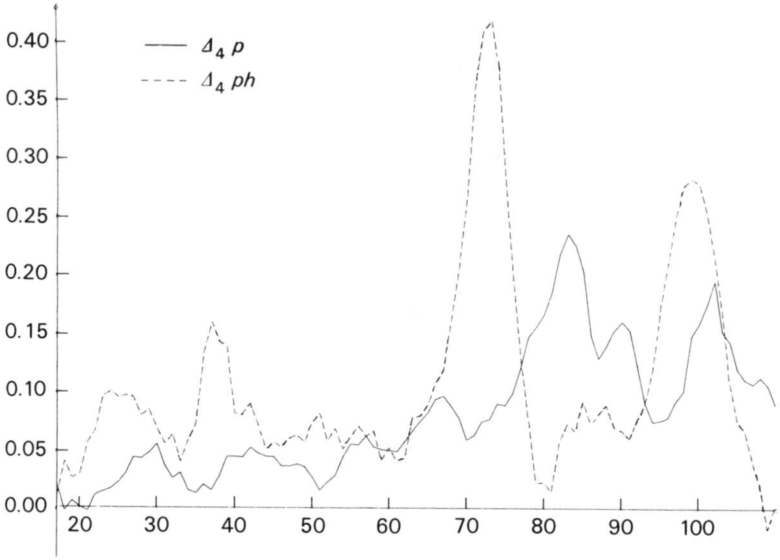

Figure 8.3 Annual rates of change in (a) house prices (broken line) and (b) retail price index (solid line).

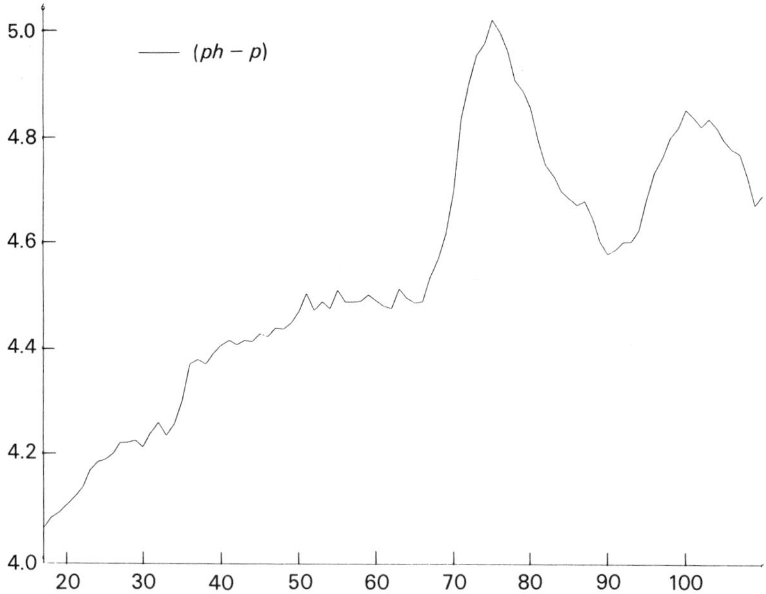

Figure 8.4 Real house prices.

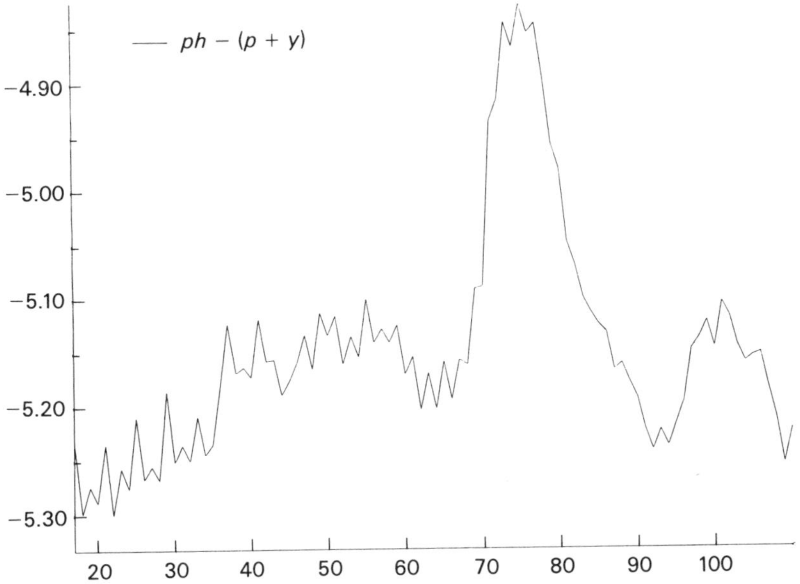

Figure 8.5 Ratio of house prices to incomes, $Ph/PY = (Ph/P)/Y$.

aggregate level, the most readily available reliable index of quarterly income is that of total personal disposable income. This measure has the drawback that changes in income distribution between owner-occupiers and others may influence house prices but are not reflected in our choice of series. Also, owner-occupation (as a percentage of the total housing stock) has increased rapidly since 1945, rising from around a third to well over half, so the constituency of owner-occupiers is variable. An aggregate income measure has the advantage that it will reflect both the 'average' ability of first-time buyers to enter the market (unless a sustained adverse redistribution of income shares is occurring) and the purchasing power of existing houseowners. Either way, figure 8.5 shows the ratio of house prices (denoted Ph) to incomes ($P.Y$) – note that this measure is independent of nominal prices, being the same for nominal house prices to nominal incomes $Ph/P.Y$ as for the equivalent real variables $(Ph/P)/Y$. The next main data phenomenon appears: despite the dramatic fluctuations over the period, $Ph/P.Y$ continually returns to a 'base level' (the value of that level is arbitrary here, being dependent on the base year for which the index *Ph* is normalized to unity). Correcting for changes in either the number of families or in the labour force would impart a slight trend to this graph.

A final but closely related data description is the average value of housing per unit income, which is a variable of the form $Ph.H/P.Y$ where H is the relevant stock of housing. There are serious difficulties in measuring this variable since *Ph* relates to owner-occupied housing, whereas $P.Y$ is aggregate disposable income. If the total housing stock is used for H, *Ph* is inappropriate (except in the highly unlikely event that houses owned by landlords and local authorities have the same average price as privately owned houses). However, if the owner-occupied stock is used for measuring H, then, $P.Y$ is not the most relevant income series for the reasons discussed above. Because of its connection with our measure of *Ph*, the owner-occupied stock of housing is used for H. Figure 8.6 reports $Ph.H/P.Y$ and the time series for the real value of the mortgage stock per house $M/P.H$. The two

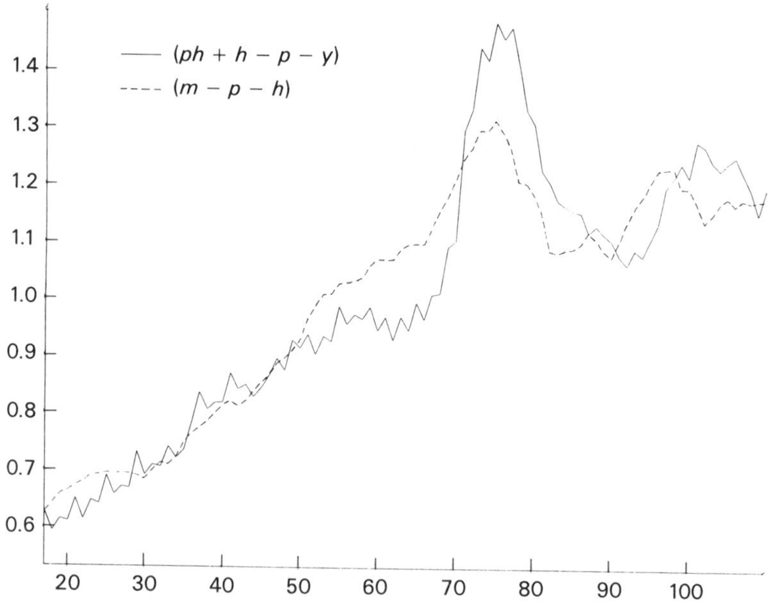

Figure 8.6 Average value of housing per unit income (solid line) and real value of the mortgage stock (broken line).

series are highly correlated, having increased at the same trend rate, evidently showing that $M/P.H$ leads $Ph.H/P.Y$. Finally, figure 8.7 shows the ratio of 'borrowed to own equity' $M/Ph.H$ which has fluctuated greatly without much sign of a trend. The average house costs more than three times average income, and the value of housing comprises over half of net total personal wealth, so the role of finance is bound to be important in housing transactions. Some institutional details relevant to that issue are provided in section 2.

Despite any appearance to the contrary in the preceding data descriptions, figures do not speak for themselves but require careful interpretation. This necessitates a theoretical framework, implicit in both the various data transformations examined above and the measures reported. The next section discusses such a framework in the usual equilibrium supply and demand paradigm of economics, but taking account of the fact that housing is an important asset as well as the source of a service flow. In section 3 the analysis is extended to allow for (a) the existence of both

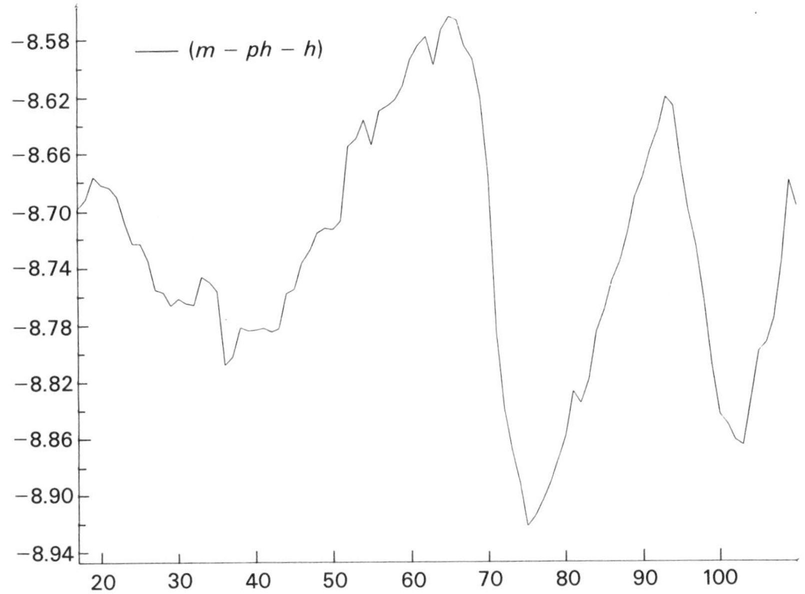

Figure 8.7 Ratio of 'borrowed to own equity', $M/Ph.H$.

stock and flow markets (existing housing and new construction respectively) so disequilibria persist unless both markets are in equilibrium, (b) the important mediating role of finance, and (c) expectations about future house price changes, which critically affect housing demand. Moreover, any postulated theory must be capable, at least in principle, of accounting for the salient data features noted in this section. Thus, the theory model of sections 2 and 3 incorporates a dynamic adjustment process whereby large disequilibria are removed very rapidly in an equation which induces a long-run 'base ratio' of $Ph.H$ to $P.Y$.

The impact of these developments on individual wealth holding can be illustrated by considering a typical individual who invested in a house in (mid) 1971 and remained an owner-occupier till (mid) 1981. The average nominal price of a house purchased on a mortgage in 1971 by a first-time buyer was £4800, with a mortgage of £3900 lent against a nominal income of £2000 p.a. By 1977, the average price of houses purchased by all buyers was £13,700 yielding a nominal capital gain of £8900 on an initial capital of £900. This gain is untaxed for owner-occupiers in the UK (for simplicity, after-tax mortgage payments are assumed equal to net rents, both calculated before adding local taxes, known as rates, which is a reasonable first approximation). The *real rate of return after tax* on the initial capital is over 25 per cent p.a. (compound)! In contrast, a *negative* after-tax real rate of return was earned on long-term bonds. In 1977, our wise individual, now earning £5200 p.a., reinvests all this net equity in a new house, borrowing a new (total) mortgage of £9100 (the average for 1977) thus purchasing a house costing £18,900. On average by 1981, such a house would exchange at £33,400, yielding a nominal gain of £14,500. Over the whole decade, the after-tax real rate of return was 20 per cent p.a. compound. At such a return real capital would increase *38-fold* in 20 years! Alternatively expressed, the total nominal gain was £23,400, approximately equal to half of his/her total *cumulative* income over the decade. A second individual entering the housing market in 1974 on the same average assumptions would have made an equivalent rate of return of 10 per cent p.a. It was difficult to become rich in the UK of the seventies on earned income alone, yet while saving none of that earned income, it was possible to convert one's wealth/income ratio from under a half to almost three by judicious timing of house purchases.

2 An Equilibrium Model of the Supply of and Demand for Housing

By 'equilibrium' here is meant 'no inherent tendency to change', where the emphasis is on inherent: that is, the situation does not contain any factors which automatically induce a different outcome in subsequent periods (as would be usual in, say, dynamic models). Thus, we are considering a static state where depreciation of the physical housing stock H is precisely matched by the rate of completion of new units C:

$$C = \delta H \tag{1}$$

where δ is the depreciation rate. We abstract from a model of the supply side (which is the subject of a separate paper – see Hendry and Ericsson (1983)), taking Ph in equilibrium to be that level which provides a 'normal profit' to the construction industry when C is produced. Land prices are taken as determined by the efficient markets hypothesis for a fixed resource so as to yield a rate of return equal to the real rate of interest. An upward sloping supply curve would not materially change the analysis, but a constant equilibrium of $Ph = Ph_0$ simplifies the exposition. Then H is determined by demand factors as in figure 8.8, given Ph_0.

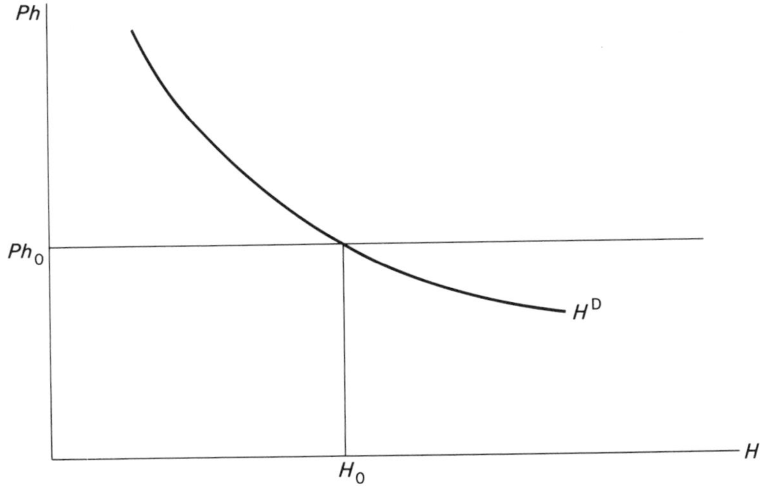

Figure 8.8 Long-run demand curve for houses.

Three sets of factors influence demand: (a) demographic (population size, average family size, etc.); (b) service flow (the utility derived from the location, size, quality, type, and environmental attributes of each individual's dwelling(s)); (c) asset demand (the relative rate of return from house ownership as against ownership of alternative assets).

These are considered in turn.

(a) The size and composition of the population obviously strongly influence the number of dwelling units and may also affect the size of the average unit. If there are N individuals and the average family is of size F, then there are N/F households. Between countries, or very different historical epochs, N/F must be a major determinant of the number of dwelling units. However, not every household unit need be housed (homelessness remains a problem even in 'developed' economies) and many may occupy several separate units (e.g. main residence, country house, and flat in London). Consequently, even conditional on N and F, H differs with economic factors such as incomes, wealth holdings, interest rates, etc. Despite the greater focus of other models on the role of demographic factors (see e.g. Buckley and Ermisch (1982)), they only enter indirectly in the empirical model below, and leave open one avenue for further improvement.

(b) Next, the demand for the flow of services provided by housing is a demand for a complex bundle of attributes. In time-series studies, such a flow is often assumed to be proportional to the stock of housing measured as a number of units, see e.g. Buckley and Ermisch (1982). This may seem extremely problematical, being dependent on an assumption of constant composition within H. For example, in a cross-section analysis, the most obvious measure of the service flow is as a proportion of the price of the dwelling – households presumably pay more for some units than others because their service flow is higher (due to higher quality, closeness to city centre, or larger size, etc., not to mention the attributes of the neighbourhood). A more appropriate stock measure would be a constant-price weighted average of the value of all existing units, which we denote by K. This is analogous to the conventional measure used for, say, the 'capital stock', so that K is the depreciated cumulation of past constant-price investment in housing. Then K and H differ over time if the relative prices of the components comprising a house change. However, from analysis of a simple model of a cost-minimizing builder who constructs homogeneous units from two inputs whose relative price alters, it emerges that H and K do not diverge substantially even if one of the relative prices doubles, so a crude approximation of K by H may be workable historically. Since no measures of private sector K are available, such an approximation must be tolerated (note that Nellis and Longbottom (1981) construct a series related to K for the total housing stock).

(c) The determinants of the asset demand are incomes and relative prices. In principle, the choice of tenure (own or rent) is separable from the level of demand, but housing taxes inextricably intermix service and asset (i.e. ownership) demands in the UK. If one acts as a landlord, then both net rental incomes (i.e. less rates and upkeep), and nominal capital gains due to house price changes are taxed (although this last state of affairs has been changed recently towards taxing only real gains). In contrast, owner-occupiers of a single unit are not taxed on either the implicit rental income or the capital gain. Also, rent controls on landlords are prevalent and tenure laws are favourable to tenants, acting as further disincentives to let properties. Yet both potential landlords and individual owner-occupiers face the same tax/return conditions in bond and equity markets. In an equilibrium in which rates of return were equal across different assets, there would be no landlords in the absence of capital rationing (see Appendix A). Matching this implication, the private rental sector has fallen from 33 per cent of the housing stock to 10 per cent over the last 25 years.

However, capital rationing is a crucial issue in the UK housing market, pervasive well beyond microeconomic imperfections. The primary suppliers of mortgage finance are Building Societies, whose assets comprise about 75 per cent of the existing total stock of mortgages. These are non-profit cooperatives or 'friendly societies', with low legal minimum reserve/asset ratios, which enable them to operate on small mark-ups of lending over borrowing interest rates. Mortgages are contracted on a variable interest rate basis which the Societies are free to alter according to market conditions. They have grown extremely rapidly over the last quarter century, their total assets increasing from round £2 billion to over £60 billion or in constant price terms by a factor of over $4\frac{1}{2}$ (around 6 per cent p.a. real growth). A further tax asymmetry now intrudes: all interest earnings of individuals are liable to tax, but for most kinds of loans interest outgoings are not deductible against tax in the UK. An exception is interest on a mortgage for a single owner-occupied unit (up to a maximum, which was constant at £25,000 from 1974 to 1983 when it was increased to £30,000). In a market-clearing equilibrium, one would anticipate this tax advantage being offset by the pre-tax interest rate rising. In practice, the rate of interest on a Building Society mortgage has been one of the *lowest* borrowing rates obtainable! A model of their functioning which accounts for this anomaly is provided in Hendry and Anderson (1977) and Anderson and Hendry (1984) but an unsurprising implication is that mortgages are generally in rationed supply. Such rationing could persist in a non-clearing equilibrium, providing Building Societies could prevent endless 'round tripping' (i.e. borrowing on a mortgage to finance purchase of other assets yielding a rate of return higher than the mortgage interest rate). For a recent analysis of mortgage lending, see Davis and Saville (1982), and for a discussion of Building Societies, see Boléat (1982).

Without specifying a formal life-cycle model, the general functional dependence can be expressed as:

$$H^D = f(\underset{-}{Ph/P}, \underset{+}{Y}, \underset{-}{\rho}, \underset{-}{R}, \underset{-}{Rm}, \underset{+}{M}, \underset{?}{T}, \underset{+}{N}, \underset{?}{F}) \tag{2}$$

(anticipated signs of partial derivatives are indicated below each variable). In (2), ρ is the real rental rate, R is a representative market interest rate, Rm is the mortgage rate of interest, M is the stock of mortgages and T is the tax rate (proxying several rates which differ across individuals). Below, a log-linear specification is chosen as consistent with the positivity of H, and this yields a flexible form for a range of transformations on the dependent variable including all of those discussed in section 1.

Then, given values for all the arguments of $f(\cdot)$, setting Ph equal to Ph_0 determines H_0. Comparative static implications follow directly from (2): viz. an increase in Ph_0/P lowers the housing stock, an increase in incomes raises H and so on. The static equilibria of both the dynamic model and the empirical model reported below will be judged in the light of such results. Nevertheless, figure 8.8 is a misleading guide as to how the housing market functions outside of a static equilibrium as discussed in the next section.

3 A Dynamic Model of the Market for Owner-occupied Housing

Intertemporally, the actual housing stock evolves according to:

$$H_t = (1-\delta_t)\, H_{t-1} + C_t \tag{3}$$

where C_t denotes net additions (private new completions plus net supply from other sectors such as the public or private rental markets). While δ_t probably varies with economic conditions, relative to other variations it is essentially constant and is treated as such. Thus, the equilibrium of (3) when $H_t = H_{t-1}$ and $C_t = C \;\forall\, t$ reproduces (1).

At any point in time, C_t is very small relative to H_{t-1} and is itself relatively predetermined by the volume of construction in progress. Thus, we treat H_{t-1} as a fixed supply of housing available in the short run. This is precisely the *opposite* fixity assumption of the previous section. The demand for the existing stock (all of which must be owned by someone) will, in consequence, determine the price *Ph*, adjustment proceeding until that stock is willingly held. Figure 8.9 illustrates the very short-run market behaviour.

A jump in demand from $H_a{}^D$ to $H_b{}^D$ induces a rise in price from Ph_a to Ph_b. Abstracting for a moment from the problem of the length of period needed for such an adjustment to occur, while the market for the stock has cleared, the new-construction market may be in considerable disequilibrium if Ph_b exceeds the Ph_0 of section 2. The prices of plots of land for new construction rise as H^D increases and a complicated dynamic interaction between land

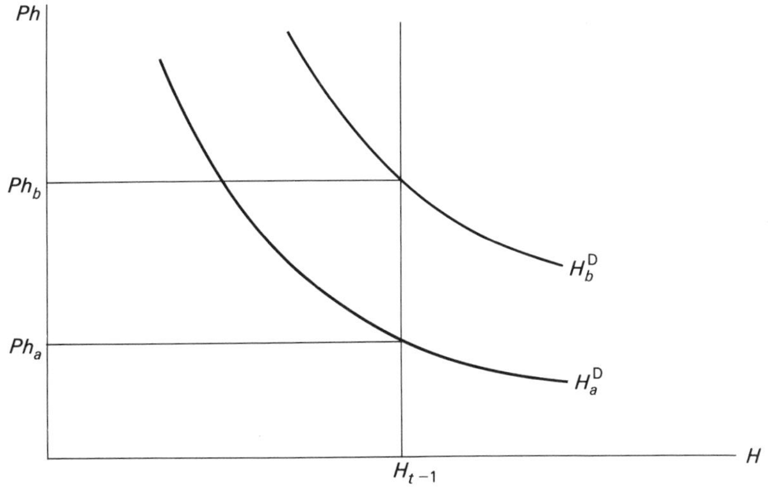

Figure 8.9 Short-run demand curve for houses.

prices and *Ph* results. Unfortunately, there is very little empirical evidence on this issue, due to the shortage of data on the price of building land (see, however, Neuberger and Nichol, 1976). Several factors operate to induce dynamic feedbacks which almost certainly alter the stock of available housing. Firstly, capital gains are made by builders on land but these are taxed, unlike those made by owner-occupiers on their houses, distorting their relative incentives. Secondly, excess profits accrue on the stock of construction in progress, which is large relative to C_t, being about five times total quarterly new completions: this is likely to alter the time profile of new construction. Finally, the relative price of land to construction cost has changed and this induces substitution, thus affecting the kind of housing desired (e.g. single dwellings may get replaced by blocks of flats). Static diagrams are unhelpful in analysing such issues, but it is clear that adjustment must continue until both markets (stock and flow) are again in joint equilibrium, with new construction yielding normal profits – i.e. until figure 8.8 becomes re-operative.

The property of switching from figure 8.9 to figure 8.8 as time evolves is a form of 'causal reversal' since, crudely expressed, in the short run, demand determines price, whereas in the long run, demand determines quantity. Certainly, strong fixity and exogeneity assumptions are needed to sustain such a clear-cut switch, and in practice both supply and demand factors influence all sample observations (a feature reflected in the overall model of the system). Models which have some degree of causal reversibility seem required on a priori grounds to characterize markets with short-run fixity but long-run flexibility of supply. The resulting framework is consistent with the earlier data descriptions, and yields insight into such debates as 'are house prices determined by construction costs or by demand?'. For example, treating the last alternatives as non-nested hypotheses creates an artificial dichotomy, since both factors operate but with different relative impacts in the short and long runs. The most important single implication for the present study, however, is that conditional on H_{t-1}, the demand equation is the equation determining *Ph*.

Out of equilibrium, expectations concerning inflation and changes in asset prices (including land and dwellings) matter so these influences need to be added to $f(\cdot)$ in (2). More crucially, a model of the dynamic adjustment implicit in figure 8.9 needs to be formulated. Here, a further institutional feature of housing markets becomes relevant, namely the role of (real) estate agents as providing information to facilitate short-run clearing by being closely in touch simultaneously with both sides of the market. Thus, very rapid adjustment of house prices to excess demand might be anticipated.

The conventional Walrasian price adjustment equation postulates that:

$$\dot{p}h = g(E) \tag{4}$$

where $dg/dE \geqslant 0$, $\dot{p}h = dph/dt$, $ph = \log Ph$ and E denotes excess demand. Throughout, lower case letters for time-dependent variables denote the natural logarithm of the corresponding capital. Often, a linear approximation is deemed adequate for $g(\cdot)$ but that does not seem appropriate for the housing market. Rather, large disequilibria should lead to very rapid price adjustment whereas small disequilibria might not be distinguishable from noise. To capture this effect, we use a cubic approximation to $g(\cdot)$:

$$\dot{p}h = g_1 E + g_2 E^2 + g_3 E^3. \tag{5}$$

If $g_2 \neq 0$, $\dot{p}h$ reacts asymmetrically to $E \gtreqless 0$. To ensure a sensible response, restrictions are required such that $\dot{p}h$ always has the same sign as E, and is monotonically increasing in E, but is no larger for a given value of $E < 0$ than when $E > 0$. Firstly, monotonicity ($d\dot{p}h/dE \geqslant 0$) requires:

$$g_1 + 2g_2 E + 3g_3 E^2 \geqslant 0 \tag{6}$$

so that $g_1 \geqslant 0$ and $g_3 \geqslant 0$ are necessary.

Since the minimum of (6) (which also must be non-negative) occurs at $E = -g_2/3g_3$, substituting this minimizing value of E into (6) implies that $3g_1 g_3 \geqslant g_2^2$. If an asymmetrical reaction is desired such that:

$$g_1 E + g_2 E^2 + g_3 E^3 \geqslant -(-g_1 E + g_2 E^2 - g_3 E^3) \tag{7}$$

then $g_2 \geqslant 0$ also is required. The three restrictions $g_i \geqslant 0$ are easily imposed by using as parameters ϕ_i such that $g_1 = \phi_1^2 \equiv 1$ (as a scale normalization) and $g_i = \phi_i^2$, $i = 2, 3$. The fourth restriction that $3g_1 g_3 \geqslant g_2^2$ follows on setting $\phi_3^2 = \phi_4^2 + \phi_2^4/3$. A typical shape of the resulting response function of $\dot{p}h$ to E is illustrated in figure 8.10, using $g_1 = 1$, $g_2 = 10$, $g_3 = 100$ (note the very different scales of the axes). While the g_i are only illustrative, a 10 per cent excess demand for the stock would generate a 30 per cent price increase, noting that the largest observed annual rate from figure 8.3 was 42 per cent. In (5), small deviations of E from

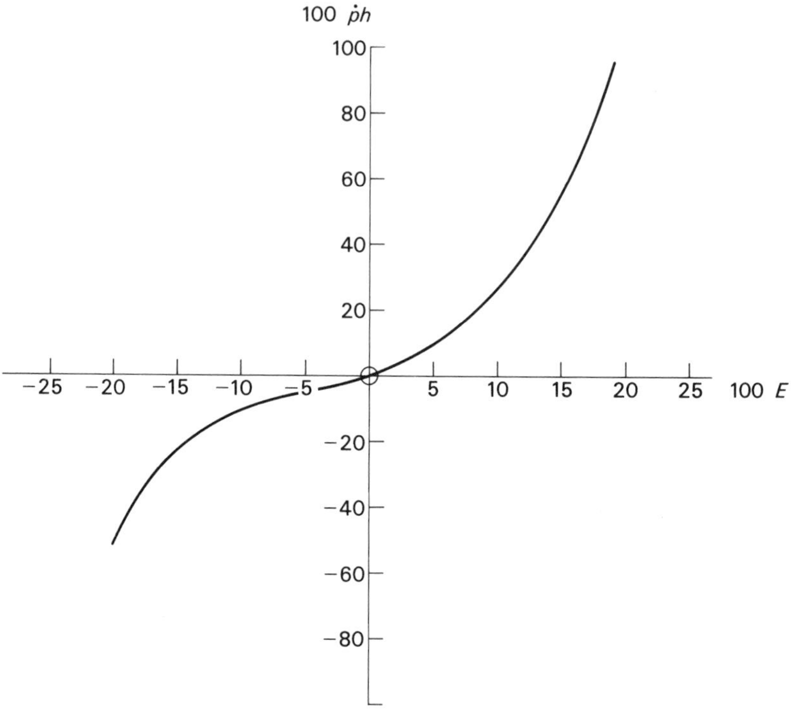

Figure 8.10 Illustrative values for $\dot{p}h$ against E from equation (5).

zero are negligible when squared and/or cubed, so the reaction of *ph* to *E* only deviates substantially from the usual linear formulation when *E* is 'large'. If so, *ph* adjusts rapidly towards a value at which $E = 0$, restoring equilibrium in the stock demand and supply. At an economy-wide level of aggregation, however, distributed lag reactions are likely to arise (see Trivedi, chapter 7 of this volume). Also, over certain ranges of real incomes, interest rates and real lending, *positive* feedback of increasing house prices (inducing expectations of higher real returns) to demand could occur leading to large price changes of the same sign over successive periods. This depends on whether $\partial E/\partial ph$ changes sign as the values of the conditioning variables alter, which seems distinctly likely given the negative influence on demand of the *level* of house prices in (2).

To implement (5) requires a model of E, which is the difference (in some scale of measurement) between the dynamic demands for and supplies of housing (*not* between the static H^D and H^S schedules of the previous section). Firstly, anticipated price rises should increase demand and lower supply transiently, thus exacerbating any adjustments due to (5). Conversely, cumulative past changes should have the opposite effects, gradually stabilizing the process. Next, the dynamic plans must reproduce the static schedules when the system is in hypothetical equilibrium, so the determinants of H^D in (2) remain relevant, but with additional factors entering as rates of change or as disequilibria from previous periods (which could be important since (5) does not ensure clearing for finite g_i). Letting z^e denote the expectation held by agents about z, schematic dynamic equations are given by:

$$h_\pi{}^d = a_0 + a_1 y + a_2(m - ph) + a_3 nf - a_4 R^* - a_5(ph - p) + a_6(\dot{m} - \dot{ph}) - a_7 \dot{R}^* + a_8 \dot{y} + a_9 \dot{ph}^e + a_{10}\dot{p} \tag{8}$$

$$h_\pi{}^s = h - b_1 \dot{ph}^e - b_2 R^* \tag{9}$$

where R^* is an after-tax interest rate, Nf is the number of families, and $h_\pi{}^d$ and $h_\pi{}^s$ are planned demand and supply respectively. Then:

$$E = h_\pi{}^d - h_\pi{}^s. \tag{10}$$

Several important issues are raised by this formulation:

(a) While (5) and (8)–(10) have been written as deterministic functions for simplicity, in principle all four equations are susceptible to innovation errors, which could induce a complicated stochastic process on the equation determining $\dot{ph}$.

(b) The translation of the operation of the adjustment mechanism into discrete time (of quarters) is far from obvious because of within period feedbacks between E and $\dot{ph}$.

(c) When $g_2 = g_3 = 0$, then $\dot{ph} = E$, which superficially resembles a 'Phillips curve' for housing (see Desai, chapter 9 of this volume), but with the crucial difference that $\dot{p}$ is one of the variables in E. Thus, the model could be re-parameterized as $(\dot{ph} - \dot{p}) = E$, so that real house prices respond to (a different measure of) excess demand. While such a re-parameterization is innocuous in the linear specification, it significantly alters the nonlinear model by changing the measurement of E. Indeed, by restricting all of the determinants of E to also enter the cubic (rather than independently influence ph) the specification is somewhat crude and a more flexible functional form would be preferable.

(d) The way in which agents actually form expectations about $\dot{p}h$ must critically affect the functioning of the process. Modelling these is more problematical if the cubic adjustment approach is adopted. Rational expectations assumptions would place excessively demanding informational requirements on agents (including knowledge of up to third moments and cross third moments of all relevant aggregate variables). Conversely, one would not wish to impute irrationality to the conduct of a most important financial transaction. Endowing agents with 'sensible' expectations – which are not systematically or persistently wrong, yet are not 'fully efficient' – potentially provides a reasonable and realistic compromise. Readily available sources of information for individuals are lagged values of $\dot{p}h$, of interest rates, of the volume of mortgage lending by Building Societies (and their average loan) and of the house price/average earnings ratio. Both suppliers and demanders know that the availability and cost of mortgage finance, the ratio of house prices to incomes, and the recent behaviour of house prices are important determinants in practice of how future house prices will behave. One feasible quarterly model embodying these considerations is

$$\Delta_1 ph_t^e = \sum_{i=1}^{2} c_i \Delta_1 ph_{t-i} - c_3(R^0 - \Delta_4 p)_{t-1} + c_4 \Delta_1 m_{t-1} - c_5(ph + h - p - y - c_a)_{t-1} + c_6(m - ph - h - c_b)_{t-1} \tag{11}$$

where c_a and c_b are the historical means of the feedbacks, and $R^0 = R^*/100$. This equation is, in essence, a special case of the actual model postulated below to be the relevant approximation to the data generation process. On the assumption that

$$\Delta_1 ph_t = \Delta_1 ph_t^e + u_t \tag{12}$$

where u_t is serially independent, and is an innovation relative to the information used for predicting ph_t, then the $\{c_i\}$ are estimable and both the predictive accuracy of (11) and the randomness of the residuals are checkable directly from the data (see e.g. Pagan, chapter 5 of this volume).

However, in the absence of tight dynamic specifications in (9) and (10), interpreting estimated parameters will be far from easy and will be contingent on (11) accurately representing the process of expectations formation.

4 Empirical Estimates of the Cubic Reaction Function

Briefly, the modelling strategy is as follows. Various descriptive statistics are examined in section 4.1, followed by the estimation of a general autoregressive-distributed lag model in section 4.2. Then an equation based on (11) is considered in section 4.3, but since it does not aid the interpretation of the parameters, the model in section 4.2 is simplified directly (section 4.4). This provides a basis both for estimating (5) (in section 4.5) and for investigating an alternative cubic reaction function in section 4.6. All of the equations were estimated using either GIVE or GENRAM from the AUTOREG library (Hendry and Srba, 1980).

In terms of the relative roles of theory and empiricism in modelling house prices (see Buckley and Ermisch, 1983, the present approach uses theoretical ideas to suggest relevant variables and equation specifications, but does not impose a theory-based model on the data. Rather (see e.g. Sargan, 1964), data-based criteria are used to select between alternative, theory-consistent equations in an error-correction framework. The focus here is on the nonlinear reaction function of excess demand, and the resulting model offers a data coherent framework within which additional explanatory factors (such as demography) could be investigated later if desired. For reviews of many previous econometric studies of UK house prices, see the Building Societies Association (1981) and Nellis and Longbottom (1981).

House purchase and mortgage acquisition decisions generally depend closely on each other, so in statistical terms, the joint density over (ph_t, m_t) should be investigated). The factorization adopted here is to study the conditional density of ph_t given m_t, and in Anderson and Hendry (1984), the marginal density of m_t is analysed. For quarterly data, when m_t is end of period and ph_t is the price at completion of contract, it seemed sensible to estimate models of ph_t given m_{t-1}, and this is followed below. However, it should be remembered that such equations are effectively conditional demand functions as well as (possibly) reflecting the rationing constraint prevalent in housing-finance markets in the UK.

4.1 Descriptive Statistics

The data are quarterly, seasonally unadjusted (with sources and definitions given in Appendix B), so the following autoregressive equation was estimated for each series:

$$\Delta_1 x_t = \alpha_0 + \sum_{i=1}^{3} \alpha_i Q_{it} + \alpha_4 x_{t-1} + \sum_{i=1}^{3} \alpha_{4+i} \Delta_1 x_{t-i} + u_t. \qquad (13)$$

The results are reported in table 8.1, and show reasonable fits, with no residual autocorrelation statistic being significant at the 1 per cent level, although several are at 5 per cent. The equations for *ph*, R^* and *h* reveal non-constant parameters and the first two also show significant ARCH errors (*a*uto*r*egressive *c*onditional *h*eteroscedasticity: see Engle (1982a)). Only for $\{h_t\}$ is $\hat{\alpha}_4$ significantly different from zero (see Dickey and Fuller (1981)). Since the α_4 coefficient represents the deviation from unity of the largest root of the dynamics, apart from $\{h_t\}$ none of the other series is stationary in levels. They all appear to be stationary in first differences, however (see Fuller, 1976, chapter 8).

This last finding does *not* entail that the differenced-data series *alone* merit analysis: any such conclusion is a *non sequitur*. For example, although *Ph*, *P* and *Y* may not be individually stationary, *Ph*/*P*.*Y* could be. One indication of whether or not some linear function of the levels of the current-dated variables is stationary is the extent of autocorrelation in the residuals from that linear equation. If the residual correlogram is close to zero, then the linear combination itself is not highly autoregressive and so stationarity is credible, whereas a substantial amount of residual autocorrelation is consistent with the linear combination still being non-stationary (or more specifically, a random walk). The following levels regression investigates such a possibility (see Granger and Weiss, 1983):

$$\begin{aligned} \hat{ph}_t &= 0.30p_t + 1.78y_t + 0.48m_t - 1.16h_t + 0.23R_t^* \\ &\quad - 3.7 + \Sigma\hat{\alpha}_i Q_{it} \end{aligned} \qquad (14)$$

$$T = 94,\ R^2 = 0.9959,\ \hat{\sigma} = 5.4\%,\ DW = 0.82$$

where the legend is as for table 8.1 and, in addition, *T* denotes the sample size (the final observation is for 1982(ii)) and DW denotes the Durbin–Watson statistic. Using the results in Sargan and Bhargava (1983) and Bhargava (1983) for the bounds of the DW test when the errors are a random walk, that null hypothesis cannot be rejected in favour of the alternative that the errors are stationary. The observed DW value lies in the inconclusive region (which is rather wide) but it is well above the lower bound. Thus,

TABLE 8.1 TIME-SERIES DESCRIPTIONS

Δx_t	x_{t-1}	Δx_{t-1}	Δx_{t-2}	Δx_{t-3}	C	$SD\%$†	R^2‡	$\hat{\sigma}\%$§	η_1¶	ξ_2‖	ξ_4††
Δph	0.001 (0.003)	0.56 (0.11)	0.26 (0.13)	−0.13 (0.12)	−0.02 (0.02)	2.7	0.52	2.0	4.0	19.4	4.0
Δy	0.024 (0.013)	−0.30 (0.10)	0.09 (0.11)	−0.26 (0.10)	0.25 (0.12)	3.4	0.60	2.2	0.5	19.4	0.1
Δm	0.0016 (0.0007)	0.91 (0.11)	−0.03 (0.15)	−0.20 (0.11)	−0.007 (0.006)	0.91	0.75	0.48	1.9	10.7	0.5
Δp	0.004 (0.003)	0.51 (0.11)	0.09 (0.12)	0.10 (0.11)	−0.011 (0.011)	1.7	0.64	1.1	1.0	4.5	2.9
ΔR^*	−0.041 (0.027)	0.48 (0.10)	0.01 (0.12)	−0.15 (0.12)	0.43 (0.20)	13.5	0.30	11.9	4.8	10.7	4.7
Δh	−0.004 (0.001)	0.56 (0.11)	0.10 (0.12)	−0.16 (0.11)	0.04 (0.01)	0.18	0.74	0.10	2.7	18.2	—

† SD, data standard deviation; ‡ R^2, squared multiple correlation coefficient; § $\hat{\sigma}$, residual standard error; coefficient standard errors in parentheses (·); ¶ η_1, Chow test for parameter constancy, distributed approximately as $F(4, 82)$ on the null (Chow, 1960); ‖ ξ_2, Box–Pierce residual autocorrelation statistic, approximately distributed as $\chi^2(9)$ on the null (Pierce, 1971); †† ξ_4, Engle's ARCH statistic, approximately distributed as $\chi^2(1)$ on the null (Engle, 1982a). The estimated seasonal effects are not reported.

it does not seem unreasonable to believe that some linear combination of the levels variables may be stationary, although the very large value of σ in (14) relative to the standard deviation of $\Delta_1 ph$ reveals how poor a characterization the static model is notwithstanding the value of R^2! Incidentally, rearranging (14) yields approximately

$$(ph - p + h - y) = 0.5(m - p - y) + 0.2R^* - 4 \qquad (15)$$

The severe residual autocorrelation of (14) precludes unbiased estimation of the coefficient standard errors, but (15) is unlikely to do great violation to the data evidence, especially given the large positive intercorrelations between the variables shown in table 8.2. Whether such high 'collinearity' poses any estimation or numerical accuracy problems for more general models is considered shortly. For the moment we note that (15) is consistent with the analysis of sections 1 and 2 but with R^* 'wrongly signed'.

4.2 *The Autoregressive-Distributed Lag Representation*

A model which embeds both (13) and (14) is a linear equation involving all the variables in (14) with the lag lengths used in (13). However, the autocorrelation of h_t with h_{t-1} was sufficiently high (>0.999) that further lags than the first seemed otiose so only h_{t-1} was retained. Moreover, the theoretical analysis in section 3 suggested that a cubic response to excess demand was likely and earlier empirical analyses had shown the linear representation to fail a RESET test against $(\Delta_1 \hat{ph}_t)^3$ (see Ramsey, 1969), consistent with the potentially important role of the nonlinearity. A simple approximation which captured much of the nonlinearity yet allowed Ordinary Least Squares (OLS) estimation was to include

TABLE 8.2 CORRELATION MATRIX OF THE DATA SERIES

	ph	*p*	*y*	*m*	*h*	R^*
p	0.98					
y	0.97	0.91				
m	0.99	0.97	0.97			
h	0.97	0.92	0.98	0.98		
R^*	0.89	0.87	0.84	0.85	0.81	
SD%	79	60	18	95	18	49

TABLE 8.3 UNRESTRICTED AUTOREGRESSIVE-DISTRIBUTED LAG ESTIMATES

x_{t-j} \ j	0	1	2	3	4	Σ
ph_{t-j}	−1	0.83 (0.15)	0.28 (0.20)	−0.37 (0.19)	0.12 (0.12)	−0.15
y_{t-j}	0.34 (0.10)	0.29 (0.12)	−0.17 (0.11)	0.01 (0.12)	0.03 (0.11)	0.49
m_{t-j}	–	0.76 (0.49)	−0.75 (0.91)	0.25 (0.91)	−0.14 (0.49)	0.12
R_{t-j}^0	−0.41 (0.36)	−0.66 (0.56)	1.13 (0.62)	−0.41 (0.62)	−0.56 (0.42)	−0.91
p_{t-j}	0.40 (0.20)	−0.22 (0.36)	−0.21 (0.35)	0.17 (0.34)	−0.09 (0.21)	0.04
Q_{jt}^0	−0.010 (1.10)	0.30 (0.95)	2.11 (0.85)	1.70 (0.85)	–	–
h_{t-1}	–	−0.52 (0.23)	–	–	–	−0.52
$(\Delta_1 ph_{t-1})^3$	–	12.4 (6.1)	–	–	–	–
D_1^0	−3.9 (1.7)	–	–	–	–	–

$T=94$ $R^2=0.99975$ $\hat{\sigma}=1.52\%$ $\eta_1(4, 60)=1.5$ $\eta_2(6, 58)=1.3$ $\xi_4(1)=0.5$.

$x_t^0 = x_t/100$ (R^* and Q_j, $j=1, \ldots, 3$); $\eta_2(\cdot)$ is the Lagrange multiplier test for sixth-order residual autocorrelation, approximately distributed as $F(6, 59)$ on the null (see Godfrey, 1978d; Breusch and Pagan, 1980; Harvey, 1981); D_1 is a dummy variable for 1967(iv).

The derived static-equilibrium solution is:

$$\underset{}{ph} = \underset{(0.75)}{3.4y} + \underset{(0.38)}{0.93m} - \underset{(3.4)}{6.3R^0} + \underset{(0.27)}{0.26p} - \underset{(1.4)}{3.6h} - \underset{(0.15)}{0.3} + \Sigma\hat{\alpha}_j Q_{jt}$$

$(\Delta_1 ph_{t-1})^3$ as a separate regressor and table 8.3 reports the results for this hypothesis.

The various diagnostic checks yield acceptable outcomes and $\hat{\sigma}$ is under 1.6 per cent. Despite the overparameterization, the very high intercorrelations between variables and the highly autoregressive nature of all of the time series, the estimated coefficients are sensibly signed and have reasonable magnitudes. Such findings certainly justify investigation of the theoretically preferred specification in (5) and (8) to (10) above.

4.3 A Possible Expectations Model

Several variants of (11) were investigated without much success in producing constant-parameter equations with white-noise residuals. Agents who formed their expectations either autoregressively or from (11) would not have achieved accurate forecasts ($\hat{\sigma}$ around 2 per cent). To obtain a significant reduction in the residual variance with random residuals required the addition of both $(y-h)_{t-1}$ (real income per household) and changes in inflation. Then $\hat{c}_1$ and $\hat{c}_2$ became negligible and estimation yielded:

$$\Delta_1 \hat{ph}_t = \underset{(0.10)}{0.28}\Delta_1{}^2 p_{t-1} + \underset{(0.30)}{0.48}\Delta_1 m_{t-1} - \underset{(0.06)}{0.12}(R^0 - \Delta_4 p)_{t-1}$$
$$+ \underset{(0.01)}{0.01}(ph + h - y - p - c_a)_{t-1}$$
$$+ \underset{(0.04)}{0.18}(m - ph - h - c_b)_{t-1} + \underset{(0.09)}{0.35}(y-h)_{t-1}$$
$$- \underset{(0.05)}{0.22} + \Sigma \hat{\alpha}_i Q_{it}. \qquad (16)$$

$T = 94, R^2 = 0.67, \hat{\sigma} = 1.74\%, \eta_1(2, 81) = 5.6,$
$\eta_2(6, 77) = 1.0, \xi_4(1) = 0.1.$

It is difficult to know precisely what properties to ascribe to (16). On the one hand, the failure to predict the last two observations is not too damaging for reasons explained below, and all of the regressors are either lagged or deterministic so (16) could be used for *ex ante* forecasts. On the other hand, its fit is significantly worse than that of table 8.3 (of which model it is a restrictive special case) and it is unclear why agents should form expectations in the way described by (16). Since using (16) (or imposing similar parametric cross-equation restrictions for fully efficient estimation) merely involved a reinterpretation of the parameter estimates of the model finally selected, it was decided to re-parameterize table 8.3 directly and not use the intermediate construction of a 'pseudo-expectations' variable.

However, there are issues of independent interest concerning (16). Firstly, its residuals are white noise (η_2 is insignificant).

Next, $(ph+h-y-p)$ has a negligible coefficient (despite any prior beliefs concerning the importance of the level of real house prices relative to household income). Finally, having rationalized the value of η_1, the equation apparently satisfies conventional criteria, yet has a residual standard deviation almost a quarter larger than the models preferred below.

4.4 A Restricted Parameterization

Because of the substantial collinearity between the levels variables in table 8.3, the strategy of simply deleting insignificant variables is unlikely to yield a useful model. Several considerations guided the simplification procedure: firstly, models with near orthogonal variables yet interpretable parameters have tended to provide 'robust' characterizations of economic time series (for extensive discussions of these and related modelling issues, see Davidson et al. (1978) and Hendry (1983); also Trivedi (chapter 7 of this volume) provides an overview of many modelling strategies). Some possible examples are that for highly autoregressive series, levels are little correlated with disequilibria or with changes; scaled variables frequently are more interpretable than unscaled (e.g. $(y-h)$ is household income and seems a plausible determinant of average house prices etc.); and the overall dynamic specification has to yield a plausible static equilibrium solution. Secondly, a model with relatively few independent parameters is not only more easily understood than an equation like that in table 8.3, but also, it avoids the danger that an excessive number of variables induces overfitting. In a multiple regression, each variable acts as a partial effect given all the other regressors. When the variables are collinear and numerous, the partials resemble dummy variables, being small for most observations, and remaining large only where not explained by the other included variables. If several of these large values happen to coincide with equivalent 'bumps' in the dependent variable (noting that many lag lengths are allowed for) a non-negligible coefficient can result even when no causal effect is present. Such a coefficient would gradually disappear as the sample size increased, perhaps incorrectly suggesting a non-constant underlying relationship, but until the spurious effect became negligible the equation would produce poor *ex ante* forecasts. Conversely, overly simplified models also would lose invariance to possible interventions, so a balance has to be struck, usually based on a mixture of judgment and data evidence. A minor benefit of simplification is that the nonlinear optimization problem to be solved shortly is somewhat easier with fewer parameters. Thirdly, where a selection is otherwise equivocal, it seems sensible to use lagged rather than contemporaneous variables both to avoid dependence on questionable exogeneity assumptions and to enhance the use of the selected equation for practical forecasting. Next, the goodness of fit of the autoregressive-distributed lag model provides a baseline against which to compare restricted equations. If the latter fit significantly worse (adjusted for degrees of freedom) then they cannot account for the estimates in table 8.3 and hence are not an acceptable simplification. Finally, the usual range of diagnostic tests for white noise, homoscedastic residuals and constant parameters is available to check any specific selection.

To *test* the resulting choice of a model which has been deliberately *designed* to account for the available evidence clearly necessitates either new evidence or new tests. Since any test available to the author could have been used in the process of selecting a model, such a task must remain for others. Nevertheless, the first public version of the present model selected as described above (see Hendry, 1979) is recorded in equation (17) so that readers can judge the constancy of the general formulation given around six years' data have appeared in the interim (the sample also has been extended to earlier years):

$$\begin{aligned}\Delta_1\hat{ph}_t = {} & \underset{(0.11)}{0.24}\Delta_1 ph_{t-2} + \underset{(4.8)}{11.4}(\Delta_1 ph_{t-1})^3 + \underset{(0.22)}{0.57}A_3(\Delta_1 y_t) \\ & + \underset{(0.026)}{0.122}(m-p-h)_{t-1} + \underset{(0.10)}{0.53}(y-h)_{t-1} \\ & - \underset{(0.05)}{0.18}(ph-p-y)_{t-1} + \underset{(0.15)}{0.45}\Delta_2(m-p)_{t-3} \\ & - \underset{(0.021)}{0.013}r_t - \underset{(0.015)}{0.027}\Delta_7 r_t - \underset{(2.3)}{3.0}\Delta_1 h_t - \underset{(0.37)}{1.01} + \Sigma\hat{\alpha}_i Q_{it}\end{aligned} \tag{17}$$

$T = 58$, $R^2 = 0.79$, $\hat{\sigma} = 1.5\%$, $\eta_1(6, 44) = 0.8$, $\eta_2(6, 44) = 1.2$, (1961(iii)–1975(iv)).

In (17), $A_n(\cdot)$ is a restricted Almon polynomial defined by

$$A_n(x_t) = \frac{2}{n(n+1)}\sum_{i=0}^{n}(n-i)x_{t-i}$$

(see Sargan, 1980a), which provides a weighted average of $(x_t, \ldots, x_{t-n})$ with linearly declining weights. The reported estimates used the six observations for 1976(i)–1977(ii) purely for forecasting tests. By way of comparison, a similar simplification strategy applied to table 8.3 yielded:

$$\begin{aligned}
\Delta_1\hat{ph}_t = {} & \underset{(0.07)}{0.22}\Delta_1 ph_{t-2} + \underset{(4.9)}{14.0}(\Delta_1 ph_{t-1})^3 + \underset{(0.07)}{0.42}A_2(\Delta_1 y_t) \\
& + \underset{(0.027)}{0.178}(m-ph-h)_{t-1} + \underset{(0.08)}{0.47}(y-h)_{t-1} + \underset{(0.12)}{0.85}F_{13}(p) \\
& + \underset{(0.11)}{0.54}F_{13}(m-p) - \underset{(0.09)}{0.22}\bar{R}_{t-3}{}^0 - \underset{(0.20)}{0.50}\Delta_1 R_{t-1}{}^0 \\
& - \underset{(0.05)}{0.30} + \Sigma\hat{\alpha}_i Q_{it} - \underset{(0.4)}{3.5}D_1{}^0 - \underset{(0.3)}{2.1}D_2{}^0 \qquad (18)
\end{aligned}$$

$T = 94$, $R^2 = 0.78$, $\hat{\sigma} = 1.43\%$, $\eta_1(2, 76) = 0.2$, $\eta_2(6, 72) = 1.0$, $\xi_4(1) = 0.01$, $\xi_5(2) = 117$.

In (18), $F_{13}(x) = \Delta_1(x_{t-1} + x_{t-3})$ and $\bar{x}_t = \frac{1}{2}(x_t + x_{t-1})$, with $\xi_5(2)$ a test for normality of the residuals, approximately distributed as $\chi^2(2)$ under the null (Jarque and Bera, 1980). The changes between (17) and (18) are the deletion of $\Delta_1 h_t$, the amalgamation of the two error-corrections into one ($(m-p-h)$ and $(ph-p-y)$ seem better parameterized as $(m-ph-h)$), the use of original rather than logarithmic interest rates (and changes in their lag specification), the addition of direct inflation effects, the two dummies D_i (discussed below), and a retiming of the effect of changes in real mortgages. Coefficients of variables in common between (17) and (18) are recognizably similar. Also refitting (17) to the new data reproduces reasonably similar estimates and fit (but (18) is better), and conversely, fitting (18) to the earlier sample yields closely similar estimates (and $\hat{\sigma} = 1.5$ per cent). Consequently, it seems worth commenting on the meaning and interpretation of (18).

In a hypothetical static equilibrium, defined by all change ceasing, (18) solves to yield

$$\frac{Ph.H}{P.Y} = K_0\left(\frac{M}{P.Y}\right)\left(\frac{Y}{H}\right)^{\underset{(0.34)}{2.65}} \exp(-\underset{(0.64)}{1.3}R^0 + \underset{(0.54)}{2.4}\dot{p}_a) \qquad (19)$$

$\xi_6(7) = 72$

where

$$K_0 = \underset{(0.2)}{\exp(-1.7} + \Sigma\hat{\beta}_j Q_j)$$

and $\dot{p}_a$ is the annual rate of inflation.

The standard errors quoted in (19) are computed (using numerical differentiation) from the coefficient covariance matrix in (18), and $\xi_6(7)$ is a Wald test of all the estimated coefficients being zero, approximately distributed as $\chi^2(7)$ on the null (see Hendry et al., 1984). Thus, the loan to income ratio, real income per household, inflation and after-tax interest rates are the 'long-run' determinants of the average house price to household income ratio. Re-expressed in terms of the normalization used in (2), we have

$$H^D = K_1\left(\frac{Y}{Nf}\right)\left(\frac{Ph}{P}\right)^{-0.27}\left(\frac{M}{P.Y}\right)^{0.27}(Nf)\exp(-0.4R^0 + 0.7\dot{p}_a). \tag{20}$$

Thus, there is a unit elasticity of H with respect to (Y/Nf) (income per family) and also to $Nf = N/F$, a substantial negative elasticity from real house prices, matched by an opposite signed effect from the loan to income ratio, and elasticities with respect to R^0 and $\dot{p}_a$ of -0.03 and 0.035 respectively (at $R^0 = 0.07$ and $\dot{p}_a = 0.05$ as representative values). The included effects seem sensible, although the implicit 'demography' is restrictive. Overall, such findings are consonant with the static analysis in section 2.

The dynamics are only approximate relative to the earlier theory, but the use of $(\Delta_1 ph_{t-1})^3$ has been successful in so far as its coefficient is significant, whereas $\Delta_1 ph_{t-1}$ has a negligible effect if added, irrespective of the inclusion of the cubic term. Even so, $\xi_5(2)$ reveals highly non-normal residuals: the skewness is 1.4 and the excess kurtosis is 5.2 so neither is close to zero (as would be required for normality). Figure 8.11 shows the plot of fitted and actual against time, and it can be seen that large changes in $\Delta_1 ph_t$ are underpredicted.

The adjustment path in (18) is locally stable (i.e. for small $\Delta_1 ph$), but once $\Delta_1 ph > 30$ per cent (per quarter), the price level diverges, which does not seem a plausible scenario. In a sense, the cubic transformation is too extreme: for $|\Delta_1 ph| < 0.1$, the effect of the cubic term is trivial, whereas it dominates for $|\Delta_1 ph| > 0.3$. Thus, (18) is an approximation that is valid only within the sample experience. Also, if one treated (18) as a potential data generation

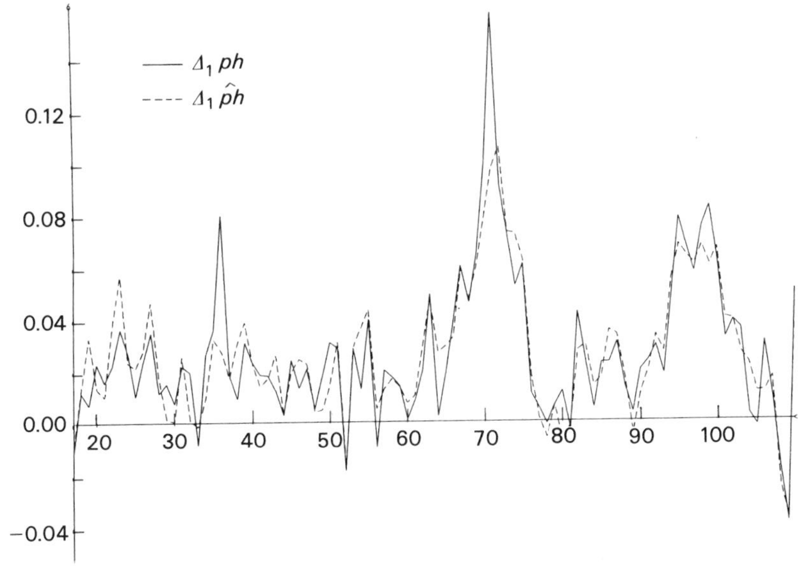

Figure 8.11 Comparison of estimates of house prices from equation (18) with actual data.

process (as in a Monte Carlo study) then the properties of the least squares estimators remain to be established and little is known about their behaviour for nonlinear dynamic processes.

There are positive impact effects from past changes in house prices, real incomes and real lending, and a negative impact from changes in interest rates, with most of the impact coefficients being well determined. Table 8.4 records both the matrix of correlations between the economics variables and the partial correlations between the regressors and $\Delta_1 ph_t$. Few of the simple correlations exceed 0.4 in absolute value (in contrast with table 8.2) so most of the effects are reasonably orthogonal (the main offender being $F_{13}(p)$, but, for example, its correlation with $\bar{R}^0$ could perhaps be reduced by using a measure of real rather than nominal interest rates). Refitting (18) in real terms (by subtracting $\Delta_1 p_t$ from $\Delta_1 ph_t$ and replacing $F_{13}(p)$ by $\Delta_1 p_{t-3}$) yields almost identical estimates.

The model highlights the important roles of the level feedback mechanisms which have small simple but large partial correlations with $\Delta_1 ph_t$. The derived levels relationship is shown in table 8.5,

TABLE 8.4 DATA CORRELATION MATRIX ($T = 94$)

	$\Delta_1 ph_t$	$\Delta_1 ph_{t-2}$	$(\Delta_1 ph_{t-1})^3$	$A_2(\Delta y_t)$	$(m-ph-h)_{t-1}$	$(y-h)_{t-1}$	$F_{13}(p)$	$F_{13}(m-p)$	$\bar{R}_{t-3}{}^0$
$\Delta_1 ph_{t-2}$	0.44 (0.27)	–	–	–	–	–	–	–	–
$(\Delta_1 ph_{t-1})^3$	0.47 (0.34)	0.49	–	–	–	–	–	–	–
$A_2(\Delta y_t)$	0.36 (0.41)	−0.03	0.16	–	–	–	–	–	–
$(m-ph-h)_{t-1}$	0.16 (0.58)	−0.26	−0.09	0.17	–	–	–	–	–
$(y-h)_{t-1}$	0.09 (0.59)	0.39	0.14	−0.22	−0.62	–	–	–	–
$F_{13}(p)$	0.02 (0.55)	0.12	0.00	−0.22	−0.36	−0.04	–	–	–
$F_{13}(m-p)$	0.27 (0.44)	0.16	0.20	0.25	0.39	−0.02	−0.84	–	–
$\bar{R}_{t-3}{}^0$	−0.17 (−0.23)	−0.08	−0.12	−0.18	−0.31	−0.08	0.75	−0.64	–
$\Delta_1 R_{t-1}{}^0$	0.05 (−0.22)	0.41	0.19	−0.12	−0.19	0.34	−0.03	0.16	−0.23

Figures in parentheses are partial correlations.

TABLE 8.5 AUTOREGRESSIVE-DISTRIBUTED LAG RELATIONSHIP DERIVED FROM EQUATION (18)

x_{t-j} \ j	0	1	2	3	4	Σ
ph_{t-j}	−1	0.82	0.22	−0.22	–	−0.18
y_{t-j}	0.28	0.33	−0.14	–	–	0.47
m_{t-j}	–	0.72	−0.54	0.54	−0.54	0.18
$R_{t-j}{}^0$	–	−0.50	0.50	−0.11	−0.11	−0.22
p_{t-j}	–	0.31	−0.31	0.31	−0.31	0.00
$Q_{jt}{}^0$	−0.30	−0.10	2.4	1.5	–	–
h_{t-j}	–	−0.65	–	–	–	−0.65
$(\Delta ph_{t-1})^3$	–	14.0	–	–	–	–

and the resulting solved coefficients are recognizably similar to those in table 8.3 given that the number of economics variables has been reduced from 25 to 9 (all but y_t being lagged).

In fact, (18) also includes two dummy variables defined as follows:

$D_1 = 1$ in 1967(iv) and zero otherwise:
$D_2 = 1$ in 1981(iv) and 1982(i), -2 in 1982(ii) and zero otherwise.

Both arise from the measure of house prices used, namely the average for houses purchased using mortgages from a Building Society. Consequently, changes in composition (especially due to source of mortgage) can alter the recorded price when the actual traded price of a 'standardized house' is unchanged. Two occasions when such compositional effects seem to have mattered were: (a) 1967(iv) when measured prices fell at an annual rate of about 8 per cent during a period of general price rises, owing to few high price houses happening to change ownership; and (b) 1981(iv)–1982(ii) when commercial banks greatly changed their mortgage lending policies and attracted a high percentage of purchasers wishing large mortgages. In turn, these were purchasers of above-average price houses, leading to a fall in the average measured price of the remaining houses transacted via Building Societies. The Banks more than doubled their nominal mortgage loans between 1981(i) and 1982(i), raising their share of new advances from under 15 per cent to over 40 per cent. In the second quarter of 1982, their lending share fell (to 35 per cent), and although it remained high during 1982, Building Societies responded to the increased competition by offering more favourable terms than previously for large mortgages. Their actions seem to have attracted back a more representative sample of buyers, leading to a jump in measured house prices. This measurement error is modelled by D_2 and significantly influences the ostensible forecast performance of the model over the last three quarters (although even if D_2 is excluded, the *level* of house prices is accurately tracked at the last observation). It is doubtful whether Bank lending should also be included in M, since there is evidence that a substantial proportion of such loans consolidate existing debt or are used for other purposes than house purchase (Davis and Saville, 1982). In fact, bank lending was excluded from M in the present study, and so the formulation in (18) was retained for the nonlinear modelling.

4.5 A Cubic Excess Demand Model

The six dummy variables in (18) (constant, seasonals, D_1 and D_2) are in essence measurement adjustment factors and to a first approximation, their effects can be accounted for by taking deviations about the relevant subgroup means (e.g. the mean for the first quarter removes Q_1 etc.). While such a procedure is exact for linear equations only, it seems unlikely to distort greatly the estimates of the remaining parameters in the cubic model. Relative to the benefits of almost halving the number of parameters in the optimization problem, the approximation errors seem acceptable. Also, $(\Delta_1 ph_{t-1})^3$ was dropped when (5) was estimated (its additional importance was checked and found to be small but not negligible). Thus, the postulated determinants of E_t in (5) are the remaining eight variables from (18):

$$\begin{aligned} E_t = {} & \theta_1 \Delta_1 ph_{t-2} + \theta_2 A_2(\Delta_1 y_t) + \theta_3 (m - ph - h)_{t-1} \\ & + \theta_4 (y - h)_{t-1} + \theta_5 F_{13}(p) + \theta_6 F_{13}(m - p) \\ & + \theta_7 \bar{R}_{t-3}{}^0 + \theta_8 \Delta_1 R_{t-1}{}^0 \end{aligned} \tag{21}$$

with

$$\Delta_1 ph_t = E_t + \phi_2{}^2 E_t{}^2 + \phi_3{}^2 E_t{}^3 + u_t \tag{5*}$$

where $\phi_3^2 = \phi_4^2 + \phi_2^4/3$. Given the prior selection of (21) from data analysis, $\{u_t\}$ is likely to be white noise, but even so such an hypothesis merits checking. The unrestricted version of (5*) is essentially not estimable so we must be content with treating it as the tentative working hypothesis.

The estimation method was least squares, minimizing

$$\sum_{t=1}^{T} u_t^2 = f(\theta, \phi)$$

with respect to the ten parameters in θ and ϕ. The numerical optimization algorithm was the Gill–Murray–Pitfield (GMP) routine using numerical derivatives from the NAG library (see Wolfe (1978) for a discussion of numerical optimization procedures). A potential drawback of the formulation in (5*), based on ϕ_i^2, is the existence of equal-valued local minima of $f(\cdot)$ at $\pm\phi_i$; in practice, however, this did not cause any difficulty, partly because good initial values could be obtained for the θ_i using $\hat{\theta}_i$ from (18) and for the ϕ_i from regressing Δph_t on a cubic on $\hat{E}_t$ (calculated from (21) using $\hat{\theta}_i$). The parameters and variables were scaled so that the arguments in $f(\cdot)$ were of similar orders of magnitude. The minimizing values of (θ, ϕ) are denoted $(\tilde{\theta}, \tilde{\phi})$ and standard errors of these were calculated from the GMP derivatives and from numerical second derivatives of $f(\cdot)$ at $(\tilde{\theta}, \tilde{\phi})$; these alternative approximations yielded generally similar values and both were checked against OLS when ϕ was fixed at zero, providing good approximations to the usual standard errors in that case. Each model required between 60 and 100 seconds central-processing-unit time on the VAX-11 system at Oxford University. Since GENRAM allowed up to cubic functions of the arguments of $f(\cdot)$, models with autoregressive error assumptions were easily estimated, but in no case yielded significant autocorrelation parameter values. Parameter constancy tests were carried out by fitting the model to various subperiods and comparing the resulting values of $f(\theta, \psi)$ (where $\psi_1 = \phi_2/5$ and $\psi_2 = \phi_4/5$ for scaling).

A potential difficulty is that the dynamic specification selected in (18) need not remain the best data characterization when the nonlinear model is estimated. Lagged responses were checked only for the levels variables (against one longer lag) and $(m-ph-h)_{t-2}$ in fact fitted rather better than the one-period lag (in contrast, (18) fits slightly worse with $\hat{\sigma} = 1.46$ per cent if $(m-ph-h)_{t-2}$ is used). For comparability, the equivalent model to (18) is reported below, and $\tilde{\sigma}$ records the residual standard deviation of the estimates with the two-period lag on the error correction.

Optimization yielded

$$\Delta_1\hat{ph}_t = \hat{E}_t + 10.7\hat{E}_t^2 + 893\hat{E}_t^3 \qquad \underset{(0.19)}{\hat{\psi}_1 = 0.65} \qquad \underset{(2.9)}{\hat{\psi}_2 = 5.8} \tag{22a}$$

$$\hat{E}_t = \underset{(0.05)}{0.14}\Delta_1 ph_{t-2} + \underset{(0.07)}{0.20}A_2(\Delta_1 y_t) + \underset{(0.025)}{0.128}(m-ph-h)_{t-1}$$
$$+ \underset{(0.07)}{0.34}(y-h)_{t-1} + \underset{(0.14)}{0.61}F_{13}(p) + \underset{(0.10)}{0.44}F_{13}(m-p)$$
$$- \underset{(0.08)}{0.14}\bar{R}_{t-3}{}^0 - \underset{(0.15)}{0.30}\Delta_1 R_{t-1}{}^0 \tag{22b}$$

$T = 94$, $\hat{\sigma} = 1.43\%$, $\tilde{\sigma} = 1.37\%$,
$R^2 = 0.78$ (fitted/actual on adjusted data).

While consistent with the section 3 analysis and suggestive of an asymmetric price response, it seemed sensible also to estimate the model with $\psi_1 = 0$ for comparison:

$$\Delta_1\hat{ph}_t = \hat{E}_t + 1806\hat{E}_t^3 \qquad \underset{(4.1)}{\hat{\psi}_2 = 8.5} \tag{23a}$$

$$\hat{E}_t = \underset{(0.05)}{0.13}\Delta_1 ph_{t-2} + \underset{(0.08)}{0.20}A_2(\Delta_1 y_t) + \underset{(0.028)}{0.116}(m-ph-h)_{t-1}$$
$$+ \underset{(0.07)}{0.30}(y-h)_{t-1} + \underset{(0.17)}{0.54}F_{13}(p) + \underset{(0.10)}{0.37}F_{13}(m-p)$$
$$- \underset{(0.07)}{0.12}\bar{R}_{t-3} - \underset{(0.13)}{0.25}\Delta_1 R_{t-1}{}^0 \tag{23b}$$

$T = 94$, $\hat{\sigma} = 1.44\%$, $\tilde{\sigma} = 1.37\%$, $R^2 = 0.76$,
$\xi_2(12) = 9.1$, $\xi_4(1) = 0.01$, $\xi_5(2) = 41$.

The parameter values are very similar, $\hat{\sigma}$ is almost unaltered, and on a likelihood-ratio test, $H_0 : \psi_1 = 0$ could not be rejected, so given $\hat{E}_t$, the quadratic and cubic terms act mainly as substitutes. In (23), $\xi_2(\cdot)$ is the Box–Pierce residual correlogram statistic. As a rough check on the difficulty noted in section 3(c) above that the determinants of E are all constrained to enter E^3 in the same way, (23a) was refitted with the optimizing value of $\hat{E}_t^3$ fixed but allowing the determinants of E_t to enter freely. The residual sum of squares only fell from 0.0164 to 0.0160 (a change of 2.5 per cent) which is consistent with the validity of the restrictions. Also, *conditional* on $\hat{\theta}$, the partial correlations of $\Delta_1 ph_t$ with $\hat{E}_t$ and $\hat{E}_t{}^3$ are almost equal at 0.43 and 0.40 respectively ($\hat{E}$ and $\hat{E}^3$ have a correlation of 0.88). One very large outlier remained at 1963(iv) (of over $4\hat{\sigma}$) when house prices jumped in that quarter at an annual rate of over 25 per cent but $\hat{E}_t$ was close to zero (see figure 8.12). If the model is re-estimated using $T = 74$ (the sample from 1964(i) onwards, which excludes the largest outlier), the parameter estimates are little altered, although the goodness of fit is improved to $\hat{\sigma} = 1.32$ per cent and $\tilde{\sigma} = 1.21$ per cent. Note that if (23a) is expressed in terms of percentage changes in house prices, the coefficient of $\hat{E}_t{}^3$ is 0.21 relative to unity on $\hat{E}_t$. Thus, for excess demand of over 3 per cent, the cubic term dominates, which seems implausible. Also, the fits of (22) and (23) are little better than that of (18) (unless $(m-ph-h)_{t-2}$ is used). Consequently, an alternative cubic specification, somewhat related to a 'Catastrophe Theory' based model, was also investigated.

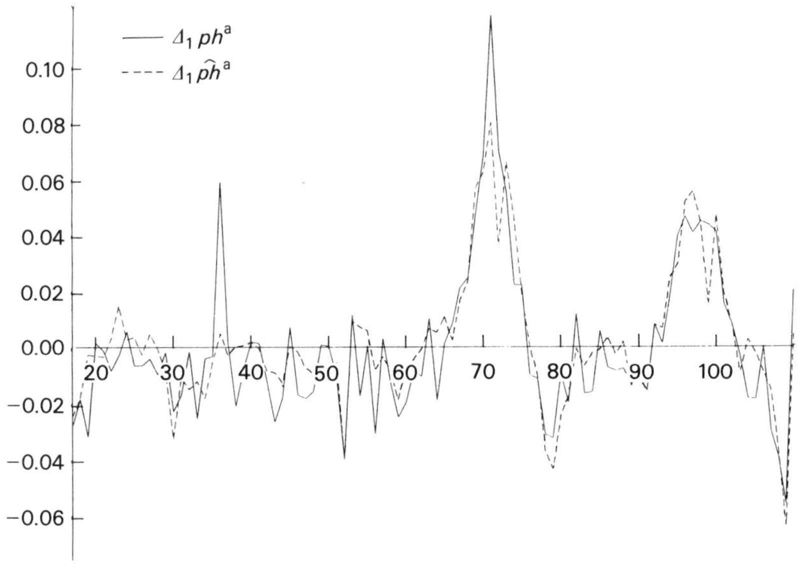

Figure 8.12 Comparison of estimates of house prices from equation (23) with actual data.

4.6 A Cubic Difference Equation

Since (5*) and (18) are only two of many approximations which could produce rapid adjustment for large discrepancies in excess demand, the following simple alternative was considered as well:

$$\Delta_1 ph_t - \alpha(\Delta_1 ph_t)^3 = E_t + u_t. \tag{24}$$

This modifies (23) by replacing the cubic in E_t by a cubic in $\Delta_1 ph_t$ or, relative to (18), makes the recursive price reaction contemporaneous. Thus, it is likely to provide a similar goodness of fit.

However, (24) is a less straightforward process than the earlier equations. Firstly, the left-hand side potentially has three solutions for $\Delta_1 ph_t$ given any value for $\{E_t + u_t\}$ and could suddenly 'jump' between solutions as in 'Catastrophe Theory' (for an introduction to that theory, see Zeeman (1976) or Woodcock and Davis (1980); Rand (1976) provides useful mathematical background). Such behaviour is at least consistent with the erratic nature of $\{\Delta_1 ph_t\}$ (see figure 8.2). Next, when $\alpha > 0$ in (24), $\Delta_1 ph_t$ responds more than proportionately to changes in E_t, until a maximum is reached at $\Delta_1 ph_t = (3\alpha)^{-\frac{1}{2}}$, after which the reaction is less than proportional. Values of $E_t + u_t > 2(3\alpha)^{-\frac{1}{2}}$ do not generate real prices, so again the nonlinearity is not entirely palatable. Finally, the likelihood function for (24) can be obtained via the data density of $\{\Delta_1 ph_t\}$, using an approach which was suggested to the author by Denis Sargan (related to that in Sargan (1964)). Given E_t, if u_t is independently normally distributed (or is a normal martingale difference sequence – see e.g. Hall and Heyde (1980) and Heijmans and Magnus (1983)) then

$$D(\Delta_1 ph_t | E_t)$$
$$= (2\pi\sigma_u^2)^{-\frac{1}{2}} \exp\left(-\frac{1}{2\sigma_u^2}(\Delta_1 ph_t - \alpha(\Delta_1 ph_t)^3 - E_t)^2\right)$$
$$\times |1 - 3\alpha(\Delta_1 ph_t)^2|. \tag{25}$$

In (25), the last term is the absolute value of the Jacobian of the transformation from u_t to $\Delta_1 ph_t$ (see e.g. Rao, 1965, chapter 3). By the independence of the u_t, the joint probability for the sample is the product of T terms like (25).

To illustrate the approach and compare the results with the earlier models, the log-likelihood for (25) was programmed in

GENRAM and maximized as a function of θ (from (21)) and α (from (24)) for the same sample as (18) and (23). Useful initial values were obtained from canonical correlation theory (see e.g. Dhrymes (1970)) as follows: given α, (24) is linear in θ which can therefore be estimated easily by least squares. The canonical correlation is simply that which maximizes the correlation between linear combinations of the two sets of variables (on the left- and right-hand sides of (24)), hence calculating R^2 over a grid of values of α allows selection of that correlation. The resulting values of $\hat{\alpha}(=10)$ and $\hat{\theta}$ initialized the nonlinear optimization routine (which was constrained to produce a positive value of $\alpha = \mu^2$). The final estimates were (again eliminating the dummies as in section 4.5):

$$\begin{aligned} \Delta ph_t - &\underset{(0.27)}{(4.63)^2}(\Delta_1 ph_t)^3 \\ = &\underset{(0.07)}{0.27}\Delta_1 ph_{t-2} + \underset{(0.09)}{0.43}A_2(\Delta_1 y_t) + \underset{(0.025)}{0.159}(m-ph-h)_{t-1} \\ &+ \underset{(0.07)}{0.43}(y-h)_{t-1} + \underset{(0.12)}{0.85}F_{13}(p) + \underset{(0.10)}{0.56}F_{13}(m-p) \\ &- \underset{(0.09)}{0.24}\bar{R}_{t-3}{}^0 - \underset{(0.22)}{0.45}\Delta_1 R_{t-1}{}^0 \end{aligned} \tag{26}$$

$T = 94$, $\hat{\sigma} = 1.32\%$, $\tilde{\sigma} = 1.30\%$, $R^2 = 0.73$.

The improved goodness of fit is unsurprising given that the left-hand side has its largest observations most attenuated, and these were precisely the worst-fitting observations in earlier models (even so, fitting (24) to the last 74 observations produces $\hat{\sigma} = 1.24$ so 1963(iv) remains poorly explained). Otherwise, however, the parameter estimates are remarkably close to those in (18) with $\hat{\mu}$ being exceptionally well determined. Since (18) only requires lagged information, and does not preclude E_t greater than 25 per cent, it seems a preferable choice for practical modelling and forecasting (see e.g. its use in Davis (1984)).

5 Conclusion

The simplified model in equation (18) appears to satisfy most of the selection criteria discussed earlier. Relative to the unrestricted formulation in table 8.1, the residuals are innovations so (18) parsimoniously encompasses the maintained model (see Mizon, chapter 6 of this volume). The coefficients have remained relatively constant since the late 1970s and all the regressors are lagged other than income, so the issue of valid conditioning on contemporaneous variables hardly arises. The model formulation is consistent with both the static and dynamic theory analyses and always ensures positive house price predictions. Less favourable evidence is the marked non-normality of the residuals despite the emphasis on a nonlinear reaction function, the crude treatment of potentially important demographic variables and the erratic behaviour of house prices during 1981 and 1982, which was attributed above primarily to measurement factors. However, D_2 could also reflect other changes in the housing market, possibly including some reduction in mortgage rationing due to Bank lending, increased sales to individuals of local authority housing, changes in capital gains taxation and the introduction of indexed government securities, a sharply higher level of unemployment – especially outside of the south of England – combined with a redistribution of income to those in work and a large increase in early retirement. Re-testing of the empirical models on more recent data seems desirable, particularly against some of these hypotheses.

Rather little has been said above about encompassing rival models, since despite a recent spate of research into house prices, none of the previous studies specifically investigates second-hand house prices. Instead, either new house prices *Pn* or overall house prices *Po* have been studied. The latter show much less variability than new or second-hand prices alone, because of offsetting variations in their relative prices, partly owing to changes in construction costs, but also owing to lags in *Pn* adjusting to changed market conditions, so that as *Ph* rises, *Pn*/*Ph* falls (Hendry and Ericsson, 1984). However, households either buy a new or a second-hand house (rather than a weighted average of the two) hence there is interest in modelling them separately. The factorization of the joint density over $\{Pn_t, Ph_t\}$ adopted in our research is

$$D(Pn_t, Ph_t | I_t) = D(Pn_t | Ph_t, I_t) \, . \, D(Ph_t | I_t)$$

where I_t is the conditioning set. The marginal density of Ph_t has been of concern here and if desired, the behaviour of a weighted average price could be derived from the joint density.

However, it is difficult to compare directly marginal models for Ph_t and Pn_t given their different lag reactions, and determinants.

For sensible overall system responses, *Pn*/*Ph* should depend on construction costs, otherwise the theory models of section 2 could not operate to determine long-run house prices, yet such a variable is generally omitted from house price equations. The importance of several potential regressors (including rents, housing taxes, long-term interest rates, the level of unemployment and the number of first-time buyers) were investigated by adding them to (18) without any positive outcomes. The last noted variable is one of the main explanatory factors in the model of Boléat (1982), although the $\hat{\sigma}$ value of his model is only 2.4 per cent.

The model of new house prices in Nellis and Longbottom (1981) is similar in several respects to (18), and it variance dominates most previous *Pn*-models including that of Mayes (1979) ($\hat{\sigma}$ of 1.6 per cent as against 2.3 per cent). The variant of (18) reported for *Po* in Davis (1984) and the model of Buckley and Ermisch (1982) fit about equally well ($\hat{\sigma} = 1.2$ per cent) despite their very different formulations (the latter emphasizing the roles of demographic changes, supply factors and the rates of return on alternative assets). Thus there remains plenty of scope for progressive improvement of existing empirical models of *Ph* although these already fit sufficiently well (as measured by the $\hat{\sigma}$ values) to justify the view that house prices can be modelled.

On the econometric theory front, many new issues require investigation including the properties of the nonlinear dynamic processes discussed above, the behaviour of estimators of their parameters in large and small samples, and methods for testing encompassing when alternative measures are used of the same underlying concept, in the present case house prices. Hopefully, further research will clarify many of these questions.

Acknowledgments

This research is based on work initially undertaken with Neil Ericsson and Geoff Heal, extended for the UK Department of the Environment in 1980 (see Hendry, 1979). I am indebted to the ESRC for continuing financial support over the eight years during which this research was in progress (Grants HR8789 and BOO 220012), to Frank Srba for considerable help in estimating prototypes of the models reported below, and to Geoff Heal for many useful suggestions in formulating the dynamics. John Parker provided invaluable research assistance. Helpful discussions with and comments from Rob Engle, Neil Ericsson, Andrew Harvey, Robert Marshall, John Muellbauer and Ken Wallis are gratefully acknowledged.

Appendix A Equilibrium Conditions Between Alternative Assets

(a) The tax structure over most of the sample period created distorting effects on the incentives of owner-occupiers and landlords between housing and other financial assets. To highlight the tendencies, we consider an abstract world of certainty and formulate the equilibrium rates of return conditions facing these two groups of agents. While only a partial equilibrium analysis is considered, the implications of the results seem unlikely to alter on endogenizing rents, house prices, etc.

(b) Consider an individual with nominal assets V choosing between either purchasing a long-term bond costing $Pg = V$ and paying a nominal rate of return Rg or purchasing a house costing $Ph = V + M$ where M is borrowed by a mortgage. Income and capital gains tax rates are Ty and Tc respectively, and inflation is at a constant rate $\dot{p}$. Under the prevailing tax laws of most of the sample period, the former asset yields a real after-tax rate of return for V of

$$\dot{p}g(1-Tc) + Rg(1-Ty) - \dot{p} - \rho(A/V). \tag{A1}$$

This expression assumes that the individual must be housed and so deducts the real rental cost of accommodation valued at A where ρ is the real rental rate and A corresponds to the individual's optimal flow of housing services.

Alternatively, if he purchases the house, paying a nominal interest rate Rm on the mortgage, and loses depreciation δ per year (not tax deductible), then his real rate of return on V is

$$(\dot{p}h - \dot{p} - \delta)(Ph/V) - (Rm(1-Ty) - \dot{p})(M/V). \tag{A2}$$

Note that capital gains tax is not charged on owner-occupied housing, nor are implicit rental incomes taxed; property taxes are implicitly included in ρ and δ, and any excess consumption of housing services owing to $Ph > A$ is valued at zero. Under a market-clearing assumption, letting $k_1 = (A/V)$ and $k_2 = (M/V)$, substitution between these alternative assets requires that (A1) and (A2) are equated:

$$(\dot{p}h - \delta) + k_2(\dot{p}h - \delta - Rm(1-Ty)) = \dot{p}g(1-Tc) + Rg(1-Ty) - \rho k_1. \tag{A3}$$

To prevent endless arbitrage by borrowing on a mortgage to invest in bonds requires that $Rm(1-Ty)$ is no less than the return on bonds or assuming their equality at the margin:

$$Rm(1-Ty) = \dot{p}g(1-Tc) + Rg(1-Ty). \tag{A4}$$

Thus, from (A3) and (A4)

$$(\dot{p}h - \delta) + \rho \frac{k_1}{(1+k_2)} = \dot{p}g(1-Tc) + Rg(1-Ty) \tag{A5}$$

(c) Next, consider the corresponding choices facing a landlord, where nominal capital gains and incomes are taxed on both assets, and depreciation is tax deductible against rental income. Taking the case where the landlord does not borrow and is already housed (to simplify the analysis), the real rates of return on bonds and housing respectively are:

$$\dot{p}g(1-Tc) + Rg(1-Ty) - \dot{p} \tag{A6}$$

and

$$\dot{p}h(1-Tc) + (\rho-\delta)(1-Ty) - \dot{p}. \tag{A7}$$

Equilibrium now requires that

$$\dot{p}h(1-Tc) + (\rho-\delta)(1-Ty) = \dot{p}g(1-Tc) + Rg(1-Ty). \tag{A8}$$

Conditions (A5) and (A8) are not mutually consistent in general owing to the differential tax treatment of both capital gains and implicit as against explicit rental incomes. If there is a free market in bonds and individuals are to own any, then a corner solution results with no landlords. Historically, the size of the UK private rental sector has diminished dramatically over the last quarter century (to under 10 per cent of the total housing market), although tenancy laws undoubtedly would also account in part for this decline.

(d) While the above analysis has abstracted heroically from many important factors (tastes, risks, expectations, and so on), its general implication of an inconsistency in the long-run real after-tax rates of return facing owner-occupiers and landlords seems reasonable. Additional complications, such as interest on loans to purchase assets other than houses not being tax deductible for individuals, serve to reinforce the conclusion. Also, mortgage interest rates often being less than anticipated rates of return on bonds (compare (A4)), entail rationing by Building

Societies to cut off arbitrage (this is consistent with the available evidence) but again support the conclusion of a corner solution. Consequently, focusing on owner-occupied housing as the factor determining house prices in general seems a useful first approximation to the UK housing market.

Appendix B Data Definitions and Sources

Ph Second-hand house price index (simple average till 1968(i), weighted average thereafter, based on houses bought with a Building Society mortgage): see *Housing and Construction Statistics*, HMSO (various issues) and *Economic Trends* (October, 1982) (respectively abbreviated to *HCS* and *ET*).

Y Real personal disposable income, 1975 prices: see, *ET* (mainly Annual Supplement, 1983).

R Minimum Lending Rate till 1981(ii) and Base Rate thereafter: see, *ET* (mainly Annual Supplement, 1983).

M Building Societies' mortgage total outstanding: see, *A Compendium of Building Society Statistics*, BSA, 1982, and BSA *Bulletins*.

P General Index of Retail Prices; see, *ET* (mainly Annual Supplement, 1983).

H Number of owner-occupied houses (quarterly interpolation from annual series of stock of dwellings, using data on completions of new houses): see, *Annual Abstract of Statistics*, 1982 (denoted *AAS*).

T Standard rate of Income Tax; see, *AAS*, 1982.

9

Wages, Prices and Unemployment a Quarter Century after the Phillips Curve

MEGHNAD DESAI

1 Introduction

The history of econometric work on wages and prices and on the Phillips curve has been a chequered one. The two main issues which pervade this history are the theoretical foundations for the observed correlation between money wage changes (or price changes) and unemployment and the empirical stability of such an observed correlation. Phillips' classic 1958 article still remains a good starting point and although the relationship has been respecified, questioned, rejected as being unstable and reinterpreted, we shall see that much of this debate is due to a misreading of the original. The bewildering course of the debate is a quintessential example in the history of econometrics of the interaction of economic theory, the nature of the data, the specification of the equation and the estimation and testing of the econometric equation.

We begin by examining in some detail Phillips' pioneering article, because it has often been ignored or its argument simplified beyond recognition. It is made to seem as if a naive economic theory was used to force the data through a misspecified relation which broke down soon after the initial publication. 'Phillips' analysis seems very persuasive and obvious, yet it is utterly fallacious. It is fallacious because no economic theorist has ever asserted that the demand and supply of labour were functions of the *nominal* wage rate' (Friedman, 1975, p. 15). By carefully rehearsing Phillips' argument we show that he had a clear appreciation of the microfoundations of the relationship, contrary to Friedman's assertion. The nature of the data also led Phillips to distinguish carefully between the long-run equilibrium and the short-run dynamics. It was perhaps his style of argument, which mixes theory and history with terse formal statements, surrounded by a mass of diagrams, that has obscured his model.

After clarifying Phillips' theoretical model and his econometric procedure, we develop in section 3 the alternative version by Lipsey around which much of the subsequent argument has centred. Lipsey altered both the theoretical basis and the econometric procedure. The debate then starts with Friedman (1968) and subsequent papers by Lucas and Rapping (1969, 1970). Sargan's Colston paper, although not in the mainstream of this debate, serves as a paradigm here since it illustrates how the adoption of a proper econometric procedure could have avoided much of this controversy. But Sargan's paper was terse and did not readily yield simple conclusions. Much is gained, however, by revisiting his paper as a code to the debate.

In the final section, we take up an issue raised in the Colston paper, namely the question of the endogeneity of the unemployment variable. The standard Phillips curve models comprise a wage equation and a price equation, with unemployment assumed to be exogenous. The question of the status of the unemployment variable pertains to whether the wage–price equations constitute a complete or an incomplete model. We survey briefly some attempts to endogenize unemployment in the literature but conclude that much work still needs to be done (compare chapter 2 of this volume).

2 The Original Phillips Curve

Phillips commences his study by stating the proposition that the price of any product changes in response to excess demand. He qualifies this for labour markets in one respect. Employers bid up wage rates when unemployment is low, and this bids labour away from other firms. When unemployment is high, labour withdraws its services at the prevailing low wage rate and hence prevents it falling further. He concludes 'the relation between unemployment and the rate of change of wage rates is therefore likely to be highly nonlinear' (Phillips, 1958, p. 283).

He adds to this the additional influence of 'the rate of change of the demand for labour, and so of unemployment'. The *acceleration* of the employers' offer of wage rates in order to bid labour away from other employers is a function of the rate of change of unemployment. This influence is symmetric and linear.

Phillips then takes up the question of the effect of 'the rate of change of retail prices, operating through cost of living adjustments in wage rates' (p. 283). Here his argument is that retail prices operating through cost of living adjustments matter only if the change in retail price is due to an *exogenous shock*, i.e. a change in import prices, and then again only if the change is so large that it disturbs the equilibrium wage/price relationship. Once again the argument is cast in terms of the behaviour of employers demanding labour. Let us suppose, Phillips says, that the demand for products grows at the same rate (2 per cent per annum) as the productivity of labour so that unemployment is constant at, say, 2 per cent. In this steady-state equilibrium, 'Assume that with this level of unemployment and *without any cost of living adjustments* wage rates rise by, say, 3 per cent per annum *as the result of employers competitive bidding for labour* and that import prices and the prices of other factor services are also rising by 3 per cent per annum' (p. 284, emphasis added). In such a situation retail prices would rise by an amount equal to 'the rate of change of factor costs minus the rate of change of productivity', i.e. 1 per cent per annum. 'Under these conditions the introduction of cost of living adjustments in wage rates will have no effect, for employers *will merely be giving under the name of cost of living adjustments part of the wage increases which they would in any case have given as a result of their competitive bidding for labour*' (p. 284, emphasis added).

Thus, Phillips' model is one where producers as employers of labour bid up wage rates competitively in order to attract labour away from other firms. We have competition, but not necessarily price-taking behaviour. In a world of price-taking agents, as Arrow has pointed out, it is difficult to model how price adjustments take place. Such price adjustments in response to excess demand are, however, necessary for stability of competitive markets (Arrow, 1959). Phillips seems to us to combine price adjusting (rather than price setting) behaviour in disequilibrium with certain regularities in steady state. The difference between price adjusting and price setting corresponds to that between differentials and levels; a price adjusting producer takes current price *level* as given and then adjusts it up or down. This adjustment ceases in equilibrium.

Phillips, however, has in mind a growing economy, where there is a constant rate of productivity growth (Δq). When aggregate demand grows at the same rate, unemployment is constant, i.e. $\Delta U = 0$, $U = U^*$. In such a steady-state equilibrium, there is an equilibrium growth of money wages Δw^* which exceeds Δq. This part of the relation is then

$$\Delta w^* - \Delta q = \alpha_0 + \alpha_1 f(U^*) > 0 \tag{1}$$

(lower case letters denote logarithms and upper case letters denote levels of variables).

Out of equilibrium we add to this the cyclical pressure of ΔU, which is symmetric and linear

$$\Delta w = \Delta w^* + \alpha_2(\Delta U/U) = (\alpha_0 + \Delta q) + \alpha_1 f(U) + \alpha_2(\Delta U/U). \tag{2}$$

Equation (1) gives us the growth of wage rate common for all producers resulting from their competitive bidding, and it is the market-clearing growth rate. (It should be obvious that our contrast between price adjusting and price setting extends to second differentials and differentials in a steadily growing economy.)

We add to this a steady-state pricing behaviour. Let F be the unit factor cost of output (either average for the economy or identical for all producers). This is a sum of unit labour cost and unit import cost. (Phillips' argument, although general, pertains to the UK economy where imports play a large role in providing raw materials as well as finished goods.) The rate of change of retail prices Δp_c then equals a weighted sum of change in labour costs, Δw, and raw material costs, Δp_m. To simplify matters let us assume the same rate of productivity growth for labour and for imported inputs, namely Δq. Then,

$$\Delta p_c = a\,\Delta w + (1-a)\,\Delta p_m - \Delta q. \tag{3}$$

Equation (3) ensures that in the steady state where $\Delta w^* = \Delta p_m{}^*$ the real wage will grow at the rate Δq. This is why the associated unemployment rate is an equilibrium one, i.e.

$$\Delta w^* - \Delta q = \Delta p_c{}^* = \alpha_0 + \alpha_1 f(U^*). \tag{4}$$

This definition of equilibrium unemployment is stated at the outset of his paper by Phillips. But while U^* is an equilibrium rate, it can be associated with a positive (as in Phillips' example) or any value of $\Delta p_c{}^*$.

Notice then that without introducing an inflation term in the wage equation, the equilibrium outcome of competitive bidding is the same as that which would come from adding such a term. The impact of price changes comes in Phillips' view in terms of an unanticipated change in its exogenous component, namely import prices.

But the size of the actual change Δp_m matters only if it exceeds the equilibrium rate. 'Assuming that the value of imports is one fifth of national income, it is only at times when the annual rate of change of import prices exceeds the rate at which wage rates would rise as a result of competitive bidding by employers by more than five times the rate of increase of productivity that cost of living adjustments become an operative factor in increasing the rate of change of money wage rates' (p. 284).

This asymmetric effect can be easily captured as follows

$$\Delta w = \Delta w^* + \alpha_2(\Delta U/U) + \alpha_3(\Delta p_c - \Delta p_c{}^*).$$

Substituting from equation (3) and its steady-state version the appropriate terms for $(\Delta p_c - \Delta p_c{}^*)$, we obtain

$$\Delta w = \alpha_0 + \alpha_1 f(U) + \frac{\alpha_2}{(1-\alpha_3 a)} \frac{\Delta U}{U} + \frac{\alpha_3(1-a)}{(1-\alpha_3 a)} (\Delta p_m - \Delta p_m{}^*).$$

The proviso here is that $\alpha_3 > 0$ if $(\Delta p_c - \Delta p_c{}^*) > 0$ and $\alpha_3 = 0$ if $\Delta p_c \leqslant \Delta p_c{}^*$. Now in the quotation above Phillips approximates $\Delta p_m{}^*$ by Δw^* ('the rate at which wage rates would rise as a result of competitive bidding') *plus* $(1-a)^{-1}\Delta q$ ('five times the rate of increase of productivity'), i.e.

$$\Delta p_m{}^* = \Delta w^* + (1-a)^{-1}\Delta q.$$

If therefore import prices rose at a rate higher than $\Delta p_m{}^*$, the wage price spiral would be set off.

Thus in his introductory section Phillips clearly poses the issue of price changes. He does not include a term for Δp_c in his wage equation since, as we have shown above, it is a reduced form expression incorporating a consistent set of equilibrium Δw^*, $\Delta p_c{}^*$ relations. In his empirical work he drops the $\Delta p_m - \Delta p_m{}^*$ term since he finds that only at the outset in 1862 did import prices rise by 12 per cent (impact of US Civil War on cotton prices?). After that seldom did they rise more than five times the rate of productivity growth. So by examining his data, in the light of his prior theory, he dropped the extra term. 'If the hypothesis stated above is correct the rise in import prices in 1862 may just have been sufficient to start up a mild wage–price spiral, but in the remainder of the period changes in import prices will have had little or no effect on the rate of change of wage rates' (p. 285).

We therefore arrive at Phillips' empirical work with a different perspective than others. He had a model of competitive price-adjusting producers generating the observed data. There is a long-run equilibrium to which cyclical dynamics is added with an occasional exogenous shock. It was the separation of these influences which informed his empirical work. Plotting his 52 annual observations for 1861–1913, Phillips noticed $6\frac{1}{2}$ regular trade cycles with an average period of about 8 years. He divided the range of U into six grids 0–2 per cent, 2–3 per cent, 3–4 per cent, 4–5 per cent, 5–7 per cent and 7–11 per cent. He obtained an average U and average Δw for each of these six grids. His purpose was to approximate a cycle free measure of U and Δw, i.e. to approximate the steady-state relation (1) above. 'Since each interval includes years in which unemployment was increasing and years in which it was decreasing the effect of changing unemployment at the rate of change of wage rates tends to be cancelled out by this averaging, so that each cross gives an approximation to the rate of change of wages which would be associated with the indicated level of unemployment if unemployment were held constant at that level.' (p. 290).

In a footnote he mentions the possibility of carrying out a multiple regresssion on a version of our equation (2) above. This is

$$\Delta w_t = \alpha_0 + \alpha_1 U_t{}^c + \alpha_2(\Delta U_t / U_t{}^m). \tag{5}$$

His notation is different and he uses differentials rather than differences in his version. Given that U was a trend free variable, his two terms on the right-hand side are uncorrelated and hence he could have carried out a stepwise regression with all the 52 observations. He argues that his averaging procedure which eliminates ΔU is 'satisfactory'. The effect of this procedure is not, however, merely computational but quite profound since it allows him to separate the long-run equilibrium relation between Δw^* and U^* from the short-run cyclical one coming from the influence of $(\Delta U/U)$ (Desai, 1975; Gersovitz, 1980).

The procedure he adopted removes the estimated equation from the time domain. The average values of U and Δw do not belong to any particular year nor are they moving averages of past actual U_t and Δw_t. This is because the averaging procedure exploits the cyclical (sinusoidal) properties of the time series and the averages thus are obtained by slicing the sine wave vertically (see Desai (1975), figure 1 for an illustration). So we have a linear filter A, say, which has the property that $A(\Delta U/U) = 0$ (we take $m = 1$), thus from equation (5),

$$A\Delta w_t = A\alpha_0 + \alpha_1 (AU)_t{}^c + \alpha_2 A(\Delta U_t / U_t)$$

$$\Delta w^* = \alpha_0 + \alpha_1 (U^*)^c. \qquad (6)$$

The equation Phillips estimated was (6). He had six data points condensed from 52 actual observations. Two of them had $\Delta w^* < 0$ associated with the two highest values of U^*. So he took the four pairs of positive Δw^*, U^* and estimated α_1 and c. He then estimated α_0 by trial and error. The equation he obtained was

$$\Delta w^* = -0.900 + 0.638 U^{-1.394}. \qquad (7)$$

He did not then proceed to estimate α_2 by a stepwise procedure. He plotted each of the actual cycles in Δw_t, U_t around the fitted equation and noticed the negative influence of $(\Delta U/U)$ as evidenced by the counterclockwise loops in each case. (For a different interpretation of Phillips' procedure, see Gilbert, 1976.)

For the next period, 1913–48, Phillips did not estimate a new relationship. The period 1915–22 was one of great variation in Δw_t, U_t, Δp_c and Δp_{mt} as Phillips noted. There was a cost of living adjustment introduced in war-time and the connection between Δw_t and Δp_{ct}, both upward and downward, is noted. For the 1923–9 period when Δp_m did not change, Phillips notes how closely his pre-war equation predicts the average wage change for 1925–9 from the average unemployment for the same five years. He rejects therefore the view that there was any downward rigidity in wages.

Throughout the discussion of this period and of the 1948–57 period, Phillips continuously notes the connection of price changes, import price changes and wage changes especially when the former were noticeably large. For the post-war period he obtains a clockwise loop around the fitted curve from 1861 to 1913 but a lag in U (seven months) eliminates the clockwise loops. The fit of the curve is so good that the loops are hardly discernible.

Phillips follows up this amended curve fitting by offering a decomposition of actual wage changes for 1948–57 into (a) a demand-pull factor, $\alpha_0 + \alpha_1 f(U)$, (b) a cost-push factor, Δp_c and (c) the extra burst due to high import price changes (Korean War years). By the post-war period, the institutional structure of the labour market had changed from the nineteenth century one of competitive bidding by producers to one of annual wage negotiations through trade unions. Also the continuous full employment in these years rendered the influence of ΔU negligible. Despite this, the original equation fits the data well, in all the three periods, and the deviations around the curve can be explained in terms of the disequilibrium variables.

3 Subsequent Developments

Phillips considered the idea of carrying out a multiple regression, but rejected it, as noted above. The independence of U_t from any differenced version of itself gave him the confidence that his results would not be biased. Gilbert (1976) argues that the averaging procedure was merely a device to aid computation of a nonlinear equation. He reproduces Phillips' results using all the observations, and adds $(\Delta U/U)_t$ for which he obtains a coefficient not significantly different from zero. Thus we have from Gilbert

$$\Delta w_t = \alpha_0 + \alpha_1 U_t^{-c} + k(\Delta U/U)_t. \tag{8}$$

He proceeds to add to this Δp_{ct} and obtains the result that the coefficient of Δp_c is less than one.

We shall return to Gilbert's results later. At this juncture, we note that it has been the usual practice for authors following Phillips to carry out a multiple regression with all the data and including besides $f(U)$ and $(\Delta U/U)$, Δp_c as well as other variables. It is best to put the debate in a common framework, as follows:

$$\begin{aligned}\Delta w_t = \alpha_0 + \alpha_1 f(U_t) + \alpha_2 \Delta U_t + \alpha_3 \Delta p_{ct} + \alpha_4(\Delta p_{ct}{}^e - \Delta p_{ct})\\ + \alpha_5(w - p_c)_{t-1} + \alpha_6 t + e_{1t}.\end{aligned} \tag{9}$$

Many of the terms have been described above; $\Delta p_c{}^e$ is the expected rate of inflation, the term $(w - p_c)$ represents real wage levels achieved in the past and t is the trend variable.

Lipsey (1960) was the first to linearize the Phillips curve and extend it by adding variables. He approximated $f(U)$ by $\Sigma \delta_i U^{-i}$ thus making the equation linear in parameters. He estimated separate regression equations for 1862–1913, 1923–47 and 1948–57. He did not test the relationship for stability across the time periods but noticed the similarity of coefficients. Lipsey also offered a theoretical argument for the nonlinearity in the $\Delta w/U$ relationship. There were many separate labour markets and in some there was excess demand and in others excess supply at the same time. This, he said, led upon aggregation to the nonlinearity.

It was not, however, his microtheoretic explanation for the nonlinearity but his inclusion of the Δp_c term that sparked off the future debate. In the context of (9) above, Lipsey assumed $\alpha_4 = \alpha_5 = \alpha_6 = 0$. So he had

$$\Delta w_t = \alpha_0 + \alpha_1 f(U_t) + \alpha_2 \Delta U_t + \alpha_3 \Delta p_{ct} + e_{1t}' \tag{9a}$$

and the coefficient of Δp_c was less than one. Lipsey also made no attempt to separate the long-run equilibrium behaviour from short-run dynamics. His equation bears the conventional interpretation of a structural single equation, i.e. a stochastic difference equation with the dependent variable on the left-hand side and independent variables on the right-hand side. Since he did not embed the wage equation in a consistent wage–price relation in equilibrium as Phillips had done, his equation is open to two objections. One, stated by Friedman (1968), concerns the size of α_3 – the parameter of 'money illusion'. The other is that of simultaneity between wages and prices.

The question of simultaneity of wages and prices was recognized by Samuelson and Solow (1960) in their paper on the analytics of an anti-inflation policy. This paper, which mainly surveys different theories of inflation – demand pull, cost push – turns its attention to what the authors call the 'fundamental Phillips schedule'. They do not carry out an econometric analysis but they present a scatter of Δw_t against U_t for US data. The scatter is discouraging 'there are points all over the place'. Undaunted by this, they add a price–wage link of the form in equation (3) above (though without Δp_m). From this they draw a smooth 'modified Phillips curve' for the US, showing 'the menu for choices between different degrees of unemployment and price stability'. Although they say it is roughly estimated, one suspects its econometric foundations.

Samuelson and Solow shift the focus to the Phillips curve as a policy tool in the short run. Indeed, they mention that if relied upon for policy, the relationship may change its shape in the long run. The reversal of Phillips' long-run equilibrium relation into a short-run policy tool was thus complete within two years of its publication. Solow has recounted how dramatic an explanation the Phillips curve seemed to offer for the inflation of 1957–9 when excess capacity and inflation coexisted. Its short-run explanatory power clinched the case for the Phillips curve.

Phillips himself was quite clear about the long run. In an exercise he carried out with Australian data for 1947–58 (during his stay as Visiting Professor at the University of Melbourne in 1959), he estimated two equations, one for price changes and one for wage changes. He is explicit about the short-run simultaneity 'Changes in wage rates are influenced by earlier changes in consumer prices; but changes in consumer prices are themselves largely determined by earlier changes in wage rates' (Phillips, 1959, p. 4). But owing to the shortness of the series, he resorts explicitly to reduced form estimation. He obtained the following two equations

$$\Delta p_t = 2.110 + 1.46 U_{t-3}^{-2} + 0.41 U_{t-3}^{-3} + 0.15[\tfrac{1}{2}(\Delta p_{x,t-1} + \Delta p_{x,t-2})] + 0.13\Delta p_{m,t-3} \quad (10a)$$

$$\Delta w_t = 0.29 + 0.93(U_{t-2} - 0.26)^{-1} + 0.05[50.0(\exp \Delta p_x - 1)] + 0.02\Delta p_{m,t-2} + 0.57\Delta w_{t-1} \quad (10b)$$

where p_x is the price of exports.

No standard errors or other statistics are provided in the paper. The variables in each case are four-quarter moving averages 'to reduce seasonal and random fluctuations'. Equations (10a) and (10b) are typical examples of Phillips' willingness to use rough-and-ready methods and ingenious nonlinear transformations of variables to explain the data.

In coming to policy analysis as Phillips says 'since we are interested here in long-run policy objectives' he takes $\Delta p_x = \Delta p_m = 0$. He then plots the two equations and remarks 'it will be seen that the two estimates agree fairly closely and at the present level of unemployment of about $2\frac{1}{2}$ per cent . . . , they indicate that, *on average over a period of years*, wage rates would rise a little over 2 per cent per year'. (1959, p. 8, emphasis in the original.)

The next stage in the analysis of wage–price data was the estimation of a simultaneous equations model of the short-run version of equations such as (2) and (3). Bodkin (1966) did this for 1900–57 for US data. Unlike Phillips, and like Lipsey, he estimated short-run structural equations with wage–price simultaneity built in. He also modelled productivity and explained cycles in productivity around the trend growth in terms of the unemployment variable. The major differences between the Bodkin and Phillips–Lipsey approaches is that Bodkin models the absolute change in money wages ΔW_t rather than percentage changes in terms of the absolute number unemployed rather than the percentage unemployed, and he explains price level rather than price change. The choice of absolute difference in money wage in Bodkin's work derived from Klein and Ball's work on the postwar UK economy (Klein and Ball, 1959).

Bodkin not only estimated his system by 2SLS but also derived the likely shape of the inflation–unemployment trade-off. This turned out to be very flat: for absolute price stability, the required rate of unemployment for the US ranged between 7.5 million unemployed (10.5 per cent) to 13.1 million (18.8 per cent). But the flatness of the (linear) trade-off implied that at zero unemployment inflation would only be 2.1 per cent. The choice for the policymaker was thus simple – a mild inflation was preferable to a horrendously high level of unemployment.

Bodkin, like Lipsey, had found that the coefficient of price change was significantly less than one. This was unlike Klein and Ball, who found a unit coefficient for a four-quarter average of absolute price changes (current plus three previous quarters) in an equation for $\Delta_4 W_t$. In a critical review article Rees and Hamilton (1967), henceforth RH, re-estimated Bodkin's equations. They changed the specification to percentage changes rather than absolute changes and also experimented with adding ΔU_t which Bodkin had tried but rejected in his final version. In arriving at their results and interpreting them RH raise many of the interesting econometric problems in this area. Their 'best' equation is

$$\begin{aligned} \Delta w_t &= \underset{(2.81)}{2.20} - \underset{(2.51)}{0.4171} U_t + \underset{(2.93)}{0.4619} U_{t-1} + \underset{(12.52)}{1.0575} \Delta p_{ct} \\ R^2 &= 0.8434, \quad DW = 2.10 \end{aligned} \tag{11}$$

On rearranging the terms in U we see that equation (11) implies a negative coefficient of ΔU_t but a small but positive coefficient for U_t, which is not likely to be significantly different from zero. It displays a coefficient for Δp_c not significantly different from unity. But RH are unhappy about this for two reasons. In a regime of stable prices ($\Delta p_{ct} = 0$) and stable unemployment ($U_t = U_{t-1}$), Δw will still grow at 2.2 per cent per annum. Secondly they are unhappy about the unit coefficient of price change. They note that the simple correlation between Δw and Δp_c is 0.875, but doubt whether this represents causal information. 'The high current correlation suggests that the causation may run in part from wages to prices or that both are simultaneously affected by powerful third forces, such as changes in aggregate demand caused by monetary and fiscal policy or autonomous shifts in investment'

(RH, p. 67). This leads them to specify an equation with lagged rather than current Δp_c:

$$\Delta w_t = \underset{(3.10)}{3.94} - \underset{(5.94)}{1.4096} U_t + \underset{(5.27)}{1.3203} U_{t-1} + \underset{(5.18)}{0.6654} \Delta p_{c,t-1}$$

$$R^2 = 0.5851, \quad DW = 1.629. \tag{12}$$

They are happier with the higher t values on the unemployment variables and do not worry about obvious misspecification signs in the drop in the DW statistic.

RH do not reproduce Bodkin's full model. They remark that the t ratios for the unemployment variable are lower in the 2SLS than in the OLS regressions and are indeed lower than unity. 'Whatever its general merits as an econometric model, Bodkin's two-stage system seems to be moving in the wrong direction for the purpose of estimating the Phillips curve' (RH, p. 68). For their preferred single equation, RH obtain a family of Phillips curves given different values for U_{t-1}. These short-run Phillips curves are steep. Then they derive the long-run Phillips curve with $\Delta U_t = 0$; '... The locus of all points on the family of Phillips curves having the property that last year's unemployment rate is equal to this year's. It may be thought of as a long-run or steady-state Phillips curve' (p. 68). The long-run Phillips curve that they obtain is flat, similar to Bodkin's. For a productivity growth of 2.5 per cent, $\Delta w = \Delta q$ at $U = 16.1$ per cent and for $\Delta q = 3.2$ at $U = 8.3$ per cent. They conclude 'The steady-state curve seems implausibly flat ...' (p. 68).

From this exercise RH conclude 'We have been astounded by how many very different Phillips curves can be constructed on reasonable assumptions from the same body of data. The nature of the relationship between wage changes and unemployment is highly sensitive to the exact choice of the other variables that enter the regression and to the forms of all the variables. For this reason the authors of the Phillips Curves would do well to label them conspicuously '*Unstable. Apply with extreme care*' (RH, 1967, p. 70).

The rejection by RH of the unit coefficient on Δp_c and their preference for equation (12) over equation (11) suggests that there was an intuitive or prior bias in favour of a downward sloping steady-state Phillips curve but there were doubts about the appropriate steepness of such a curve. Empirical work, it seemed, gave a bewildering variety of choice of short-run curves, though the similarity of the shape of the long-run curve of Bodkin's and their own calculations should have suggested an empirical stability rather than instability of the long-run Phillips curve.

It is in this context that Friedman's Presidential Address, later in the year in which RH's review appeared, is interesting (Friedman, 1968). He offered no empirical estimates but an a priori argument for the shape of the Phillips curve. His Presidential Address is remarkable for the total lack of any discussion of the details of Phillips' paper (indeed even any bibliographical reference to it) or details of any other empirical study. In Friedman's model monetary authorities can alter unemployment below (or above) its equilibrium level. This equilibrium level is consistent with any level of inflation as long as real wage changes are in line with productivity changes very much as in equation (4) above. It is unanticipated price change and the divergence between *ex post* fall in real wages for employers and the rise in *ex ante* real wages for workers (given their false anticipations) which causes the change in unemployment. It is because product prices change more rapidly than factor prices that this divergence occurs.

But Friedman leaves unclear the question as to who initiates the change in product prices. We have price-taking behaviour on both the demand and the supply side but product prices change and change faster than money wages. Whereas Phillips clearly attributes price adjusting behaviour to producers, with workers reacting passively by going to the highest bidder, Friedman leaves this anomaly unclear. In the standard textbook model, *levels* of demand for and supply of labour depend on the *level* of real wages. The Friedman model conflates this with a world where *changes* in prices and wages determine *changes* in excess supply or demand for labour. The switch between levels and differences is not merely one of mathematical convenience. It leaves a behavioural problem open: who changes the prices in a Walrasian competitive model? The problem remains whether one talks of actual or anticipated quantities.

The econometric form of Friedman's model can be easily set out. We have equation (9) above with $\alpha_5 = 0$. To this we can add an adaptive expectations scheme for $\Delta p_c{}^e$:

$$\Delta p_c{}^e = \frac{(1-\lambda)}{(1-\lambda L)}\,\Delta p_c + \frac{1}{(1-\lambda L)}\,e_2, \qquad 0 \leqslant \lambda < 1 \qquad (13)$$

where L is the lag operator. Combining (9) with (13) gives

$$(1-\lambda L)\,\Delta w = \alpha_0(1-\lambda) + \alpha_1(1-\lambda L)\,f(U) + \alpha_2(1-\lambda L)\,\Delta U + (\alpha_3-\alpha_4\lambda)\,\Delta p_c + (\alpha_4-\alpha_3)\,\lambda\,\Delta p_{c,-1} + (1-\lambda L)\,e_1 + \alpha_4 e_2. \tag{14}$$

Equation (14) has a moving average error as well as a lagged dependent variable. A real wage Phillips curve requires $\alpha_3 = \alpha_4 = 1$ but the econometric estimation of equation (14) is not straightforward.

Such econometric issues are of concern in Sargan's Colston paper, as its subtitle says. The approach is to tackle the estimation of an equation with a lagged dependent variable and a first-order autoregressive (1AR) error. But much greater interest should attach to the specification of the wage equation. Sargan considers both the Klein–Ball and the Lipsey specifications and chooses the logarithmic one. His specification allows the determination of an equilibrium real wage/unemployment relationship, with the wage change relation being a disequilibrium dynamic one around the equilibrium. Thus

$$(w - p)^* = b_0 + b_1\Delta p_t + b_2 U_t + b_3 t + \epsilon_{1t}, \tag{15}$$

$$\Delta w_t = \gamma[(w-p)_{t-1}{}^* - (w_{t-1} - p_{t-1})] + \epsilon_{2t}. \tag{16}$$

Combining (15) and (16) gives

$$\Delta w_t = \gamma(b_0 - b_3) + \gamma b_1 \Delta p_{t-1} + \gamma b_2 U_{t-1} + \gamma b_3 t - \gamma(w_{t-1} - p_{t-1}) + \epsilon_{2t} + \gamma\epsilon_{1,t-1}. \tag{17}$$

The similarity of (17) to (9) is obvious: $f(U) = U_{t-1}$ and $\alpha_2 = 0$. The parallel between Phillips' implicit equations (1) and (4) and equation (15) is clear. But Phillips has no explicit adjustment process of actual to equilibrium levels; he separates the equilibrium process from the actual by his averaging device. Sargan adds an explicit adjustment process. Thus his stochastic structural equation is similar to Lipsey's but still allows the separation of the two parts of the process. But for any such separation to be valid, the dynamic specification must be free of omissions. The major likely omission that Sargan focuses on concerns the error process; hence the importance of specifying an explicit 1AR process.

In computing the steady-state equilibrium, all the variables in change form are set to zero. Sargan adds a price equation in level terms but otherwise similar to our equation (3) above. The long-run equilibrium is

$$(w-p)^* = 0.0049t - 0.0443U, \tag{18}$$

$$(p-w)^* = 0.198(p_m - w) + 0.875\tau - 0.115q - 0.0018t. \tag{19}$$

In (19), τ is the log of factor cost adjustment. Solving (18) and (19) gives a consistent set of *levels* of wage and price for given levels of the variables U, τ, p_m and q. A powerful implication of (18) and (19) is that the natural rate of unemployment is explicitly a function of a competitiveness variable $(w - p_m)$ as well as taxes, productivity and trend. Thus,

$$U^* = -4.47(w - p_m) + 0.07t + 19.75\tau - 2.60q. \tag{20}$$

Contrast (20) with a natural rate derived from (9) with $\alpha_2 = \alpha_5 = 0$ and $\alpha_3 = \alpha_4 = 1$: if we put $\Delta w = \Delta p_c$ we obtain

$$U^* = -f^{-1}((\alpha_0 + \alpha_6 t)/\alpha_1). \tag{21}$$

Sargan does not spell out the theory underlying his wage and price equations in any detail but it would seem that his wage change equation is a bargaining equation on the part of workers, given a level of excess demand in the labour market U. Producers are price setters who decide the price level (or the product real wage) in light of costs. The producers are thus able to adjust product prices instantaneously (or at least within the unit time period) but workers adjust wages slowly in the bargaining process to attain their desired level of real wage.

4 The Treatment of Unemployment

Sargan has another innovation in his paper which has gone relatively unnoticed. While wage–price simultaneity was usually assumed by previous model builders, the unemployment variable was always taken as exogenous. Sargan, however, uses instruments for not only the price variable but also the unemployment variable in his Phillips curve equation. Thus the wage–price subsystem is implicitly part of a larger model within which unemployment is an endogenous variable. Sargan uses import and export prices and expenditure variables, all lagged, as instruments. The Phillips curve is thus seen as an incomplete system even after the addition of a price equation. We need an equation for the unemployment variable to move towards a complete system.

The theoretical basis of the wage–price equations in early econometric work is only barely sketched out, as we have seen. Thus Phillips in his introductory section envisages a world of wage- and price-adjusting producers who via competitive bidding hire workers. Workers' behaviour is passive in this model. Friedman's model is one with price changes being more rapid than wage changes, but the initiators of the price changes are unspecified. Sargan has instantaneous price adjustment and lagged wage adjustment by producers and workers respectively. Lucas and Rapping (1969), henceforth LR, propose a model which turns the logic of the Phillips curve into one where workers adjust the quantity of labour services supplied in the light of unanticipated changes in real wages. The forces initiating the unanticipated changes in real wages are, however, left unspecified because here, as in Friedman's model, agents are price takers.

LR discriminate between the long-run equilibrium and short-run adjustment in their theoretical model. They have a 'normal' labour supply N_t^* and an actual labour supply N_t. Normal supply reacts to changes in permanent real wage as well as the inflation rate measured as the deviation of last period's actual price level from the permanent price level. Actual supply reacts to deviations of actual real wage from permanent real wage, the level of permanent real wage and anticipated inflation. Actual observed unemployment is the discrepancy between the actual and normal labour supply. Thus

$$U_t = \beta_0 + \beta_1[(w_t - p_t) - (\bar{w}_{t-1} - \bar{p}_{t-1})] + \beta_2(p_t - \bar{p}_{t-1}) + \xi_1 \tag{22}$$

where bars over variables indicate permanent values. These are in turn generated by an adaptive scheme as in (13), with parameter $(1-\lambda)$ identical for both $\bar{w}$ and $\bar{p}$. Substituting this gives

$$\begin{aligned}\Delta U_t = {} & \beta_0(1-\lambda) + \beta_1 \Delta w_t + (\beta_2 - \beta_1)\,\Delta p_t \\ & -(1-\lambda)\,U_{t-1} + (1-\lambda L)\,\xi_1 - \beta_2 e_{2,\,t-1}.\end{aligned} \tag{23}$$

Writing (23) in this way brings out one important aspect of the LR specification: equation (23) is a rewritten version of equation (9), i.e. Lipsey's equation with $f(U) = U_{t-1}$, but with ΔU as the dependent variable rather than Δw. This reversal of the dependent and independent variables represents a continuing controversy in the wage–price literature. Econometrically an equation in g separate endogenous variables can be trivially normalized on any one of them. What is at stake here, however, is that the Lipsey specification presumes that the causation runs from U_t to Δw_t, given Δp_t etc. The LR specification argues that the causation runs from Δw_t to U_t given Δp_t etc. It is not possible, however, to discriminate between these two alternative models on the basis of single equation estimates. Although much controversy has centred on whether $\alpha_3 = \alpha_4$ was one (equivalently whether $\beta_2 = 0$), the important problem is that of the status of U and Δw.

The next step in the wage–price debate did not, however, tackle the exogeneity issue. Lucas in his 1972 paper proposed a substitution of a rational expectations (RE) scheme in place of adaptive expectations (AE). This meant going back to equation (22), imposing $\beta_2 = 0$ and treating the deviation from permanent real wage as an innovation. The Lucas argument generalized the LR specification to real output (via an implicit use of Okun's Law) and turned (22) into the now famous 'surprise-only' supply relation

$$(U_t - U_t^*) \simeq y_t - y_{nt} = \beta_1 [p_t - E_{t-1} p_t] + \zeta_1. \qquad (24)$$

To compare with (22) set $U_t^* = \beta_0$. Equation (24) then follows given the redefinition of the permanent real wage as the rationally expected price level. We no longer need an adjustment equation to translate (24) into an estimable equation: we need a complete model to generate the conditional expectation of p_t. Equation (24) is then one equation embedded in a complete model but the remainder, which generates $E_{t-1} p_t$, is assumed to be recursive with respect to (24).

The Lucas RE model comprises apart from equation (24) and a price–money link via the quantity theory, an explanation for the natural level of output y_{nt}. Unlike in the Lipsey, Sargan or LR versions of the Phillips curve, the natural rate is not given by the parameters of that curve, but must be specified from outside. Here the economic theoretic story is that y_{nt} is aggregated from real supply response in individual markets, all depending on the appropriate relative prices as in the N^* relationship in the LR models. The econometric measurement either assumes y_{nt} to be the trend level of output (Lucas, 1973) or models it in terms of an aggregate production function with labour force and a trend variable as surrogate for capital stock (Sargent, 1976). But a trend level of output can be the natural level of output only if all observed deviations are random, i.e. if equation (24) is assumed to be true. It cannot be used in testing equation (24) if it presumes its validity.

The separation of long-run equilibrium from the short-run dynamics is again a problem here. The Lucas model predicates that the economy is in short-run and long-run equilibrium. All observed deviations are random. This brings to the fore the problem of testing the observed series on output (or unemployment) for serial correlation. Since what is usually tested is not the series itself but some residuals from an estimated equation purporting to explain output, it is of utmost importance that there be no dynamic misspecification in such an equation.

There is now a substantial body of literature on the problem of dynamic misspecification. Much of this stems from Sargan's Colston paper, which rigorously formulated the issue of dynamic specification in the presence of serially correlated errors. Subsequent generalizations of Sargan's 1AR model to higher-order processes (Wallis, 1972; Hendry, 1974) led to improved formulations of the sequential hypothesis testing procedure (Mizon, 1977a). An important implication is that it is best to formulate a general model with a very high order of dynamics and then specialize it down to a specific equation by a stepwise test procedure, instead of starting with a static formulation and adding lags or autoregressive errors only when something 'goes wrong' (Hendry and Mizon, 1978).

This principle of starting from the general formulation holds equally for a multiple equation system. Thus in testing the Lucas hypothesis, Sargent (1976) formulated a model which imposed a recursive structure a priori so that the nominal variables do not influence the real variables in equilibrium. As Cuddington (1980) shows, the imposition of such a recursive structure is a misspecification, and a general formulation of the model yields a test of exogeneity of the real variables with respect to the nominal variables which leads to a rejection of the exogeneity hypothesis.

As yet there are few attempts to treat endogenous unemployment jointly with wages and prices. I argued in an earlier paper (Desai, 1975) that Phillips' estimate should be considered to be that of a steady-state locus corresponding to a differential equation which was written in terms of unemployment. Thus take the LR specification in equation (23). Phillips' estimated equation with the transformed data, I argued, was obtained by setting $\Delta U_t = 0$ for all t. Since there is no simple way of generating observations for such a steady state, the transformation procedure served precisely that function. Then the Phillips curve is an incomplete model, since we have only one steady-state locus in a space of two variables. So I proceeded to specify, admittedly informally, the second differential equation in terms of $\Delta^2 w$. Such an equation comes from a wage-bargaining model with adaptive expectations, such as equation (14). This could be easily rewritten with $\Delta^2 w$ as the dependent variable. Setting $\Delta^2 w = 0$, which is equivalent to a $\Delta p_c = \Delta p_c^e$ equilibrium, we could obtain the other steady-state locus which along with the Phillips curve solves for the equilibrium values of U *and* of Δw. (An extra equation for Δp raises no problems.) This argument is valid in so far as it points to the incompleteness of the single equation for Δw or for ΔU. Its interpretation of Phillips' procedure for transforming the data as having the special significance of separating the long run from the short run has been challenged by Gilbert (1976) who, as noted above, was able to reproduce Phillips' results without the transformation, but did not address the issue of the incompleteness of the single equation for Δw, whether with raw or transformed data.

In the light of our discussion of Phillips' paper, I would now argue that Phillips, in setting $\Delta U = 0$, was merely trying to observe $\Delta w = \Delta w^*$ as in equation (2). Thus although he did not formulate his equation that way, one should reformulate equation (2) or equation (5) with $\Delta^2 w$ as the dependent variable. Thus following Sargan, we take the equilibrium wage equation to be (1). Then the adjustment equation becomes

$$\Delta^2 w = a_0 + a_1 \Delta U + a_2(\Delta p_c - \Delta p_c^e) + a_3[\Delta w - \alpha_0 - \alpha_1 f(U) - \alpha_3 \Delta p - \alpha_5 (w-p)_{-1} - \alpha_6 t]_{-1} + \zeta_2. \tag{25}$$

Equation (25) is then a combination of Phillips' short-run dynamics with Sargan's equilibrium formulation. We may replace the $(\Delta p_c - \Delta p_c^e)$ term by $(\Delta p_m - \Delta p_m^*)$ etc. In addition to (25) we should have a price adjustment equation. Here again, following Sargan's procedure, we should combine a price-change equation with an implicit price-level term. Keeping to the cost-plus argument, we can write the price equation as

$$\Delta^2 p_c = b_0 + b_1 \Delta U + b_2(\Delta p_m - \Delta p_m^*) + b_3[\Delta p_c - b_4 \Delta w - b_5 \Delta p_m - b_6 \Delta q - b_7(p_c - w - p_m - q - k)] + \zeta_3. \tag{26}$$

In equation (26) we have deliberately specified a second-order process for p_c. Here ΔU is taken to represent aggregate demand pressure and $(\Delta p_m - \Delta p_m^*)$ an exogenous price shock. The term in square brackets incorporates equation (4) but adds a level term whereby equilibrium price level is unit factor cost plus (the logarithm of) mark-up factor k. As before identical productivity has been assumed for labour and imports. We also take output price to be the same as p_c.

This system still leaves unemployment as an unexplained endogenous variable. There have been two attempts, apart from Sargent's, to endogenize unemployment which are of some interest. One is an eclectic neo-Keynesian model by Stein (1974) which makes unemployment a function of unanticipated inflation and of the change in real government expenditure, i.e.

$$\Delta U = d_0 + d_1 U_{-1} + d_2(\Delta p_c - \Delta p_c{}^e) + d_2 \Delta G + \zeta_4. \tag{27}$$

This equation, along with a price-change equation similar to (26) but with $b_1 = 0$, an elaborate specification for aggregate demand pressure and an adaptive expectations scheme as in (13), was the Stein model. It turns out, however, that the model suffers from severe dynamic misspecification and must be rejected (Desai, 1981, pp. 172–84).

An alternative is a classical model by Goodwin (1967). Here we have a bargaining model that gives real wage change in terms of unemployment

$$(\Delta w - \Delta p) = \alpha_0 + \alpha_1 U + e_1'. \tag{28}$$

To this equation, Goodwin adds a classical savings hypothesis – all wages are consumed, all profits saved and invested. A constant capital–output ratio and a constant growth rate for labour productivity gives a relation between unemployment and the share of wages in total output:

$$(\Delta U/U) = \Delta u = g_0 + g_1 \frac{W}{PQ} + e_2'. \tag{29}$$

This is simplified somewhat (see Desai, 1973) but gives a model which is nonlinear in parameters and in variables and is closed; there are no exogenous variables except, implicitly, trend. Both U and (W/P) appear in levels and in rate of change form. This model needs to be embedded in a more conventional wage–price model such as that given by (25) and (26), but it is found here again that the classical model, suggestive though it is, is misspecified (Desai, 1984).

The unemployment equation thus continues to be elusive but the importance of arriving at a robust specification of this 'missing equation' cannot be exaggerated. A general model in which wages, prices and unemployment (plus some other variables) are jointly endogenous is still needed. This involves making explicit assumptions about who sets and who adjusts prices, who decides on quantities, and how is the aggregate outcome consistent with individual actions. Since the data to be explained are aggregative, we need also a macroeconomic model with an explicit account of the likely effects, if any, of the policy variables. The econometric issues which arise from these considerations concern the choice of levels or first differences, the separation of the long-run equilibrium from the short-run dynamics and the completeness or otherwise of the model being estimated. This last issue of course relates to the exogeneity or otherwise of the right-hand side variables in any equation. No separation is possible of the economic theoretic and the econometric, which has been a basic theme of this chapter.

Acknowledgments

Helpful comments by Andrew Harvey, David Hendry and Steve Nickell are gratefully acknowledged.

10

Wages and Prices in the United Kingdom: A Study in Econometric Methodology

J. D. SARGAN

1 Introduction

The primary intention of this study was to develop methods of estimation, and to compare different methods of estimation when estimating structural relationships from economic time series when the errors in the relationships are autocorrelated. The methods used are based upon the theoretical treatment of the problem in Sargan (1959, section 6), and are closely related to those given by Durbin (1960).

The study was intended to consider practical problems in the use of the methods in a typical econometric investigation. It was decided to consider wages and prices in the United Kingdom since this is a subject of economic interest and substantial studies were available (Dicks-Mireaux and Dow, 1959; Klein et al., 1961; Lipsey and Steuer, 1961; Phillips, 1958) to form a springboard. Both wage and price determination equations were based on those used by Klein et al. (1961).

2 Alternative Methods of Estimation

We consider the case where a set of variables x_{it}, $i = 1, \ldots, n$, $t = 1, \ldots, T$, are connected by a relationship

$$\alpha_0 + \sum_{i=1}^{n} \alpha_i x_{it} = u_t. \tag{1}$$

We adopt the convention that $x_{0t} = 1$ for all t, so that the equation can be written

$$\sum_{i=0}^{n} \alpha_i x_{it} = u_t. \tag{2}$$

The u_t are determined by a first-order autoregressive relation

$$u_t - ku_{t-1} = e_t \tag{3}$$

where the e_t are independent random variables.

Combining equations (2) and (3)

$$\sum_{i=0}^{n} \alpha_i x_{it} - \sum_{i=0}^{n} k\alpha_i x_{i(t-1)} = e_t. \tag{4}$$

This equation will be referred to as the transformed equation. Using vector notation equations (2) and (4) can be rewritten

$$\boldsymbol{\alpha}\mathbf{x}_t' = u_t, \qquad \boldsymbol{\alpha}\mathbf{x}_t' - k\boldsymbol{\alpha}\mathbf{x}_{t-1}' = e_t.$$

It is sometimes useful to introduce vectors of length $2n+2$ by the equations

$$\mathbf{a} = (\boldsymbol{\alpha}, -k\boldsymbol{\alpha}), \qquad \boldsymbol{\xi}_t = (\mathbf{x}_t, \mathbf{x}_{t-1})$$

and then to write the transformed equation as

$$\mathbf{a}\boldsymbol{\xi}_t' = e_t. \tag{5}$$

It is sometimes appropriate to consider the problem of estimating the coefficients a_i, $i = 0, \ldots, 2n+1$, of equation (5) subject to a set of n nonlinear restrictions of the form

$$a_0 a_{i+n+1} = a_{n+1} a_i, \qquad i = 1, \ldots, n. \tag{6}$$

Alternatively we may consider the problem as a special case of the more general form where the coefficients of a linear equation a_i are functions of a set of parameters forming a vector $\boldsymbol{\theta}$, so that $\mathbf{a} = \mathbf{a}(\boldsymbol{\theta})$. In this case the parameters form the vector $\boldsymbol{\theta} = (\boldsymbol{\alpha}, k)$ of order $n+2$. This viewpoint was adopted in my article on the estimation of such equations by the use of instrumental variables (Sargan, 1961).

Consider first the case where all the variables x_t except one are predetermined variables and the e_t are normally and independently distributed with mean zero and variance σ^2. Then it is clear that the maximum likelihood estimates in this case are generalized least squares estimates obtained by minimizing

$$\sum_{t=1}^{T} e_t^2$$

considered as a function of the α_i and k.

If we number the variables so that x_{nt} is the dependent variable it will be useful to normalize the coefficients so that $\alpha_n = -1$, so that the equation can be written

$$x_{nt} = \sum_{i=0}^{n-1} \alpha_i x_{it} - u_t.$$

Writing $\mathbf{M}_{\xi\xi}$ for the matrix whose elements are

$$(1/T) \sum_{t=1}^{T} \xi_{it} \xi_{jt}$$

the sum of squares is

$$\sum_{t=1}^{T} e_t^2 = T\mathbf{a}(\boldsymbol{\theta})\, \mathbf{M}_{\xi\xi} \mathbf{a}'(\boldsymbol{\theta})$$

and the problem is to minimize this function of the parameters $\boldsymbol{\theta}$. The function is biquadratic in the parameters k and α_i so that an explicit solution is not possible, but an iterative solution is comparatively easy. Since the second-order derivatives of the likelihood function are continuous functions of the variables and parameters and have finite expectations, an estimate of the error variance matrix of the maximum likelihood estimates is obtained from the usual formula. Defining

$$s^2 = (1/T) \sum_{t=1}^{T} \hat{e}_t^2 = \hat{\mathbf{a}}(\boldsymbol{\theta})\, \mathbf{M}_{\xi\xi} \hat{\mathbf{a}}'(\boldsymbol{\theta})$$

where the hat (ˆ) indicates the estimated value, the asymptotic error variance matrix of the $\hat{\boldsymbol{\theta}}$ can be estimated as

$$\frac{s^2}{T}\left[\left(\frac{\partial \hat{\mathbf{a}}}{\partial \boldsymbol{\theta}}\right) \mathbf{M}_{\xi\xi} \left(\frac{\partial \hat{\mathbf{a}}}{\partial \boldsymbol{\theta}}\right)'\right]^{-1}. \qquad (7)$$

It is not necessary to include a term of the type

$$\frac{1}{T}\left(\hat{\mathbf{a}}(\boldsymbol{\theta})\, \mathbf{M}_{\xi\xi} \frac{\partial^2 \hat{\mathbf{a}}}{\partial \boldsymbol{\theta}\, \partial \boldsymbol{\theta}'}\right)$$

in expression (7) since $\mathbf{a}(\boldsymbol{\theta})\, \mathbf{M}_{\xi\xi}$ is $O(1/T)$ except for its $(n+1)$th element, whereas the corresponding elements of $\partial^2\hat{\mathbf{a}}/\partial\boldsymbol{\theta}\, \partial\boldsymbol{\theta}'$ are zero, since $a_{n+1} = -1$, and so has second-order derivatives equal to zero. It is clear that an asymptotic significance test for any coefficient is obtained by assuming that the coefficient is asymptotically normally distributed, with the given standard error.

A significance test is also available for the general formulation against the assumption that there is a relationship of the form (5) with the coefficients a_i unrestricted. In order to consider this it is necessary to take account of the fact that the matrix $\mathbf{M}_{\xi\xi}$ is usually singular. If there is present among the set of variables x_{it} a variable which is an exact linear function of any set of $x_{j(t-1)}$ this variable will be called redundant. Examples of redundant variables are the constant term, any polynomial trend (provided all lower order powers of t are included in the equation), the seasonal shift variables, and any variable which is the lagged value of another variable in the structural equation.

For example if $x_{1t} = t$, then $x_{1t} = x_{1(t-1)} + x_{0(t-1)}$ and if we define the seasonal shift variables by $S_{1t} = 1$ in the first quarter of each year but is zero in any other quarter; $S_{2t} = 1$ in the second quarter of each year but is zero otherwise; and $S_{3t} = 1$ in the third quarter of each year but is zero otherwise: then $S_{2t} = S_{1(t-1)}$, $S_{3t} = S_{2(t-1)}$, and $S_{1t} = x_{0(t-1)} - S_{2(t-1)} - S_{3(t-1)}$.

Although the presence of redundant variables is not the only reason why $\mathbf{M}_{\xi\xi}$ should be singular, in practice it does appear to be the most usual cause of singularity. We use a likelihood ratio test which considers the ratio of the maximum likelihood achieved on the assumptions summarized at the start of this section, with the maximum likelihood achieved using the unrestricted equation of form (5) omitting, however, those variables ξ_{it} which make $\mathbf{M}_{\xi\xi}$ singular; in particular omitting redundant variables. If m is the number of omitted variables then twice the log of the likelihood ratio is asymptotically distributed as χ^2 with $n-m-1$ degrees of freedom. If we write $\mathbf{Q}$ for the matrix obtained from $\mathbf{M}_{\xi\xi}$ by omitting its $(n+1)$th row and column, $\mathbf{q}$ for the vector obtained by taking the $(n+1)$th row of $\mathbf{M}_{\xi\xi}$ and omitting its $(n+1)$th element, and p for this latter element, then an equivalent asymptotic test is obtained by using the fact that, if the autoregressive assumption is correct, then the criterion

$$T[1+(1/s^2)\,(\mathbf{q}\mathbf{Q}^{-1}\mathbf{q}'-p)]$$

is distributed asymptotically as χ^2 with $n-m-1$ degrees of freedom. If the criterion is judged significant at some conventional level of significance (for example, 5 per cent), then the autoregressive hypothesis is rejected in favour of the unrestricted equation (5). This can often be interpreted to mean that a more complicated structure of lags, or a longer lag is required in the structural equation on at least one of the variables. The modification required to the structural equation can be indicated by the coefficients of the unrestricted equation. If one of the lagged variables in the unrestricted equation has a much larger coefficient proportionally than the other lagged variables, it seems reasonable to introduce the lagged value of this variable into the structural equation, and to estimate the new form of the structural equation, assuming as before a first-order autoregressive equation for the error. This process of modifying the form of the structural equation can continue until the criterion ceases to be significant. Of course at some stage in the process the autoregressive coefficient k may not be significantly different from zero, indicating that its significance in the original form of the structural equation was due to the variables in the equation having the wrong lags.

Finally a test for the first-order autoregressive equation as against a second-order autoregressive equation was made. This will be described in section 4.

Considering now the case where the variables are subject to measurement errors or where there is more than one endogenous variable in the equation, it is necessary to consider a set of instrumental variables z_{jt}, $j=1, \ldots, N$, $t=1, \ldots, T$. Some of the variables ξ_{it} may be included among the instrumental variables. Introducing the matrices $\mathbf{M}_{zz}$ with elements

$$(1/T) \sum_{t=1}^{T} z_{it} z_{jt}$$

and $\mathbf{M}_{z\xi}$ with elements

$$(1/T) \sum_{t=1}^{T} z_{it} \xi_{jt}$$

then the instrumental variables estimates of Sargan (1961) are obtained by minimizing

$$\mathbf{a}(\boldsymbol{\theta})\, \mathbf{M}_{\xi z} \mathbf{M}_{zz}{}^{-1} \mathbf{M}_{z\xi} \mathbf{a}'(\boldsymbol{\theta})$$

considered as a function of the parameters $\boldsymbol{\theta}$. Mathematically the minimization problem is exactly similar to that arising in the least squares case, the only difference being the substitution of the matrix $\mathbf{M}_{\xi z} \mathbf{M}_{zz}{}^{-1} \mathbf{M}_{z\xi}$ in the instrumental variables case for the matrix $\mathbf{M}_{\xi\xi}$ in the least squares case. The problem of computing the estimates will be considered in the next section.

Defining as before $s^2 = \hat{\mathbf{a}}(\boldsymbol{\theta})\,\mathbf{M}_{\xi\xi}\hat{\mathbf{a}}'(\boldsymbol{\theta})$ an estimate of the asymptotic error variance matrix of $\boldsymbol{\theta}$ is given by

$$(s^2/T)\left[\left(\frac{\partial \mathbf{a}}{\partial \theta}\right)\mathbf{M}_{\xi z}\mathbf{M}_{zz}{}^{-1}\mathbf{M}_{z\xi}\left(\frac{\partial \mathbf{a}}{\partial \theta}\right)'\right]^{-1}.$$

Finally a criterion (similar to the χ^2 criterion of the least squares case) for the assumed form of the structural equation and the autoregressive equation is given by the consideration that

$$(T/s^2)\,(\hat{\mathbf{a}}(\boldsymbol{\theta})\,\mathbf{M}_{\xi z}\mathbf{M}_{zz}{}^{-1}\mathbf{M}_{z\xi}\,\hat{\mathbf{a}}(\boldsymbol{\theta}))$$

is distributed asymptotically as χ^2 with $N-n$ degrees of freedom.

The method of estimation can be described by saying that it is equivalent to the method of two-stage least squares applied to the transformed equation taking account of the restrictions (6); it can be considered to be an extension of the method of two-stage least squares, in the case where all the variables are free of measurement errors and so all the predetermined variables in the stochastic model can be used as instrumental variables. The limited information maximum likelihood estimates considered in Sargan (1959) are asymptotically equivalent to these autoregressive two-stage least squares estimates but are a good deal more difficult to compute. Since there is no reason to believe that they have any advantage over the two-stage least squares estimates it was decided not to use the maximum likelihood estimates.

3 Computing Methods

The mathematical formulation of the minimization in both cases is the same. The function to be minimized can be written

$$\alpha(\mathbf{A}-k(\mathbf{B}+\mathbf{B}')+k^2\mathbf{C})\,\alpha' \tag{8}$$

where in the least squares case

$$\mathbf{M}_{\xi\xi}=\begin{bmatrix}\mathbf{A} & \mathbf{B}\\ \mathbf{B}' & \mathbf{C}\end{bmatrix}$$

and in the instrumental variables case

$$\mathbf{M}_{\xi z}\mathbf{M}_{zz}{}^{-1}\mathbf{M}_{z\xi}=\begin{bmatrix}\mathbf{A} & \mathbf{B}\\ \mathbf{B}' & \mathbf{C}\end{bmatrix}$$

and **A**, **B**, and **C** are in both cases square $n+1$ order matrices. The traditional way of minimizing this function, suggested by several writers, notably Orcutt, is an iterative minimization. Starting with some arbitrary value of k, say $k = 0$, minimize with respect to α keeping k constant. Since (8) is a quadratic in α the minimization only requires the solution of linear equations. Now keep α constant at the new value and minimize with respect to k. Repeat the iteration starting with this new value of k, and continue until the iteration converges.

Although this process has often been discussed in the literature, its convergence has not been discussed theoretically and several writers have doubted whether it can be relied upon to converge. In Appendix A a general discussion of this type of iteration shows that the process will always lead to a stationary value of (8), moreover to a point where the function is a minimum with respect to α and k separately. There is a possibility, although a very unlikely possibility, that the point is a saddlepoint. However, there is the possibility of the existence of several local minima, and in this case the iteration might converge to any one of them depending on the starting point. The discussion of Sargan (1961) makes it clear that any of these local minima is an equally valid estimate provided it satisfies the appropriate criterion of the previous section. If there are several local minima satisfying the χ^2 criterion, then there are multiple solutions in the sense discussed in Sargan (1961), a case where it is impossible to distinguish between several alternative and equally valid estimates. It is therefore important to find all local minima of (8). Finally there may occur the case where the equation is unidentifiable in the instrumental variables case. This is the case where for all values of k, $-1 \leqslant k \leqslant +1$, the corresponding χ^2 criterion is not significant.

The simplest way to consider the possibility of multiple minima is to minimize (8) with respect to α for a set of values of k covering the whole range from -1 to $+1$. The actual computing routine used by the author used the set of values $k = -1, -0.9, -0.8, -0.7, -0.6, -0.5, -0.4, -0.3, -0.2, -0.1, 0, 0.1, 0.2, 0.3, 0.4, 0.5, 0.6, 0.7, 0.8, 0.9, 1.0$. When using quarterly data with seasonal variables, it was found convenient to omit $k = -1$, since this value of k makes the transformed seasonals linearly dependent; the minimum of (8) was never found in practice to be near $k = -1$ so there was no loss from the omission of this value. The calculation of this set of values of (8) not only gave material for considering whether the function had multiple minima, but also provided a suitable starting point for the iteration.

The actual computations were carried out on a Ferranti Pegasus 2 computer at the University of Leeds Computing Laboratory.[1] A program was written which read the time-series data, computed the matrices **A**, **B**, and **C**, and minimized the function (8) for the above values of k. The computer chose the minimum value of the function to start the iteration. At each stage of iteration the computer printed the next value of k and the current value of the function. The iteration finished when successive values of k differed by less than a preset constant, or if the value of the function (8) increased (because of rounding errors), or the finish could be controlled by the operator. The computer then printed out the last value of $\hat{k}$, $\boldsymbol{\alpha}$, the coefficient error variance matrix, s^2 and the χ^2 criterion.

In all the 53 cases which are reported here, and in the use of the same program by research students at the University of Leeds, there has been no case of the occurrence of multiple minima. However, an alternative defect of this procedure is the possibility of slow convergence, so that a large number of iterations are required to obtain adequate accuracy. If α and k are close to the stationary value of the function it can be approximated by a Taylor expansion quadratic in the variables. Writing ϕ for the function and ϕ_{kk} for the second derivative with respect to k, $\boldsymbol{\phi}_{\alpha k}$ for the vector of cross second derivatives with respect to k and any component of $\boldsymbol{\alpha}$ and $\boldsymbol{\phi}_{\alpha\alpha}$ for the matrix of derivatives with respect to two components of $\boldsymbol{\alpha}$ we have

$$\Delta k_r \simeq \mu \Delta k_{r-1} \tag{9}$$

where Δk_r is the error in k at the rth stage of the iteration, and

$$\mu = \frac{1}{\phi_{kk}} (\boldsymbol{\phi}_{k\alpha} \boldsymbol{\phi}_{\alpha\alpha}{}^{-1} \boldsymbol{\phi}_{\alpha k}).$$

If we assume that (9) is sufficiently accurate for all r including the initial $r = 1$, and if we assume that the initial error in k is less than 0.1, then if $\mu = 0.5$ the error is reduced to less than 10^{-6} after 17 iterations. On the Pegasus using the author's program, one iteration took 18 seconds when $n = 10$ or 31 seconds when $n = 13$. If $\mu = 0.25$ the number of iterations is halved and if $\mu = 0.7$ the number of iterations is doubled. Even in the worst case in this set, where $\mu = 0.7$ and $n = 13$, the total time for the iteration is

[1] I am grateful to Leeds University, and to the Director and staff of the Leeds University Computing Laboratory for their help and advice.

16 minutes, which is relatively small compared with the time required to compute the rest of the program (perhaps 30 minutes). The advantages of this method are the simplicity of the program and the relative certainty of convergence, but occasionally the convergence is very slow. To assess this it would be necessary to know how frequently in practice values of μ close to one occur. It was therefore arranged that the computer calculated and printed out $(k_r - k_{r-1})/(k_{r-1} - k_{r-2})$ at each stage of the iteration since this approximates μ, and also printed out the total number of iterations. Although the author is aware that his results do not constitute in any sense a random or representative sample, in the 53 cases covered here, the distributions as shown in table 10.1 were obtained.

It is clear from this that occasionally the number of iterations required was large, but even in the worst case the total time required was only 20 minutes. However, more efficient iteration procedures are available. One possibility is to make use of the Aitken method of speeding the convergence. This consists in taking the values of k from two successive stages of the previous iteration, calculating $\mu_r = (k_r - k_{r-1})/(k_{r-1} - k_{r-2})$ and then obtaining an estimate of k from the equation $k = (k_r - k_{r-1})/(1 - \mu_r)$. However, considering this whole process of taking two stages of the previous iteration and deriving the Aitken estimate of k, as one stage in an iteration, it was realized that it was more complex and took more time than a Newton–Raphson iteration would do. The Newton–Raphson iteration consists of approximating the

TABLE 10.1

		Distribution of final limit of μ	
Number of iterations	*Frequency*	*Final limit of μ*	*No. of cases*
5–15	7	Less than 0.3	0
16–20	10	0.3–	7
21–24	12	0.5–	25
25–29	18	0.6–	15
30–37	5	0.7–0.8	6
Total	53	Total	53

equations $\phi_\alpha = 0$, $\phi_k = 0$ which hold at the minimum by the first order Taylor series approximation to them

$$\phi_{\alpha\alpha}(\alpha_r - \alpha_{r-1}) + \phi_{\alpha k}(k_r - k_{r-1}) + \phi_\alpha = 0$$
$$\phi_{k\alpha}(\alpha_r - \alpha_{r-1}) + \phi_{kk}(k_r - k_{r-1}) + \phi_k = 0$$

and all the derivatives are worked out at α_{r-1}, k_{r-1}. This procedure, like the Aitken procedure in this case, is a second order procedure, in the sense that if the errors at any stage are of order ϵ then the errors at the next stage are of order ϵ^2. The Newton–Raphson iteration was tested by using it on 21 of the previous cases. Although in general there is the possibility of non-convergence in this procedure, since in contrast with the previous iteration it is not necessarily true that the function is reduced at each stage, with the comparatively simple function (8) in the cases that are reported here convergence was in all cases rapid. Although the stage in the iteration took slightly longer, 23 seconds for $n = 10$ and 39 seconds for $n = 13$, the reduction in the number of iterations was more than sufficient to compensate in all cases.

It was also decided to introduce a new way of selecting the starting point for the iteration, by considering the unrestricted estimate of the coefficients of equation (5). In the least squares case this is obtained by running a regression of the endogenous variable on the non-redundant variables and all the variables lagged; that is, on all the variables ξ_{it}, except those that are redundant. The coefficient of $x_{n(t-1)}$ then provides a consistent estimate of k. If we maximize (8) with respect to α for this value of k this will provide a consistent estimate of α, and this provides a starting point for the iteration. In the instrumental variables case exactly the same procedure is followed using the unrestricted instrumental variables estimate of equation (5). The method fails if $x_{n(t-1)}$ is included among the set of variables x_{it}. If for example $x_{1t} = x_{n(t-1)}$ the transformed equation takes the form

$$\alpha_0(1-k) + \sum_{i=2}^{n-1} \alpha_i x_{it} - k \sum_{i=2}^{n-1} \alpha_i x_{i(t-1)} - k\alpha_1 x_{n(t-2)}$$
$$+ (k + \alpha_1) x_{n(t-1)} - x_{nt} = e_t.$$

It is clear that in this case it is possible to estimate $k + \alpha_1$, and $k\alpha_1$ from the coefficients of $x_{n(t-1)}$ and $x_{n(t-2)}$, but impossible to distinguish between the estimates of k and α_1. However, if there is any non-redundant variable x_{jt}, such that $x_{j(t-1)}$ does not occur among the remaining x_{it}, then it is possible to get a consistent estimate of k by taking the ratio of the coefficient of $x_{j(t-1)}$ to the coefficient of x_{jt} in the unrestricted equation. This can be used as before to obtain a starting point for the iteration.

Durbin (1960) has shown that in the least squares case if all the variables except one are completely exogenous, then the initial value defined above is already an asymptotically efficient estimate of k and α. A sufficient condition for this is that u_t should be independent of x_{it} and $x_{i(t-1)}$ for all $i \neq n$. However, if the x_{it} include some lagged endogenous variables, these are partly determined by the past values of e_t, which also determine u_t. Thus it is impossible to assume that u_t is independent of x_{it} and $x_{i(t-1)}$ for all $i \neq n$ unless these are all completely exogenous variables. However, it is clear that these initial values have standard errors of order $1/\sqrt{T}$. Also the Newton–Raphson method has the property that if the errors at one stage are of order ϵ then the errors at the next stage are of order ϵ^2. It follows that from the given starting point after the first stage of the method the errors in the coefficients compared with the minimum values are of order $1/T$. It follows that asymptotically the values of the coefficients at this stage are equivalent to the minimum values and, in particular, if these latter are asymptotically efficient then so are the values at the end of the first stage. It was therefore decided to run a set of estimates in which the value at the first stage was compared with the initial value and the final value. This was done for ten equations each with $T = 51$. It was decided to compare only the values of k, since the values of α in the three cases were related to the values of k by almost the same relationship. The difference between the final and the initial values of k, and the final and first stage values of k were divided by the sample error of the coefficient estimated from the final values of the coefficients. The resulting ratios were averaged (RMS) and the results were: for the initial value 0.77, and for the first stage value 0.34. Again the ten cases considered give a small and non-random sample but the advantage should be with the more efficient method in large enough samples.

4 An Asymptotic Test for Higher Order Autoregression

Probably the best way of considering the possibility of higher-order autoregression is to fit a second-order autoregressive equation in the same way that the first-order autoregressive equation was fitted and then consider the significance of the second coefficient in this equation. However, since in any case only an asymptotic test was wanted, and it was intended to print out the $\hat{e}_t$ as part of a program for computing and printing out the separate contributions of each variable x_{it} to the u_t in each period, it was decided to use the following simple and asymptotically efficient test criterion

$$r = \sum_{t=2}^{T} \hat{e}_t \hat{e}_{t-1} \Big/ \sum_{t=1}^{T} \hat{e}_t^2$$

where

$$\hat{e}_t = \mathbf{a}(\hat{\theta})\,\mathbf{x}_t{}' = e_t + \Delta\theta \left(\frac{\partial \mathbf{a}}{\partial \theta}\right)' \mathbf{x}_t{}' + \mathrm{O}(1/T)$$

and

$$\Delta\theta = \hat{\theta} - \theta.$$

Since

$$\operatorname{plim}\left(\frac{1}{T}\sum_{t=1}^{T} \hat{e}_t{}^2\right) = \sigma^2$$

$\sqrt{T\sigma^2 r}$ is asymptotically distributed as

$$(1/\sqrt{T}) \sum_{t=2}^{T} e_t e_{t-1} + \frac{\Delta\theta}{\sqrt{T}} \left(\frac{\partial \mathbf{a}}{\partial \theta}\right)' \left[\sum_{t=2}^{T} (\mathbf{x}_t{}' e_{t-1} + \mathbf{x}_{t-1}{}' e_t)\right].$$

Let

$$\operatorname*{plim}_{T \to \infty} \left(\frac{1}{T} \sum_{t=2}^{T} \mathbf{x}_t e_{t-1}\right) = \mathbf{h}$$

and assume

$$\operatorname*{plim}_{T \to \infty} \left(\frac{1}{T} \sum_{t=2}^{T} \mathbf{x}_{t-1} e_t\right) = \mathbf{0}.$$

In the least squares and two-stage least squares cases the $x_{i(t-1)}$ are predetermined variables and are independent of e_t, and in the instrumental variables case it seems appropriate to set up the test on the basis that the autoregressive transformation has yielded an e_t which is independent of the measurement errors on all the variables in previous periods. Cramer's theorem on asymptotic limits of linear functions shows that $\sqrt{T}\sigma^2 r$ is asymptotically distributed as

$$\frac{1}{\sqrt{T}}\sum_{t=2}^{T} e_t e_{t-1} + \sqrt{T}\Delta\boldsymbol{\theta}\left(\frac{\partial \mathbf{a}}{\partial \boldsymbol{\theta}}\right)' \mathbf{h}'. \tag{10}$$

Since each term of (10) is asymptotically normally distributed with mean zero and known variance a further application of Cramer's theorem shows that (10) is asymptotically normal with mean zero and variance determined by the covariance matrix for the separate terms of (10). Now in any case we can write $\sqrt{T}\Delta\boldsymbol{\theta} = -\mathbf{wKH}^{-1}$ where

$$\mathbf{w} = (1/\sqrt{T})\left(\sum_{t=1}^{T} e_t \mathbf{z}_t\right)$$

and $\mathbf{z}_t$ is the vector of all the predetermined (including lagged) variables and in the least squares case includes all the current independent variables. In the least squares case

$$\mathbf{K} = \frac{\partial \mathbf{a}}{\partial \boldsymbol{\theta}} \qquad \text{and} \qquad \mathbf{H} = \left(\frac{\partial \mathbf{a}}{\partial \boldsymbol{\theta}}\right)' \mathbf{R}\left(\frac{\partial \mathbf{a}}{\partial \boldsymbol{\theta}}\right)$$

where $\mathbf{R}$ is the population moment matrix of the predetermined variables. In the instrumental variables case

$$\mathbf{K} = \mathbf{R}^{-1}\mathbf{Q}\left(\frac{\partial \mathbf{a}}{\partial \boldsymbol{\theta}}\right) \qquad \text{and} \qquad \mathbf{H} = \left(\frac{\partial \mathbf{a}}{\partial \boldsymbol{\theta}}\right)' \mathbf{Q}'\mathbf{R}^{-1}\mathbf{Q}\left(\frac{\partial \mathbf{a}}{\partial \boldsymbol{\theta}}\right)$$

where $\mathbf{R}$ is the moment matrix of all the instrumental variables and $\mathbf{Q}$ is the moment matrix of the instrumental variables $\mathbf{z}_t$ with the variables $\mathbf{x}_t$. The equation for the instrumental variables case is given in Sargan (1961), the equation in the least squares case can be regarded as derived from the instrumental case when all the independent variables are treated as instrumental variables (noting that $\partial a_n/\partial\boldsymbol{\theta} = \mathbf{0}$ since the coefficients have been standardized by assuming $a_n = -1$).

Since the asymptotic variance matrix of $\mathbf{w}$ is $\sigma^2\mathbf{R}$ the asymptotic variance of the terms specified last in equation (10) is

$$\sigma^2\mathbf{h}\left(\frac{\partial \mathbf{a}}{\partial \boldsymbol{\theta}}\right) \mathbf{H}^{-1}\left(\frac{\partial \mathbf{a}}{\partial \boldsymbol{\theta}}\right)' \mathbf{h}'$$

and the variance of the first term is σ^4. It remains to compute the asymptotic covariance between the first and last terms.

The asymptotic covariance of

$$(1/\sqrt{T})\sum_{t=2}^{T} e_t e_{t-1} \qquad \text{and} \qquad \mathbf{w} = (1/\sqrt{T})\sum_{t=2}^{T} e_t \mathbf{z}_t$$

is obtained by taking expectations, using

$$E(e_t e_{t-1} e_{t'} \mathbf{z}_{t'}) = \begin{cases} 0, & t \neq t' \\ \sigma^2 E(e_{t-1}\mathbf{z}_t), & t = t' \end{cases}. \tag{11}$$

Writing $\mathbf{v}_t = \mathbf{x}_t - \mathbf{z}_t \mathbf{R}^{-1}\mathbf{Q}$, the $\mathbf{v}_t$ are random variables which are the errors on the reduced form equations. We assume that $E(\mathbf{v}_t e_{t-1}) = \mathbf{0}$ which is equivalent to assuming that the first order autoregressive transformation of the original structural equation has removed all the autocorrelation and serial correlation connecting e_{t-1} with the set of variables $\mathbf{v}_t$. This is certainly correct in the least squares and two-stage least squares cases where the $\mathbf{z}_t$ are taken to include all the lagged values of all the variables in the model as well as all the current predetermined variables. In the instrumental variables case the assumption is not a necessary consequence of the general assumptions of the model, i.e. this is a separate assumption, but the simplification that follows from this assumption makes it worth while. Then

$$E(e_{t-1}\mathbf{z}_t)\mathbf{K} = E(e_{t-1}\mathbf{x}_t)\left(\frac{\partial \mathbf{a}}{\partial \theta}\right) = \mathbf{h}\left(\frac{\partial \mathbf{a}}{\partial \theta}\right).$$

The covariance between

$$\mathbf{w}\mathbf{K}\mathbf{H}^{-1}\left(\frac{\partial \mathbf{a}}{\partial \theta}\right)'\mathbf{h}' \qquad \text{and} \qquad \frac{1}{\sqrt{T}}\sum_{t=2}^{T} e_t e_{t-1}$$

is therefore

$$\sigma^2\left\{\mathbf{h}\left(\frac{\partial \mathbf{a}}{\partial \theta}\right)\right\}\left[\mathbf{H}^{-1}\left(\frac{\partial \mathbf{a}}{\partial \theta}\right)'\mathbf{h}'\right]$$

so that the variance of (10) is

$$\sigma^4 - 2\sigma^2\mathbf{h}\left(\frac{\partial \mathbf{a}}{\partial \theta}\right)\mathbf{H}^{-1}\left(\frac{\partial \mathbf{a}}{\partial \theta}\right)'\mathbf{h}' + \sigma^2\mathbf{h}\left(\frac{\partial \mathbf{a}}{\partial \theta}\right)\mathbf{H}^{-1}\left(\frac{\partial \mathbf{a}}{\partial \theta}\right)'\mathbf{h}'$$

and the asymptotic variance of $\sqrt{(T)}\,r$ is

$$1 - 1/\sigma^2\left[\mathbf{h}\left(\frac{\partial \mathbf{a}}{\partial \theta}\right)\mathbf{H}^{-1}\left(\frac{\partial \mathbf{a}}{\partial \theta}\right)'\mathbf{h}'\right].$$

Now $(\sigma^2/T)\,\mathbf{H}^{-1}$ is the asymptotic error variance matrix of the coefficients $\hat{\theta}$ and an estimate of this has already been computed and printed out. The $\hat{\mathbf{h}}$ can also be estimated using

$$\hat{\mathbf{h}} = \frac{1}{T}\sum_{t=2}^{T} \hat{e}_{t-1}\mathbf{x}_t.$$

In order to calculate this it is necessary to calculate $\hat{e}_t$, but this is done in any case, so that the results can be printed out for the scrutiny of the experimenter who will be interested in detecting any anomalous behaviour in the computed residuals. It was therefore arranged that a program computed $\hat{e}_t$, r, $\hat{\mathbf{h}}$, and took s^2 and $\mathbf{V}$ the estimated error variance matrix of the coefficients and from them computed

$$1 - \frac{T}{s^4}\left[\hat{\mathbf{h}}\left(\frac{\partial \mathbf{a}}{\partial \theta}\right)\mathbf{V}\left(\frac{\partial \mathbf{a}}{\partial \theta}\right)'\hat{\mathbf{h}}'\right]; \tag{12}$$

r was then divided by the standard error derived from (12).

(*Note added:* This was done for 30 different estimations. Unfortunately because of a minor error in the algebra, which was not uncovered at the time, the actual test statistics used were incorrectly computed. However, the results do not in retrospect appear to be inconsistent with the first order autoregressive specification.)

5 The Econometric Model

In considering a model for the determination of wages and prices a starting point was the equations used by Klein et al. (1961).

For wages they use an equation of the form

$$\begin{aligned} w_t - w_{t-4} = a_0 + a_1(p_t + p_{t-1} + p_{t-2} + p_{t-3} - p_{t-4} - p_{t-5} \\ - p_{t-6} - p_{t-7}) + a_2(U_t + U_{t-1} + U_{t-2} + U_{t-3}) \end{aligned} \tag{13}$$

where the data are quarterly, and w_t is the wage rate index in quarter t, p_t is the index of retail prices in period t, and U_t is a percentage index of the number wholly unemployed (i.e. this number expressed as a percentage of the corresponding number in 1948). In the Klein–Ball case the variables are absolute values but it is convenient to use the same symbols for later equations and in some cases to use the symbols to mean the logarithms of the corresponding absolute variables. It will be convenient to refer to a version of the equation linear in the absolute values of the variables as the absolute form of the equation, and a version linear in the logarithms of the corresponding variables as the corresponding logarithmic form of the equation.

The argument for the equation above is that wage-raises in any occupation are annual events, and if we consider the raises being made in any one quarter, they are assumed to be based upon the price change over the whole year and the unemployment in the same quarter. The percentage change in the wage rate over the whole year is a weighted average of the percentage raises in each quarter, and if we approximate by taking the weights to be equal we get the form (13).

However, it is unnecessary to consider an equation explaining the rise in the wage index over a full year. If we consider the change in the index for one quarter only, this is due to the wage-raise given to those workers whose rates change in this quarter. On the equal weights assumption the percentage change in the wage rates index will equal one quarter of the percentage raise. This leads to the equation

$$w_t - w_{t-1} = \tfrac{1}{4}a_0 + a_1(p_t - p_{t-4}) + a_2 U_t. \qquad (14)$$

Klein says that he considered this form of equation but used (13) in preference because it appeared a more stable form of relation. Now if any kind of stochastic equation is considered and an unweighted moving average of the equation is taken, since the error on the average equation is the moving average of the original random error, if the original error is non-autocorrelated there will be a considerable reduction in the variance of the moving average error (it will be halved for the four-quarter moving average). If there is a positive autocorrelation the reduction will be less but will still be present. So the multiple correlation will be increased by taking the moving average, although estimates of the moving average equation using least squares or two-stage least squares may be inconsistent and inefficient. To argue about the most appropriate form of equation to use, the only criterion is that the optimum form should have errors which are independent in different time periods. Since form (14) is derived most directly from the raises negotiated in successive quarters, it seems most likely to give independent errors. If anything, there may be positive autocorrelation, but in any case the moving average form will give larger autocorrelation. A study of the equation using

Klein's coefficients in form (13) and then in form (14) showed nothing which could not be explained by the averaging process so that all work was done with the equation (14), and with this form the autocorrelations were low.[2]

The author was, however, not satisfied with equation (14) because it is in effect non-homogeneous in money prices. Suppose that over some time interval a large change in the price level occurs with the level of unemployment normal. According to the equation estimated by Dicks-Mireaux and Dow (1959) money wages rise by a smaller percentage than prices, and real wages fall. But unions are very conscious of the effect of price rises, and it is possible that if past changes have unfavourably affected the level of real wages, they will increase their pressure so as to correct the level of real wages again. It is possible to test this possibility by introducing one extra variable into equation (14) representing real wage rates. Using a Klein linearization, $w_{t-1}-p_{t-1}$ was used. When this was done the corresponding coefficient had the right sign and was significant with t-ratio greater than three. However, as explained in the next paragraph, it seemed likely that a linear trend was needed to explain the continuous growth in real wages over the sample period. This was also found significant. Previous writers had considered it necessary to include a political factor F_t to represent the wage freeze at the end of the 1940s. Initially the Klein–Ball factor was used, defined by $F_t = 0$ up to 4th quarter, 1951, and $F_t = 1$ thereafter. This F_t had negative non-significant coefficients. However, it was then realized that to get a change in the rate of trend of wages a trend type variable was required. A new variable F_t was defined so that $F_t = 0$ up to the 4th quarter of 1951, and $F_t = t - 16$ thereafter. This can be regarded as obtained by cumulating the previous F_t. This variable turned out to have a positive significant coefficient in the first estimates, although in some of the later estimates it became non-significant.

The form of the wage-determination equation at this stage is

$$\begin{aligned} w_t - w_{t-1} = a_0 &+ a_1(p_{t-1} - p_{t-4}) + a_2 U_{t-1} \\ &+ a_3(w_{t-1} - p_{t-1}) + a_4 F_t + a_5 t\,. \end{aligned} \tag{15}$$

It will be noted that at this stage $p_{t-1}-p_{t-4}$ has been substituted for $p_t - p_{t-4}$ of (14). This was done because it was not thought likely a priori that this made much difference to the theoretical

[2] The suggestion that the first difference of equation (13) should be used, since this gives a form with small autocorrelation, offers no advantages over the simpler (14).

interpretation of the equation; because in practice the coefficient of this variable was small and insignificant in all the many versions of the equation which the author tried; and finally because at this early stage in estimation of the equations a direct comparison of estimates using the two different forms showed no significant difference in the other coefficients. Form (15) has the advantage that all the variables on the right-hand side of the equation are predetermined so that in the absence of measurement errors autoregressive least squares estimates are consistent and unbiased. The economic interpretation of the equation can take several forms. First it is possible to consider a desired or equilibrium level of real wages w_{Et} given by the equation

$$w_{Et} = -\frac{a_0}{a_3} - \frac{a_1}{a_3}(p_t - p_{t-3}) - \frac{a_2}{a_3}U_t - \frac{a_4}{a_3}F_{t+1} - \frac{a_5}{a_3}(t+1) \quad (16)$$

and a dynamic adjustment equation

$$w_t - w_{t-1} = a_3[w_{t-1} - p_{t-1} - w_{E(t-1)}].$$

Equation (16) says that the desired level of real wages is determined by a linear trend (politically affected) and by the level of unemployment. The presence of the term $p_t - p_{t-3}$ may be regarded as an extrapolation of past price movements into the future, so that the desired level of real wages should be attained at these extrapolated prices. If the adjustment equation is to be stable $a_3 < 0$, and we then expect $a_1 > 0$, $a_2 < 0$, $a_4 > 0$, $a_5 > 0$.

If we stress that in full employment periods union pressure is the only important determinant of wages, then equation (16) can be regarded as representing the influence of unemployment on union demands. The equation can more realistically be interpreted as representing the joint nature of wage-bargaining procedure if the use of U_t as a crude measure of the excess supply of labour is stressed. If we take the actual demand for labour as strongly correlated with the number employed, this could be used as an indicator of the willingness of the employers to grant higher wages. The number unemployed is obviously also an indicator of the difficulty experienced by the employer in finding labour. Unemployment also is a good indication of the bargaining strength of the union.

Alternatively we can consider that equation (15) represents a correction to a 'Phillips' type equation (Phillips, 1958) where the crude measure of excess supply of labour represented by U_t has been refined by introducing

$$E_t = U_t + (a_3/a_2)(w_t - p_t) + (a_4/a_2)F_{t+1} + (a_5/a_2)(t+1)$$

and taking E_t as a more exact measure of the excess supply of labour. The difference between E_t and U_t is positively related to the real wage because there is a supply of part-time and temporary labour which does not maintain its unemployment benefit or continue to seek work when the real wage is relatively low, and possibly because of labour hoarding which inflates the apparent demand for labour at times of low real wages.

The author on the whole prefers the justification in terms of union pressure, but whatever the economic justifications, the mathematical effect on the model is the same.

The dynamic adjustment equation can be solved in the form

$$w_t = -a_3\left[\sum_{s=-\infty}^{t-1} (1+a_3)^{s+1-t}(p_s + w_{Es})\right]$$

and this shows w_t as a weighted average of past prices and equilibrium real wages, the weights being geometrical or exponential. There is a geometrical distributed lag of money wages behind money prices and unemployment equal to $-1/a_3$. For example with $a_3 = -0.5$ the lag is two quarters or six months; with $a_3 = -0.375$ the lag is two and two thirds quarters or eight months. Since these are the extremes of the range of the estimates of a_3 found in the author's work, it follows that a fairly short lag is suggested in money wages on the equilibrium value. This will be considered later when the price equation has been estimated.

The data used were obtained by continuing the wage-rates index, consumption price index, and unemployment index, of Klein et al. (1961) up to the fourth quarter of 1960. Appendix C gives the continuations used. Appendix B gives a brief summary of the various alternative forms of equations tried. The final form of the equation used was (15) and this was finally estimated by three different methods, first by autoregressive least squares, then the same equation by the single-stage iteration method of section 2 on least squares assumptions, and finally using instrumental variables with complete iteration. The instrumental variables used were an index of total import prices, of export prices, the current value of total exports, consumption, and government expenditure on goods and services (all lagged one quarter, but consumption lagged two quarters, and all defined as in Klein et al. (1961)), F_t,

TABLE 10.2

Method used	$\hat{a}_1$	$\hat{a}_2$	$\hat{a}_3$	$\hat{a}_4$	$\hat{a}_5$	$\hat{k}$	s^2	χ^2
Autoregressive least squares	−0.015 (0.090)	−0.017 (0.007)	−0.497 (0.148)	+0.391 (0.161)	+0.038 (0.056)	+0.231 (0.159)	0.846	9.17 4 D.F.
L.S. single-stage iteration	+0.053 (0.102)	−0.015 (0.008)	−0.438 (0.137)	+0.231 (0.148)	+0.057 (0.061)	+0.178 (0.163)	0.921	8.76 4 D.F.
Inst. variables	+0.062 (0.262)	−0.289 (0.145)	−0.388 (0.512)	+0.283 (0.456)	+0.049 (0.110)	+0.441 (0.597)	1.022	0.51 2 D.F.

t and three seasonals. Table 10.2 compares the results. The second line in each case contains standard errors. Comparing first the instrumental variable estimates with the full least squares estimates, the standard errors of the instrumental variables estimates are much larger, but the coefficients are not greatly different except the coefficient of *U*. This difference could be a result of the presence of measurement error of a definitional kind, but it is less than twice the instrumental variables standard error. The author was prepared to take the difference as sampling error and accept the least squares estimates. As a consequence there seemed little point in trying to find a better set of instrumental variables to reduce the standard errors.

Comparing the two sets of least squares estimates the differences in coefficients are small and certainly not significant. The average distributed lag $-1/\hat{a}_3$ is approximately half a year. Doubling the 1948 level of unemployment produces a 3.5 per cent change in the equilibrium real wage (cf. (16)). Using (16) it can be seen that the *equilibrium* real wage grows at 2.5 points a year under a Conservative government, but not significantly under a Labour government. The χ^2 criterion is quite close to the 5 per cent significance limit. This suggested that longer lags might be required in some of the variables in the equation. However, at this stage it was decided to look for further data. None of the different forms of the equation considered by the author had a significant $\hat{k}$; the use of the author's quarterly form of the wage determination equation had been only too successful in removing the autocorrelation of the residuals in the equation, so that the use of a method of estimation designed to take account of autocorrelation is unnecessary. However, from previous work with prewar data the author was aware that with the same type of equation and using the official Ministry of Labour Index of Wage Rates, the residuals of the equation have a first-order autocorrelation close to one. It is also clear that the official index is a poor index; that is, it has a relatively large measurement error, so that these data could be used to give some practical experience of the relative advantages of the use of least squares and instrumental variable methods in these circumstances. Since the results are mainly of methodological interest a full description of the data and the different forms of equation considered will not be given but a brief summary is given here.

The wage rates index was taken from the *Ministry of Labour Gazette* (various dates). The consumption prices index was taken from 'The Consumption Function in the U.K. 1924–38', by El Imam (unpublished PhD thesis at Leeds University). It differed from the official cost of living index mainly in correcting the gross overweight of food prices in the latter index. Unemployment was included as an index of the number unemployed estimated from the unemployment insurance data by correcting for changes in coverage. Initially all the data were used on a quarterly basis from the first quarter 1922 to the last quarter 1938, but it was evident from a consideration of the residuals of the fitted equations that the results for 1922 and 1923 were much worse than for the other years so that later estimates were made omitting the first two years. A political factor of the trend shift type was included defined in exactly the same way as the postwar political factor. When using the instrumental variable method, exactly the same set of instrumental variables was used as in the postwar case.

Although nine estimates of different versions of the equation were made, no very satisfactory estimates were obtained. Using least squares and the same form of equation as (15) the results were as in table 10.3 (the second line in each case gives standard

TABLE 10.3

Method used	$\hat{a}_1$	$\hat{a}_2$	$\hat{a}_3$	$\hat{a}_4$	$\hat{a}_5$	$\hat{k}$	s^2	χ^2
Least squares	−0.362	+0.004	+0.207	−0.534	−0.009	+0.807	0.306	12.65
	(0.056)	(0.011)	(0.192)	(0.073)	(0.073)	(0.047)		4 D.F.
Inst. variables	+0.334	−0.006	−0.320	−0.164	+0.219	+0.792	0.449	0.92
	(0.279)	(0.029)	(0.409)	(0.508)	(0.398)	(0.565)		2 D.F.
Omitting F_t	+0.406	+0.003	–	–	−0.008	+0.585	0.359	2.33
and	(0.166)	(0.009)			(0.016)	(0.391)		4 D.F.
$(w_{t-1} - p_{t-1})$								

errors). Notable are the facts that the coefficient $\hat{a}_1$ of the rate of change of prices is significant and negative; that the only other significant coefficient is that of the political factor which is also negative; that $\hat{k}$ is quite close to one, and that the χ^2 criterion is significant. The latter result alone gives sufficient reason for rejecting the present estimates, but the pattern of coefficients looks unsatisfactory on a priori grounds. The instrumental variables estimates given in the third and fourth lines of the table agree much better with a priori expectation, but none of them is significantly different from zero. In particular it is to be noted that $\hat{k}$ is not significant. This may be taken as an indication that the strong autocorrelation is present in the measurement errors but not in the random error in the structural equation. Because of the non-significance of the coefficients the author tried various equations in which sets of the coefficients were assumed to be zero. The form of most interest among these is given in lines five and six of the table. Real wages and the political factor have been omitted. Since the coefficient of the price change is close enough to one third, one may interpret this to mean that money wage rates in each quarter rise at the same rate as the average increase in prices in the previous three quarters. However, the results are not very satisfactory. They might be improved by the use of a wider set of instrumental variables, but a more obvious method would be to use a better index of wage rates. The author did not pursue this matter since he considered that greater value would result from a further study of the postwar data.

6 The Logarithmic Model

The discussion of the choice between using equations linear in the variables or alternatively of using equations linear in the logarithms of the variables has usually been carried on using a priori arguments only. Klein used a linear form for his equaton because he was estimating a large model, and the prediction problem becomes difficult if non-linear equations are used. It is usually assumed that since any simple mathematical form for the structural relationships is only an approximation, the mathematical form of the approximation is not important. However, this is incorrect. The choice of model to use should be based on the data available; the choice between a linear and log-linear form of equation should be made using the theories of statistical decisions in the same way as the choice between different values for the coefficients.

It is not difficult to embed the problem in a continuum of models in such a way that the linear and log-linear models are just two special cases out of the continuum. The consideration of this suggests that asymptotically it is efficient to use a likelihood ratio criterion. It is not difficult to develop this for a general linear model, but for reasons of relevance and simplicity only the single equation least squares case is considered here.

Suppose that the dependent variable Y_t is determined by the equation

$$Y_t = \sum_{i=0}^{n} A_i X_{it} + U_t$$

where the X_{it} are a set of variables independent of the U_t and the coefficients A_i may be subject to any a priori restrictions such as those of section 1 which would make the above equation a transformed form of a structural equation with autoregressive error. Suppose now that $x_{it} = \log X_{it}$ and $y_t = \log Y_t$. The second hypothesis is that the structural equation is of the form

$$y_t = \sum_{i=0}^{n} a_i x_{it} + u_t.$$

In order to use the likelihood ratio method it is assumed that both random errors form independently normally distributed time series with constant standard deviations Σ and σ respectively.

Suppose that the likelihood function defined in the normal way for the first hypothesis is $F(A, \Sigma)$ and for the second hypothesis is $F(a, \sigma)$. These likelihood functions differ in that the first is the joint frequency density function of the Y_t while the second is the joint distribution function of the y_t. If the ratio of the likelihood functions is to be used as a criterion it is necessary to transform the variable so that both are density functions for the same set of sample variables. We can do this by changing the likelihood function for the second hypothesis so that it becomes a density function for the Y_t by introducing the factors $\mathrm{d}y_t/\mathrm{d}Y_t = 1/Y_t$. The likelihood function for the second hypothesis is then

$$\left(\prod_{t=1}^{T} 1/Y_t\right) F(a, \sigma).$$

Now maximizing both likelihoods with respect to A, Σ and a, σ respectively, and introducing $S = \hat{\Sigma}$ and $s = \hat{\sigma}$ respectively, the maxima of the two likelihood functions are $(1/S^T)\,e^{-\frac{1}{2}T}$ and

$$\left(\prod_{t=1}^{T} 1/Y_t\right)(1/s^T)\,e^{-\frac{1}{2}T}$$

where T is the number of time periods. Defining the geometric mean of the Y_t by

$$Y_G{}^T = \prod_{t=1}^{T} Y_t$$

the likelihood ratio is $(S/Y_G s)^T$. This suggests that we use $S/Y_G s$ as a criterion for deciding between the two models. A conventional discussion would now require us to obtain the distribution function of the criterion on each hypothesis; possibly to use a continuous sampling plan so that we sample until we can reject one hypothesis or the other. However, the distribution of the criterion is a very complicated function of the parameters of the true model, so that the author has decided not to develop this type of solution here. Since there seems no a priori reason to prefer one model to the other, it seems simplest to accept the first hypothesis if $S/Y_G s$ is less than one, and vice versa. This corresponds to a maximum likelihood choice.

A more sophisticated argument is obtained by using decision theory. Suppose we are only interested in using the right type of model, so that our loss function is $+1$ if we have the wrong model and 0 if we have the right model. We then want to compare the total a posteriori probability of the first hypothesis with the second. Writing R for the ratio of the a posteriori probabilities it can be shown that $\log R = T \log (S/Y_G s) + f(T)$ where $f(T)$ is $O(1)$ as $T \to \infty$. $f(T)$ is a complicated function of the a priori distributions and data. However, when T is sufficiently large the decision turns on the value of $S/Y_G s$.

Since the ratio $S/Y_G s$ for the standard form of equation was 0.987, the criterion on the whole indicated that the non-logarithmic form of equation was better. However, the advantage was very slight, $(S/Y_G s)^T$ being 0.513, so that the data cannot be regarded as being strongly in favour of the linear form of equation. It was therefore decided to explore further the logarithmic form of relation. The initial form of equation considered was exactly the same as (15) except that the symbols are to be interpreted as meaning the logarithms of the corresponding variables. The estimate of this equation was

$$w_t - w_{t-1} = \underset{(0.086)}{-0.005}(p_{t-1} - p_{t-4}) - \underset{(0.0064)}{0.0143}U_{t-1}$$
$$\underset{(0.136)}{-0.395}(w_{t-1} - p_{t-1}) + \underset{(0.00074)}{0.00085}F_t + \underset{(0.00037)}{0.00119}t.$$

The figures in brackets are standard errors. $\hat{k} = 0.189\ (0.157)$, $s^2 = 0.479 \times 10^{-4}$ and $\chi^2 = 11.88$ (4 D.F.).

It is notable here that the coefficient of F_t is not significant and that the χ^2 is significant at the 5 per cent level. The latter suggests that a more complicated structure of lags was required.

It is a rather unsatisfactory feature of the above equation that the linear trend forms an important part of explanation of wages. It was decided to experiment with new variables which might be important in explaining the trend. First of these was real profits, defined as an index of gross company profits deflated by an index of consumption goods prices. In terms of the symbols of Klein et al. (1961) this was D/p, and the data were taken from the same sources. When this variable was put into the equation and the coefficients estimated by least squares, the corresponding coefficient was positive but small and not significant. In an effort to improve this a moving average of real profits for the previous 12 quarters was used, the three-year period being chosen by analogy with the three-year period used by Milton Friedman for 'permanent income'. The estimate of the corresponding coefficient was increased to 0.021 (0.013). It was decided that the profit variable did not give much promise of improving the explanation of wage determination. As an alternative it was decided to use a variable representing productivity. The simplest variable to estimate quarterly is industrial productivity which was obtained by dividing the official index of industrial production by the number of employed workers in the appropriate industries, in terms of Klein's symbols P/E_p. When this variable was introduced into the standard equation it was found to have a positive but relatively small and non-significant coefficient. This variable was then also subject to a three-year moving average, and the resulting average substituted in the standard equation. Although the estimated coefficient was increased, it was still not significant. The resulting equation was estimated as below

$$w_t - w_{t-1} = \underset{(0.055)}{-0.005}(p_{t-1} - p_{t-4}) - \underset{(0.0067)}{0.0129}U_{t-1} + \underset{(0.00079)}{0.00085}F_t$$
$$- \underset{(0.139)}{0.386}(w_{t-1} - p_{t-1}) + \underset{(0.00049)}{0.00104}t + \underset{(0.072)}{0.053}(I_{t-1})$$

where I_t is the moving average of productivity for the three years up to and including the current quarter.

All these alternative variables were introduced into the log-linear form of equation, and all these equations gave significant χ^2 criteria. However, before pursuing this matter it was decided to simplify the equation by omitting the non-significant $p_{t-1}-p_{t-4}$ and F_t. The resulting equation estimated by least squares was

$$w_t - w_{t-1} = \underset{(0.0058)}{-0.0120}U_{t-1} - \underset{(0.073)}{0.271}(w_{t-1}-p_{t-1}) + \underset{(0.00036)}{0.00133}t, \quad (17)$$

$\hat{k} = 0.206$ (0.151), $s^2 = 0.496 \times 10^{-4}$, and $\chi^2 = 2.59$ (2 D.F.). The non-significant χ^2 compared with the previous results suggested that it might be worth considering equations with more complicated lags in prices and with lagged values of F_t. The author considered various combinations of lagged political factors plus rates of price change without finding any combination of variables which satisfied the two statistical conditions, that all the coefficients are significant, and the χ^2 criterion is not significant. However, consideration of the unrestricted form of the transformed equation suggested that longer lags on the other variables were appropriate, and the author was led to consider equations involving U_{t-2}, U_{t-3}, U_{t-4}, $w_{t-2}-p_{t-2}$, $w_{t-1}-w_{t-2}$, and $w_{t-2}-w_{t-3}$. Various combinations of these variables were considered, new forms of equation being obtained by modifying previous forms, omitting variables whose coefficients were non-significant, and increasing the lag on variables when this was suggested by the coefficients of the unrestricted estimate of the transformed equation. The author does not feel it to be worth while to give details of all the equations tried but some information is given in Appendix B. It was found better to include a long lag on unemployment and in the later estimates unemployment was represented by U_{t-4}. The coefficient of $(w_{t-2}-w_{t-3})$ was also significant whereas the political factor was frequently insignificant and it was ultimately decided to omit this variable. The form of equation which was judged most satisfactory of those considered was the following

$$\begin{aligned} w_t - w_{t-1} = & \underset{(0.008)}{-0.018}U_{t-4} - \underset{(0.119)}{0.375}(w_{t-1}-p_{t-1}) + \underset{(0.0008)}{0.0019}t \\ & + \underset{(0.064)}{0.106}(w_{t-1}-w_{t-2}) - \underset{(0.157)}{0.524}(w_{t-2}-w_{t-3}) \end{aligned} \quad (18)$$

$s^2 = 0.353 \times 10^{-4}$, $\hat{k} = 0.441$ (0.186), $\chi^2 = 0.12$ (4 D.F.).

All the coefficients are significant except that of $w_{t-1}-w_{t-2}$; it was decided to retain this variable because of the presence of $w_{t-2}-w_{t-3}$. It is to be noted that $\hat{k}$ is significant. This was true of the $\hat{k}$ of several forms of equation considered.

One possible explanation of the rather complex set of lags of w_t in this equation is got by considering what happens when all w_{t-i}, $i>0$, are eliminated from this equation by using lagged versions of the equation. By such a procedure it is possible to express w_t as a linear function of U_{t-i} for all $i \geqslant 4$, and p_{t-i} for all $i \geqslant 1$. The result can be summarized as expressing w_t as a weighted moving average of past unemployment and prices. If we carry out this process with equation (18) not all the coefficients are positive but relatively trivial changes in the coefficients of (18) will produce two moving averages with positive weights. For example the equation

$$\begin{aligned} w_t - w_{t-1} = &-0.018U_{t-4} - 0.328(w_{t-1} - p_{t-1}) \\ &+ 0.128(w_{t-1} - w_{t-2}) - 0.512(w_{t-2} - w_{t-3}) \\ &+ 0.0019t \end{aligned}$$

can be solved to give

$$x_t = \phi(\mathrm{L})\,(-0.055U_{t-4} + p_{t-1}) + 0.0058t$$

where $\phi(\mathrm{L})$ is the infinite series

$$\begin{aligned} \phi(\mathrm{L}) = &\ 0.328 + 0.262\mathrm{L} + 0.134\mathrm{L}^4 + 0.107\mathrm{L}^5 + 0.055\mathrm{L}^8 \\ &+ 0.044\mathrm{L}^9 + \ldots \end{aligned}$$

and L is a lag operator interpreted for a general variable x_t as meaning that $\mathrm{L}^r x_t = x_{t-r}$. The general structure of the weights in the above distributed lag operator may not be very realistic; possibly it may be interpreted as an approximation to the idea that there is an immediate impact effect, represented by the first two weights, and then a much longer-lagged distributed long-term effect, but certainly if we work out the average lag corresponding to these weights we find that the lag of wages on prices is 4.02 quarters, and the lag of wages on unemployment is 7.02 quarters. These are longer than the lags associated with equation (17), which gives a lag of 3.69 quarters on both prices and unemployment. It will be noted that in the above calculations of lags the price index has been treated as an exogenous variable; we have assumed it possible to change prices to a new level and hold them there while observing the consequent change in wages. However, if prices are treated as endogenous, so that the rise in wages produces a consequent change in prices, as in section 8, the lag in the wage on unemployment and other exogenous variables is found to be much greater.

An alternative explanation of equation (18) to which the author attaches some probability, is in terms of the demonstration effect of recent wage increases. It seems reasonable to assume that if one union sees an earlier union in the sequence of yearly wage bargains obtain a large rise, then it is encouraged to increase its wage demands. This would lead to a direct relationship between the wage increases in one quarter and those in previous quarters. But a more fundamental problem with the general form of wage determination equation studied here is that the use of a general index of real wages obscures the important distinction between the wage rates of the individual union and the wage rates of other unions. If a union is relatively satisfied with its own real wage rates (i.e. if they are high compared with some normal level), then it will not press for a large increase. If on the other hand the real wage rates of workers belonging to other unions are relatively high, this will encourage the union to press for a larger raise to preserve differentials. These influences, the effect of recent raises and other wage rates, on the wage bargain are almost impossible to study with aggregate data. The author did not proceed further with the current investigation, because he became dissatisfied with its aggregative form. A study using disaggregated data is obviously needed.

7 The Price Determination Equation

In order to discuss the policy implications of the wage determination equation, it must be considered in relation to a price determination equation. The author decided to estimate equations similar to the Klein et al. (1961) equations 3.20, 3.22, 3.23, 3.24, The main differences between the sets of estimates were that the data used here were quarterly from beginning 1948 to end 1961 although most of the data were defined as in Klein et al., that the equations were in log-linear form, and that they were made homogeneous in money prices.

Apart from this it was decided to include both wage rates and average earnings in the equations, since it is not clear which is the most appropriate in determining changes in the marginal cost or average cost of output. For example if differences between the two variables occur because of changes in overtime working, it is not clear that the entrepreneur would take overtime rates into account in fixing prices, since the extra labour costs are to some extent compensated by reduced overhead cost. If wage drift is caused by movement of labour between different occupations this is not increasing the costs of production in either industry. If the wage drift is caused by the earnings of piece workers increasing because of increased productivity with no change in the piece rate, this may lead to no increase in unit costs. In fact the coefficient of the wage rate was relatively large compared with the coefficient of earnings. The latter coefficient was never significant at the 5 per cent level. The estimates were made for each equation using both the autoregressive least squares and instrumental variables programmes, the set of instrumental variables being the same as those used for the wage determination equation. It was found worthwhile to modify Klein's tax variable and to introduce productivity variables so that in all 13 separate estimates of the different equations were made.

The final estimates of the different equations were as below:

$$\begin{aligned} p_t - w_t = {} & \underset{(0.054)}{0.012}(w_{et} - w_t) + \underset{(0.014)}{0.198}(p_{I(t-2)} - w_t) + \underset{(0.706)}{0.875}T_{it} \\ & - \underset{(0.052)}{0.115}R_t - \underset{(0.0008)}{0.0018}t \end{aligned} \tag{3.20}$$

$$\hat{k} = 0.587\ (0.115), \quad s^2 = 0.745 \times 10^{-4}, \quad \chi^2 = 0.55\ (4\ \text{D.F.})$$

$$\begin{aligned} p_{ft} - w_t = {} & \underset{(0.042)}{0.182}(p_{if(t-2)} - w_t) - \underset{(0.022)}{0.027}(S_{ut} - w_t) \\ & - \underset{(0.00075)}{0.0037}t + \underset{(0.008)}{0.016}Z_t \end{aligned} \tag{3.22}$$

$$\hat{k} = 0.460\ (0.147), \quad s^2 = 0.169 \times 10^{-3}, \quad \chi^2 = 3.44\ (3\ \text{D.F.})$$

$$p_{dt} - w_t = \underset{(0.188)}{0.890}(p_t - w_t) + \underset{(0.025)}{0.134}(p_{me(t-2)} - w_t) - \underset{(0.0009)}{0.0029}t \tag{3.23}$$

$$\hat{k} = 0.568\ (0.129), \quad s^2 = 0.179 \times 10^{-3}, \quad \chi^2 = 5.06\ (2\ \text{D.F.})$$

$$p_{ot} - w_t = \underset{(0.108)}{0.737}(p_t - w_t) + \underset{(0.020)}{0.040}(p_{im(t-2)} - w_t) - \underset{(0.0009)}{0.0028}t \tag{3.24}$$

$$\hat{k} = 0.781\ (0.090), \quad s^2 = 0.660 \times 10^{-4}, \quad \chi^2 = 4.35\ (2\ \text{D.F.})$$

w_e Average weekly wage earnings
p_I Index of total import prices
T_i Ratio of consumption expenditures at market prices to consumption expenditures at factor cost
R Ratio of index of industrial production to number employed in the same industries
p_f Retail price index for food, drink and tobacco
P_{if} Price index for food, drink and tobacco imports
S_u Index of subsidies on food and agricultural products
Z $=1$ in 1954 and 1955, $=0$ otherwise
p_d Price index of consumer durables
p_{me} Price index of imported non-ferrous metals
p_o Price index of non-food, non-durable consumer goods
p_{im} Price index of basic material imports.

The definitions and sources are as in Klein et al. (1961) except for the definition of T_i. This definition was used because it was realized that if the entrepreneur passed on the tax to the consumer the coefficient of T_{it} would be one. In fact the coefficient had a relatively large standard error, and the difference between it and one was small and certainly not significant. In all the estimates the $\hat{k}$ was significant. There seemed no reason to depart from the structure of lags used by Klein et al., and in particular no lag was introduced in the wage rate variable. Despite this the estimates using least squares and instrumental variables differed by only relatively trivial amounts, and the differences were certainly not significant.

8 Economic and Policy Implications

This section considers the economic implications of the wage and price determination equations by first looking at the moving equilibrium solution, and then considering the time lags in the movement to equilibrium.

The static implications of both equations (17) and (18) are almost identical. Those for equation (17) are

$$w-p=0.00491t-0.0443U.$$

The first coefficient shows that real wages in the moving equilibrium increase at a rate of roughly 2 per cent per annum. The second coefficient can be interpreted by saying that if unemployment doubles, thereby adding 0.69 to U since the units are in natural logarithms, this produces a 3 per cent fall in the real wage in equilibrium. To obtain the corresponding changes in money wages and prices account must be taken of the static equivalent of equation (3.20) of the last section. This is

$$p-w = 0.198(p_I - w) + 0.875T_i - 0.115R - 0.0018t.$$

Eliminating $p-w$ and solving for w the resulting equation is

$$w = p_I + 4.4T_i - 0.22U + 0.015t - 0.58R. \tag{19}$$

Similarly for p we obtain

$$p = p_I + 0.010t - 0.58R + 4.4T_i - 0.18U.$$

Concentrating on the trend in money wages and prices, the equations suggest that if prices are to be stabilized, R must increase at 6.7 per cent per annum; and that if wages are to be stabilized in relation to import prices then R must increase at 10 per cent per annum. Alternatively if R is increasing at 2.7 per cent per annum as it did in the sample period, the total trend in (3.20) because of this and the linear trend, is roughly equivalent to 1 per cent per annum. If money prices are to keep in line with the prices of imports this trend must be increased to 1.6 per cent; if money wages are to keep in line with the prices of imports the trend on the price equation must be increased to 2 per cent. The objective of stabilizing money wages in relation to import prices looks rather difficult, but the objective of stabilizing home prices in relation to import prices looks more capable of realization. The estimate of the required change in the rate of growth in industrial productivity may be too large since it depends upon an estimate of a coefficient of R which has a large standard error, and no allowance is made for an improvement in non-industrial productivity.

Considering now the influence of unemployment on money wages and prices, doubling unemployment would ultimately reduce money wages by 15 per cent and prices by 12 per cent. It also follows that a 1 per cent change in indirect tax rates ultimately changes both prices and money wages by 5 per cent, a relatively large multiplier effect. Finally note that prices and money wages ultimately change in proportion to a change in import prices. This means that in this model devaluation has a purely temporary effect. In equilibrium internal costs are changed proportionally to the extent of the devaluation.

Considering now the dynamic behaviour of the model eliminate $w_{t-1} - p_{t-1}$ from equation (17) using equation (3.20) and the result is

$$w_t - w_{t-1} = -0.012U_{t-1} - 0.054(w_{t-1} - p_{I(t-3)}) + 0.271T_{i(t-1)} + 0.00084t - 0.031R_{t-1}. \quad (20)$$

This can be interpreted in terms of an exponentially weighted distributed lag of average length 18.5 quarters. The effect of this can be illustrated by considering a once for all change in one of the variables p_I, U, or T_i. Suppose for the sake of simplicity that all the variables except the trends have been held constant for a sufficient length of time for the model to be in its moving equilibrium, and then a change is made in U to a new constant level, which will lead to a change in the equilibrium level given by equation (19). Since the difference between w_t and the new equilibrium level is being reduced by the factor 0.946 per quarter, it will take 13 quarters before the wage rate has moved half-way to its new equilibrium value, and 43 quarters before the wage rate has moved 90 per cent of the way to the equilibrium.

Applying the same type of analysis to a devaluation, and assuming that this has an immediate full impact on import prices, according to the equation it will be three quarters before money wage rates are at all affected. It will be a further 13 quarters before money wage rates have risen by half the change in import prices, and 43 quarters before they have risen by 90 per cent of the change in import prices. More crudely, half the initial impact of the devaluation has disappeared by the end of four years, and 90 per cent by the end of 11 years. In the light of these rather long lags, the force of the statement that devaluation has only a temporary impact is weakened.

Consider finally the immediate impact of government policy on the rate of change of money wages. For the first year after the change in the policy variable, the model shows that the effect of the second term on the right of the previous equation can be neglected, so that the effect of a change in U or T_i is to change the rate of change in money wage rates. It is of some interest to compare this initial impact with those obtained by previous investigators. Considering again the effect of a doubling of the level of unemployment this increases log (unemployment) by 0.69

and decreases the rate of change of money wage rates by 3.3 per cent per annum. Comparing this with Klein et al. equation (3.18e) where the equivalent change is an increase in the unemployment index of 100, according to their equation a doubling of unemployment would reduce the rate of change of money wage rates by 9.1 per cent per annum. Our results show a much smaller effect. The difference might to some extent be explained by sampling error but not entirely. It is to be noted that in our model there is no level of unemployment which will lead to stationary wage rates. The presence of the trend in (20) ensures that the trend in money wages can only be suppressed by a change in the rate of increase of productivity.

The previous discussion has been carried on making use of wage determination equation (17). If instead equation (18) is used the equilibrium results are very little changed. In place of equation (20) the following equation is obtained for the dynamic behaviour of the model

$$\begin{aligned} w_t - w_{t-1} = {} & -0.018U_{t-4} - 0.075(w_{t-1} - p_{I(t-3)}) \\ & + 0.375T_{i(t-1)} + 0.106(w_{t-1} - w_{t-2}) \\ & - 0.524(w_{t-2} - w_{t-3}) + 0.0012t - 0.042R_{t-1}. \quad (21) \end{aligned}$$

Solving this to give w_t in terms of previous values of U, p_I, and T_i we get a distributed lag formula with average lag of 17.9 quarters. Considering the time taken for the wage rate to reduce the initial difference from the equilibrium value, it is necessary to consider the latent roots of equation (21). These are the roots of the equation

$$\lambda^3 - 1.031\lambda^2 + 0.630\lambda - 0.524 = 0.$$

This has one real root, 0.949, and two complex roots with a period of approximately one year and a damping factor of 0.74 per quarter. In the medium period of 10 to 40 quarters with which we are concerned the large real root dominates the solution, so that a process of approximation can be used to estimate the time period required for the solution to approach within any distance of the equilibrium value. It is found that the time for the distance to halve its initial value is 11 quarters approximately, and the time for the distance to become one tenth is 33 quarters. These are somewhat smaller lags than with equation (17), but not sufficiently so to affect general policy conclusions.

The initial impact is also increased. Doubling the level of unemployment will initially reduce the rate of increase in money wage rates by 5 per cent per annum. The difference between this and the Klein–Ball result is reduced, and could be due to sampling errors.

9 General Conclusions

This study has shown that it is relatively simple to take account of first order autoregression in estimating the coefficients of a structural equation if it is possible to use an electronic computer. The method could easily be generalized to take account of higher order autoregressions, but in no case in the present investigation did the data warrant the fitting of a higher order autoregression.

The wage-determination equation used in this paper leads to policy conclusions which differ fundamentally from those implied by previous investigators. In particular they suggest that the effect of devaluation is only temporary, and that it is impossible to restrain money wages indefinitely by maintaining unemployment at some appropriate level. An increase in unemployment has a once-for-all effect on money wages. However, the lags in the model are of order several years so that the immediate short period prediction from the model is not greatly different in kind, but rather smaller quantitatively than in previous models.

Appendix A The Method of Iterative Maximization

Consider the general method of maximizing a function $f(\mathbf{a}, \mathbf{b})$ which is a function of two vectors **a** and **b** by the following iterative procedure. First maximize with respect to **b** keeping **a** constant, and then maximize with respect to **a** keeping **b** constant, and iterate. Although the procedure may not be very efficient, it converges to a local maximum in a very wide class of cases.

Basic Assumptions

(i) For some c the set of points $f(\mathbf{a}, \mathbf{b}) > c$ is bounded, and (ii) the function is continuous throughout this region.

Take as arbitrary starting point some point within the region, and label the successive points obtained by the iteration $(\mathbf{a}_i, \mathbf{b}_i)$ and the successive values of the function f_i, $i = 1, 2, 3, \ldots$

Since the function cannot decrease at any stage, the points must stay within the bounded region. Since f_i is a positive monotonic sequence with an upper bound (since the function is continuous on a closed set) the sequence converges to its upper bound f^*. Also since the sequence $(\mathbf{a}_i, \mathbf{b}_i)$ is bounded it possesses limit points. Consider any limit point $(\mathbf{a}^*, \mathbf{b}^*)$. Since there is a subsequence of points, denoted by $(\mathbf{a}_i^*, \mathbf{b}_i^*)$, which converges to the limit point and the function is continuous, $f(\mathbf{a}^*, \mathbf{b}^*) = f^*$.

There are three possibilities to be considered. Either all except a finite number of the subsequence are obtained by maximizing with respect to **a**, when the limit point is called of type *a*, or all except a finite number are obtained by maximizing with respect to **b**, when the limit point is of type *b*, or the subsequence has an infinite number of points of both types when the limit point is of type *ab*. We suppose that the limit point is of type *a* or *ab*; the limit point of type *b* can be considered by interchanging *a* and *b* in the following argument.

Suppose $f(\mathbf{a}, \mathbf{b}^*)$ had not a maximum at $\mathbf{a} = \mathbf{a}^*$. Then there exists $\mathbf{a}^{**}$ such that $f(\mathbf{a}^{**}, \mathbf{b}^*) > f(\mathbf{a}^*, \mathbf{b}^*) = f^*$. By continuity there exists δ_1 such that $f(\mathbf{a}^{**}, \mathbf{b}) > f^*$ if $|\mathbf{b} - \mathbf{b}^*| < \delta_1$. Now since the subsequence $(\mathbf{a}_i^*, \mathbf{b}_i^*)$ tends to the limit point of type *a* or *ab* there exists a point of this subsequence obtained by maximizing with respect to **a**, such that $|\mathbf{b}_i^* - \mathbf{b}^*| < \delta_1$. And then $f(\mathbf{a}^{**}, \mathbf{b}_i^*) > f^* \geqslant f(\mathbf{a}_i^*, \mathbf{b}_i^*)$. But $\mathbf{a}_i^*$ was obtained by maximizing $f(\mathbf{a}, \mathbf{b}_i^*)$ with respect to **a**. This is a contradiction showing that

$$f(\mathbf{a}^*, \mathbf{b}^*) \geqslant f(\mathbf{a}, \mathbf{b}^*)$$

for all **a**.

Suppose now that $f(\mathbf{a}^*, \mathbf{b})$ had not a maximum at $\mathbf{b} = \mathbf{b}^*$, so that there exists $\mathbf{b}^{**}$ such that $f(\mathbf{a}^*, \mathbf{b}^{**}) > f^*$. There exists δ_2 such that $f(\mathbf{a}, \mathbf{b}^{**}) > f^*$ if $|\mathbf{a} - \mathbf{a}^*| < \delta_2$ from continuity. We can find a point of the subsequence obtained by maximizing with respect to **a** such that $|\mathbf{a}_i^* - \mathbf{a}^*| < \delta_2$. At the next stage of the iteration we choose **b** so as to maximize $f(\mathbf{a}_i^*, \mathbf{b})$. If we take $\mathbf{b} = \mathbf{b}^{**}$ we obtain $f(\mathbf{a}_i^*, \mathbf{b}^{**}) > f^*$. This contradicts the definition of f^* as an upper bound of the sequence. Thus $f(\mathbf{a}^*, \mathbf{b}^*) \geqslant f(\mathbf{a}^*, \mathbf{b})$ for all values of **b**. From these two results it follows that if $f(\mathbf{a}, \mathbf{b})$ has all first order derivatives at $(\mathbf{a}^*, \mathbf{b}^*)$ this is a stationary point of the function.

Since the presence of more than one limit point would require that the function had several stationary points of this type each with a value of the function equal to f^*, in general there will only be one limit point. Indeed it can be shown that the stationary points must satisfy further very restrictive conditions. It must be possible to link the points in a cyclic chain so that each pair in the chain differs only in the value of one of the vectors **a** or **b**. In practice only the presence of a single limit point need be considered and in this case the sequence of points converges to this limit point. So the original sequence will converge to one of the stationary values in the region. Furthermore only maxima or saddle points need be considered.

However, the likelihood of the limit point being a saddlepoint is low. Suppose that the limit point were a saddlepoint and that at some stage of the iteration the current point had been obtained by maximizing with respect to **b**. The linear space $\mathbf{b} = \mathbf{b}_i$ must not intersect the region where $f > f^*$ for then the sequence would obviously not converge to the saddlepoint. This condition is unlikely to be fulfilled for all i.

In particular if the vector **b** has only one component, as in the case considered in the body of the paper, convergence to a saddle point is extremely unlikely. If there is a direction through the saddle point (α, β) such that $f(\mathbf{a}^* + k\alpha,\ b^* + k\beta) > f^*$ for all $|k| < \delta$, and this condition is certainly satisfied if the function has continuous second order derivatives at the saddlepoint, then we can find a point of the sequence obtained by maximizing with respect to **b** which lies within a distance $\delta\beta$ of the limit point. If this point is $(\mathbf{a}_i, b_i)$ take $k = (b_i - b^*)/\beta$. The corresponding point on the line defined above could be taken as the next point in the iteration, and unless $k = 0$, $f_{i+1} > f^*$. This is a contradiction showing that the sequence does not converge to the saddlepoint. The only case where the sequence does converge to the saddlepoint is where for some finite i, $b_i = b^*$. In this case the next point in the sequence is the saddlepoint, and so are all subsequent points. This case, however, occurs with probability zero.

Appendix B Summary of Equations Estimated

For each equation estimated a list of the symbols for the variables in the equation is given, using the symbols defined in the body of the paper or in Klein et al. (1961), preceded by the method of estimation. For this L.S. means ordinary least squares, I.V. means instrumental variables, A.L.S. means autoregressive least squares, and A.I.V. means autoregressive instrumental variables. The addition of a star means that the equation was also estimated by single iteration method.

Postwar Non-logarithmic Wage Determination Equation

In all these equations $w_{t-1}-p_{t-1}$, and U_{t-1} were included, and seasonal shifts.

(1) L.S. Old F_t, $p_{t-1}-p_{t-4}$.
(2) A.L.S. Old F_t, $p_{t-1}-p_{t-4}$.
(3) A.L.S. Old F_t, $p_{t-1}-p_{t-4}$, t.
(4) A.L.S.* New F_t, $p_{t-1}-p_{t-4}$, t.
(5) A.L.S. New F_t, $p_{t-1}-p_{t-4}$, t, three seasonal trend variables.
(6) A.I.V. New F_t, $p_{t-1}-p_{t-4}$, t.
(7) A.I.V. New F_t, p_t-p_{t-4}, t.
(8) A.L.S. New F_t, $p_{t-1}-p_{t-5}$, t.
(9) A.L.S. New F_t, F_{t-1}, $p_{t-1}-p_{t-4}$, t.

Prewar Non-logarithmic Wage Determination Equation

In all these equations t and the seasonal shift variables were included.

(10) L.S. F_t, $w_{t-1}-p_{t-1}$, $p_{t-1}-p_{t-4}$, U_{t-1}.
(11) A.L.S. F_t, $w_{t-1}-p_{t-1}$, $p_{t-1}-p_{t-4}$, U_{t-1}.
(12) A.I.V. F_t, $w_{t-1}-p_{t-1}$, $p_{t-1}-p_{t-4}$, U_{t-1}.

In this and all subsequent estimates the years 1922 and 1923 were omitted.

(13) A.I.V. F_t, $w_{t-1}-p_{t-1}$, $p_{t-1}-p_{t-4}$, U_{t-1}.
(14) A.I.V. $w_{t-1}-p_{t-1}$, $p_{t-1}-p_{t-4}$, U_{t-1}.
(15) A.I.V. $w_{t-1}-p_{t-1}$, $p_{t-1}-p_{t-4}$, U_{t-2}.
(16) A.I.V. $w_{t-1}-p_{t-1}$, U_{t-1}.
(17) A.I.V. $w_{t-1}-p_{t-1}$, $p_{t-1}-p_{t-4}$.
(18) A.I.V. $p_{t-1}-p_{t-4}$, U_{t-1}.

Postwar Logarithmic (Wage Determination) Equations

In all these equations t and the seasonal shift variables were included.

(19) A.L.S. F_t, $w_{t-1}-p_{t-1}$, U_{t-1}, $p_{t-1}-p_{t-4}$.
(20) A.I.V. F_t, $w_{t-1}-p_{t-1}$, U_{t-1}, $p_{t-1}-p_{t-4}$, $(D/p)_{t-1}$.

(21) A.I.V. F_t, $w_{t-1}-p_{t-1}$, U_{t-1}, $p_{t-1}-p_{t-4}$.
(22) A.L.S. F_t, $w_{t-1}-p_{t-1}$, U_{t-1}, $p_{t-1}-p_{t-4}$, $(D/p)_{t-1}$.
(23) A.L.S. F_t, $w_{t-1}-p_{t-1}$, U_{t-1}, $p_{t-1}-p_{t-4}$, $(\bar{D}/\bar{p})_{t-1}$. This last variable was a three-year average of past profits deflated.
(24) A.L.S. F_t, $w_{t-1}-p_{t-1}$, U_{t-1}, $p_{t-1}-p_{t-4}$, $(P/E_p)_{t-1}$.
(25) A.L.S. F_t, $w_{t-1}-p_{t-1}$, U_{t-1}, $p_{t-1}-p_{t-4}$, $(\bar{P}/\bar{E}_p)_{t-1}$. This last variable was a three-year average of past labour productivity.
(26) A.L.S.* $w_{t-1}-p_{t-1}$, U_{t-1}.
(27) A.L.S. $w_{t-1}-p_{t-1}$, U_{t-1}, $p_{t-1}-p_{t-4}$, $p_{t-2}-p_{t-5}$, F_t.
(28) A.L.S. $w_{t-1}-p_{t-1}$, U_{t-1}, $p_{t-1}-p_{t-4}$, $p_{t-1}-p_{t-2}$, F_t, $w_{t-1}-w_{t-2}$.
(29) A.L.S. $w_{t-1}-p_{t-1}$, U_{t-1}, $p_{t-1}-p_{t-4}$, F_t, $w_{t-1}-w_{t-2}$.
(30) A.L.S. $w_{t-1}-p_{t-1}$, U_{t-1}, U_{t-2}, $p_{t-1}-p_{t-4}$, F_t, $w_{t-1}-w_{t-2}$.
(31) A.L.S. $w_{t-1}-p_{t-1}$, U_{t-1}, $p_{t-1}-p_{t-4}$, F_t, $w_{t-1}-w_{t-2}$, $w_{t-2}-w_{t-3}$.
(32) A.L.S. $w_{t-1}-p_{t-1}$, U_{t-1}, U_{t-2}, U_{t-3}, $p_{t-1}-p_{t-4}$, F_t, $w_{t-1}-w_{t-2}$.
(33) A.L.S. $w_{t-1}-p_{t-1}$, U_{t-3}, $p_{t-1}-p_{t-4}$, $p_{t-2}-p_{t-5}$, $p_{t-1}-p_{t-2}$, F_t, $w_{t-1}-w_{t-2}$, $w_{t-2}-w_{t-3}$.
(34) A.L.S. $w_{t-1}-p_{t-1}$, U_{t-3}, $p_{t-1}-p_{t-4}$, $p_{t-2}-p_{t-5}$, $w_{t-1}-w_{t-2}$, $w_{t-2}-w_{t-3}$, $w_{t-3}-w_{t-4}$.
(35) A.L.S. $w_{t-1}-p_{t-1}$, U_{t-3}, $p_{t-1}-p_{t-4}$, F_t, F_{t-1}, $w_{t-1}-w_{t-2}$, $w_{t-2}-w_{t-3}$.
(36) A.L.S. $w_{t-1}-p_{t-1}$, $w_{t-2}-p_{t-2}$, U_{t-3}, $p_{t-1}-p_{t-4}$, F_t, F_{t-1}, $w_{t-1}-w_{t-2}$, $w_{t-2}-w_{t-3}$.
(37) A.L.S. $w_{t-1}-p_{t-1}$, U_{t-3}, U_{t-4}, $w_{t-1}-w_{t-2}$, $w_{t-2}-w_{t-3}$.
(38) A.L.S. $w_{t-1}-p_{t-1}$, U_{t-4}, F_t, F_{t-1}, $w_{t-1}-w_{t-2}$, $w_{t-2}-w_{t-3}$.
(39) A.L.S. $w_{t-1}-p_{t-1}$, U_{t-4}, F_t, F_{t-1}, F_{t-2}, $w_{t-1}-w_{t-2}$, $w_{t-2}-w_{t-3}$.
(40) A.L.S. $w_{t-1}-p_{t-1}$, U_{t-4}, F_{t-2}, $w_{t-1}-w_{t-2}$, $w_{t-2}-w_{t-3}$.
(41) A.L.S.* $w_{t-1}-p_{t-1}$, U_{t-4}, $w_{t-1}-w_{t-2}$, $w_{t-2}-w_{t-3}$.
(42) A.L.S. $w_{t-1}-p_{t-1}$, U_{t-4}, F_{t-2}, $w_{t-1}-w_{t-2}$.

Price Determination Equations

3.20 All these equations included $w_{et}-w_t$, $p_{I(t-2)}-w_t$, t and seasonal shifts.

(43) A.L.S. Old T_i.
(44) A.L.S. New T_i.
(45) A.I.V. New T_i.
(46) A.L.S.* New $T_i.(P/E_p)_t$.
(47) A.L.S.* New $T_i.(\bar{P}/\bar{E}_p)_t$.

3.22 All these equations included $p_{if(t-2)} - w_t$, $S_{ut} - w_t$, Z_t, t, and seasonals.

(48) A.L.S.* $w_{et} - w_t$.
(49) A.I.V. $w_{et} - w_t$.
(50) A.L.S.*

3.23 All these equations included $p_t - w_t$, $p_{me(t-2)} - w_t$, t, and seasons.

(51) A.L.S.* $w_{et} - w_t$.
(52) A.I.V. $w_{et} - w_t$.
(53) A.L.S.*

3.24 Both equations included $p_t - w_t$, $p_{im(t-2)} - w_t$, t and seasonals.

(54) A.L.S.* $w_{et} - w_t$.
(55) A.L.S.*

Appendix C Data Used

TABLE 10.4

	p	w	U	p_f	p_d	p_0	S_u	p_{if}	p_{im}	p_{met}
1958	141.3	165.8	137.8	143.5	130.5	132.4	59.5	131.6	133.2	148.0
	143.4	166.4	146.4	146.8	129.3	130.4	59.5	135.8	133.8	144.0
	142.2	168.1	146.7	144.0	128.2	129.9	59.5	135.8	128.6	149.5
	142.5	171.0	173.7	144.3	128.0	129.9	59.5	138.8	125.5	152.8
1959	143.7	171.7	195.4	145.1	129.7	131.1	56.0	136.7	117.1	145.1
	142.7	172.1	156.6	144.2	126.1	129.6	56.0	133.9	128.6	149.0
	142.2	172.6	134.8	142.4	124.3	129.8	56.0	135.8	130.1	146.6
	142.5	173.1	139.8	144.2	125.1	129.2	56.0	140.4	125.0	150.0
1960	143.3	174.9	145.4	143.5	125.6	131.6	56.2	136.2	125.4	155.7
	143.5	176.8	114.0	145.2	126.2	129.6	56.2	132.5	121.3	150.4
	145.3	177.7	100.8	146.1	126.2	130.7	56.2	133.5	127.2	150.0
	145.6	179.1	115.6	145.8	126.2	131.7	56.2	137.6	121.2	148.1
1961	145.8	182.5	–	145.0	126.2	134.1	71.1	133.0	124.7	146.4
	146.3	183.9	–	144.8	127.0	133.2	71.1	133.5	126.0	148.5
	150.3	184.9	–	151.4	127.9	135.2	71.1	127.4	121.7	150.2
	150.6	186.3	–	151.3	127.2	135.8	71.1	128.8	116.3	152.1

I am grateful to J. E. Tozer for compiling the above data. The prewar data are given in full in table 10.5

The data used were a continuation of those given in Klein et al. (1961), Table VII. For the wage equation these were continued for 3 years, for the price equation 4 years. Only the continuations are given in table 10.4.

TABLE 10.5

	w	p	U		w	p	U		w	p	U
1921		145.3		1927	102.0	104.8	73.0	1933	95.0	92.1	164.8
		137.8			101.0	103.9	59.7		95.0	91.3	149.1
		131.8			101.0	103.4	60.8		95.0	91.5	138.9
	130.0	118.9	103.7		100.0	101.9	64.3		95.0	91.5	131.4
1922	118.1	117.2	112.4	1928	100.0	104.1	66.6	1934	95.0	91.3	133.4
	111.2	111.1	99.6		100.0	103.1	64.9		95.5	91.1	122.6
	106.6	111.0	84.0		100.0	103.5	74.7		95.5	92.0	122.6
	99.1	110.6	81.7		100.0	103.3	78.8		95.5	91.6	122.2
1923	98.0	108.3	81.7	1929	100.0	102.5	78.2	1935	96.0	91.6	130.6
	98.0	106.7	72.4		100.0	102.6	65.5		96.0	92.1	117.6
	98.6	107.4	73.6		99.5	102.4	66.6		97.0	92.4	113.6
	99.1	107.2	72.4		99.5	102.9	74.2		97.0	92.6	110.1
1924	99.1	106.7	68.4	1930	99.5	101.5	89.2	1936	98.5	92.7	117.1
	99.7	105.9	59.7		99.5	100.3	102.0		99.0	93.2	101.2
	100.3	105.6	64.3		99.5	100.0	118.8		99.5	93.6	94.4
	100.9	107.0	69.5		99.0	98.8	133.1		100.0	93.8	93.9
1925	101.5	107.1	71.8	1931	98.5	97.2	151.9	1937	101.0	94.3	95.0
	102.0	107.0	70.7		98.0	96.7	149.1		102.5	95.4	82.3
	101.5	106.4	74.7		97.0	95.4	158.4		103.5	96.3	79.7
	101.5	104.5	69.5		96.5	94.9	154.6		104.5	97.3	88.6
1926	101.5	105.2	66.0	1932	96.0	94.9	154.7	1938	106.5	96.7	104.8
	101.0	106.0	80.5		96.0	94.9	157.2		107.0	97.3	103.6
	101.0	106.8	91.5		95.5	93.4	164.7		107.0	97.2	103.6
	101.0	107.4	86.3		95.5	93.4	159.7		107.0	97.2	105.8

Reprinted from Vol. XVI of the Colston Papers, being the Proceedings of the Sixteenth Symposium of the Colston Research Society held in the University of Bristol, 6–9 April 1964. Published by Butterworths Scientific Publications, London.

The Published Works of J. D. Sargan

A new approach to the general distribution problem. *Metroeconomica*, **3**, 108–116 (1951).

An illustration of duopoly. *Yorkshire Bulletin of Economic and Social Research*, **4**, 133–145 (1952).

An approximate treatment of the properties of the correlogram and periodogram. *Journal of the Royal Statistical Society* B, **15**, 140–152 (1953).

Subjective probability and the economist. *Yorkshire Bulletin of Economic and Social Research*, **5**, 53–64 (1953).

The period of production. *Econometrica*, **23**, 151–165 (1955).

A note on Mr. Blyth's article. *Econometrica*, **24**, 480–481 (1956).

The danger of over-simplification. *Bulletin of Oxford Institute of Statistics*, **19**, 171–178 (1957).

The distribution of wealth. *Econometrica*, **25**, 568–590 (1957).

The estimation of economic relationships using instrumental variables. *Econometrica*, **26**, 393–415 (1958).

The instability of the Leontief dynamic model. *Econometrica*, **26**, 381–392 (1958).

Mrs. Robinson's warranted rate of growth. *Yorkshire Bulletin of Economic and Social Research*, **10**, 35–40 (1958).

The estimation of relationships with autocorrelated residuals by the use of instrumental variables. *Journal of the Royal Statistical Society* B, **21**, 91–105 (1959).

Linear models for the frequency distributions of economic variables. (Abstract). *Econometrica*, **27**, 315–316 (1959).

Lags and the stability of dynamic systems: a reply. *Econometrica*, **29**, 670–673 (1961).

The maximum likelihood estimation of economic relationships with autoregressive residuals. *Econometrica*, **29**, 414–426 (1961).

Wages and prices in the United Kingdom: a study in econometric methodology. In *Econometric Analysis for National Economic Planning*, ed. P. E. Hart, G. Mills and J. K. Whitaker. London: Butterworths (1964).

Three-stage least-squares and full maximum likelihood estimates. *Econometrica*, **32**, 77–81 (1964).

An approximate distribution of the two-stage least squares estimators. (Abstract). *Econometrica*, **32**, 660 (1964).

Production functions. In *Qualified Manpower and Economic Performance: An Inter-Plant Study in the Electrical Engineering Industry*. With P. R. G. Layard, M. E. Ager and D. J. Jones, Part V. London: Penguin (1971).

A study of wages and prices in the U.K. 1949-1968. In *The Current Inflation*, ed. H. G. Johnson and A. R. Nobay. London: Macmillan (1971).

A general approximation to the distribution of instrumental variables estimates. With W. M. Mikhail. *Econometrica*, **39**, 131-169 (1971).

The validity of Nagar's expansion for the moments of Econometric estimators. *Econometrica*, **42**, 169-176 (1974).

Missing data in an autoregressive model. With E. G. Drettakis. *International Economic Review*, **15**, 39-58 (1974).

Some discrete approximations to continuous time stochastic models. *Journal of the Royal Statistical Society* B, **36**, 74-90 (1974).

Gram-Charlier approximations applied to *t* Ratios of *k*-class estimators. *Econometrica*, **43**, 327-346 (1975).

Asymptotic theory and large models. *International Economic Review*, **16**, 75-91 (1975).

Some discrete approximations to continuous time stochastic models. In *Statistical Inference in Continuous Time Economic Models*, ed. A. R. Bergstrom. Amsterdam: North-Holland (1976). (Full length version of *JRSS* (1974).)

Econometric estimators and the Edgeworth approximation. *Econometrica*, **44**, 421-428 (1976). (erratum, **45**, 272.)

The spectral estimation of simultaneous equation systems with lagged endogenous variables. With A. Espasa. *International Economic Review*, **18**, 583-605 (1977).

The existence of the moments of 3SLS estimators. *Econometrica*, **46**, 1329-1350 (1978).

Some approximations to the distribution of Econometric criteria which are asymptotically distributed as chi-squared. *Econometrica*, **48**, 1107-1138 (1980).

Some tests of dynamic specification for a single equation. *Econometrica*, **48**, 879-897 (1980).

A model of wage-price inflation. *Review of Economic Studies*, **47**, 97-112 (1980).

The consumer price equation in the post war British economy: an exercise in equation specification testing. *Review of Economic Studies*, **47**, 113-135 (1980).

Edgeworth approximations to the distribution of various test statistics. With Y. K. Tse. In *Proceedings of the Econometric Society European Meeting 1979. Selected Econometric Papers in Memory of Stefan Valavanis*, ed. E. G. Charatsis. Amsterdam: North-Holland (1981).

On Monte Carlo estimates of moments that are infinite. *Advances in Econometrics*, **1**, 267-99.

Testing residuals from least squares regression for being generated by the Gaussian random walk. With A. Bhargava. *Econometrica*, **51**, 153–174 (1983).

Maximum likelihood estimation of regression models with first order moving average errors when the root lies on the unit circle. With A. Bhargava. *Econometrica*, **51**, 799–820 (1983).

A generalization of the Durbin significance test and its application to dynamic specification. With F. Mehta. *Econometrica*, **51**, 1551–1567 (1983).

Identification and lack of identification. *Econometrica*, **51**, 1605–1633 (1983).

Estimating dynamic random effects models from panel data covering short time periods. With A. Bhargava. *Econometrica*, **51**, 1635–1659 (1983).

Identification in models with autoregressive errors. In *Studies in Econometrics, Time Series, and Multivariate Statistics*, ed. S. Karlin, T. Amemiya and L. A. Goodman. New York: Academic Press (1983).

Dynamic specification. With D. F. Hendry and A. R. Pagan. In *Handbook of Econometrics*, Vol. II, ed. Z. Griliches and M. D. Intriligator. Amsterdam: North-Holland (1984).

References

Akaike, H. (1973). Information theory and the extension of the maximum likelihood principle. In *2nd International Symposium on Information Theory*, ed. B. N. Petrov and F. Csaki, pp. 277-281. Budapest: Akailseonia-Kindo.

Akaike, H. (1983). The selection of smoothness priors for distributed lag estimation. In *Bayesian Inference and Decision Techniques with Applications: Essays in Honor of Bruno de Finetti*, ed. P. K. Goel and A. Zellner. Amsterdam: North-Holland.

Almon, S. (1965). The distributed lag between capital appropriations and expenditures. *Econometrica*, **33**, 178-196.

Alogoskoufis, G. (1983). The labour market in a model of the equilibrium business cycle. *Journal of Monetary Economics*, **11**, 117-128.

Alt, F. L. (1942). Distributed lags. *Econometrica*, **10**, 113-128.

Amemiya, T. (1977). A note on a heteroscedastic model. *Journal of Econometrics*, **6**, 365-370.

Amemiya, T. (1981). Qualitative response models: a survey. *Journal of Econometric Literature*, **19**, 1483-1536.

Amemiya, T. and Morimune, K. (1974). Selecting the optimal order of a polynomial in the Almon distributed lag. *Review of Economics and Statistics*, **56**, 378-386.

Anderson, B. D. O. and Moore, J. D. (1979). *Optimal Filtering*. Englewood Cliffs: Prentice-Hall.

Anderson, G. J. and Hendry, D. F. (1984). An econometric model of United Kingdom Building Societies. *Oxford Bulletin of Economics and Statistics*, **46**, 185-209.

Andrews, D. F. (1971). Significance tests based on residuals. *Biometrika*, **58**, 139-148.

Anscombe, F. J. (1961). Examination of residuals. *Proceedings of the Fourth Berkeley Symposium on Mathematical Statistics and Probability*, Vol. 4, 1-36.

Arrow, K. J. (1959). Towards a theory of price adjustment. In *The Allocation of Economic Resources*, ed. M. Abramovitz. Palo Alto, California: Stanford University Press.

Ashenfelter, O. and Brown, J. N. (1983). Testing the efficiency of employment contracts. Unpublished paper, Princeton University.

Ashley, R. A. and Granger, C. W. J. (1979). Time-series analysis of residuals from the St. Louis model. *Journal of Macroeconomics*, **1**, 373–394.

Balestra, P. (1975). *La Dérivation Matricielle*. Paris: Sirey.

Barro, R. J. (1977). Unanticipated money growth and unemployment in the United States. *American Economic Review*, **67**, 101–115.

Bartlett, M. S. (1946). On the theoretical specification and sampling properties of autocorrelated time series. *Journal of the Royal Statistical Society* B, **8**, 27–41.

Bera, A. K. and Jarque, C. M. (1981). An efficient large sample test for normality of observations and regression residuals. Working Papers in Economics and Econometrics No. 049, Australian National University.

Bera, A. K. and Jarque, C. M. (1982). Model specification tests: a simultaneous approach. *Journal of Econometrics*, **20**, 59–82.

Bera, A. K., Jarque, C. M. and Lee, L. F. (1982). Testing for the normality assumption in limited dependent variable models. Unpublished paper, University of Minnesota.

Berenblutt, I. I. and Webb, G. I. (1973). A new test for autocorrelated errors in the linear regression model. *Journal of the Royal Statistical Society* B, **35**, 33–50.

Bergstrom, A. R. (ed.) (1976). *Statistical Inference in Continuous Time Economic Models*. Amsterdam: North-Holland.

Bergstrom, A. R. (1983). Gaussian estimation of structural parameters in higher order continuous time dynamic models. *Econometrica*, **51**, 117–152.

Berkson, J. (1980). Minimum chi-square, not maximum likelihood! *Annals of Statistics*, **8**, 457–487.

Berndt, E. R. and Savin, N. E. (1977). Conflict among criteria for testing hypotheses in the multivariate linear regression model. *Econometrica*, **45**, 1263–1278.

Bhargava, A. (1983). On the theory of testing for unit roots in observed time series. Unpublished paper, London School of Economics.

Blatt, J. M. (1978). On the econometric approach to business-cycle analysis. *Oxford Economic Papers*, **30**, 292–300.

Blaug, M. (1980). *The Methodology of Economics*. Cambridge: Cambridge University Press.

Bodkin, R. G. (1966). *The Wage-Price-Productivity Nexus*. Philadelphia: University of Pennsylvania Press.

Boléat, M. (1982). *The Building Society Industry*. London: George Allen and Unwin.

Bowman, K. O. and Shenton, L. R. (1975). Omnibus contours for departure from normality based on $\sqrt{b_1}$ and b_2. *Biometrika*, **62**, 341–348.

Box, G. E. P. and Cox, D. R. (1964). An analysis of transformations. *Journal of the Royal Statistical Society* B, **26**, 211–243.

Box, G. E. P. and Jenkins, G. M. (1976). *Time Series Analysis: Forecasting and Control* (revised edn). San Francisco: Holden-Day.

Box, G. E. P. and Pierce, D. A. (1970). Distribution of residual autocorrelations in autoregressive-integrated moving average time series models. *Journal of the American Statistical Association*, **65**, 1509–1526.

Breusch, T. S. (1978). Testing for autocorrelation in dynamic linear models. *Australian Economic Papers*, **17**, 334–355.

Breusch, T. S. (1979). Conflict among criteria for testing hypotheses: extension and comment. *Econometrica*, **47**, 203-208.

Breusch, T. S. and Godfrey, L. G. (1981). A review of recent work on testing for autocorrelation in dynamic economic models. In *Macroeconomic Analysis: Essays in Macroeconomics and Economics*, ed. D. A. Currie, R. Nobay and D. Peel. London: Croom Helm.

Breusch, T. S. and Pagan, A. R. (1979). A simple test for heteroscedasticity and random coefficient variation. *Econometrica*, **47**, 1287–1294.

Breusch, T. S. and Pagan, A. R. (1980). The Lagrange multiplier test and its applications to model specification in econometrics. *Review of Economic Studies*, **47**, 239–253.

Brewer, K. R. W. (1973). Some consequences of temporal aggregation and systematic sampling for ARMA and ARMAX models. *Journal of Econometrics*, **1**, 133–154.

Buckley, R. and Ermisch, J. (1982). Government policy and house prices in the United Kingdom: an econometric analysis. *Oxford Bulletin of Economics and Statistics*, **44**, 273-304.

Buckley, R. and Ermisch, J. (1983). Theory and empiricism in the econometric modelling of house prices. *Urban Studies*, **20**, 83–90.

Building Societies Association (1981). *The Determination and Control of House Prices.*

Building Societies Association (1982). *A Compendium of Building Society Statistics*, 4th edn.

Building Societies Association. *BSA Bulletin*, quarterly.

Chesher, A. D. (1983). Residuals and diagnostics for Probit, Tobit and related models. Unpublished paper, University of Bristol.

Chow, G. C. (1960). Tests of equality between sets of coefficients in two linear regressions. *Econometrica*, **28**, 591-605.

Cooley, T. F. and Prescott, E. C. (1976). Estimation in the presence of stochastic parameter variation. *Econometrica*, **44**, 167–184.

Cox, D. R. (1961). Tests of separate families of hypotheses. *Proceedings of the Fourth Berkeley Symposium on Mathematical Statistics and Probability*, Vol. 1, 105–123.

Cox, D. R. (1962). Further results on tests of separate families of hypotheses. *Journal of the Royal Statistical Society* B, **24**, 406–424.

Cragg, J. G. (1982). Estimation and testing in time-series regression models with heteroscedastic disturbances. *Journal of Econometrics*, **20**, 135–157.

Crowder, M. J. (1976). Maximum likelihood estimation for dependent observations. *Journal of the Royal Statistical Society* B, **38**, 45–53.

Cuddington, J. (1980). Simultaneous-equations tests of the natural rate and other classical hypotheses. *Journal of Political Economy*, **88**, 539-549.

Dastoor, N. K. and McAleer, M. (1983). Testing separate models with stochastic regressors. Unpublished paper, Australian National University.

Davidson, J. E. H. and Hendry, D. F. (1981). Interpreting econometric evidence: the behaviour of consumers' expenditure in the UK. *European Economic Review*, **16**, 177-192.

Davidson, J. E. H., Hendry, D. F., Srba, F. and Yeo, J. S. (1978). Econometric modelling of the aggregate time-series relationship between consumers expenditure and income in the United Kingdom. *Economic Journal*, **88**, 661-692.

Davidson, R. and MacKinnon, J. G. (1981). Several tests for model specification in the presence of alternative hypotheses. *Econometrica*, **49**, 781-793.

Davis, E. P. (1984). A recursive model of personal sector expenditure and accumulation. Technical Series Discussion Paper 6, Bank of England.

Davis, E. P. and Saville, I. D. (1982). Mortgage lending and the housing market. *Bank of England Quarterly Bulletin*, 390-398.

Deaton, A. and Muellbauer, J. (1980). *Economics and Consumer Behaviour*. London: Cambridge University Press.

De Groot, M. H. and Goel, P. (1981). Information about hyperparameters in hierarchical models. *Journal of the American Statistical Association*, **76**, 140-147.

Desai, M. (1973). Growth cycles and inflation in a model of the class struggle. *Journal of Economic Theory*, **6**, 527-545.

Desai, M. (1975). The Phillips curve: a revisionist interpretation. *Economica*, **42**, 1-19.

Desai, M. (1981). *Testing Monetarism*, London: Frances Pinter.

Desai, M. (1984). An econometric model of the share of wages in national income. In *Studies in Non-linear Dynamic Models*, ed. M. Kruger and A. Vercelli. Berlin: Springer Verlag.

Dhrymes, P. J. (1970). *Econometrics*. New York: Harper and Row.

Diaconis, P. and Effron, B. (1983). Computer-intensive methods in statistics. *Scientific American*, **248**, 96-109.

Dickey, D. A. and Fuller, W. A. (1981). Likelihood ratio statistics for autoregressive time series with a unit root. *Econometrica*, **49**, 1057-1072.

Dickey, J. (1975). Bayesian alternatives to the *F*-test and least-squares estimates in the normal linear model. *Studies in Bayesian Econometrics and Statistics*, ed. S. E. Fienberg and A. Zellner, Chapter 19. Amsterdam: North-Holland.

Dicks-Mireaux, L. A. and Dow, J. C. R. (1959). The determinants of wage inflation: United Kingdom, 1946-56. *Journal of the Royal Statistical Society* A, **122**, 145-184.

Dolde, W. C. (1975). Forecasting the consumption effects of stabilization policies. *International Economic Review*, **16**, 431-438.

Drèze, J. H. (1977). Bayesian analysis using poly-*t* densities. *Journal of Econometrics*, **6**, 329-354.

Drèze, J. H. and Richard, J. F. (1983). Bayesian analysis of simultaneous equation systems. In *Handbook of Econometrics*, ed. Z. Griliches and M. D. Intriligator, vol. I. Amsterdam: North-Holland.

Duncan, D. B. and Horn, S. D. (1972). Linear dynamic regression from the viewpoint of regression analysis. *Journal of the American Statistical Association*, **67**, 815-821.

Durbin, J. (1954). Errors in variables. *Review of the International Statistical Institute*, **22**, 23-32.

Durbin, J. (1957). Testing for serial correlation in systems of simultaneous regression equations. *Biometrika*, **44**, 370-377.

Durbin, J. (1960). The estimation of parameters in time-series regression models. *Journal of the Royal Statistical Society* B, **22**, 139-153.

Durbin, J. (1970). Testing for serial correlation in least squares regression when some of the regressors are lagged dependent variables. *Econometrica*, **38**, 410-421.

Durbin, J. and Watson, G. S. (1950). Testing for serial correlation in least squares regression I. *Biometrika*, **37**, 409-428.

Durbin, J. and Watson, G. S. (1971). Testing for serial correlation in least squares regression III. *Biometrika*, **58**, 1-19.

Eicker, F. (1967). Limit theorems for regressions with unequal and dependent errors. *Proceedings of the Fifth Berkeley Symposium on Mathematical Statistics and Probability*, Vol. 1, 59-82.

Engle, R. F. (1982a). Autoregressive conditional heteroscedasticity with estimates of the variance of UK inflations. *Econometrica*, **50**, 987-1007.

Engle, R. F. (1982b). A general approach to Lagrange multiplier model diagnostics. *Journal of Econometrics*, **20**, 83-104.

Engle, R. F. and Watson, M. (1981). A one-factor multivariate time series model of metropolitan wage rates. *Journal of the American Statistical Association*, **76**, 774-781.

Engle, R. F., Hendry, D. F. and Richard, J. F. (1983a). Exogeneity. *Econometrica*, **51**, 277-304.

Engle, R. F., Lilien, D. M. and Robbins, R. P. (1983b). Estimating time varying risk premia in the term structure. Discussion Paper No. 82-4, University of California, San Diego.

Epps, T. W., Singleton, K. J. and Pulley, L. B. (1982). A test of separate families of distributions based on the empirical moment generating function. *Biometrika*, **69**, 391-399.

Evans, G. B. A. and Deaton, A. S. (1980). Testing linear versus logarithmic regression models. *Review of Economic Studies*, **67**, 275-281.

Evans, G. B. A. and Savin, N. E. (1981). Testing for unit roots I. *Econometrica*, **49**, 753-777.

Evans, G. B. A. and Savin, N. E. (1984). Testing for unit roots II. *Econometrica*, forthcoming.

Farebrother, R. W. (1979). A grouping test for misspecification. *Econometrica*, **47**, 209-210.

Fisher, G. and McAleer, M. (1981). Alternative procedures and associated tests of significance for non-nested hypotheses. *Journal of Econometrics*, **16**, 103-119.

Florens, J. P., Mouchart, M. and Richard, J. F. (1979). Specification and inference in linear models. CORE Discussion Paper No. 7943, Université Catholique de Louvain.

Foutz, R. V. and Srivastava, R. C. (1977). The performance of the likelihood ratio test when the model is incorrect. *Annals of Statistics*, **5**, 1183-1194.

Friedman, M. (1968). The role of monetary theory. *American Economic Review*, **58**, 1-17.

Friedman, M. (1975). Unemployment vs inflation: an evaluation of the Phillips Curve. Occasional Paper 44. Institute of Economic Affairs.

Frisch, R. (1933). Editorial. *Econometrica*, **1**, 1-4.

Fuller, W. A. (1975). Regression analysis for sample survey. *Sankhya, Series C*, **37**, 117-132.

Fuller, W. A. (1976). *Introduction to Statistical Time Series*. New York: John Wiley.

Garbade, K. (1977). Two methods of examining the stability of regression coefficients. *Journal of the American Statistical Association*, **72**, 54-63.

Gersovitz, M. (1980). Mis-specification and cyclical models: the real wage and the Phillips curve. *Economica*, **47**, 433-441.

Geweke, J. (1978). Temporal aggregation in the multiple regression model. *Econometrica*, **46**, 643-662.

Gilbert, C. (1976). The original Phillips curve estimates, *Economica*, **43**, 51-57.

Godfrey, L. G. (1976). Testing for serial correlation in dynamic simultaneous equation models. *Econometrica*, **44**, 1077-1084.

Godfrey, L. G. (1978a). A note on the use of Durbin's *h* test when the equation is estimated by instrumental variables. *Econometrica*, **46**, 225-228.

Godfrey, L. G. (1978b). Testing for higher order serial correlation in regression equations when the regressors include lagged dependent variables. *Econometrica*, **46**, 1303-1310.

Godfrey, L. G. (1978c). Testing for multiplicative heteroskedasticity. *Journal of Econometrics*, **8**, 227-236.

Godfrey, L. G. (1978d). Testing against general autoregressive and moving average error models when the regressors include lagged dependent variables. *Econometrica*, **46**, 1293-1302.

Godfrey, L. G. (1981). On the invariance of the Lagrange multiplier test with respect to certain changes in the alternative hypothesis. *Econometrica*, **49**, 1443-1455.

Godfrey, L. G. (1983a). Testing non-nested models after estimation by instrumental variables or least squares. *Econometrica*, **51**, 355-365.

Godfrey, L. G. (1983b). Comment. *Econometric Reviews*, **2**, 229-233.

Godfrey, L. G. and Pesaran, M. H. (1983). Small sample adjustments for the J-test. Working Papers in Economics and Econometrics No. 084, Australian National University.

Godfrey, L. G. and Poskitt, D. S. (1975). Testing the restrictions of the Almon technique. *Journal of the American Statistical Association*, **70**, 105-108.

Godfrey, L. G. and Wickens, M. R. (1981). Testing linear and log-linear regressions for functional form. *Review of Economic Studies*, **48**, 487-496.

Goodwin, R. M. (1967). A growth cycle. In *Socialism, Capitalism and Economic Growth*, ed. C. H. Feinstein, pp. 54-58. London: Cambridge University Press.

Gourieroux, C., Monfort, A. and Trognon, A. (1984). Pseudo maximum likelihood methods: theory. *Econometrica*, **52**, 681-700.

Granger, C. W. J. (1969). Investigating causal relations by econometric models and cross-spectral methods. *Econometrica*, **37**, 424-438.

Granger, C. W. J. and Andersen, A. P. (1978). *An Introduction to Bilinear Time Series Models.* Gottingen: Vandenhoeck & Ruprecht.

Granger, C. W. J. and Weiss, A. A. (1983). Time series analysis of error-correction models. In *Studies in Econometrics, Time Series and Multivariate Statistics*, ed. S. Karlin, T. Amemiya and L. A. Goodman. New York: Academic Press.

Gregory, A. W. and McAleer, M. (1981). Simultaneity and the demand for money in Canada: comments and extensions. *Canadian Journal of Economics*, **14**, 488-496.

Gregory, A. W. and McCurdy, T. H. (1982). Efficiency of the forward foreign exchange market: a stability analysis using Canadian/United States weekly and monthly data. Unpublished paper, Queen's University.

Grout, P. A. (1983). The level of employment in management union bargaining. Unpublished paper, University of Birmingham.

Hall, P. and Heyde, C. C. (1980). *Martingale Limit Theory and Its Application.* New York: Academic Press.

Harrison, M. J. and McCabe, B. P. M. (1979). A test for heteroscedasticity based on ordinary least squares residuals. *Journal of the American Statistical Association*, **74**, 494-499.

Harrison, P. J. (1967). Exponential smoothing and short-term sales forecasting. *Management Science*, **13**, 821-842.

Harvey, A. C. (1977). Discrimination between CES and VES production functions. *Annals of Economic and Social Measurement*, **6**, 463-472.

Harvey, A. C. (1981a). *The Econometric Analysis of Time Series*. Deddington, Oxford: Phillip Allan.

Harvey, A. C. (1981b). *Time Series Models.* Deddington, Oxford: Phillip Allan.

Harvey, A. C. (1983a). A unified view of statistical forecasting procedures. *Journal of Forecasting* (forthcoming).

Harvey, A. C. (1983b). The formulation of structural time series models in discrete and continuous time. *Questiio*, **7**, 563-575.

Harvey, A. C. and McKenzie, C. R. (1984). Missing observations in dynamic econometric models: a partial synthesis. In *Time Series Analysis of*

Irregular Observations, ed. E. Parzen. Berlin: Springer-Verlag.
Harvey, A. C. and Peters, S. (1983). Estimation procedures for structural time series models. Unpublished paper, London School of Economics.
Harvey, A. C. and Phillips, G. D. A. (1981). Testing for heteroscedasticity in simultaneous equation models. *Journal of Econometrics*, **15**, 311-340.
Harvey, A. C. and Pierse, R. G. (1984). Estimating missing observations in economic time series. *Journal of the American Statistical Association*, **79**, 125-131.
Harvey, A. C. and Stock, J. H. (1983). The estimation of higher order continuous time autoregressive models. Econometrics Programme Discussion Paper, No. A.38, London School of Economics.
Harvey, A. C. and Todd, P. H. J. (1983). Forecasting economic time series with structural and Box-Jenkins models. *Journal of Business and Economic Statistics*, **1**, 299-315.
Hausman, J. A. (1978). Specification tests in econometrics. *Econometrica*, **46**, 1251-1272.
Heijmans, R. D. H. and Magnus, J. R. (1983). On the asymptotic normality of the maximum likelihood estimator with dependent observations. Discussion paper, London School of Economics.
Hendry, D. F. (1974). Stochastic specification in an aggregate demand model of the United Kindom. *Econometrica*, **42**, 559-578.
Hendry, D. F. (1976). The structure of simultaneous equations estimators. *Journal of Econometrics*, **4**, 51-85.
Hendry, D. F. (1979). A model of UK house prices. Paper presented to the Centre for Environmental Studies Conference, Manchester.
Hendry, D. F. (1980). Predictive failure and econometric modelling in macroeconomics: the transactions demand for money. In *Economic Modelling*, ed. P. Ormerod, pp. 217-242. London: Heinemann.
Hendry, D. F. (1983a). Econometric modelling: the consumption function in retrospect. *Scottish Journal of Political Economy*, **30**, 193-220.
Hendry, D. F. (1983b). Monte Carlo experimentation in econometrics. In *Handbook of Econometrics*, ed. Z. Griliches and M. D. Intriligator, Vol. II. Amsterdam: North-Holland.
Hendry, D. F. and Anderson, G. J. (1977). Testing dynamic specification in small simultaneous systems: an application to a model of building society behaviour in the United Kingdom. In *Frontiers in Quantitative Economics*, ed. M. D. Intriligator, Vol. 3A, pp. 361-383. Amsterdam: North-Holland.
Hendry, D. F. and Ericsson, N. R. (1984). Econometric modelling of the market for new housing in the United Kingdom. In *A Celebration of Statistics*, ed. A. C. Atkinson and S. Feinberg. International Statistical Institute (forthcoming).
Hendry, D. F. and Mizon, G. E. (1978). Serial correlation as a convenient simplification, not a nuisance: a comment on a study of the demand for money by the Bank of England. *Economic Journal*, **88**, 549-563.
Hendry, D. F. and Richard, J.-F. (1982). On the formulation of empirical models in dynamic econometrics. *Journal of Econometrics*, **20**, 3-33.

Hendry, D. F. and Richard, J.-F. (1983). The econometric analysis of economic time series. *International Statistical Review*, **51**, 111-163.

Hendry, D. F. and Srba, F. (1980). AUTOREG: A computer program library for dynamic econometric models with autoregressive errors. *Journal of Econometrics*, **12**, 85-102.

Hendry, D. F. , Pagan, A. R. and Sargan, J. D. (1984). Dynamic specification. In *Handbook of Econometrics*, ed. Z. Griliches and M. Intriligator, Vol. II. Amsterdam: North-Holland.

Her Majesty's Stationary Office (1982). *Housing and Construction Statistics*. London.

Her Majesty's Stationary Office (1982). *Annual Abstract of Statistics*. London.

Her Majesty's Stationary Office (1983). *Economic Trends* (Annual Supplement). London.

Hoerl, A. E. and Kennard, R. W. (1970). Ridge regression: biased estimation for non-orthogonal problems. *Technometrics*, **12**, 55-67.

Holly, A. (1982). A remark on Hausman's specification test. *Econometrica*, **50**, 749-760.

Huber, P. J. (1967). The behaviour of maximum likelihood estimates under non-standard conditions. *Proceedings of the Fifth Berkeley Symposium on Mathematical Statistics and Probability*, Vol. 1, 221-233.

Imhof, J. P. (1961). Computing the distribution of quadratic forms in normal variables. *Biometrika*, **48**, 419-426.

James, W. and Stein, C. (1961). Estimation with quadratic loss. *Proceedings of the Fourth Berkeley Symposium on Mathematical Statistics and Probability*, Vol. 1, 361-397.

Jarque, C. M. and Bera, A. K. (1980). Efficient tests for normality, homoscedasticity, and serial independence of regression residuals. *Economics Letters*, **6**, 255-259.

Jarque, C. M. and Bera, A. K. (1982). Efficient specification tests for limited dependent variable models. *Economics Letters*, **9**, 153-160.

Jones, G. (1982). Scientific consistency, two-stage priors and the true value of a parameter. *British Journal for the Philosophy of Science*, **33**, 133-160.

Jones, R. H. (1981). Fitting a continuous time autoregression to discrete data, In *Applied Time Series Analysis*, Vol. II, ed. D. F. Findley, pp. 651-682. New York: Academic Press.

Jones, R. H. (1984). Fitting multivariate models to unequally spaced data. In *Time Series Analysis of Irregular Observations*, ed. E. Parzen. New York: Springer-Verlag.

Jorgenson, D. W. (1966). Rational distributed lag functions. *Econometrica*, **34**, 135-149.

Judge, G. G. and Bock, M. E. (1978). *The Statistical Implications of Pre-test and Stein-Rule Estimators in Econometrics*. Amsterdam: North-Holland.

Judge, G. G., Griffiths, W. E., Hill, R. C. and Lee, T.-C. (1980). *The Theory and Practice of Econometrics*. New York: John Wiley.

Kelejian, H. H. (1982). An extension of a standard test for heteroskedasticity to a systems framework. *Journal of Econometrics*, **20**, 325–333.

Kendall, M. G. and Stuart, A. (1967). *The Advanced Theory of Statistics*, Vol. 2 (2nd edn). London: Griffin.

Kent, J. T. (1982). Robust properties of likelihood ratio tests. *Biometrika*, **88**, 19–27.

Kiefer, N. M. and Richard, J.-F. (1979). A Bayesian approach to hypothesis testing and evaluating estimation strategies. CORE Discussion Paper No. 7927, Université Catholique de Louvain.

King, M. L. (1982a). A bounds test for heteroscedasticity. Working Paper No. 5/82. Monash University.

King, M. L. (1982b). A locally optimal bounds test for autoregressive disturbances. Paper presented at the European Meeting of the Econometric Society, Dublin.

King, M. L. (1983). Testing for autocorrelation in linear regression models: a survey. In *Specification Analysis in the Linear Model: Essays in Honour of Donald Cochrane*, ed. M. L. King and D. E. A. Giles.

King, M. L. and Hillier, G. (1980). A small sample power property of the Lagrange multiplier test. Discussion Paper, Monash University.

Kirby, M. G. (1981). An investigation of the specification and stability of the Australian aggregate wage equation. *Economic Record*, **57**, 35–46.

Kiviet, J. F. (1982). Size, power and interdependence of tests in sequential procedures for modelling dynamic relationships. Unpublished paper, University of Amsterdam.

Kiviet, J. F. (1984). Model selection procedures in a single linear equation of a dynamic simultaneous system. Unpublished paper, University of Amsterdam.

Klein, L. R. and Ball, R. J. (1959). Some econometrics of the determination of absolute prices and wages. *Economic Journal*, **69**, 465–482.

Klein, L. R., Ball, R. J., Hazelwood, A. and Vandome, P. (1961). *An Econometric Model of the United Kingdom*. Oxford: University Press.

Kloek, T. and van Dijk, H. K. (1978). Bayesian estimates of equation systems parameters: an application of integration by Monte Carlo. *Econometrica*, **46**, 1–19.

Kmenta, J. (1967). On the estimation of the CES production function. *International Economic Review*, **8**, 180–189.

Koenker, R. (1981). A note on Studentising a test for heteroscedasticity. *Journal of Econometrics*, **17**, 107–111.

Kolmogorov, A. N. (1956). *Foundations of the Theory of Probability*. New York: Chelsea.

Kooiman, P. and Kloek, T. (1979). Aggregation of micro markets in disequilibrium. Econometric Institute Working Paper, Erasmus University, Rotterdam.

Koyck, L. M. (1954). *Distributed Lags and Investment Analysis*. Amsterdam: North-Holland.

Leamer, E. E. (1972). A class of informative priors and distributed lag analysis. *Econometrica*, **40**, 1059–1081.

Leamer, E. E. (1978). *Specification Searches*, New York: John Wiley.

Leamer, E. E. (1983). Let's take the con out of econometrics. *American Economic Review*, **73**, 31-44.

Leamer, E. E. and Leonard, H. (1983). Reporting the fragility of regression estimates. *Review of Economics and Statistics*, **65**, 306-317.

Lee, B. M. S. (1979). *On the Use of 'Improved' Estimators in Econometrics*. Unpublished Ph.D. Thesis, Australian National University.

Lindley, D. V. and Smith, A. F. M. (1972). Bayes estimates for the linear model. *Journal of the Royal Statistical Society* B, **34**, 1-41.

Lipsey, R. G. (1960). The relation between unemployment and the rate of change of money wage rates in the United Kindom 1862-1957: a further analysis. *Economica*, **27**, 1-31.

Lipsey, R. G. and Steuer, M. D. (1961). Relations between profits and wage rates. *Economica*, **28**, 137-155.

Litterman, R. B. (1980). A Bayesian procedure for forecasting with vector autoregressions. Unpublished paper, Massachusetts Institute of Technology.

Loeb, P. D. (1976). Specification error tests and investment functions. *Econometrica*, **44**, 185-194.

Lubrano, M. (1979). Consistent approximations of the maximum likelihood estimator in linear models. CORE Discussion Paper No. 7924. Université Catholique de Louvain.

Lubrano, M. and Richard, J.-F. (1981). Specification of the prior density in single equation errors-in-variable models: an application to a U.K. money demand equation. CORE Discussion Paper No. 8101. Université Catholique de Louvain.

Lubrano, M., Pierse, R. and Richard, J.-F. (1984). Stability of a U.K. money demand equation: a Bayesian approach to exogeneity testing. CORE Discussion Paper, Université Catholique de Louvain.

Lucas, R. E. (1973). Econometric testing of the natural rate hypothesis. In *The Econometrics of Price Determination*, ed. O. Eckstein. Washington: Board of Governors of the Federal Reserve System.

Lucas, R. E. and Rapping, L. A. (1969). Real wages, employment and inflation. *Journal of Political Economy*, **77**, 257-305.

Lucas, R. E. and Rapping, L. A. (1970). Price expectations and the Phillips curve. *American Economic Review*, **59**, 342-349.

McAleer, M., Fisher, G. and Volker, P. A. (1982). Separate misspecified regressions and the U.S. long run demand for money function. *Review of Economics and Statistics*, **64**, 572-583.

MaCurdy, T. E. and Pencavel, J. (1982). Testing between competing models of wage and employment determination in unionized markets. Unpublished paper, Stanford University.

McDonald, I. M. and Solow, R. M. (1981). Wage bargaining and employment. *American Economic Review*, **71**, 896-908.

MacKinnon, J. White, H. and Davidson, R. (1983). Tests for model specification in the presence of alternative hypotheses: some further results. *Journal of Econometrics*, **21**, 53-70.

Maddala, G. S. (1977). *Econometrics*, New York: McGraw-Hill.

Maddala, G. S. (1983). *Limited Dependent and Qualitative Variables in Econometrics*. Cambridge: Cambridge University Press.

Mayes, D. G. (1979). *The Property Boom*. Oxford: Martin Robertson.

Miller, P. W. and Volker, P. A. (1983). A cross-section analysis of the labour force participation of married women in Australia. *Economic Record*, **59**, 28–42.

Milliken, G. A. and Graybill, F. A. (1970). Extensions of the general linear hypothesis model. *Journal of the American Statistical Association*, **65**, 797–807.

Minford, P. (1983). Labour market equilibrium in an open economy. *Oxford Economic Papers*, (supplement), **35**, 207–244.

Mizon, G. E. (1977a). Model selection procedures. In *Studies in Modern Economic Analysis*, ed. M. J. Artis and A. R. Nobay. Oxford: Basil Blackwell.

Mizon, G. E. (1977b). Inferential procedures in nonlinear models: an application in a UK industrial cross section study of factor substitution and returns to scale. *Econometrica*, **45**, 1221–1242.

Mizon, G. E. and Hendry, D. F. (1980). An empirical application and Monte Carlo analysis of tests of dynamic specification. *Review of Economic Studies*, **47**, 21–46.

Mizon, G. E. and Richard, J.-F. (1983). The encompassing principle and its application to testing non-nested hypotheses. Unpublished paper, Southampton University.

Morales, J. A. (1971). *Bayesian Full Information Structural Analysis*. Berlin: Springer-Verlag.

Mortensen, D. T. (1970). A theory of wage and employment dynamics. In *Micro-economic Foundations of Employment and Inflation Theory*, E. S. Phelps et al., pp. 167–211. London: Macmillan.

Muellbauer, J. and Winter, D. (1980). Unemployment, employment and exports in British manufacturing: a non-clearing markets approach. *European Economic Review*, **13**, 383–409.

Muth, J. (1960). Optimal properties of exponentially weighted forecasts. *Journal of American Statistical Association*, **55**, 299–306.

Nakamura, A. and Nakamura, M. (1981). On the relationships among several specification error tests presented by Durbin, Wu and Hausman. *Econometrica*, **49**, 1583–1588.

Nellis, J. G. and Longbottom, J. A. (1981). An empirical analysis of the determination of house prices in the United Kingdom. *Urban Studies*, **18**, 9–21.

Nerlove, M. (1967). Distributed lags and unobserved components in economic time series. In *Ten Essays in the Tradition of Irving Fisher*, ed. W. Fellner, pp. 127–169. New York: Wiley.

Nerlove, M. (1972). On lags in economic behaviour. *Econometrica*, **40**, 225–252.

Nerlove, M., Grether, D. M. and Carvalho, J. L. (1979). *Analysis of Economic Time Series*. New York: Academic Press.

Neuberger, H. I. L. and Nichol, B. H. (1976). The recent course of land and property prices, and the factors underlying it. Research Report 4, Department of the Environment.

Nicholls, D. F. and Quinn, B. G. (1982). *Random Coefficient Autoregressive Models: An Introduction: Lecture Notes in Statistics*, ed. D. Brillinger et al., Vol. 11. New York: Springer-Verlag.

Nickell, S. J. (1978). *The Investment Decisions of Firms*. London: Cambridge University Press.

Nickell, S. J. (1980). Some disequilibrium labour market models: further formalisation of a Muellbauer type analysis. Centre for Labour Economics Working Paper No. 205, London School of Economics.

Nickell, S. J. (1982). A bargaining model of the Phillips curve. Centre for Labour Economics Discussion Paper No. 130, London School of Economics.

Nickell, S. J. and Andrews, M. (1983). Unions, real wages and employment in Britain 1951–79. *Oxford Economic Papers*, (supplement), **35**, 183–206.

Oswald, A. and Ulph, D. (1982). Unemployment and the pure theory of the trade union. Unpublished paper, Oxford University.

Pagan, A. R. (1978). Some simple tests for nonlinear time series models. CORE Discussion Paper 7812, Université Catholique de Louvain.

Pagan, A. R. (1980). Some identification and estimation results for regression models with stochastically varying parameters. *Journal of Econometrics*, **13**, 341-363.

Pagan, A. R. (1984). Econometric issues in the analysis of regressions with generated regressors. *International Economic Review*, **25**, 221-247.

Pagan, A. R. and Hall, A. D. (1983). Diagnostic tests as residual analysis. *Econometric Reviews*, **2**, 159–218.

Pagan, A. R. and Nicholls, D. F. (1984). Estimating predictions, prediction errors and their standard deviations using constructed variables. *Journal of Econometrics*, **24**, 293-310.

Pagan, A. R. and Volker, P. A. (1981). The short-run demand for transactions balances in Australia. *Economica*, **48**, 381–395.

Pagan, A. R., Hall, A. D. and Trivedi, P. K. (1983). Assessing the variability of inflation. *Review of Economic Studies*, **50**, 585–596.

Pagano, M. and Hartley, M. (1981). On fitting distributed lag models subject to polynomial constraints. *Journal of Econometrics*, **16**, 171–198.

Pesaran, M. H. (1974). On the general problem of model selection. *Review of Economic Studies*, **41**, 153–171.

Pesaran, M. H. (1982a). A critique of the proposed tests of the natural rate/rational expectations hypothesis. *Economic Journal*, **92**, 529–554.

Pesaran, M. H. (1982b). On the comprehensive method of testing non-nested regression models. *Journal of Econometrics*, **20**, 263-274.

Pesaran, M. H. and Deaton, A. S. (1978). Testing non-nested nonlinear regression models. *Econometrica*, **46**, 677–694.

Phadke, M. S. and Wu, S. M. (1974). Modelling of continuous stochastic processes from discrete observations with application to sunspots data. *Journal of the American Statistical Association*, **69**, 325–329.

Phelps, E. S. (1967). Phillips curves, expectations of inflation and optimal unemployment over time. *Economica*, **34**, 254–281.

Phelps, E. S. (1970). Money wage dynamics and labour market equilibrium. In *Micro-economic Foundations of Employment and Inflation Theory*, E. S. Phelps et al. London: Macmillan.

Phillips, A. W. H. (1958). The relation between unemployment and the rate of change of money wage rates in the United Kingdom, 1861–1957. *Economica*, **25**, 283–299.

Phillips, A. W. H. (1959). Wage changes and unemployment in Australia 1947–1958. The Economic Society of Australia and New Zealand (Victoria Branch) Economic Monograph No. 14.

Phillips, A. W. H. (1959). The estimation of parameters in systems of stochastic differential equations. *Biometrika*, **46**, 67–76.

Phillips, P. C. B. and Wickens, M. R. (1978). *Exercises in Econometrics*, Vol. I. Deddington, Oxford: Phillip Allan.

Pierce, D. A. (1971). Distribution of residual autocorrelations in the regression model with autoregressive-moving average errors. *Journal of the Royal Statistical Society* B, **33**, 140–146.

Pierce, D. A. (1977). Relationships and the lack thereof between economic time series, with special reference to money and interest rates. *Journal of the American Statistical Association*, **72**, 11–21.

Pierce, D. A. and Haugh, L. D. (1977). Causality in temporal systems: characterizations and a survey. *Journal of Econometrics*, **5**, 265–293.

Plosser, C. I., Schwert, G. W. and White, H. (1982). Differencing as a test of specification. *International Economic Review*, **23**, 535–552.

Poirier, D. J. and Ruud, P. A. (1979). A simple Lagrange multiplier test for lognormal regression. *Economics Letters*, **4**, 251–255.

Priestley, M. B. (1980). State-dependent models: a general approach to non-linear time series analysis. *Journal of Time Series Analysis*, **1**, 47–71.

Priestley, M. B. (1981). *Spectral Analysis and Time Series*, Vol. 2. London: Academic Press.

Quandt, R. E. (1974). A comparison of methods for testing non-nested hypotheses. *Review of Economics and Statistics*, **56**, 92–99.

Raiffa, H. and Schlaifer, R. (1961). *Applied Statistical Decision Theory*. Cambridge: Massachusetts Institute of Technology Press.

Ramsey, J. B. (1969). Tests for specification errors in classical linear least-squares regression analysis. *Journal of the Royal Statistical Society* B, **31**, 350–371.

Ramsey, J. B. (1974). Classical model selection through specification error tests. In *Frontiers in Econometrics*, ed. P. Zarembka, pp. 13–47. New York: Academic Press.

Ramsey, J. B. and Alexander, A. (1982). The econometric approach to business cycle analysis reconsidered. Discussion Paper 82-08, New York University.

Ramsey, J. B. and Gilbert, R. (1972). A Monte Carlo study of some small sample properties of tests for specification error. *Journal of the American Statistical Association*, **67**, 180-186.

Ramsey, J. B. and Schmidt, P. (1976). Some further results on the use of OLS and BLUS residuals in specification error tests. *Journal of the American Statistical Association*, **71**, 389–390.

Rand, D. (1976). Catastrophes and economic models. Discussion Paper, University of Southampton.

Rao, C. R. (1965). *Linear Statistical Inference and its Applications*. New York: John Wiley.

Rees, A. and Hamilton, M. (1967). The wage-price-productivity perplex. *Journal of Political Economy*, **75**, 63–70.

Richard, J.-F. (1973). *Posterior and Predictive Densities for Simultaneous Equation Models*. Berlin: Springer-Verlag.

Richard, J.-F. (1979). Exogeneity, inference and prediction in so-called incomplete dynamic simultaneous equation models. CORE Discussion Paper No. 7922, Université Catholique de Louvain.

Richard, J.-F. (1980). Models with several regimes and changes in exogeneity. *Review of Economic Studies*, **47**, 1-20.

Richard, J.-F. and Tompa, H. (1980). On the evaluation of poly-*t* density functions. *Journal of Econometrics*, **12**, 335-351.

Romer, D. (1981). Rosen and Quandt's disequilibrium model of the labour market: a revision. *Review of Economics and Statistics*, **62**, 145-146.

Rosen, H. S. and Quandt, R. E. (1978). Estimation of a disequilibrium aggregate labor market. *Review of Economics and Statistics*, **60**, 371–379.

Rosenberg, B. (1973). Random coefficient models: the analysis of a cross section of time series by stochastically convergent parameter regression. *Annals of Economic and Social Measurement*, **2**, 399–428.

Sachs, J. D. (1983). Real wages and unemployment in the OECD countries. *Brookings Papers on Economic Activity*, **1**, 255–289.

Salkever, D. S. (1976). The use of dummy variables to compute predictions, prediction errors and confidence intervals. *Journal of Econometrics*, **4**, 393-397.

Samuelson, P. and Solow, R. (1960). The analytics of an anti-inflation policy. *American Economic Review*, **50**, 177–194.

Sargan, J. D. (1958). The estimation of economic relationships using instrumental variables. *Econometrica*, **26**, 393–415.

Sargan, J. D. (1959). The estimation of relationships with autocorrelated residuals by the use of instrumental variables. *Journal of the Royal Statistical Society*, **21**, 91-105.

Sargan, J. D. (1961). The maximum likelihood estimation of economic relationships with autoregressive residuals. *Econometrica*, **29**, 414-426.

Sargan, J. D. (1964). Wages and prices in the United Kingdom: a study in econometric methodology. In *Econometric Analysis for National Economic Planning*, ed. P. E. Hart, G. Mills and J. K. Whitaker. London: Butterworths. (Reprinted as Ch. 10 of this book.)

Sargan, J. D. (1974). Some discrete approximations to continuous time stochastic models. *Journal of the Royal Statistical Society* B, **36**, 74–90.

Sargan, J. D. (1975). Discussion on misspecification. In *Modelling the Economy*, ed. G. A. Renton, pp. 321-322. London: Heinemann.

Sargan, J. D. (1980a). The consumer price equation in the post-war British economy: an exercise in equation specification testing. *Review of Economic Studies*, **47**, 113–135.

Sargan, J. D. (1980b). A model of wage-price inflation. *Review of Economic Studies*, **47**, 97–112.

Sargan, J. D. (1980c). Some tests of dynamic specification for a single equation. *Econometrica*, **48**, 879-897.

Sargan, J. D. and Bhargava, A. (1983). Testing residuals from least squares regression for being generated by the Gaussian random walk. *Econometrica*, **51**, 153-174.

Sargan, J. D. and Drettakis, E. G. (1974). Missing data in an autoregressive model. *International Economic Review*, **15**, 39–58.

Sargan, J. D. and Sylwestrowicz, J. D. (1976). COMFAC: Algorithm for Wald Tests of Common Factors in Lag Polynomials. Users' Manual, London School of Economics.

Sargent, T. J. (1976). A classical macroeconometric model for the US. *Journal of Political Economy*, **84**, 207–237.

Sargent, T. J. (1978). Estimation of dynamic labor demand schedules under rational expectations. *Journal of Political Economy*, **86**, 1009–1044.

Sargent, T. J. (1979). *Macro-economic Theory*. London: Academic Press.

Sato, K. (1967). A two level constant elasticity of substitution production function. *Review of Economic Studies*, **34**, 201–218.

Sawa, T. (1978). Information criteria for discriminating among alternative regression models. *Econometrica*, **46**, 1273–1292.

Sawyer, K. R. (1983). Testing separate families of hypotheses: an information criterion. *Journal of the Royal Statistical Society* B, **45**, 89–99.

Schwarz, G. (1978). Estimating the dimension of a model. *Annals of Statistics*, **6**, 461- 464.

Shiller, R. J. (1973). A distributed lag estimator derived from smoothness priors. *Econometrica*, **41**, 775–788.

Sims, C. A. (1971). Discrete approximations to continuous time distributed lags in econometrics. *Econometrica*, **39**, 545-563.

Sims, C. A. (1974). Distributed lags. In *Frontiers of Quantitative Economics*, ed. M. D. Intriligator and D. A. Kendrick, Vol. 2, Chapter 5. Amsterdam: North-Holland.

Sims, C. A. (1982a). Scientific standards in econometric modelling. In *Current Developments in the Interface: Economics, Econometrics, Mathematics*, ed. M. Hazewinkel and A. H. G. Rinnooy Kan. Dordrecht: Reidel.

Sims, C. A. (1982b). Policy analysis with econometric models. *Brookings Papers on Economic Activity*, **11**, 107–164.

Solow, R. M. (1960). On a family of lag distributions. *Econometrica*, **28**, 393–406.

Spencer, G. (1976). *A Comparison of Some Alternative Estimators for Some Distributed Lag Models.* Unpublished M.Sc. Thesis, London School of Economics.

Stein, J. L. (1974). Unemployment, inflation and monetarism. *American Economic Review*, **64**, 867–887.

Stewart, M. B. and Wallis, K. F. (1981). *Introductory Econometrics* (2nd edn). Oxford: Blackwell.

Stewart, M. B. (1983). Relative earnings and individual union membership in the United Kingdom. *Economica*, **50**, 111–125.

Symons, J. S. V. (1981). The demand for labour in British manufacturing. Centre for Labour Economics Discussion Paper No. 91, London School of Economics.

Szroeter, J. (1978). A class of parametric tests for heteroscedasticity in linear economic models. *Econometrica*, **46**, 1311–1327.

Tallis, G. M. (1961). The moment generating function of the truncated multinormal distribution. *Journal of the Royal Statistical Society* B, **23**, 223–229.

Terasvirta, T. (1980). The polynomial distributed lag revisited. *Empirical Economics*, **6**, 69–81.

Terasvirta, T. (1982). Superiority comparisons of heterogeneous linear estimators, Discussion Paper No. 127, ETLA, Helsinki.

Terasvirta, T. and Mellin, I. (1983). Estimation of polynomial distributed lag models. Paper presented to Econometric Society European Meeting, Pisa.

Theil, H. (1961). *Economic Forecasts and Policy* (2nd edn). Amsterdam: North-Holland.

Thursby, J. G. (1979). Alternative specification error tests: a comparative study. *Journal of the American Statistical Association*, **74**, 222–225.

Thursby, J. G. (1981). A test strategy for discriminating between autocorrelation and misspecification in regression analysis. *Review of Economics and Statistics*, **63**, 117–123.

Thursby, J. G. (1982). Misspecification, heteroscedasticity and the Chow and Goldfeld-Quandt tests. *Review of Economics and Statistics*, **64**, 314–321.

Tong, H. (1977). Discussion on 'Stochastic modelling of riverflow time series' by Lawrence and Kottegoda. *Journal of the Royal Statistical Society* A, **140**, 34–35.

Tong, H. and Lim, K. S. (1980). Threshold autoregression, limit cycles and cyclical data. *Journal of the Royal Statistical Society* B, **42**, 245–292.

Toyoda, T. and Wallace, T. D. (1976). Optimal critical values for pre-testing in regression. *Econometrica*, **44**, 365–375.

Trivedi, P. K. (1978). Estimation of a distributed lag under quadratic loss. *Econometrica*, **46**, 1181–1192.

Trivedi, P. K. and Lee, B. M. S. (1981). Seasonal variability in a distributed lag model. *Review of Economic Studies*, **47**, 497–505.

Trivedi, P. K. and Pagan, A. R. (1979). Polynomial distributed lags: a unified treatment. *Economic Studies Quarterly*, **30**, 37–49.

Trivedi, P. K. and Rayner, J. (1978). Wage inertia and comparison effects in the Australian award wage determination. *Economic Record*, **54**, 195–218.

Trivedi, P. K., Lee, B. M. S. and Yeo, J. S. (1979). On using ridge-type estimators for a distributed lag model. Unpublished paper, Australian National University.

Trognon, A. (1983). Pseudo-asymptotic tests based on linear exponential families. Document de Travail No. 8305, ENSAE, Paris.

Ullah, A. and Raj, B. (1980). A polynomial distributed lag model with stochastic coefficients and priors. *Empirical Economics*, **5**, 219–232.

van Dijk, H. K. and Kloek, T. (1980). Further experience in Bayesian analysis using Monte-Carlo integration. *Journal of Econometrics*, **14**, 307–328.

Vinod, H. D. (1973). Generalization of the Durbin–Watson statistic for higher order autoregressive processes. *Communications in Statistics*, **2**, 115–144.

Vinod, H. D. (1978). A survey of ridge regression and related techniques for improvement over OLS. *Review of Economics and Statistics*, **60**, 121–131.

Vinod, H. D. and Ullah, A. (1981). *Recent Advances in Regression Methods.* New York: Marcel Dekker.

Wadhwani, S. (1984). Inflation, bankruptcy and employment. Centre for Labour Economics, Discussion Paper No. 592, London School of Economics.

Wallis, K. F. (1972). Testing for fourth order autocorrelation in quarterly regression equations. *Econometrica*, **40**, 617–636.

Watson, M. (1980). Testing for varying regression coefficients when a parameter is unidentified. Discussion Paper No. 80-8, University of California, San Diego.

Wecker, W. E. and Ansley, C. F. (1983). The signal extraction approach to nonlinear regression and spline smoothing. *Journal of the American Statistical Association*, **78**, 81–89.

Wei, W. W. S. (1978). The effects of temporal aggregation on parameter estimation in distributed lag models. *Journal of Econometrics*, **8**, 237–246.

Weiss, A. A. (1982). Systematic sampling and temporal aggregation in time series models. Unpublished paper, University of California, San Diego.

Weiss, A. A. (1983). ARCH and bilinear time series models, comparison and combination. Unpublished paper, University of California, San Diego.

White, H. (1980). A heteroskedasticity-consistent covariance matrix estimator and a direct test for heteroskedasticity. *Econometrica*, **48**, 817–838.

White, H. (1982a). Maximum likelihood estimation of misspecified models. *Econometrica*, **50**, 1–26.

White, H. (1982b). Instrumental variables regression with independent observations. *Econometrica*, **50**, 483–500.

White, H. and MacDonald, G. M. (1980). Some large sample tests for non-normality in the linear regression model. *Journal of the American Statistical Association*, **75**, 16–28.

Wolfe, M. A. (1978). *Numerical Methods for Unconstrained Optimization.* New York: Van Nostrand Reinhold.

Woodcock, A. and Davis, M. (1980). *Catastrophe Theory.* Harmondsworth (Middlesex): Penguin Books.

Wu, D. M. (1973). Alternative tests of independence between stochastic regressors and disturbances. *Econometrica*, **41**, 733–750.

Zeeman, E. C. (1976). Catastrophe theory. *Scientific American*, April.

Zellner, A. (1962). An efficient method of estimating seemingly unrelated regressions and tests for aggregation bias. *Journal of the American Statistical Association*, **57**, 348–368.

Zellner, A. (1971). *An Introduction to Bayesian Inference in Econometrics.* New York: John Wiley.

Zellner, A. (1980). On Bayesian regression analysis with *g*-prior distributions. Paper presented at the Econometric Society Meeting, Denver, Colorado.

Zellner, A. (1983). Statistical theory and econometrics. In *Handbook of Econometrics*, ed. Z. Griliches and M. D. Intriligator, Vol. I. Amsterdam: North-Holland.

Zellner, A. and Montmarquette, C. (1971). A study of some aspects of temporal aggregation problems in econometric analysis. *Review of Economics and Statistics*, **53**, 335–342.

Zellner, A. and Vandaele, W. (1975). Bayes–Stein estimators for *k*-means, regression and simultaneous equation models. In *Studies in Bayesian Econometrics and Statistics*, ed. S. E. Fienberg and A. Zellner. Amsterdam: North-Holland.

Zellner, A. and Williams, A. D. (1973). Bayesian analysis of the Federal Reserve–MIT–Penn model's Almon lag consumption function. *Journal of Econometrics*, **1**, 267–299.

Author Index